A HISTORY OF JAPANESE LITERATURE

Also by Shuichi Kato (in English)
FORM, STYLE, TRADITION
THE JAPAN-CHINA PHENOMENON

A HISTORY OF JAPANESE LITERATURE

The First Thousand Years

c. 1

SHUICHI KATO

TRANSLATED by DAVID CHIBBETT

FOREWORD by RONALD DORE

KODANSHA INTERNATIONAL LTD
Tokyo, New York and San Francisco

First published 1979 by
MACMILLAN PRESS LTD
London and Basingstoke
Associated companies in Delhi
Dublin Hong Kong Johannesburg Lagos
Melbourne New York Singapore

Published in Japan and the USA by
KODANSHA INTERNATIONAL LTD
2–12–21 Otowa, Bunkyo-ku, Tokyo 112 and
KODANSHA INTERNATIONAL/USA LTD
10 East 53rd Street, New York, N.Y. 10022
and 44 Montgomery Street, San Francisco,
California 94104

LCC 77–75967
ISBN 0–87011–307–0
JBC 1095–785901–2361

Printed in Great Britain

To Midori and Paul
and
in memory of David

Contents

Foreword

In the 1970s, with paperback editions of novels by Mishima and Kawabata in every bookstore, it is hard to recapture the sense of wonder and discovery with which the ordinary reader of the English-speaking world made his first acquaintance with Japanese literature, in limited circles through Fenollosa's translations of Nō plays published by Yeats and Pound in the middle of the First World War, then, much more widely, in the mid-twenties, through Arthur Waley's elegant and imaginative translation of the *Tale of Genji*.

It is not just that Japanese literature was new and hardly yet assimilated into Western consciousness, though that was part of it: when W. G. Aston wrote the first history of Japanese literature in 1899 he could reflect that 'only forty years ago no Englishman had ever read a single line of Japanese'. But that was not all. Ever since the missionaries and scholar diplomats first began to publish translations and their commentaries, Japanese literature has always been in severe danger in the West of being captured for desiccated academic scholarship. Doubtless there are some people who can read Beowulf for pleasure or for the access it gives them to an esthetic experience, but for most of us Beowulf belongs firmly to the sphere of EngLit, as distinct from the English literature of Shakespeare or Donne or Dickens which still has something to say to modern sensibilities. Japanese literature was in danger of being thought all Beowulf, exclusively a matter for specialist analyses of JapLit. In the universities it was gaining a bare respectability as a branch of Oriental Studies – a strange ghetto category which largely derived its original respectability from the fact that Hebrew was the language of the Old Testament and was subsequently extended to include anything beyond the Southern shores of the Mediterranean. Oriental Studies was the heading, for instance, in the 1920s, under which the *Times Literary Supplement* classified a new book on the Bantu languages. JapLit had claims to respectability as a branch of Oriental Studies which

put it in a different category from Bantu languages, for its oldest
texts were undoubtedly ancient, and written in a language which
was sufficiently removed from modern speech to be genuinely
Classical. Waley's own first work on Japanese poetry is a scholarly little treatise with explanatory notes intended to help the
serious student to gain access to the original.

The Tale of Genji put things in a different light, opening up a
world of delicacy and refined conventions, of acute observation
and subtle emotion, which was recognizably a 'civilization' worth
learning one's way around in, worth the effort of trying vicari-
ously to experience. It was still a remote world, however,
glimpsed as in the Genji picture scrolls as if through swirling
clouds of mist by an observer twelve feet off the ground. How
remote, perhaps, the translation itself showed, for Waley did not
hesitate to embellish the original text without acknowledgement.
His elaborations, most would agree, were improvements, but
they betray, nevertheless, a sense of the moral gulf between
that world and ours which made respect for the integrity of the
original a matter of minor importance.

That world is less remote for the modern reader half a century
later. The novelists of twentieth-century Japan, particularly men
like Tanizaki, who was translating the Tale of Genji for the modern
Japanese reader at the same time as he was writing the Makioka
Sisters, have served as intermediaries, leading us to the sensibilities of the traditional culture through literary skills
nourished also in European traditions, writing about a modern
Japanese society which is familiarly urban, industrial and
bureaucratic. The film makers have given us graphic images of
the Japan which has vanished: for anyone who has seen Ugetsu
Monogatari Professor Kato's remarks in this book about the 'prevalent feelings of faintness and mistiness' in Heian literature will
have an immediate resonance. Gifted Western students like
Keene and Morris and Seidenstecker have made a wide range of
diaries and plays, short stories and poems, Japanese works and
Japano-Chinese works, accessible through their translations and
intelligible through their commentaries. Japanese Zen has
become the archetypal form of Buddhism for the questing,
alternative-culture-seeking youth of Europe and North America:
the young Frenchman seeking enlightenment on a motorbike,
following in the Haiku footsteps of Basho's poetic seventeenth-

century pilgrimage through Northern Japan, can serve as a symbol of one kind of 1970s-style encounter between traditional Japan and the West.

Another is represented by this book. Since Aston's pioneering work at the end of the nineteenth century, with its compilation of facts and bland judgements (and general tendency to interpret Japanese literary history as steady progress in moral and esthetic standards which held great promise of the Japanese eventually embracing Christianity), there have been several histories and anthologies of traditional Japanese literature, but this is the first such history in English from a Japanese author. Its publication, in a splendid translation by the late David Chibbett, is an event to be warmly welcomed.

It was originally written for a Japanese audience; serialized, in fact, in the *Asahi Journal*, a leading weekly review. That it has been possible to translate it for a quite different audience with minimal modification is an indication, not just of how little a modern critic can take a modern Japanese readership's knowledge of Japanese traditions for granted, but also of the wide ranging, and in the best sense cosmopolitan, perspectives which inform Professor Kato's judgements, his comparisons and his explications. It is because he can both feel Japanese literature from the inside and see it from the outside – through the eyes of one familiar with French and German as well as English and Japanese literature – that the English reader will find the things he needs explaining explained, will find comparisons rather more subtle than the usual jejune attempts to identify the Japanese Blake or the Japanese Shakespeare, and above all will find a view of the way literature relates with the rest of society which draws its subtlety from a deep familiarity with European and North American societies and their histories. It is partly just his capacity for creative speculation that leads him to consider, say, the affinities between Japanese sentence structure and Japanese architecture, but it is partly also his knowledge of other languages, other architectures.

Japan's post-war intellectual ferment has sometimes been dubbed a cultural renaissance, but there are, perhaps, few among those who participated in it who have quite the renaissance-man breadth of interests and accomplishments of Shuichi Kato – doctor, poet, novelist, medical researcher, literary critic, professor, political commentator, but above all a citizen of the world with an insatiable curiosity about all things human. As a medical student during the war, when patriots looked askance at anything that smacked of xenophilia, he joined a French literature study group, learnt Latin, and read those poets of the *Shin kokinshū* who symbolized a distant Japan very different from the contemporary one with which he was so little in sympathy. His determination to go to Europe – more specifically to France – grew from his eager post-war encounter with the literature of the French Resistance. Why had *they* been so active, and so purposefully active, when their Japanese counterparts could merely sulk and read the *Shin kokinshū*? And why, for that matter, for all his reading on Mauriac, had his sense of the man been so imperfect that he was surprised to discover that he made common cause with the Communists in the Resistance? What of the inner meanings of French literature was he missing?

My own friendship with Professor Kato dates back to the mid-1950s towards the end of his four years as a medical researcher in Paris. We discovered that we were going to Japan about the same time, and arranged to take a boat together. I had a solid programme of reading on Japanese land reform to get through on that long voyage, but I didn't complete it. Meals lengthened as Shu's inexhaustible supply of things to talk about was restocked by the large store of reading matter he brought with him. I recall being so taken with his enthusiasm for Virginia Woolf's *A Room of One's Own* that I borrowed it from him, though for me it failed to ignite. There was another afternoon when we tried to work out an obscure passage of Rimbaud. But there was also a lot of talk about the land reform too, for Shu was even then also a political animal, and a sociologically sophisticated political animal who was fascinated by the whys and wherefores of major social trends and not just by the Manichaean struggles between good and evil which are the sort of politics those of a predominantly literary imaginative are generally attracted to.

And so it has been whenever we have met since – at conferences summoned to consider the 'modernization' of Japan, in Vancouver where for several years he was a professor of Asian Studies, in Princeton when he was on his way to become a professor of Japanese Studies at the Free University of Berlin, in each other's homes in England and Japan. Shu is always full of some new experience, alive with some new plan or enthusiasm, and at the same time, almost like a skilled debriefer, wanting to know what one has been doing and what news one can bring; what is happening in the London theatre, what the Berufsverbot portends, what private jealousies lie behind the latest row in the *TLS*?

His history of Japanese literature cannot convey the warmth of his friendship, but the reader will discern, and gain from, the breadth of sympathies, the awareness of the range and variety of human sentiment and institutions which Shu derives from his wide international network of friends and acquaintances, and from his own widespread travels. (One of his books of essays is called *From Uzbekistan to Croatia and Kerala*, another is about China, and yet another, called *Words and Tanks*, takes off from a visit to Prague during its Spring.) They will gain, too, from his equal facility as sociologist and as literary critic; his combination of intellect and intuition; his ability to see the *Kokin denjū*, say, as a means for reinforcing the self-identification of the aristocracy on the one hand, and to judge it as a literary work on the other. (In this case as an example of 'appalling triviality': no pious respect here for antiquity *qua* antiquity.)

There is, perhaps, a certain tension between the analysing Kato and the appreciating (or deprecating) Kato. Is literature to be loved, or to be explained? It is a tension the author is familiar with and has learnt to live with. In his autobiography he describes it in a very different context. As a member of a joint Japanese–American research team he went soon after the war to the cinder waste of Hiroshima, to do research on the effects of the atom bomb. Science required the collocation of facts, the correlation of symptoms with reported experience at the time of the explosion, etc. It required eliciting these facts from, say, children still speechless from the shock of seeing a parent turned into a charred corpse. He describes how it outraged every decent instinct to ask those questions, to be concerned in their presence not just with sympathy but with statistics. We murder to dissect, said Wordsworth about another kind of literary criticism. Readers will find that Shuichi Kato can still be concerned with 'structures', but murder rather less than most.

R. P. Dore
June 1979

Glossary of Literary, Historical and Buddhist terms used in the text

Ato Shite   The second appearance of the protagonist in a *Nō* play, often as a ghost.

Azuma-uta   A group of poems or 'songs', principally comprising the 14th *maki* of the *Manyōshū*, composed by the common people of the eastern provinces of Japan.

Bakufu   Literally, 'bent government'. The name given to the military administrations of the Kamakura, Muromachi and Edo periods.

Banka   The generic name given to the elegies of the *Manyōshū*.

Biwa   A traditional Japanese stringed musical instrument, rather resembling a lute.

Biwa hōshi   Blind itinerant Buddhist monk of the medieval period who toured Japan singing lays and ballads to the accompaniment of the *biwa*. In some ways equivalent to the medieval European minstrel, the *Biwa hōshi* disseminated news and played an important role in the genesis of works such as the *Heike monogatari*.

Bugaku   An ancient form of ceremonial court music imported from T'ang China.

Bushidō   The unwritten ethical code of the *samurai*.

Chadō   'The way of tea.' General name for the tea cult.

Chika renga   'Underground *renga*.' The popular, as opposed to the aristocratic, branch of *renga* poetry, represented by such figures as the monk Guzai.

Chōka   A poem of alternating five and seven syllable lines culminating with a seven syllable line. One of the few forms of Japanese poetry in which the length of the poem is not pre-determined.

Chōnin 'Townsfolk.' The name given to the artisan and merchant class of the Edo period who lived in the big towns and cities.

Chūnagon A Heian period court rank.

Daimyō The feudal lords of the late Muromachi and Edo periods.

Dengaku Dance entertainment of agrarian origins which was practised from early times, but died out in the seventeenth century. Acrobatics were an important part of *Dengaku*, which is regarded as one of the ancestors of the *nō* drama.

Ekō A key concept in the Pure Land Buddhist teachings of Shinran. Its basic meaning is 'transference of merit', which can be accomplished by such acts as copying sacred texts etc. To Shinran it meant, more specifically, Amida's transference of his accumulated store of merit to mankind.

Emakimono 'Picture scrolls.' Narrative scrolls with painted illustrations of the Heian, Kamakura and Muromachi periods, e.g. the *Genji emaki*.

Fudoki Gazetteers for each province of Japan which were compiled following a central government decree in 713. Each *fudoki* (the concept has something in common with the English *Domesday Book*) contained information on the nature of the land, crops, roads, bridges, provincial history, etc. Only the *Izumo fudoki* survives in anything like complete form.

Fūzoku-uta One of the categories which come under the general heading of *kodai kayō* or 'ancient ballads', *fūzoku-uta* were a kind of pre-Nara period folk song particularly associated with the eastern provinces.

Gagaku A form of stately music and dance imported into the ancient Japanese court from T'ang China.

Gensei rieki 'Profit in this world.' The Japanese Buddhist concept of performing prayers, ceremonies, rituals etc., with the object of obtaining practical benefits in this life.

Gō A popular Japanese board game which originated in China, involving the placing of stones on the interstices of a chequered playing area in such a manner as to acquire the maximum possible territory.

Gokenin 'Honourable-House-Men.' Warriors from the eastern provinces who regarded themselves as the personal retainers of Minamoto Yoritomo.

Gozan-ban   The generic name for books printed at the Gozan temple complexes of Kamakura and Kyoto (particularly the latter), from the Kamakura to the Muromachi periods. The Gozan temples were of the Zen sect, but not only Zen texts but also Chinese classics and even medical works were printed there.

Gozan bungaku   The generic name for the literature, normally written in the Chinese language, produced by the Zen monks of the Gozan temples.

Gunki monogatari   'War tales.' Generic term for works such as the *Heike monogatari* and the *Taiheiki* of the medieval period which took the events of war for their basic themes.

Haibun   An Edo period literary phenomenon, *haibun* was a mixture of *haiku* poetry and prose in which the prose (as in Basho's travel diaries) served as a linking vehicle for the poetry.

Haikai renga   Humorous *renga*-style poems which derived the main part of their humour from parody and crudity.

Handen nōmin   'Allotment-land farmers.' Peasants who held their land under the *Handen shujū* system (q.v.).

Handen shujū   A system of land-holding under which peasants had a lifetime's interest in a piece of arable land which reverted to the state after death. Under this system non-arable land could be inherited.

Hanka   An 'envoy' poem. A *waka* poem appended to the end of a *chōka*. Also known as *kaesiuta*, *hanka* are almost exclusively associated with the *Manyōshū*.

Heikyoku   The text of the collection of ballads relating the rise and fall of the Taira family which was recited to musical accompaniment by the *Biwa hōshi* (q.v.), and which formed the basis of the *Heike monogatari*.

Hinayana   A Sanskrit word meaning the 'Lesser Vehicle', applied scornfully by *Mahayana* (q.v.) Buddhists to Theravada Buddhism (primarily associated with India and South East Asia), which is largely concerned with the individual achieving *Nirvana* (q.v.) through his own efforts.

Hokku   The initial verse of a *renga*.

Honji suijaku   The theory states that Shinto *kami* or 'gods' can be identified with specific Buddhas or Bodhisattvas; for example the god Hachiman was regarded as a manifestation of Amida Buddha.

Honkadori A *waka* poem based on a *waka* from earlier times. The idea was to compose a new poem giving a different slant on an older work, and then to compare the new poem with the original. *Honkadori* are particularly associated with the *Shin kokinshū*.

Ichinen sanzen The Tendai/Nichiren teaching that all worldly phenomena (*sanzen*) are included in one thought (*ichiren*) which humans think in their daily lives.

Ikkō ikki The name given to the Amidist-inspired peasant riots of the Muromachi period.

Insei The system of rule by a Retired Emperor in which the Retired Emperor maintained a court which was parallel to but independent of that of the reigning Emperor.

Jinshin no ran The Jinshin rebellion. The dispute for the imperial succession in 672 by which the Emperor Temmu came to rule.

Jōkamachi 'Castle towns.' Towns which developed around military castles in the feudal period.

Jōkyū no ran The name given to Retired Emperor Go-Toba's unsuccessful attempt to overthrow the Kamakura Shogunate in 1221. Also known as the *Shōkyū no ran*.

Joshi An introduction (of varying length) to a *tanka* (q.v.) poem which was often linked to the poem by a pivot word.

Kabuki One of the national drama forms of Japan.

Kaeri-ten A form of reading mark used to enable Japanese to interpret a text in Chinese.

Kagura *Kagura*, also known as *kamiasobi*, were an early form of music and dance ballad associated with the worship of Shinto deities. They date back to at least the ninth century.

Kakekotoba A pivot word (used in poetry). A word which has two meanings according to the way a line of poetry is parsed. For example, in the expression 'Osaka barrier', the *Ō* of *Ōsaka* was sometimes written *au* (in *kana*) with the meaning of 'meet'. Thus the expression meant either 'Osaka barrier' or 'to meet at the Osaka barrier'. A kind of pun.

kakemono A hanging scroll of painting or calligraphy.

Kambun Chinese text with reading marks inserted to enable a

Japanese to reconstruct the Chinese sentence according to his own grammar.

Kami The 'gods' of Shintoism.

Kana General term covering the two native Japanese syllabaries – *hiragana* and *katakana*.

Kana-majiri A text written using a combination of Chinese characters and one of the native syllabaries.

Kana monogatari A novel of the *monogatari* (q.v.) genre, written primarily in *kana*.

Kanō-ha A school of painting founded in the Muromachi period by Kanō Masanobu (1454–1550) and patronized by the feudal nobility in particular.

Karma A Sanskrit Buddhist term often translated as 'fate'. Its actual meaning is the accumulated deeds of one's life which are stored up and have consequences either in this life or the next. What happens to a person in this life is a consequence of previous *Karma*.

Karon A treatise on *waka* poetry.

Katarimono A recited narrative tale, the recitation usually accompanied by music.

Kōan Insoluble or nonsense problem posed in Zen Buddhism to stir the mind of the meditator into intuitive enlightenment.

Kodai kayō Referred to throughout this book as 'ancient ballads'. A generic term for the various categories of songs and ballads of the pre-Nara period contained in such works as the *Kojiki*.

Kokin denju The 'esoteric' teaching and transmission of knowledge of the *minutiae* of the *kokinshū*.

Kokubunji The name given to the official monastery and nunnery established in each province of Japan as the result of a decree made by the Emperor Shomu in 741.

Kokugaku An Edo period school of learning and philosophy which emphasized the native Japanese tradition and culture in opposition to government-sponsored Confucian learning.

Kokushi Provincial officials.

Koto A thirteen-stringed musical instrument somewhat resembling a zither.

Kouta Short songs of the Muromachi period for which the *Kanginshū* is the principal source.

Kyōgen Short and humorous plays staged between performances of the *Nō* drama.

Mae shite   The first appearance of the protagonist in a *Nō* play.

Mahayana   Sanskrit word for the so-called 'Greater Vehicle' of Buddhism, principally associated with the Far East. Whereas the ideal of *Hinayana* Buddhism was the *Arhat* who achieved *Nirvana* by his own efforts, the ideal of *Mahayana* Buddhism was the *Bodhisattva* who refused to accept Buddhahood until all mankind was also 'saved',

Maki   Originally meant a roll or scroll, dating from the time when books were in scroll form. When codex forms were introduced, the term was retained to mean something like a chapter but generally longer.

Makura kotoba   A 'pillow word'. A fixed epithet (usually of 5-syllable length) qualifying or modifying a name in a *tanka* poem. An idea of how this worked can be gained from such an expression as 'Manchester where it always rains'. 'Where it always rains' would always appear with 'Manchester' whenever that name was used in a poem.

Mana   A system of rendering the Japanese language into written form by means of Chinese characters used phonetically.

Monogatari   Literally means 'talk of things'. A general term for narrative material, particularly fiction, associated with the Heian, Kamakura and Muromachi periods.

Monogatari-e   Illustrated *monogatari*. Basically the same as *emakimono* (q.v.), but specifically applied to *monogatari*.

Mono no aware   Usually translated as 'pathos' or 'the sadness of things' (literally). The closest Western equivalent is perhaps the Latin expression *lacrimae rerum* ('tears of things').

Momiji   Maple leaves in their autumnal tints.

Nembutsu   The Pure Land Buddhist invocation of Amida. The words of the *Nembutsu* are *Namu Amida Butsu* or 'Praise be to Amida Buddha'.

Nirvana   The goal of *Hinayana* Buddhism. Although the term literally means 'emptiness' or 'extinction', *Nirvana* was a more positive concept – a state in which the chain of existence was broken and all earthly desires ended.

Nō   One of the national drama forms of Japan, originating in the fourteenth century.

Nyobō bungaku   'Court lady literature.' Although this term has come to be applied to works written by any female aristocrat

of the Heian period, it specifically means works of literature
written by ladies in direct service of the court.

Okurigana Kana following a Chinese character to show its
'declension' in Japanese.

Otogi-zōshi 'Companion stories.' Specifically a body of 23
Japanese short stories of the Muromachi period, printed *c*.
1700 by the Osaka publisher Shibukawa Seieimon. By extension the whole corpus of Muromachi period short stories
from which Shibukawa made his selection.

Rekishi monogatari 'Historical tales.' A term devised in the Meiji
period (1868–1912) to cover eight works of historical narrative composed in the Heian, Kamakura and Nambokucho
period and centring on court life. The most important works
in this category are the *Eiga monogatari* and the *Okagami*.

Renga 'Linked verse.' Originally a *tanka* in which the first three
5–7–5 syllable lines were composed by one person and the
concluding two 7–7 syllable lines by another. This concept
from the thirteenth century onwards was extended until the
classical 100-poem sequence was developed with different
poets each picking up an idea from a 'start' poem and developing it in turn. Each new poet had to pick up his theme from
the preceding poem.

Ritsuryō The code of penal (*ritsu*) and administrative (*ryō*) law
by which Japan was governed, in imitation of T'ang China,
from the late seventh century until its final collapse was
brought about during the period of the Kamakura Bakufu.

Sabi An aesthetic concept which is basically untranslatable, but
which seems to have meant something like an austere sim-
plicity tinged with melancholy. It was a highly desirable
quality to be found in everything from poetry to the tea
ceremony.

Saibara A group of ballads or songs of ancient origin which in
the Heian period were adapted for the *koto* and performed at
court.

Sakamori Frontier guards, some of whose poems appear in the
Manyōshū.

Sake Fermented rice wine – the national drink of Japan.

Samurai Japanese warrior.

Sangaku An early form of entertainment, originating in China,
consisting of music, dancing, magicians, acrobats, jugglers,

contortionists, etc. Popular in Japan during the tenth century.

Sansui 'Mountain and water' landscape paintings.

Sarugaku 'Monkey music.' One of the antecedents of the *Nō* drama, *Sarugaku* is believed by some to have developed from *Sangaku* and by others to have been a separate form contemporary with *Sangaku*. It was very similar in nature to *Sangaku*, but seems to have aspired to higher artistic motives.

Satori 'Awakening.' The Zen Buddhist concept of enlightenment.

Sedōka 'Head-repeated' poems. Poems, particularly associated with the pre-*Manyōshū* and *Manyōshū* periods, consisting of six lines in a 5–7–7/5–7–7 syllable pattern with the final line of each half identical.

Seii Taishōgun 'Barbarian-Subduing-Generalissimo.' A title awarded to Japanese generals intermittently from the time of the eighth-century wars against the Ainu onwards. From the time of Minamoto Yoritomo onwards it came to be used as the title for the head of the military government and is generally abbreviated to *Shōgun*.

Sessuō The earliest title used to mean 'Regent' (acting for the Emperor during his minority).

Setsuwa Stories of either a secular or religious nature which flourished in Japan from the eighth century through the medieval period. Although not genuine folk literature (since they were not intended for a popular audience), they do cast a revealing light on contemporary popular life. Religious *setsuwa* were usually adapted from earlier stories with a Buddhist gloss added. The *Nihon ryōiki* and the *Konjaku monogatari* are perhaps the outstanding *setsuwa* collections.

Shikken Another term meaning 'Regent'. In this case, however, the title, first adopted by the Hōjō family, meant Regent for the *Shōgun* and not for the Emperor.

Shingaku A moral and ethical philosophy founded in the Edo period by Ishida Baigan (1685–1744).

Shite The protagonist or principal actor of a *Nō* or *Kyōgen* play.

Shōen Large 'manors' owned by the imperial house, the aristocracy and the great Buddhist temples. They originated in grants of tax-free lands to notables which over the centuries were built up and expanded.

Shōgun   See *Seii Taishōgun*.

Shōji   Sliding doors or screens made from paper.

Shōmyō   Buddhist 'hymns' (of Indian origin) of the ancient period.

Sōmonka   Generic term for the love poems of the *Manyōshū*.

Sokushin Jōbutsu   Shingon Buddhist concept of 'achieving Buddhahood in this life' by practise of the 'Three Secrets'.

Suiboku   A style of ink painting (primarily associated with landscapes) imported from China to Japan following the introduction of Zen Buddhism.

Taihō Ritsuryō   The *Ritsuryō* (q.v.) code promulgated in the first year of the Taiho reign period (i.e. 701).

Taika reforms   The series of reforms dating from 645 and afterwards imposing a Chinese style administrative and government system on Japan.

Taisaku   The questions (as contained in the *Keikokushū*) posed to candidates taking examinations for advancement within the bureaucracy.

Tanka   These days the term *tanka* is used interchangably with *waka* (q.v.), but originally it meant the five-line 'short' poem in the 5–7–5–7–7 syllable pattern which became the principal Japanese form of lyric poetry. *Waka* or 'Japanese poetry' was a more general term which included not only *tanka* but other forms such as *sedōka* (q.v.).

Tengu   Long-nosed goblins or demons of Japanese mythology.

Udaijin   Heian period court rank usually translated as Minister of the Right.

Ushin   An aesthetic concept implying elegant and refined taste.

Uta-awase   Poetry contexts which became popular in Japan from the early tenth century onwards. Poets were given a theme and each had to compose a poem on that theme. A judge (or two judges) was appointed to decide which was the best poem.

Utagaki   Ancient village entertainments or festivals where young people could meet and exchange love poems.

Uta-makura   Place names used over and over again in poetry because of their romantic and poetic associations.

Uta monogatari   Novels, such as the *Ise monogatari*, in which the prose text served as a connecting background for *waka* poems.

Waka See *Tanka*.

Waki The deuteragonist in a *Nō* play.

Watkakushi shōsetsu A form of novel which evolved in the Meiji period (1868–1912) told in the first person and directly based on the author's own personal emotions and reactions.

Yamato-e 'Japanese painting.' The name (first used in 999) given to the evolving style of Japanese genre painting which was beginning to supplant styles of painting directly imitative of Chinese models.

Yayoi One of the three prehistoric cultures of Japan dating from about 200 B.C. to A.D. 250.

Yōeki An early form of labour tax.

Yūgen An aesthetic concept implying the conveyance of an emotion in a poem without explicitly stating it.

Yūsoku kojitsu Works relating to correct behaviour and etiquette at court or in military society.

Zazen 'Sitting in meditation.'

Glossary of selected literary works mentioned in the text

Fudoki   General name given to a collection of accounts of various ancient Japanese provinces compiled by government order in the Nara period. The *fudoki* contained information on various aspects of economics, agriculture, folklore and similar matters pertaining to the province in question. Many *fudoki* were subsequently lost, and perhaps the best known of the survivors is *Izumo fudoki*. The various fudoki bear some relation to the English *Domesday Book*.

Genji monogatari   One of the world's oldest novels, and the most celebrated novel of the Heian period. It was written in 54 chapters by the court lady Murasaki Shikibu, probably at the beginning of the eleventh century, and deals with the life and amorous adventures of 'Hikaru Genji', often known as the 'Shining Prince'.

Hagi daimyō   A *kyōgen* play of unknown authorship.

Heike monogatari   A long novel of the *gunki monogatari* genre written by an unknown author towards the end of the twelfth century and dealing with the rise and fall of the house of Taira, which ruled Japan between about 1160 and 1185.

Hizakurige   An Edo period humorous novel of the *kokkei-bon* genre, written by Jippensha Ikku (1765–1831). The first part of this long novel was published in 1802, and the whole work relates the adventures of two young men as they journey along the *Tōkaidō*. The *Hizakurige* inspired many other similar novels and is one of the most important works of its type of the Edo period.

Kojiki   The oldest extant history of Japan, the *Kojiki* was compiled by imperial order by Ono Yasumaro and submitted to Emperor Gemmei in A.D. 712. It relates the history of Japan from the age of the gods down to the reign of Empress Suiko (592–628), but largely consists of myth and legend rather than real history.

Kokinshū   Also known as the *Kokin waka-shū*. An anthology of *waka* poems compiled at the order of Emperor Daigo by Kino Tsurayuki (d. 946) and others in 905. It consists of 20 *maki* and more than 1100 poems, and is the earliest of what are known as the *chokusenshū*, *waka* anthologies compiled by imperial command.

Kokon chōmon-jū   A collection of *setsuwa* tales compiled by Tachibana Narisue (fl. *c.*1250) and completed in 1254.

Konjaku monogatari   A collection of *setsuwa* tales in 31 *maki* (of which three no longer survive) compiled in the late Heian period. Tradition ascribes the compilation to Minamoto Takakuni (1004–97), but this is very dubious. A valuable source for popular folklore and for the literature of the people outside the court aristocracy.

Kyōun-shū   A collection of Chinese poems by the priest Ikkyū (1394–1481) on Buddhist themes. Ikkyū was a Zen monk noted for his wit and eccentricity, and these poems were collected by his disciples.

Manyōshū   Japan's oldest anthology of *waka* poetry, compiled probably at the end of the eighth century by persons unknown. It consists of 20 *maki* and contains more than 4500 poems by a very wide range of poets, of whom Hitomaro is probably the best known.

Masu kagami   A semi-historical narrative of the *rekishi monogatari* genre, of unknown authorship and probably written about the middle of the fourteenth century. Told in the form of an old nun speaking to a young novice, the *Masu kagami* relates the history of Japan from about 1184 to 1333.

Meigetsu-ki   The diary of the poet and courtier Fujiwara Teika (1162–1242), covering the period 1180–1235. A valuable source for both the politics and literature of the period.

Nihon ryōiki   A collection of 112 *setsuwa* tales compiled by the priest Keikai at the beginning of the ninth century.

Nihon shoki   The second-oldest extant history of Japan, compiled in 30 *maki* by imperial order by Prince Toneri (d. 735), Ono

Yasumaro and others and completed in 720. It covers roughly the same period as the *Kojiki*, but the narrative is extended to the year A.D. 697. The text is written in Chinese.

Shasekishū   A collection of *setsuwa* tales in 10 *maki*, compiled by the monk Mujū. The work was begun in 1279 and completed in 1283, but additions were made in 1295 and 1308. The tales and anecdotes illustrate the teachings of Buddhism in popular form.

Shin kokinshū   Also known as the *Shin Kokin waka-shū*. Another of the *chokusenshū*, the *Shin kokinshū* is a collection of almost 2000 *waka* poems compiled by order of Emperor Go-Toba and completed in 1205. The editors were Fujiwara Teika, Minamoto Michitomo, Fujiwara Ariie, Fujiwara Ietaka and Fujiwara Masatsune.

Taiheiki   A *gunki monogatari* work in 40 *maki* of unknown authorship, believed to have been written in the late fourteenth century. The work deals with the civil wars in Japan between 1319 and 1371.

Tsukuba-shū   An anthology of *renga* poetry compiled in the fourteenth century by Nijō Yoshimoto (1320–88) and the monk Gusai.

Ukiyoburo   A long *kokkei-bon* novel written by Shikitei Samba (1797–1844) and published between 1809 and 1812. The novel is set against the background of an Edo bath-house and is based on stories told by male and female customers of the bath-house.

Utsuho monogatari   A long novel of the late tenth century, of unknown authorship.

Note on
Japanese names

According to Japanese convention, all names in this volume are set out with the family name first and the given name second. The exception is that of the author's where Western convention is applied because of his international reputation; the same criterion has been applied in the omission of the macrons in the spelling of his name.

Note on
Japanese names

Introduction
The Distinctive Features
of Japanese Literature

The literature of Japan has a number of distinctive features in relation to Chinese and Western literature. These features are related to five main factors: the role of literature in Japanese culture as a whole; the pattern of its historical development; the Japanese language and its writing system; the social background to literature; and, finally, the underlying Japanese world-view to life, death, religion and philosophy. By tracing these factors and seeing how they interrelate, a clear picture of the structure of Japanese literature emerges and it becomes possible to present an orderly account of the history of that literature as it has changed and developed within that structure. The hypothesis of a synchronic structure is the starting point for seeking a diachronic order. What follows in this introduction is not meant to have any universal application to the methodology of literary history in general, but without touching on the features which distinguish it from the literature of other countries it is impossible to explain a methodology for Japanese literature in particular.

1. THE ROLE OF LITERATURE IN JAPAN

The role of literature and the visual arts in Japanese culture is of enormous importance. In every age of their history, the Japanese have expressed their thought not so much in abstract philosophical systems as in concrete literary works. The *Manyōshū*, for example, far more clearly expresses the thoughts and attitudes of the Japanese of the Nara period (710–94) than do all the Buddhist doctrinal works of the same period put together. The culture of the Heian court, to take another example, gave birth to poetry and fiction of a very high degree of refinement, but it did not produce any original philosophical system. There are, in fact, only two exceptions to this general rule in the history of Japan, and these are to be found in the Buddhism of the Kamakura period (1185–1333) and the Confucianism of the Tokugawa (Edo) period (1603–1868).

However, even in the case of Kamakura Buddhism, the religious philosophy taught by men such as Hōnen and Dōgen was not completely systematized by their successors, and the learning of Edo period Confucianists such as Itō Jinsai and Ogyū Sorai may have had an influence on the thought of subsequent philosophers, but it did not lead to more abstract and wide-ranging speculative thinking. The undeniable tendency of Japanese culture is to avoid logic, the abstract and systematization, in favour of emotion, the concrete and the unsystematic.

The world of Japanese feeling and sentiment found its expression not so much in abstract art forms such as music, but chiefly in the visual arts and hand crafts. The artists of the Heian period (794–1185), for example, displayed surprising originality in such forms as Buddhist sculpture and painted *emakimono*, but it is doubtful whether native Japanese genius added much of significance to musical forms such as *shōmyō* and *gagakū*.

Certainly, the Japanese created music for the Nō drama in the Muromachi period (1392–1568) and for the *Jōruri* drama in the Edo period, but in both cases, once the form had been created there was little subsequent development, and there is nothing in music which parallels the phenomenal development in Japanese painting. Rather than creating a structural order from the abstract components which make up music, the Japanese preferred to paint the objects before their eyes – cherry blossoms, pines, people – and excelled at the aesthetic refinement of ordinary utensils.

Literature and art lie at the heart of Japanese culture. Probably the reason that Japanese culture as a whole has maintained close contact with the realities of everyday life is that the Japanese people have always disliked leaving the real physical world behind them and ascending into the ethereal realms of metaphysics.

This characteristic could hardly be more alien to the underlying features of ancient Mediterranean and medieval European cultures. In Europe, there were abstract and comprehensive systems of ideas, which later led to a great variety of modern European philosophies; similarly, in the field of music, polyphony gradually developed into the vast range of modern European instrumental music. The cornerstones of medieval European culture were not art or literature, but religion and philosophy, and the concrete manifestation of this is to be found in the great cathedral. Painting and sculpture were for the adornment of the cathedral. Mystery plays were performed outside the cathedrals and music echoed in the interiors.

In Japan at that time art was related not just to Buddhism, but to popular literature, and music found expression in religious ceremonial, as well as in drama and popular ballads. In Japan, literature, at least to a certain degree, fulfilled the role of philosophy in Europe and at the same time influenced art to a level unparalleled in Europe. By contrast, in medieval Europe, theology made the arts and even music its servants, whereas in Japan the history of literature is to a large extent the history of thought and sensitivity.

In China, literature and art, particularly through the medium of calligraphy, were often inseparable. Music was not really independent of literature and there was never the same development of instrumental music as there was in the West. Excluding for the moment the question of mutual influences, there are many superficial resemblances between the cultures of China and Japan. However, where the countries markedly differ, culturally speaking, is that in Chinese tradition there is the unyielding will for comprehensive systematization which is typified by the teachings of the Sung period (960–1279) philosopher Chu Hsi.

The same kind of phenomenon does not really exist in Japan and never has existed. Even when Sung Confucianism was adopted by the Japanese authorities as a formal educational vehicle at the beginning of the Tokugawa period, it was less than a century before it had been adapted to Japanese patterns. What the Japanese did was to de-systematize it and reduce it to a system of values which related to politics and practical ethics. The Chinese approached the question of concrete, practical considerations via the route of universal principles, wrapping up the parts in the whole.

The Japanese, however, concentrating from the outset on practicalities, began with the parts and built them into the whole. The reason for the importance of literature in Japanese culture is not the same reason for its importance in Chinese culture. Metaphorically speaking, in Japan literature took over the role of philosophy; in China, even literature was treated philosophically.

2. LITERATURE – THE PATTERN OF HISTORICAL DEVELOPMENT

The history of written Japanese literature can be traced back to at least the eighth century. Many of the world's literatures go back further, but few have such a long, unbroken tradition of writing in the same language which extends to the present day. For example, there is no Sanskrit literature being written today, and the flourishing literatures of England, France, Germany and Italy cannot for the most part trace their origins much further back than the Renaissance. Only the literature of China has a longer unbroken tradition.

The history of Japanese literature is not only long, but also displays an extraordinarily wide number of distinctive features in its pattern of development. In Japanese literary history it has never been simply the case of one particular form and style being influential in one period only to be succeeded by a new form in the next. In Japan the new did not replace the old, but was added to it. For example, the principal form of Japanese lyrical poetry has always been the *waka* which was already in existence by the eighth century. In the seventeenth century a new and influential poetic form – the *haiku* – appeared, and in the present century the lengthy free-verse forms enjoy widespread use. However, the *waka* has not ceased to be one of the principal forms of lyric poetry. Naturally, there have been cases where popular literary forms have disappeared such as the 'envoy poems' of the Nara period, but even at that time such poems were probably not a representative form.

The Chinese style poetry so widely practised among the intelligentsia of the Tokugawa period has also almost passed out of use, but this again is a rather special case since it was a poetic form based on a foreign language. The new being added to the old 'instead of supplanting it' is fundamental to understanding the pattern of Japanese literary development; this tenet, in fact, does not apply solely to poetry. For example, the practice can be seen very vividly at work in Japanese drama after the Muromachi period. Fifteenth-century dramatic forms such as *Nō* and *Kyōgen* were joined by *Kabuki* and the puppet drama in the seventeenth century and by *Shingeki* in the twentieth century, and it is a fact that none of these forms has been swallowed up by subsequent developments.

This pattern of development applies as much to aesthetic values in each age as it does to literary forms. Aesthetic concepts such as *mono no aware* in the Heian period, *yūgen* in the Kamakura period, *wabi* and *sabi* in the Muromachi period, and *iki* in the Tokugawa period did not perish in the age in which they were created, but survived to exist alongside the aesthetic thought of the succeeding age. Even after the Meiji period (1868–1912) poets continued to strive for *mono no aware*, *Nō* actors for *yūgen*, tea masters for *sabi* and *geisha* for *iki*, and all this is just as true today.

Because of this basic pattern of historical development in the sense that the old is never lost, there is a considerable unity and continuity in Japanese literary history. At the same time, since new is always being added to old, with each new age literary forms and aesthetic values become more diverse and multi-faceted.

Japanese achievement in all varieties of literature is unrivalled except in some Western languages, and again, with the exception of the modern Western world, there is nothing to rival Japan in the variety of aesthetic values manifested in art and literature. In China too, up to the end of the Ch'ing dynasty in 1911, traditional literary forms were carefully preserved, but the situation in China was always different to that in Japan where new forms normally found ready acceptance.

When a new literary form appeared in China, historical continuity and cultural integrity were threatened, there was a fierce conflict between the old and the new, and one had to give way. This never happened in Japan because the expectation was not that the old should be replaced by the new, but that the two should co-exist. The fact that modern Japanese society is extremely conservative, but that at the same time there is a love for all things new, are two sides of the same coin and reflect the same pattern of cultural development.

It is not possible here to go thoroughly into the reasons why this pattern appears in all fields of Japanese cultural development, but in literature at least part of the answer lies in the 'dual structure' which permeates the Japanese linguistic, social and 'world-view' background.

3. THE JAPANESE LANGUAGE AND WRITING SYSTEM

The languages of China and Japan have different origins and their sound systems, vocabulary and grammar are very different indeed. However, since the Japanese had no writing system of their own when Asian continental culture was first encountered, the already highly developed Chinese writing system was adopted, and this happened as early as the fifth century A.D. Chinese characters (*Kanji*) are ideographic and since one character represents one monosyllabic word, some special device was necessary to adapt this system to the writing of Japanese. Two methods of adaptation were possible; either the meaning of the character could be retained and its sound rejected, or the sound retained and the meaning rejected. In fact both methods were used at times. Chinese sounds were largely retained, for example, in the *Kojiki*, and the *Manyōshū* (where southern Chinese pronunciation of the fifth and sixth centuries was used), and for some words in the *Nihon shoki* (where seventh-century northern Chinese pronunciation was used). It was not until the ninth century that the native Japanese syllabary (*kana*) was invented and adopted, and in this sense the early Heian period marks a turning point in the writing of the Japanese language.

Japanese using Chinese characters to write their own language also devised a method of reading original Chinese poetry and prose in the Japanese manner. By the use of *Kaeri-ten* (a kind of reading mark) the correct word order of the sentence was established, and individual word inflexions and word endings were indicated by *okuri-gana* (another kind of reading mark). By using these methods of 'translating' Chinese, the Japanese were also able to write their own poetry and prose in the Chinese language. Consequently, from the seventh to the nineteenth centuries Japanese literature was written in two languages, Japanese and Chinese (or at least the Japanese version of Chinese).

It goes without saying that the Japanese normally expressed their emotions in poetry – using the native language *waka* form which, for the purpose, was far richer and far more subtle than Chinese poetry. However, as time went by, greater weight was attached to the use of the Chinese language in poetry, and the lyrical world of the Muromachi period, for example, is represented typically not only by native language *renga* verse, but also by the Chinese poetry of the Gozan monks. It is difficult to know which is more replete with the sentiment of the period – the *Tsukuba-shū* or the *Kyōun-shū*, and if such judgements are difficult to make for the Muromachi period, how much more difficult they are for the Tokugawa period. In some senses there are parallels in this situation with the use of Latin in medieval Europe, but the major contrast is that, with a few exceptions, Latin and the various European languages are not so linguistically disparate as are Chinese and Japanese. Again, after the Renaissance Latin literature was gradually absorbed into the literatures of the various European nations whereas in Japan the two-language literature situation survived until the Meiji Restoration.

Naturally, native literature composed in Chinese (known in Japanese as *Kambun*) influenced the vocabulary of native Japanese literature, and there was an equally marked Japanese influence on the kind of Chinese that was written. The *Konjaku monogatari* and the *Meigetsu-ki* are respectively two good examples of this phenomenon. In fact the birth of two literary styles, one with a pronounced Chinese influence, and the other with almost none that was very close to the colloquial language, considerably enriched Japanese literature.

The usefulness of Chinese words long absorbed into the Japanese language at the time of the Meiji Restoration and afterwards when the Japanese were under pressure to introduce Western concepts into their language goes without saying. The ability to use such Chinese terms to translate Western words into Japanese is in marked contrast to the situation in most non-Western cultures where such words had to be adopted into the language of origin without being translated. The fact that Japanese possessed these Chinese words undoubtedly played an important role in the modernization of Japan after the Meiji Restoration. On the other hand, their adoption weakened the traditional flavour of the Japanese language and, in the literary sense, especially in the composition of poetry, introduced many, complicated problems.

Leaving aside the question of a dual language structure in literature, it seems to me that the Japanese language itself has several characteristic features closely related to the nature of literary works produced in Japan. To begin with, Japanese writing bears a close relationship to the situation in everyday life when one person speaks to another. For example, when highly developed respect language is used in speech, it indicates the comparative social relationship of the speaker and the listener. Again in speech, personal pronouns are frequently omitted. Whether the subject of a sentence is mentioned or not depends entirely on the situation in which the speaker and the listener find themselves which means that, in comparison with Chinese and Western languages, the structure of the Japanese language is extremely limited in its ability to transcend particular concrete situations. In other words, Japanese places more emphasis on the spoken language than the written, and it is difficult to avoid the conclusion that Japanese culture as a whole does not place that much emphasis on the universal validity of written statements.

It can easily be imagined how in such a culture and under certain conditions two people could communicate without words. Similarly, the custom of using words which do not transcend a particular situation in the language also parallels the general Japanese cultural tendency for values not to transcend a particular situation. The result of this is that Japanese writers in the native language have excelled at abbreviated forms of literature, at brief and pithy descriptions of particular objects or thoughts. This is an explanation of the Japanese preference for poetic forms such as the *waka* and *haiku* in which a writer conveys his perceptions in just a few words.

Secondly, almost invariably the Japanese sentence begins with a phrase which modifies the noun and then ends with a verb; in other words it begins with the details and builds into the whole. This is in marked contrast to Chinese and Western languages and is in fact parallel with a part of Japanese architecture which was not subject to Chinese influences.

In Japanese mythology time is conceived as something without beginning or end. This is a reflection of the general Japanese attitude towards history in which the whole continuous thread of history is not broken down into parts and periods, but is made up of those parts and periods. The Japanese sentence order reflects the Japanese sense of cultural order, and it is quite natural that what is true of culture as a whole is true of literature also. Almost all Japanese prose, with a number of exceptions, is more or less broken into small, limited sections with seldom any consideration of the whole structure. The Heian period *monogatari* provide the ideal example of this phenomenon. The *Utsubo monogatari*, for example, ostensibly a novel, is really a collection of independent chapters with only the most tenuous of connections. Even with the *Genji monogatari*, although the various sections are written with an eye to the structure as a whole, each individual section, in the vast majority of cases, also stands by itself and can be enjoyed as a separate entity. Again, the *Konjaku monogatari* is a compilation of many short legends which are classified under various headings. However, apart from a loose classification by subject matter, there is no attempt to place each legend in context with the whole. Several stories, however, do have a life of their own and can be read as independent works of excellent quality.

This is in great contrast to the literature of T'ang and Sung China which was standardized into various patterns having regard for the structure of the whole, and to French classical literature of the seventeenth and eighteenth centuries which was also extremely conscious of order within the whole structure. This point can be made clear by a comparison between different descriptions of the same story in Chinese collections of legends and in Japanese collections, such as *Nihon ryōiki*. The Chinese version tells the essentials of the story in a concise way, while the Japanese version provides more vivid details. In these two collections one becomes aware of two fundamentally different cultural backgrounds.

4. THE SOCIAL BACKGROUND TO JAPANESE LITERATURE

One of the most marked characteristics of Japanese literature is its centripetal tendency. Almost all authors and the majority of readers lived (and live) in the cities with city life providing the background for a very large number of literary works. It is true that in the regions there were orally transmitted ballads and folk stories, but it was in the cities that these were first collected and written down. For example, the *Kojiki*, and, even more so, the *Fudoki*, both of which were compiled in the eighth century, contain a large number of legends and popular ballads from the regions, but there is no doubt that it was because of an order from the *central* government that these were collected and written down. This is also true of the various *setsuwa* collections which contain tales set in the regions, ranging from the *Nihon ryōiki* to the *Konjaku monogatari*, and from the *Kokon chōmon-jū* to the *Shasekishū*.

In Japan in any given period one city tended to be the country's cultural centre. This was not the case in China, where it was normal for literary men to travel through the provinces writing poems on the notable features of each area as they passed through it. The T'ang poets, for example, did not always take their material from the city streets of the capital, Ch'ang-an. On the other hand, the poets of Heian Japan stayed in Kyoto, the capital, and wrote poems about famous places in the provinces – places they had never visited themselves – using conventionalized epithets to describe them.

In the West the centrifugal tendency in literature was even more pronounced than it was in China. The European Middle Ages was the period of the minstrel and of the scholar who travelled from university to university, writing Latin poems as he went. Even in modern times there is not a single instance of German or Italian literary activity being concentrated on a single city. As far as Europe as a whole is concerned, the only notable exception is France where Paris has become the centre of modern French literature. In Japan it is notable, for example, that from Hitomaro to Saitō Mokichi there has not been a single great poet who even made use of regional dialect in his work.

The tendency for literature to centre on one large city society was most marked in Kyoto from the ninth century. Although in the previous period the administrative machinery of the *ritsuryō* system had been centred on Nara, Nara itself did not truly represent a large city society either economically or culturally. It was simply the entrepot whereby the government and the great Buddhist temples received the culture of the Asian continent. It was only in the Heian period that the economy developed sufficiently to support a large city society and that a monopoly of cultural activity went hand-in-hand with a monopoly of political power. Kyoto's position as the literary centre of Japan was not challenged by any provincial city until the rise of Osaka in the seventeenth century. The age of Edo literature was from the eighteenth century onwards, but at that time, although the cultural centre of Japan had passed from Kyoto-Osaka to Kyoto-Edo, Kyoto itself did not cease to be a cultural centre.

After the Meiji Restoration in 1868 Tokyo became the cultural centre of Japan and today the overwhelming majority of authors live in or near Tokyo, and the majority of publishers are situated there. It is only the readership which has expanded to a nation-wide scale, and of course this is closely related to the fact that not only books, but all goods, are now produced for a national market place. What Tokyo decides is followed by the rest of the country and in this respect the centripetal tendency of Japanese culture as a whole and of literature in particular is even more pronounced than it was in the Tokugawa period.

A large city society was the centre of literature and the elements of that society manifesting the strongest literary capacity varied from period to period. If one calls the group of people who participate in the production of literature and its enjoyment the 'literary class', the fact is that in Japan this class has varied from age to age bearing a close resemblance to the historical situation in the West, while being in marked contrast to that in China. The literary class in China – and this applies from the T'ang dynasty right through to the end of the Ch'ing dynasty – was the 'shih' or 'gentleman scholar'. It was almost solely this class which received higher education and filled positions in the government and administration, and it was they alone who could read and write the literary language of China. Because this was so, there was a strong adherence to the forms of classical literature with all that phenomenon's implied resistance to anything which was new and against tradition.

In Japan the literary class had not been properly formed by the Nara period. The *Manyōshū* contains poems primarily written in the seventh and eighth centuries, but the authors were not only members of the nobility, but also monks, peasants and soldiers with a large number of anonymous folk ballads. The authors of the poems of the *Kokinshū*, compiled about a hundred years later than the *Manyōshū*, were members of the ninth-century nobility or monks. Thus during the Heian period an exclusive literary class emerged. As indicated before, this does not mean that there was no orally transmitted literature independent of the Kyoto ruling class. In all probability there was a great wealth of legends, folk stories and folk ballads, and we can get a glimpse of what there must have been in this field from the various *setsuwa* collections compiled by the nobility.

There are two noteworthy features about the Heian nobility as the literary class. First, among the authors of the masterpieces of the period, there were a very large number of members of the lower nobility; and, second, there were many women. In other words, a large part of the fiction and lyrical poetry representative of the period was produced not by those who were at the centre of power, but by those on the fringes of that power. It is not difficult to deduce the reason for this. The lower nobility were close enough to the court to be able to observe its life and far enough away to be able to avoid becoming embroiled in its power struggles.

Men sent into the provinces as officials must have had in addition numerous opportunities for contact with society outside that of the capital. The ladies of the Kyoto court were free from economic considerations and political ambition and free from having to learn the Chinese language which was the official language for public business. Consequently they were in an ideal position to present their own private thoughts and feelings in their native language. Heian literature cannot truly be described as women's literature, but there can be few parallels in history, either Eastern or Western, of women playing such an important literary role.

When the political centre of Japan moved from Kyoto to Kamakura the nobility were replaced as the rulers of Japan by the military class, but the nobility did not immediately cease to be the literary class. From the thirteenth to sixteenth centuries the prime literary creative forces continued to be the nobility and the Buddhist priesthood. From the *Shin Kokinshū* to the *Tsukuba-shū*, from the *Nō* drama to the *gunki monogatari*, from the *Masu kagami* to the poetry and prose of the Gozan monks, the higher echelons of the military class acted as patrons of the literary arts, and their lives and deeds frequently served as models for literary works. But they seldom wrote works and even when they did, they

attempted to absorb the styles and tastes laid down and standardized by the nobility and priesthood. The inferiority complex of
the rising class of the period in relation to traditional aristocratic
culture is ideally demonstrated by the *Kyōgen* play *Hagi daimyō*, a
Japanese counterpart of Molière's *Bourgeois Gentilhomme*.

The writers and artists who had been so highly integrated into
the aristocratic society of the Heian period were more or less
estranged from the warrior society after the Kamakura period.
The poets of the *Shin Kokinshū* were the first 'alienated' intellectuals in Japan's literary history. During the next few hundred years
it became quite usual for poets to 'abandon the world' and live in
grass huts or in temples. This is one reason why the literature of
the period is so often termed 'recluse literature'. However, not all
writers of aristocratic or monkish origin abandoned the world
and hid themselves away. Some authors took a keen interest in
the deeds and ethics of the new class and frequently wrote in
praise of it.

It was in the Tokugawa period that the military class began
themselves to read, write and produce literature. They were the
writers of Chinese Confucian poetry and prose. Yet at the same
time a new class of readers arose among the *chōnin* or townsmen.
In the early Tokugawa period up to the middle of the eighteenth
century authors were in the main of *samurai* background but in
the later Tokugawa period they were not only *samurai*, but also
chōnin and even peasants. For example, Ogyū Sorai and Arai
Hakuseki, the former of medical background, the latter of *samurai*
background, both became Confucianists in the Genroku period
(1688–1704) and lived in the warrior society. Matsuo Bashō was
born a *samurai*, but did not live as one and instead became a
master *haiku* poet living on the fringes of society. Chikamatsu
Monzaemon was born of a *samurai* family, but wrote plays for
chōnin audiences. Apart from Ihara Saikaku, an Osaka towns-
man, there were very few authors who did not come from a
samurai background, and Genroku literature was very clearly not
townsmen literature.

A further distinction can be made between those authors of
samurai background who wrote for the warrior intelligentsia and
those who wrote for the higher *chōnin* classes. The family background of all such writers changed in the later part of the
Tokugawa period. Novelists included not only such men of the

samurai class as Kyokutei Bakin and Jippensha Ikku, but also townsmen such as Ueda Akinari, Santō Kyōden and Shikitei Samba. The same was true even among authors of Chinese-style poetry with *samurai* writers such as Rai Sanyō and writers of peasant, merchant and artisan background such as Kan Sazan, Chō Baigai and Emura Jotei.

The literary class after the Meiji Restoration was the urban middle class, and writers can be divided between those of *samurai* or *chōnin* Tokugawa period origins and those who came from regional middle and small landowning stock. Mori Ōgai and Nagai Kafū are model examples of the former who wrote 'city literature' and Shimazaki Tōson of the latter who wrote about matters removed from the refinements of city life. For example, the origins of the 'Naturalist' movement in Japanese literature are explained far better by the rural backgrounds of the writers in question rather than in terms of any direct relationship with Western Naturalism.

There is no room for doubt that the fact that the Japanese literary class changed from period to period gave many new dimensions to the way literature was written, its aesthetic values and its material. However, it must also be admitted that the literary class in any given period were a cultural elite. There are three kinds of source material extant today on what kind of literature was produced by the common people and how the spirit of the masses was reflected in literature.

First, there are the popular ballads and legends produced by the people which were collected, recorded and illustrated by the cultural elite, such as the poems of the *Nihon Shoki* and the *Kojiki*. Second, there is the work written by the cultural elite for the popular audience, thus closely reflecting the life-styles and standards of the masses. Good examples here are the novels of Saikaku and such works as the *Hizakurige* and the *Ukiyoburo*. Third, there was the kind of work which was frequently originated and always enjoyed by the people such as the Kyōgen drama, *rakugo* and *senryū*.

One final social peculiarity of Japanese literary history is the way writers have always been wrapped up with the group to which they belong and their closed-shop attitude towards other groups. There are two aspects to this. The first is the thorough integration of literature into the culture of the ruling class. The

literature of the Heian period held its place among the aristocracy, while the literature of the Tokugawa period was at once
enjoyed and supported both by the bureaucratized warrior society and by the *chōnin* society which ruled the economy of the
cities (kabuki, yomihon, sharebon etc.).

Writing poetry at the Heian court was an indispensable part of
everyday culture, while the education of the warrior bureaucrats
in the Tokugawa period followed continental patterns and rested
on the basis of classical Chinese literature. As far as Kabuki is
concerned, in the Japan of the eighteenth and early nineteenth
centuries, the theatre played a central role in city culture as a
whole, perhaps more than any other factor. The Japanese theatre
of that period was in many senses like the church of medieval
Europe – a place where ideology, music, art and literature met, a
place which epitomized the whole of the cultural activities of the
cities.

However, there were exceptions to this integration of writers
into the ruling classes. One cannot say that literary activities from
the Kamakura to Muromachi periods involved the ruling classes
very much. At that time, literature was not necessarily critical of
the system, but it frequently escaped from the power of the
military. I have already touched on the fact that for this reason the
period is often termed that of 'recluse literature'. This term,
however, is something of an exaggeration (for example, *Nō* and
Kyōgen could not have developed as well as they did without the
patronage and support of the military class), but it satisfactorily
indicates the special features of the period.

The phenomenon of the social estrangement of writers followed the collapse of the aristocratic regime and lasted for several
centuries. It might be said that the difficulties of living in the
warrior society encouraged writers to form their own groups and
the *bundan* resulted. Model examples of this are the *waka* circles of
the aristocracy which lived on and the Chinese poetry circles of
the Gozan monks. Military power protected the Gozan temples,
but the literary circles which developed within the temples and
participated in the production of poetry in a foreign language,
had no external contact with the military class and created, as it
were, an autonomous, closed world of their own. Estrangement
from large groups was compensated for by thoroughgoing integration into a small group. The 'recluses' of the Muromachi

period did not simply live alone in grass huts, but drank sake with others of their kind; they did not wander in the wilderness, but visited their fellows and travelled with them. This is another aspect of the phenomenon of integration into a group of writers.

In the age of bureaucratic government and capitalism which followed the Meiji Restoration, literary estrangement and the formation of closed *bundan* can be seen emerging. That this phenomenon survived the Pacific War into the present day is seen on one hand in the involvement of writers in mass society while on the other there is the tendency still for authors to be estranged extremely from mass society, forming small groups with their own magazines.

This tendency of writers to become integrated into groups has naturally had the effect of limiting material in Japanese literature. There is, for example, a surprising uniformity of theme in the poems of the imperial anthologies of the Heian period from the *Kokinshū* to the *Shin Kokinshū*. There are seasonal poems, love poems and travel poems, with spring invariably meaning cherry blossoms, and autumn invariably maple leaves. Since the types of plants mentioned in poems of the period were fixed, it would be impossible to gain any real idea of the flora of the period and its distribution from the poetry. There are countless poems about the moon, and hardly any about the stars (if one excepts poems about the Milky Way and Tanabate). Almost to a man the poets of the period ignored stars and violets in their poems. Again almost to a man they ignored the grief of wars, the hardships of poverty and resentment of corrupt politics.

This closed tendency in *monogatari* fiction after *The Tale of Genji* grew more and more marked. These *monogatari* concerned themselves exclusively with the emotional life of the aristocracy and ignored other sections of society. Apart from touching on them as incidentals to round out a picture, the artisans of the cities, the peasants of the country, soldiers and robbers make no appearance in their pages. The *monogatari* are the exclusive product of the closed aristocratic society and we do not catch even a glimpse of the ordinary crude but spirited common people of the type with which the *Canterbury Tales* abounds. There is a part of the *Konjaku monogatari* which is an outstanding exception to this general rule, but exceptions do not disprove rules; they prove them.

Fundamentally, this state of affairs did not change from the

Kamakura to the Muromachi periods. *Renga* and *Nō* inhe
court culture as their themes, the *gunki monogatari* from the *I
monogatari* to the *Taiheiki* depicted the life of the military society,
but none of these types of works even touched on the life of the
peasantry. The poetry and prose of the Gozan monks added the
new dimension of introspective Zen philosophy; yet they not
only wrote of the daily lives of the monks but added another new
dimension by mentioning political matters through their connections with the higher classes of the warrior society. These were all
themes untouched by the Heian period poets. However, it is clear
that the monks never left the temples, and there was no place in
their work for the common people. Also they wrote in a foreign
language, and as they took T'ang and Sung Chinese writers as
their models, they seldom transcended the traditional themes of
T'ang and Sung writing and added something new.

Kyōgen is the only exception. Here one finds that the characters
are servants of *samurai* warriors, peasants, independent artisans
and their wives, blind men, robbers and swindlers. *Kyōgen* certainly had its life close to the people, but rather than giving this as
the reason, it owed its nature to the stage improvization of the
actors who were 'common people'. From the fourteenth and
fifteenth to the early sixteenth centuries, these improvised
dramatic sketches were the oral traditional literature of the common people. Therefore, the more different the material of *Nō* and
Kyōgen the more it becomes clear how closely involved the
cultural elite were with small, closed groups.

In Edo period society there was a sharp differentiation between
the various classes and their cultures. The cultures of the military
bureaucracy, the *chōnin* and the peasantry differed from one
another. Consequently, as already touched upon, the forms of
literature, subject matter and even language that became integrated into culture differed greatly. However, there was a
marked tendency for literary subject-matter of any one class in
any one period to be of limited range. A model example of this is
the novel forms of the late eighteenth century called *sharebon*,
kibyōshi and *ninjōbon* each of which was almost entirely concerned
with the activities of the red-light districts. It is noteworthy that
the same theme often appeared in *Kabuki* drama in the same
period and was the chief topic of wood-block prints. Even Chinese style poets wrote on the same theme.

Among the groups of Chinese-style poets who proliferated from the late eighteenth century onwards, the brothels which formed the centre of culture were a common theme in their writing. In the early Edo period the Chinese-style poets never expanded on the limited themes of T'ang and Sung poetry, but in the latter part of the same period they did at least acknowledge in their writing the existence of the red-light districts.

In the early twentieth century the *watakushi-shōsetsu* novels engendered by the *bundan* were even more limited in their themes than were the entertaining novels of the Tokugawa period, for the authors wrote about nothing other than their own daily lives which seldom strayed outside their own families and their relations with magazine editors.

Between the wars the influence of Marxism gave birth to a type of novel which depicted the working-class, but if one excludes these works, there have been extremely few novels in the modern period which have depicted such figures as politicians, businessmen, engineers and farmers. The reason is not difficult to find. Professional writers became so integrated into their *bundan* that they knew nothing of what went on in the outside world. An author who is thoroughly integrated into society cannot truly criticize that society's system of values, nor, through criticism, can he transcend those values, but taking those given values as a basis, he is at least able to refine his perception of them. Sei Shōnagon, for example, did not in any sense transcend the court society of the Heian period, but she did succeed in portraying its trivialities with remarkable insight. Her tradition is still alive in modern Japanese literature and reflects the peculiarities of the general structure of Japanese society.

5. THE JAPANESE WORLD-VIEW

Historical transformations in the Japanese world-view have been characterized not so much by the infiltration of various foreign thought systems as by an obstinate clinging to an indigenous attitude and over and over again imparting a Japanese flavour to those systems. The most representative examples of foreign thought systems to have influenced the Japanese are to be found in Mahayana Buddhism, Confucianism, Christianity and Marxism. There is no strict chronological order in the influence of Buddhism and Confucianism for both reached Japan at about the same time. However, Buddhism achieved the position of exerting profound influence on Japanese culture far more quickly than did Confucianism. From the seventh to the sixteenth centuries, Buddhism played a vital role in Japanese cultural background, but in the case of Confucianism, although it had an influence from quite early on, and this influence did become stronger after the fourteenth or fifteenth century, it was only after the seventeenth century that the influence of Sung Confucianism as a background to a world view became of decisive importance. Christianity had an influence only in the late sixteenth and early seventeenth centuries and from the late nineteenth century onwards, whereas Marxism exerted an influence between the two wars, mostly on the Japanese intelligentsia. Taoism is also worthy of mention as is Western scientific thought from the nineteenth century, but although both these had an undeniable influence on literature, neither presented comprehensive systems for the interpretation of nature, man, society and history as a whole.

Buddhism, Confucianism, Christianity and Marxism all do have such comprehensive systems. Each is possessed of an abstract theory; each recognizes either a transcendent supernatural existence or defines a universal system of values related to a basic principle. In Mahayana Buddhism there is the 'Buddhahood'; in Christianity, God; in Confucianism *T'ien* or *li*; in Marxism, History. Since the Buddhahood is transcendent, the compassion of the Bodhisattvas transcends conventional standards and reaches all people; since God is absolute, all men are equal in his sight and that justice which is guaranteed by God transcends historical culture; since *T'ien* transcends the ruler, revolution (in the classical sense) comes about, and since *li* is universal, standards based on it do not change with changing social conditions; since the laws of History transcend subjectivity they can be used to interpret thought in terms of progress and reaction. When that which acts as the transcendent element is not of this world, then the system it engenders is concerned primarily with the other world; whereas if it *is* of this world, then the system engendered is concerned with the matters of this world.

Traditionally, the Chinese world view is of the latter type, in contrast to that of India and the West. Since Indian influence reached Japan through the medium of Chinese civilization and since it was only very much later that Western influence reached Japan at all, it might be thought that because the Chinese were this-worldly, the indigenous Japanese world view, similar to the Chinese, would have been protected. Indeed this may have been the case and it might well be true to say that concern with matters of this world, almost to the exclusion of the next, is a special characteristic of East Asian philosophy and culture. However, laying aside that aspect for the moment, in respect of their aims to provide a transcendental basic principle and universal values with an abstract, logical and comprehensive basis, foreign thought systems as a whole influenced Japanese culture precisely because they were in such marked contrast to the native world-view.

Basically, to describe the structure of the Japanese world view is not nearly so easy to enumerate as is, say, the special features of an articulate theoretical system. The theoretical side of the Shinto system, from Urabe Kanetomo to Hirata Atsutane, borrowed from Confucianism, Buddhism, Taoism and even Christianity. There is no Shinto theory which does not owe something to a foreign thought system. Since, however, the *Kojiki* and the various *fudoki* have little Buddhist or Confucian influence, we must be able to deduce from them a way of thought which we can imagine as indigenous. We can check conclusions against folk-lore material and we can compare and contrast them with later literature.

The world-view which was emerging in Japan about the fourth and fifth centuries was made up of a polytheistic, complex system of belief containing elements of ancestor worship, shamanism and animism, and there were differences in content from region to region. It was neither an abstract nor theoretical view, but tended towards the material and the practical; it did not involve a comprehensive philosophical system, but rather a system of customs which involved special attention being paid to the intrinsic nature of individual phenomena. There was no transcendent basic principle. *Kami* were entities of this world and there was, historically speaking, a direct relationship between the age of the gods and the age of man. Moreover, *kami* were innumerable and not mutually exclusive, and naturally, therefore, there was no absolute entity. Since basic principles were concrete and did not transcend the special conditions for which they were devised, there was no question of any universal system of values which could be defined in terms of that transcendental basic principle. Of course, this does not mean that there were no individuals who did possess an absolute set of values. On the contrary heads of special groups frequently had absolute authority over the groups' members, and loyalty became an absolute value, as, for example, in the Emperor System. However, this authority did not extend over the membership of other groups and loyalty to *their* leaders was not a value. For example, Yamato Takeru-no-Mikoto's conquest of Kumano was for the purpose of enlarging his own group and not for the purpose of realizing values fundamental to the persons concerned. This differs fundamentally from the intentions of the Crusaders, for example, who waged holy war to free the Holy Land.

What happened when this indigenous world view encountered the highly organized, intellectually sophisticated, transcendental world views of foreigners? In some cases the foreign world view was accepted for itself; in some cases it was rejected; but in the majority of cases, the foreign thought system was adapted to Japanese needs. This adaptation was in standard form when the foreign thought system was highly organized and sophisticated as in the case of Buddhism, Confucianism, Christianity and Marxism. Abstract, theoretical aspects were weeded out, the transcendental basic principle was excluded, the comprehensive system was dismantled and only that proportion of it retained which had value in terms of practical application. What remained was a 'Japanized' foreign world view.

From the first the material advantages of Buddhism, which was used by the Yamato court along with other continental imports such as legal systems, magic and writing, were stressed. The Buddhist monks played an important role in the Japanese state in that through prayer they sought to preserve the peace of the country, they provided other prayers and incantations to bring rainfall for the crops and to cure sickness, and in the temples they provided education. Even today, Buddhism's vast influence on Japanese culture can be seen in temple architecture and Buddhist images of the time. However, it is difficult to imagine that Buddhism fundamentally altered the world-view of the Japanese of the

Nara period. It is true that poets of the *Manyōshū* wrote about 'jinsei no hakanasa' (the transience of human life) and this may have been through Buddhist influence, but this concept is by no means an essential component of Buddhist doctrine, and there are several examples of the same feeling in aspects of non-Buddhist culture in the same period. It is not the transience of life which lies at the core of Buddhist philosophy, but the means of combating it. However, in the *Manyōshū* virtually no mention is made of Buddhism's unique contribution to resolving the problems of life and death. Nowhere does it display any real evidence that Buddhism had thoroughly permeated the hearts of the Nara period Japanese. Its poems in the vast majority of cases evince no Buddhist influence, and in a small number of cases influence which may or may not have been Buddhist-inspired.

The stress on the worldly benefits of Buddhism continued in the Heian period, and a kind of Shinto-Buddhist philosophical amalgam emerged so that Buddhism, which may have had a distinct identity at the end of the sixth century, lost its exclusive identity through being Japanized. In China it was during the Sung period that the idea of 'Three in One' (Buddhism, Confucianism and Taoism) emerged, but in Japan from very early on in the Heian period, the joint existence of indigenous beliefs and Buddhism was accepted as not being mutually contradictory.

However, in the thirteenth century came the phenomenon known as Kamakura Buddhism, pursuing a denial of worldly benefits and with its emphasis on the role of a transcendental absolute (Amida in the case of Jōdo Shinshū, Satori in the case of Zen and the Lotus Sutra in the case of Nichiren Buddhism). Clearly, it forms an exception to the general rule in the history of Japanese thought. Such purity of purpose, however, did not last as is vividly demonstrated by the case of Zen. The Zen sect, which became thoroughly secularized during the course of the Muromachi period, was broken down into two major components – aesthetics and practical ethics. Zen did not, for example, as is commonly stated, give rise to *suiboku* painting and the tea ceremony; it simply became those things. The warrior class may have seen in Zen a means of controlling their emotions and fears even on the battlefield, but this is an ethical, not a religious question.

By the beginning of the Tokugawa period, three centuries after its rise, Kamakura Buddhism which in the thirteenth century had been a transcendental religion, had become completely secularized and was no more than a cultural phenomenon. The religion of Dōgen had developed simply into a secular scholarship of Chinese classical literature and art and Tokugawa political power ushered in a new age in which Buddhism was abandoned as a value system in favour of Sung Confucianism.

Basically, Sung Confucianism attempted to explain the universe as a whole and led to a comprehensive system in which human affairs were a part of that whole. However, this system was gradually dismantled by the Japanese Confucianists into political and economic studies on the one hand, and into ethics on the other. The terminology of Sung Confucianism survived, but scholars who displayed an interest in its comprehensive system were rare, Miura Baien being something of an exception. Attention tended to move away from abstract, intellectual problems posed by Confucianism to those of concrete practicality – a very typical example of how foreign thought systems underwent Japanese influence.

Thus the world-view background to Japanese literature may be divided into three types. On one extreme there were foreign thought systems in their original form, which were different in different periods, while on the other there was indigenous Japanese thought which remained unchanged through history. In between lay the various systems of foreign thought which had undergone thorough Japanese influence. Naturally enough, each of these three types was represented in literature, though the third was the most predominant.

The history of modern Japanese literature can also be interpreted in terms of responses to these three underlying types of world-view. Uchimura Kanzō for example represents the writers who accepted foreign thought systems in their original form, while Masamune Hakuchō represents the other extreme. Mori Ōgai and Natsume Sōseki represent the mainstream view. These are all writers of the Meiji period, but even in more modern times, the same has remained true with Miyamoto Yuriko and Kawabata Yasunari representing the two extremes, and Kobayashi Hideo and Ishikawa Jun in the middle.

It would not be true to say that there is no Western influence at play in the works of Hakuchō and Yasunari, but the world-view they present adheres completely to indigenous traditions, contrasting greatly with the Christian influence underlying the works of Kanzō and the Marxist influence underlying the works of Yuriko. In the case of Ōgai and Sōseki, and probably also in the case of Hideo and Jun, the world-views presented are not on the indigenous pattern. In their writings one finds a common individualism which does not come through the medium of religious belief. They have a tendency towards self-definition in terms of historical society and culture as a whole, but their world views do not include a transcendental absolute as in the case of Kanzō's God and Miyamoto's 'history'. Their views are rational and fundamentally this-worldly, with Ōgai leaning towards scepticism and agnosticism and Kobayashi Hideo leaning towards subjectivism and aestheticism.

6. THE INTER-RELATION OF THESE SPECIAL CHARACTERISTICS

I have already outlined the special characteristics of Japanese literature, some of which are shared with Chinese literature, others with Western literature. However, the whole represents something distinctively Japanese, and it remains to enquire how all these special characteristics inter-relate.

Socially speaking, it is remarkable how not only writers, but Japanese individuals as a whole are highly integrated into the groups to which they belong. For the sake of brevity, let us call this group-consciousness. Philosophically speaking, the special characteristic of indigenous Japanese thought is that it does not have a world-view which recognizes beings or values which transcend ordinary everyday practicalities (this contrasting slightly with the Chinese situation and markedly with that in India and the West). These two factors inter-relate in the following way. If one does not believe in values which transcend the group, it is impossible for members to be independent of the group. It is also very difficult, when people are so integrated into a group, to develop a world-view which will transcend the group. It will be seen, therefore, that these two special characteristics closely relate to one another and must be treated as two sides of the same coin.

The structure of language also relates to the special characteristics of the Japanese world-view, although one cannot say that one is the result of the other. Language is built up from parts into a whole while the indigenous world-view places emphasis on the special nature of concrete parts and pays little attention to the universal nature of the abstract whole. In this way the special features of language and the world-view correspond and it was convenient for the Japanese to express their view through the vehicle of language in literary form rather than devise speculative philosophical systems. Naturally, as a consequence the role played by literature in culture as a whole was correspondingly larger than is usual.

Having a world-view which does not include transcendental values implies that when searching for the new it is not necessary to discard the old. When new thought was brought to Japan from abroad, the special characteristics of the indigenous world-view were seldom damaged, and the question of a crisis in cultural integrity and autonomy never arose. Moreover, the two-language literature system corresponded to the twin social stratification of the cultural elite and the masses which served to reinforce the steady procedure of new being added to old. The cultural elite may have used foreign languages and explained new ways of thought, but it is difficult to imagine that this fundamentally affected the Japanese language world of the masses through a few generations. When, as in the case of Buddhism, foreign thought did permeate to the masses, it was the thought, not the people, which was changed.

However, the contrasts between the new and old are not necessarily overlapped with those between foreign and indigenous thought, between the cultural elite and the masses, and between Chinese and Japanese languages. Among the cultural elite, among the literary classes as a whole, and even in the cases of some individual writers, foreign thought affected the shallower levels of consciousness and reason, while indigenous thought and feeling affected the deeper levels of emotional life. These shallower and deeper levels corresponded, as it were, to the public and private domains of the individual's life. Quite usually thorough integration into a group meant that the relationship between the group and its members crossed from the public domain into the private domain, and it was never easy for foreign thought to penetrate into the depths of emotional life.

Because, however, Japanese society never stagnated, Japanese literature did not cease to develop. The political ruling classes and the cultural ruling classes were constantly changing and it is in this that the origin of development of cultural values lay. On the other hand, the successive importation of Buddhism, Confucianism and Western philosophy provided not only a foreign stimulus to thought, but also the techniques and general skills necessary for internal development. The history of Japanese literature is, therefore, a subtle combination of diversity and unity, of change and continuity.

Chapter 1

The Age of the *Manyōshū*

From extant written materials, the history of Japanese literature can be traced back as far as the seventh or eighth century A.D. It was during this period that Japanese forces were finally withdrawn from Korea after having been involved in the strife of the Three Kingdoms ever since the sixth century, and throughout the period envoys continued to be sent and tribute paid to the courts of first Sui and then T'ang China. During the same period each of the constantly warring Three Kingdoms of Korea concentrated power in the hand of one ruler, while the imperial family of Japan gradually extended its power and influence. This was accomplished in three stages; first, through the charismatic power of the Regent Shōtoku Taishi towards the end of the sixth century at the court of the Empress Suiko; second, through the bureaucratization of the machinery of government which was engendered at the end of the seventh century as a result of the Taika Reforms of 645; and, third, through the complete systematization of centralized authority which arose from the introduction of the Taihō Ritsuryō code in 701.

The *Ritsuryō* system, which was adopted in imitation of T'ang China, consisted of three components – the hereditary ruling authorities, the central administrative machinery, and the provincial officials (*kokushi*) who were appointed by the central government. This in effect confirmed the country's social stratification which had been in force since the sixth and seventh centuries. Under the *Ritsuryō* system the aristocratic ruling class lived by means of a tax on farmers. There was then a class of farmer, normally known as *Handen nōmin* (allotment-land farmers) who held land in fairly equal proportions per capita, and finally there was a slave class which owned no land, nor indeed any private possessions.

The allotment-land farmers held a lifetime's tenure on a fixed area of agricultural land, but as, after their death, the land reverted to the government, there was no private landownership in the feudal sense. However, non-agricultural land could be inherited. Under the *Ritsuryō* system, the allotment-land farmer had no political rights but was obliged to offer his labour and his crop taxes. In this sense his position differed from that of the farmer during the feudal period and also differed from that of the 'citizen' of the ancient Roman Empire. The farmer of the Nara period used iron implements, but the yield on his crops was generally poor as is indicated by the fact that the tax on crops was often no more than 3 per cent of the total yield. The slave population, according to one theory, reached some 10–15 per cent of the total population of 6,000,000 in the Nara period.

Just as the ruling artistocracy adopted the *Ritsuryō* administrative system from China, so their ideological background too was adopted from the continent. Nowhere is this more concisely and explicitly revealed than in the Seventeen Clause Constitution (*Jūshichi-jō kempō*) traditionally attributed to Shōtoku Taishi. There is no incontrovertible evidence that Shōtoku Taishi was the author of the *Jūshichi-jō kempō*, and it may be that it was written by someone else at the end of the seventh century after the time of the Taika Reforms. The ancient historical chronicle *Nihon shoki* has an entry for the 'fourth month, summer, of the twelfth year of the reign of Empress Suiko' (603) stating that at that time an imperial prince wrote a constitution and that it had seventeen clauses. However, the historical accuracy of the *Nihon shoki* can sometimes be relied on and sometimes not and truly reliable evidence, such as would have been provided by mention of it in a contemporary Chinese chronicle, is entirely lacking.

Therefore the *Nihon shoki* cannot simply be believed as it stands. The fact that the text of the 'Constitution' did not refer to the actual systems in operation after the Taika Reforms is not necessarily in itself proof that the work was written before that time. Also the fact that some of the vocabulary which suggests the existence of bureaucracy is used in the Constitution does not prove it could not have been written before the Reforms. It is not clear who wrote the 'Constitution'; nor is it clear whether it was written at the beginning of the seventh century or at the end of the seventh century, but there is no room for doubt that the work summarizes the ideology of the Taika Reforms. This is the important point and whether the work was in existence before those reforms or not is not of great consequence.

The original text of the *Jūshichi-jō kempō* is in Chinese and simply presents the articles of the 'Constitution' without any kind of preamble. The articles deal with the duty and conduct of officials and range from general principles such as 'Good faith is the foundation of right . . .' (article 9) to specific exhortations such as 'Ministers should attend court early in the morning and not retire until late in the evening' (article 8). No attempt was made to place these articles in any sort of order and general principles and specific instructions are intermingled at random. There are many remarkable characteristics to be found in the articles of general principles.

First the basic principles to create a united country are written from the point of view of Confucian concept. Article 12, for example, contains the words: 'A country does not have two lords, nor the people two masters. The king is the master of all the people.' This saying parallels numerous others found in Chinese Confucian literature. The relationship between the ruler and the people as a whole is clearly laid down as are the duties owed by the latter to the former, such as 'loyalty'. As far as the country's officials are concerned, great stress is placed on the harmony which should exist between them and the people.

The first article opens with the line, 'Harmony is to be valued', and the final article contains the stricture, 'Weighty matters should not be considered by one person alone; they should be discussed with many people'. Some scholars have seen Buddhist influence, as well as Confucian influence, in this emphasis on 'harmony'. Be that as it may, it is possible that the opening statement on harmony which is re-iterated in article 15 represents the subjective view of the author of the 'Constitution'. If this is so, it may well be that here one is seeing one of the highest values of the individual man, that of harmony within the group, being consciously and explicitly stated.

There is also the same kind of implicit emphasis on harmony in article 17 where it is stated that important matters should be considered by a number of people and not just by a single individual. The argument of article 17 is emphasized in article 10 which contains the words, 'although we alone may be right, let us follow the multitude and act like them'. Thus if we consider articles 1, 10, 15 and 17 together, we can see that the purpose of the 'Constitution' was to emphasize the necessity and desirability of discussion within the 'group', and of the overriding virtue of harmony within the 'group'. At this point comes the obvious problem of practical relationships between the aristocratic bureaucracy at the centre of government and regional official-dom. The purpose of the Taika Reforms was to centralize and reconstruct the regional bureaucracy, and this is a clear indication that in the past there had been considerable tension between the central government and the regional officials. Thus the emphasis on harmony was not merely a platitude imported from foreign thought, but a practical solution to a very real problem within Japan itself.

The 'Constitution' goes on to reveal a deep respect for and concern with the universal principles of Buddhism. Article 2 opens with the words, 'Sincerely revere the Three Treasures, for these Three Treasures (i.e. the Buddha, the Law and the Priest-hood) are the final refuge of the four regenerated beings and are the supreme objects of faith in all countries'. 'The four regener-ated beings' means all living creatures and in this context 'all countries' can be taken to mean China, Korea and Japan.

This emphasis on the universality of Buddhism is natural for a ruling class conscious that they were making use of a foreign religion and needing to defend it against indigenous beliefs. The influence of Buddhism is again present in the 'Constitution' in the form of a kind of egalitarian thought. Article 10 says, 'All men have different opinions. We are not unquestionably wise, and they are not unquestionably fools', which is another way of saying 'let us follow the multitude and act like them'. Several conclusions could have been derived from this Buddhist egalitarianism. Among them, however, the 'Constitution' chose such propositions as: 'let us follow the multitude and act like them'. The reason for this choice lies in the need for harmony within the group, in the background of which there existed the actual regional communities and the clan system. Put another way, these are not simply the views of an aristocratic ruling class converted to Buddhism, but those of seventh-century Japanese rulers making use of Buddhist ideas to put across their own values.

Written in a foreign language, the 'Constitution' clearly shows

the influence of foreign thought, notably Buddhist and Confucian. It does not, however, simply mimic foreign ideas, but
unceasingly emphasizes values deeply related to the realities of
Japanese society of the period, that is to say a kind of co-operative
harmony in the context of the establishment of the power of the
Emperor system. The Seventeen Articles, which in simple form
summarize these two things, even when read in the Japanese as
opposed to Chinese style, must be regarded as a splendid piece of
prose.

The establishment of a unified country implies the existence of
a permanent capital city and the compilation of some kind of
national history. At the beginning of the eighth century the
Emperors of Japan who during the seventh century had lived in
the Asuka region, created the city of Nara in imitation of the
Chinese capital of Ch'ang-an. Nara was at the time Japan's only
real city; it was about a quarter the size of Ch'ang-an and had a
population of some 200,000. The labour for building the city was
obtained by levying a labour tax (yōeki) on the allotment-land
farmers in the regions, and the collection of the necessary re-
sources and materials was done through the forcible use of central
power which also employed various other forms of taxation.

Nara did not develop as a market town through the development of commerce, but rather as a kind of jōkamachi ('castle town')
by virtue of being the centre of the operation of the Ritsuryō
system. Nara was established as the capital in 710 and within ten
years, through the use of the same central power, two national
histories had been written, the Kojiki (completed in 712) and the
Nihon shoki (completed in 720). The Kojiki was written in a rather
odd style of Chinese which contained elements of Japanese,
while the Nihon shoki was written in pure Chinese on the pattern
of the Chinese historical chronicles. Both were arranged in
chronological order and can be divided into two parts: one dealing with the divine and mythical origins of the Japanese imperial
house, and one dealing with the historical activities of the
Emperors.

The circumstances in which these two works came to be written are not entirely clear. Work on them seems to have been
begun at the end of the seventh century but the primary sources
for both works, the Teiki and the Kyūji (neither of which now
exists – the former being a genealogy of the imperial family and

the latter a record of stories current at court) seem to have been compiled in the sixth century.

The studies of Tsuda Sōkichi and others since have made it clear that by detailing in the *Kojiki* and *Nihon shoki* the events of the age of the gods and then following these with actual historical occurrences without any clear indication of where myth ends and history begins, the powers behind the *Ritsuryō* system were consciously attempting to justify their own position. Doubtless stories current at court and among the people at large were to some extent used as raw material, but these were sought out and embellished for inclusion in the two histories from a viewpoint which clearly was primarily concerned with the legitimacy of imperial rule. That the rulers of seventh- and eighth-century Japan felt the necessity to explain the legitimacy of imperial rule in historical terms was probably due to the diplomatic prestige and benefits it conferred in dealing with the kingdoms of Korea and the tributary relationship which existed with China at that time.

The customs of the advanced countries of East Asia reached more backward Japan and in his work *Nihon no kodai kokka* (1971), the historian Ishimoda Tadashi described very specific events relating to this question. On the basis of records scattered in the *Nihon shoki*, the *Sung Shih* and the *Sui Shu*, he deduces that when the T'ang Emperors received Japanese envoys in public audience questions were frequently asked relating to the geography of Japan and to the names of its gods. He suggests that the same must have applied in the case of Japanese envoys visiting Sui China in the pre-T'ang period and argues that this fact was one of the reasons for the history of the age of the gods being written into the two national histories. Looked at against the background of Japan's tributary relationship to China, it may well be that the 'age of the gods' sections had to be written, against the will of the Japanese, for purely technical reasons relating to external affairs. Why was the *Nihon shoki* compiled less than ten years after the *kojiki*? It may have been that in the circumstances of its compilation, its source materials and its prose style the *Kojiki* was deemed not sufficiently suitable for the purpose for which, as we have seen, it was designed and that it was important to produce an official national history in good Chinese. We shall come later to the myths and legends of the two works.

In the seventh and eighth centuries Buddhism, which reached Japan in the sixth century, became welded to the power of the secular state. As is well known, great temples were constructed and Buddhist-associated art developed. This period began with the building of the Hōryūji (607) and reached its zenith with the construction of the Great Buddha (*Daibutsu*) of the Tōdaiji in 752. During this span of years the style of Buddhist sculpture and iconography progressed from that of Asuka Buddhism in which models of the Chinese Six Dynasties period were imitated to that of Tempyō Buddhism with its adherence to T'ang models. Virtually nothing is known about the architects and sculptors responsible for these works of art, but probably many of them were of foreign origin who became naturalized Japanese. However, this does not necessarily mean that the Buddhist images made in Japan were no more than purely mechanical copies of mainland originals. Stylistically there were no important discoveries made, but in individual images one finds slight idiosyncratic developments and refinements, and certainly Buddhist art formed the nucleus of the culture of the aristocratic ruling classes.

However, the literature produced in the same period, insofar as it is possible to make comparisons with art, was not Buddhist in this way. As we shall see later, there is some slight Buddhist influence to be seen in the *Manyōshū*, the great collection of lyric poetry particularly of the seventh and eighth centuries, but this was confined to a sparse scattering of Buddhist vocabulary in just a few of the more than 4500 poems contained in the anthology. In other words, the Golden Age of Buddhist art in Japan was also the age in which native lyric poetry was almost completely unrelated to Buddhism. It was the age of the Tōdaiji *Daibutsu* and of the *Manyōshū*. This surprising contrast indicates the enormous difference between the role played by Buddhism in ancient Japanese culture and the role played by Christianity in medieval European culture. It does not need to be overstressed that in the Golden Age of cathedral architecture and Christian art in the medieval period, there was no literature which was not at least tinged with Christianity. There was, in the twelfth century, for example, secular European literature, but the values which appear even in such works were defined within the framework of the Christian world view.

Why then in Nara period Japan were there both the *Daibutsu*

and the *Manyōshū*? Why this contrast? Probably because Buddhism, a foreign religion, was used by the upper echelons of society
and did not permeate lower to any great extent, and because even
within the same aristocratic ruling class abstract thought expressed in a foreign language (Chinese) was greatly influenced
by Buddhism, while the inner emotions of the Japanese expressed in the Japanese language remained untouched by
Buddhism. In terms of artistic expression this can be best
explained by noting that Tempyō Buddhist art, of which the
Daibutsu is representative, was largely the work of foreign
craftsmen.

The Seventeen Article 'Constitution' of Prince Shōtoku, with
its use of ideas taken from both Confucianism and Buddhism,
and its quotations from the Chinese classics, was an expression of
the individual viewpoint of the ruling class of the seventh century. At about the same period monks seem to have written
highly abstract, speculative works relating to the Buddhist scriptures. The *Sangyō gisho*, traditionally ascribed to Prince Shōtoku,
is an example of this kind of work, being a commentary on the
Shōman-gyō, the *Yuima-kyō* and the *Hokke-kyō*. It is not clear
whether the same author was responsible for all three commentaries and even if they were the work of one man we are not sure
who he was. They may have been produced by a group of learned
monks working under the direction of Prince Shōtoku.

The *Sangyō gisho*, in comparison with similar Chinese under-
takings, seems to have had little, if any, originality, but there are
some points worth noting. First, in the choice of sutras taken for
commentary, there is some indication of a tendency towards an
interest in Buddhism for the laity. At any rate both the *Shōman-
gyō* and the *Yuima-kyō* explain the essence of Buddhism and
matters of importance relating to the daily lives of lay believers.
Probably a certain section of the ruling class of Japan who envisaged the creation of a Buddhist state saw their own aspirations
reflected in these sutras. Second, although in parts the contents
of the commentaries are no more than naively far-fetched, in
other parts (notably in the celebrated *Jisshu mondō* of the *Yuima-
kyō gisho*) there are some highly abstract arguments and discussions. Even in assuming that the author in such sections plagiarized other original works, it can be imagined that he was at least
familiar with abstract, theoretical modes of thought. In other

words, the *Sangyō gisho* indicates that Japanese intellectuals and monks of the seventh century had reached a sufficiently advanced stage to be able to assimilate the speculative philosophical elements of Buddhism. If such had not been the case, then probably there could have been no *Kūkai* in the ninth century.

The aristocratic intellectuals of Japan who between the seventh and eighth centuries wrote 'legal' works, compiled national histories and composed treatises on Buddhist theory, all in Chinese, wrote poetry in the same language. The composition of poetry and prose in classical Chinese formed an important part of the training of government officials in China who had to pass examinations in such subjects. The circumstances in which such composition in Chinese played a role in the examinations of government officials in Japan, where the T'ang *Ritsuryō* system was adopted, can be deduced from the examination papers contained in the *Keikokushū* of 827.

The *Kaifūsō* (751) contains 120 Chinese poems and is the first national anthology of lyric poetry, pre-dating the *Manyōshū* by some thirty years. The poets represented include various Emperors, members of the imperial family, aristocrats, monks, naturalized Chinese etc., and the poems mostly date from the seventh and eighth centuries, corresponding to the date of the majority of *Manyōshū* poems.

The form of the poems is principally that of five graphs to the line, and there are many four and eight line poems. The influence of Six Dynasty poetry is said to be marked here, but the rarity of long poems with seven graphs to the line is an indication of the difficulties encountered by foreigners not used to the Chinese language. Court banquets and sight-seeing excursions form the main subject matter of the poems and by comparison with contemporary Chinese poetry there is remarkably little by way of political comment on the part of the poets. It is also noticeable by comparison with the *Manyōshū*, in which there are many such, that the *Kaifūsō* contains only two love poems. Philosophically speaking, the influence of Chinese thought (Confucius, Lao-tse and Chuang-tse especially) is all pervasive, while the influence of Buddhism is perfunctory.

To sum up, what the *Kaifūsō* reveals is that Chinese poetry written by the courtiers of the Nara period was simply imitative of

Chinese models. Its use was, so to speak, part of general court etiquette and the poetry itself did not present either the emotions or the thoughts of the authors.

We have already spoken of the traces of original Japanese thought to be found in the *Sangyō gisho*. It goes without saying that the representation of genuine emotion to be found in the Japanese language poetry of the *Manyōshū* is remarkable, but it is significant that there is very little influence in the *Manyōshū* not only from Buddhism but from any other foreign philosophy. This is especially true when one looks not at the poems of courtiers but at the anonymous poems of popular origin where there is hardly a trace of Confucian, Buddhist or other Chinese philosophical vocabulary. The *Kojiki* and the *Nihon shoki*, standing in between, relying on foreign concepts and a foreign language, arranged and structured indigenous legends, ballads and attitudes with the specific intention of supporting the *Ritsuryō* system itself.

THE KOJIKI AND NIHON SHOKI

The *Kojiki* (3 vols., 712) begins with an account of the creation of Heaven and Earth, the birth of the gods and the formation of the Japanese islands, and the relationships between the gods and their various deeds; it proceeds to an account of the semi-legendary Emperors of Japan beginning with Emperor Jimmu and finally deals with the historical Emperors, concluding with the Empress Suiko who ruled in the late sixth and early seventh centuries. The *Nihon shoki* (30 vols., 720) likewise begins with an account of the Creation and the various gods and then gives a chronological record (which is in many cases suspect) of the reigns of the Emperors of Japan from Emperor Jimmu to the late seventh-century Empress Jitō. The *Kojiki* contains a preface in Chinese by Ōno Asomi Yasumaro and the main text is written partly in Chinese, partly in Chinese characters used phonetically to represent the syllables of Japanese names etc., and partly in characters used to convey the whole meaning of Japanese words. The *Nihon shoki* has no preface and is written entirely in Chinese.

The *Kojiki* was not widely read until the development of *Kokugaku* ('national' studies) in the Tokugawa period, while the *Nihon shoki* was revered as Japan's first authentic history. Court chronicles continued to be written to supplement it. Modern historians value highly the records provided by the *Nihon shoki*, for the period of the late seventh century was not covered by the *Kojiki*. However, as works of literature, both are coherent and are of profound interest in the history of thought in that they provide accounts of the age of the gods and the legendary Emperors.

We have already touched briefly on the circumstances surrounding the compilation and source materials of the two histories. As far as the basic contents are concerned, the compilers sought out fragmentary myths and stories originally transmitted in the provinces, interwove ballads known at court and among the people at large and embellished and organized the whole of this material through the medium of adopted figures of speech from China, historical formats similarly adopted and Confucian philosophy. In other words in the *Kojiki* and *Nihon shoki* there was an encounter between popular indigenous culture spanning from the Yayoi period to as late as the seventh century and the foreign culture which had been learned by the intellectuals of the court between the late seventh and early eighth centuries. However, there was more to it than that. The way the source materials of popular indigenous culture was sought out and even the way the narrative as a whole was treated were not as simple imitations of mainland models, and in the very way the stories are told the structure of the indigenous spirit emerges.

The most ancient portions of the source material, that is to say the fragmentary myths concerning the gods, were not unique to Japan. For example, the Sun Goddess (Amaterasu) is a figure by no means entirely associated with Japan and her grandson Ninigi no Mikoto and the story of how he descended from Heaven to the mountains of Kyūshū has many parallels in Northern Asia. There is for example a very similar myth concerning the origin of Korea when the God Kan'yū is supposed to have descended to the summit of Mt. Taihaku.

Many other Japanese myths included in the *Kojiki* and *Nihon shoki* have parallels in Southern Asia. How and when these myths were transmitted is not clear, but at the time the source material for the two histories was being collected, these stories which had become an intrinsic part of indigenous belief and legend were a complex synthesis of North and South Asian elements. That much is certain. There was nothing unique or original about the source material. However, the collation of so much material from the provinces and the compilation of it into a kind of compendium of mythology was specific to ancient Japan.

When one examines the contents of the *Kojiki* and *Nihon shoki*, it seems to emerge, generally speaking, that before the time when they were compiled there were two major lines of gods identifiable in provincial tradition – the Izumo line and the Yamato line. The Izumo line concentrated on Kami-musuhi, Susanoo (the Storm God) and Susanoo's sons, particularly Ōnamuchi (or Ōkuninushi). The Yamato line was concentrated on Takami-musuhi, Amaterasu and her sons, and it seems that the ruling families of Izumo and Yamato claimed descent respectively from these different groups of gods. It is easy to see that the Yamato clan combined these two lineages of deities within the *Kojiki* and *Nihon shoki* as there are inconsistencies in the relationships between gods of different lineages, and also because there are narrative discrepancies between the *Izumo fudoki* and the *Kojiki* and *Nihon shoki*.

In the text of the *Kojiki* and the *Nihon shoki* Susanoo appears as the brother of Amaterasu and as an evil god who ascends to Heaven and makes all kinds of mischief on account of which he is expelled from Heaven. However, when driven back to earth, instead of performing evil deeds, he overcomes evil and assists good. Moreover, his son Ōkuninushi is a good god. No reason is given for this sudden change of character. If forced to make an explanation one can only think that Susanoo symbolized two originally different gods – one the evil god driven from Heaven, the other the good god living on Earth.

The reason that Susanoo had to represent in one entity the evil god as depicted by the Yamato clan, and the good god as depicted by the Izumo clan, was doubtless that the various gods of the Izumo line had to be tied by blood with the gods of Heaven of the Yamato line. The discrepancies between the *Izumo fudoki* and the *Kojiki* and *Nihon shoki* are vividly demonstrated by the story of *Kuni-yuzuri* ('surrendering the country'). According to the *Izumo fudoki*, the god Ōkuninushi gave the country to the descendants of Amaterasu (the symbol of the Yamato Court), but Izumo itself was not included in the gift and continued to be independent. However, according to the *Kojiki* and *Nihon shoki*, he handed over all the provinces of the Reed Plain (i.e. Japan) to an envoy from Amaterasu.

The compiler of the *Izumo fudoki* was a provincial man, but the work was compiled in the early eighth century at the request of the Yamato court. To say that Izumo was the province of Ōkuninushi while all the rest of Japan belonged to the descendants of Amaterasu was perhaps a compromise on the compiler's part. The compilers of the *Kojiki* and *Nihon shoki* had no need for such a compromise and in telling the story of the 'surrendering' of the country took the stance that Ōkuninushi had made a complete submission.

The basic reason why the *Kojiki* and *Nihon shoki* attempted to incorporate all the provincial deities into one system was to legitimize the imperial power in Yamato by pretending that the Emperors were blood descendants of the gods. The Emperor Temmu who is said to have ordered the compilation of both works must have felt the need for such legitimization particularly intensely. In 672 he only just managed to emerge victorious in a violent dispute over the imperial succession.

The preface to the *Kojiki* which goes into some detail about the Emperor Temmu describes how when ordering the compilation of the work he said 'This is the framework of the state, the great foundation of imperial influence'. (In describing the Jinshin Rebellion, the *Nihon shoki* says that the future Emperor Temmu recaptured the imperial power which had once been bequeathed to him through a war waged in legitimate self-defence. In this case too the basic justification for the inheritance of imperial power was the right of blood and the dispute between the two princes who had legitimate claim to the succession was justified with moral reasons. This moralistic justification is in general terms much more heavily emphasized in the *Nihon shoki* than in the *Kojiki*, which however contained no record of the 672 conflict.)

In neither the *Kojiki* nor the *Nihon shoki* can one find any other basic principle for the assumption of imperial power than the right to hold it through blood descent. This is in marked contrast to the Chinese tradition where great emphasis was placed on justifying the holding of imperial power by the 'Mandate of Heaven'. Another special feature of the blood relationship situation, again vastly different from the Chinese custom, was the intermarriage·that was permitted between very close relations. (For example, if the mothers were different, marriage between half-brothers and sisters was permitted.) The consanguineous marriages mentioned in the *Kojiki* and *Nihon shoki* must have been reflections of a common practice in a certain period of the development of ancient Japan and it may well be imagined that for a single family concentrated in one region, marriages outside the family were by no means compulsory. If this hypothesis is correct it would perhaps be one explanation of the extremely 'closed' nature of regional communities and the consequent high degree of integration that existed within them.

When one examines the structure of the unified mythology which is principally manifested in the *Kojiki* (there are certain differences in the records of the *Nihon shoki*, but the basic structure of the mythology is the same), the following scenario emerges.

In the beginning there were three gods in Heaven – Amano-minakanushi, Takami-musuhi, and Kami-musuhi. The first of these features hardly at all in later stories and the probability is that he was a god created from the formal necessity of adhering to continental patterns where normally three original gods were recognized. The highly abstract nature of his name also tends to confirm this; the name meaning something like the Heavenly-Central-Lord.

These three gods produced many offspring culminating with Izanagi and Izanami, respectively the male and female deities who gave birth to the Japanese islands. These two gods stirred up the sea to create land, descended to that land and were married, whereupon they proceeded to give birth to the islands of Japan and to a number of other gods. Izanami died after giving birth to the Fire God who was slain by the furious Izanagi. Izanagi then visited Izanami in the lower regions (the land of the dead or Yomi). After returning Izanagi performed a ritual cleansing of himself to rid himself of impurity. When he washed his left eye, the Sun Goddess Amaterasu was born as was the Moon Goddess Tsukuyomi when he washed his right eye; and when he washed his nose Susanoo, the Storm God, appeared.

Izanagi then divided the world among these three children, giving to Amaterasu the 'Plain of Heaven', to Tsukuyomi the 'Realm of Night', and to Susanoo the 'Sea Plain'. (According to the *Nihon shoki* he gave to Susanoo the *Ne no Kuni* which seems to have meant the Underworld.) Thereafter the Moon Goddess virtually disappears from the scene.

According to the *Kojiki* and *Nihon shoki*, the world consists of the Plain of Heaven given to Amaterasu, the Earth (Middle Earth of the Reed) – who should rule it would become the main plot of the history of the divine age in both the *Kojiki* and *Nihon shoki* – and the Sea Plain or Underworld given to Susanoo. In other words the world concept of the *Kojiki* and the *Nihon shoki* was the three-fold division between Heaven, Earth and the Sea or Heaven, Earth and the Underworld. Stories appear in both works about events on the surface of the sea and under the waves and about the worlds beneath the surface of the earth. The former was a world of light approximating to the Taoist concept of Paradise, while the latter, the Underworld, was a place of darkness and shadows.

It is hard to decide which world was the older in Japanese thought, but both had in common that it was possible for a mortal man from this Earth to live there for a time and then return. In this sense both were extensions of the Earth. The gods who lived in Heaven sometimes visited the Earth and in exceptional cases a mortal had the power to transform himself after death (into a white bird who flew up to Heaven in the case of Yamato Takeru) and join the gods. In other words, Heaven too was not totally divorced from this world. Moreover, in the myths of the *Kojiki* and the *Nihon shoki* it is sometimes difficult to tell whether a given event is taking place in Heaven or on Earth. The gods conspired, fought one another, were jealous of one another, threatened, punished, married, danced, laughed and cried. It would be better to consider the Plain of Heaven as an extension of the Yamato Court – or rather, as a kind of ancestor of that court set in space. Heaven was not a place where the gods were born but rather a necessary meeting place where the gods who roamed the earth could be united. The Heaven of the *Kojiki* and *Nihon shoki* was inspired by the Chinese world view. Heaven and Earth were not divorced from one another and it is perhaps not surprising that the age of the gods became inextricably involved with the ancestry of the rulers of men. The indigenous world view which runs through the pages of the *Kojiki* and the *Nihon shoki* did not imply a world which transcended the realities of this earth but was totally of this world.

The stories of Amaterasu and Susanoo (and later Ōkuninushi) which form part of the central development of the *Kojiki* deal with the fight between the two gods in Heaven and Susanoo's banishment to Earth; the famous incident in which Amaterasu retires into a cave because of the mischief made by Susanoo and the antics of the gods to lure her from the cave; the deeds of Susanoo on Earth; and the activities of Susanoo's son (or grandson) Ōkuninushi in Izumo.

The accounts of the last of these are particularly detailed, and many stories about him are included such as the incident in which he was killed in a fight for one woman with the '80 gods' (Yasogami) and restored to life by an envoy sent from Heaven by Kami-musuhi. There are a great many other stories about him; going down to the *Ne no kuni* to see Susanoo and escape with his daughter Suseri-bime; his love affair with a woman in *Koshi no kuni*, and the jealousy of Suseri-bime; the foundation of the Middle Earth of the Reed in co-operation with Sukunahikona, the son of Kami-musuhi. During this long series of stories, however, the gods of the line of Takami-musuhi and Amaterasu seem to have been entirely forgotten. The only intermediary deity from Heaven who appears in these stories is Kami-musuhi and he is not described as having played any role at all in the *Kojiki* stories about Heaven.

Susanoo himself is the main linking character between events prior to and post his banishment from Heaven. However, there is more to it than that. In the Yamato tradition it was Izanagi and Izanami who created the Japanese islands; in the Izumo tradition it was Ōkuninushi and Sukunahikona. Therefore in order to have some consistency about the stories of Heaven and Earth at about the time of Susanoo's banishment from Heaven it was essential to introduce some kind of link between the Amaterasu line and the Ōkuninushi line. This link in the *Kojiki* is provided by the story of 'surrendering the country'.

However, this transference was not easily accomplished. Twice envoys sent by Takami-musuhi and Amaterasu returned with their mission unfulfilled. The third envoy, Take-mikazuchi, conquers Izumo and brings about the fulfillment of the 'surrender of the country', although, as has already been suggested, the account of this provided in the *Izumo fudoki* is substantially different.

After this the gods of Izumo disappear as a separate line. Ninigi, grandson of Amaterasu, descends to Earth and lays the foundation of the Yamato Court while his great-grandson, the Emperor Jimmu founds the line of Emperors who complete the conquest of Japan and descend thereafter in an unbroken line.

This at any rate is the general outline of the story, although, of course in the accounts given in the two chronicles there are obscurities and inconsistencies. However, to rationalize the blood relationships of the various gods and the legends associated with them even to the extent that was achieved is indicative of a remarkable talent in the compiler of the account. We are not sure exactly who was the man who put all this together but there is no room for doubt that he had clarity of purpose and selected, organized and structured his material to the highest intellectual standards. In the *Kojiki* at least the work bears the vivid stamp of the intellectual selectiveness of the times rather than revealing the influence of compartmentalized continental culture. The so-called myths included in the *Kojiki* and *Nihon shoki* were not the true myths which lived in the hearts of the people at large, but were rather 'mythological literature' created by the ruling class.

However, there is something of the spirit of the ordinary people captured by the literary ruling class, as shown in the *way* of telling the story of the *Kojiki* and *Nihon shoki*. The special feature here was the tendency to wander from the main point of the story and give detailed anecdotes and tales which were out of proportion to their significance in the whole work. This tendency was definitely not continental in nature. Traditional Chinese thought tends towards an ordered whole and the breaking down of the whole into parts was doubtless symptomatic of indigenous Japanese thought patterns free from the influence of the mainland.

The aims of the *Kojiki* and *Nihon shoki*, the actual literary framework used to encompass those aims and the way of interweaving stories into the chronological narrative style were the consequence of Continental culture having been thoroughly assimilated by the upper class intelligentsia. The insertion of stories irrelevant to the main thread of the narrative simply because they were of interest and the intense concentration on details were the consequence of the heart of the people at large still beating in the chests of those same upper class intellectuals.

This phenomenon is much more pronounced in the *Kojiki* than it is in the *Nihon shoki* and for that reason the *Kojiki* is interesting to the modern reader as literature but unsatisfactory as general history or indeed dynastic history.

Stories concerning the Emperor Nintoku, for example, appear in both the *Kojiki* and *Nihon shoki*. They include the account of how he earned the title of Sage-Emperor when he ascended to a high place and seeing that no smoke was rising from the houses of the people gathered that they were poor and accordingly abolished taxes and compulsory labour for three years. The concept of 'Sage-Emperor' clearly has a Confucian flavour. The episode is essentially moralistic and lacking in real colour, so that from it we can gain no clear idea of the character and psychology of Nintoku. What formed the principal subject matter of the lengthy section following this incident? The word 'Sage-Emperor' first appears here in the two histories and if he had been a Sage-Emperor in the Confucian concept, what followed should have dealt with the way in which he ruled the country and his attitudes towards his people. However, especially in the *Nihon shoki* where the account is very detailed indeed, it is not Nintoku's ruling of the country and people which is described but his relationships with women. We see no reason in all this to justify his being called Sage-Emperor. Moreover, the further the deviation from matters of state to private affairs, the clearer the narrative becomes.

In all the accounts of Nintoku's relationship with his Empress and their various personal tribulations a vivid and lively picture of the psychology of the Emperor emerges. One such tribulation involves various aspects of the Empress' jealousy; how she decides not to return to the court but to seclude herself in the mountain out of spite, yet is unable to get her husband out of her mind. A modern reader might even feel in this some suggestion that the ancestry of the modern period's 'I-novel' novels could be traced back to the *Kojiki* and *Nihon shoki*. However, the Sage-Emperor's relationships with women were not necessarily confined to the sphere of simple everyday life. Nintoku wanted his Empress' sister Medori as a concubine and sent his younger brother Hayabusawake as an intermediary. However, Medori and Hayabusawake themselves fell in love. Nintoku did not kill his brother at that stage but thinking his brother guilty of treachery, sent soldiers in pursuit of the couple and killed them – this, remember, the Nintoku who was labelled 'Sage-Emperor'.

The editor of the *Nihon shoki* apparently felt that such an action was a barrier to Nintoku's sagacity, and made the moralistic explanation that the couple were not killed for reasons of Nintoku's private jealousy but because his younger brother had betrayed his trust. However, the compiler of the *Kojiki* seems not even to have considered any moralistic explanation necessary. Of course we have no way of knowing how true any of these stories of Nintoku are, but to reach the following conclusions such knowledge is unnecessary. First, the compilers of the *Kojiki* and the *Nihon shoki* introduced the concept of a Sage-Emperor under the direct influence of Chinese thought. Second, the account of the Sage-Emperor is scanty in providing stories explaining where Nintoku's wisdom actually lay and rich in anecdotes concerning his private life, totally unconnected with his supposed wisdom. Third, the abundance of perceptive and vivid stories concerning Nintoku's private life are indicative of the literary talents of the compilers. Moreover, such stories are told not only of Nintoku but of many other characters from both works.

It has already been said that the indigenous Japanese world view which permeates the *Kojiki* and *Nihon shoki* was 'this-worldly' and not transcendental. Thus the gods are not represented as one transcendental entity. The gods who are united into one system in the two chronicles and whose development was closely related to agrarian society and subject to influences from the mythology of other parts of Asia, were not incarnations of justice, beauty, truth or fate. Since they did not exist as absolute entities there were no tragic stories of heroes battling unavailingly against the absolute.

If anything at all was absolute it was the community itself which was intensified through the legitimacy of imperial rule. Since even the gods were reflections of the community's past and extensions of human society, human beings lived in a direct relationship with other human beings and the essentially 'human' gods. In this sense, and in this sense only, the world of the *Kojiki* and the *Nihon shoki* could be described as 'humanistic'.

A great many ballads which probably were transmitted by the peasantry were incorporated into the two chronicles as supposedly the work of the gods, the Emperors and the imperial family – the dramatic heroes of the narrative. These ballads were never related to noble missions, to the world after death or to absolute and abstract ideas, but were direct expressions of love for the native province and love between men and women. Moreover, that so many of these ballads were appropriate, coming from the mouths of dramatic heroes, is probably a reflection of the fact that the structure of the emotions of these demi-god heroes was in essence no different from that of the peasantry.

For example, before sacrificing her life to appease the anger of the god of the sea-crossing in order to get him to spare the life of Yamato-takeru, Oto-tachibana-hime sings this song:

> O you, my lord, alas –
> You who once, standing among the flames
> Of the burning fire, spoke my name
> On the mountain-surrounded
> Plain of Sagamu!

Again Yamato-takeru when sorely ill on one of his expeditions of conquest puts his nostalgia and love of country into this song:

> Yamato is
> The highest part of the land;
> The mountains are green partitions
> Lying layer upon layer.
> Nestled among the mountains,
> How beautiful is Yamato!

Few poems show more clearly than these how suitable peasant songs were to their adapted use as ballads of the dramatic heroes.

According to the *Kojiki*, after Yamato-takeru has with due despatch accomplished the mission set him by his father the Emperor to kill the two unruly brothers Kumaso in the West, he visits his aunt at the great shrine of Ise. Having just been given a new mission to subdue the East, he weeps and asks his aunt whether the mission has been given to him because his father wants him to die. Together with several tales of his amorous adventures, there are other of this type of peasant ballad sung as if composed by Yamato-takeru himself, expressing the love for home and reluctance to leave it.

When the *Nihon shoki* borrowed from foreign thought and made a hero and idol of Yamato-takeru, it to a great extent destroyed the man as a character. According to the *Nihon shoki*, after Yamato-takeru's return from slaying the brothers Kumaso-takeru, the Emperor his father praised him and bestowed 'extraordinary affection' on him. As far as subduing the East is concerned, the *Nihon shoki* has it that Yamato-takeru volunteered for the mission after the task had been given to his elder brother and he had run away in terror. The peasant ballads would not have been suitable coming from the mouth of such a character.

The most beautiful and most inspired sections of the *Kojiki* almost always are related to love stories, especially those having to do with elopement. For example, take the tragic love of the full brother and sister Karuno-miko and Karuno-ōiratsume. Because of the forbidden love affair, Karuno-miko was sent into exile where his sister followed him. According to the *Kojiki*, together in exile the couple decide that, without love, home and country mean nothing and after a long exchange of love songs they commit suicide together. The idea thus presented that love finds complete fulfillment in death is widespread in Japanese literature from the *Kojiki* onwards. Basically, within the structure of the 'This-worldly' world view of the Japanese, this may be seen as an attempt to give a kind of eternalism to the strong emotions of human love.

FOLK TALES AND BALLADS

What do we know of the beliefs and feelings of the mass of the people living in the provinces before the Nara period? Two important materials for the study of this are the *fudoki* and the so-called 'ancient ballads'.

The *fudoki*, written mostly in Chinese, were records of each province of Japan compiled in the first half of the eighth century as the result of an order made by the central government in 713. They contained the names of each place in each province together with their origins, a record of the produce and nature of the soil in each province and ancient stories. Many of these last were extremely fragmentary, but some of them comprise the mythology and secular folk tales of the provinces. -

The only *fudoki* to have survived to the present in reasonably

complete form are the *Hitachi fudoki*, the *Harima fudoki* and, especially, the *Izumo fudoki* which appear to have been completed respectively *c*. 715, *c*. 723 and in 733. Small sections from the *Hizen
fudoki* and the *Bungo fudoki* have also survived and these seem to
have been completed at some time between the *Harima* and *Izumo
fudoki*. In addition fragments of other *fudoki*, otherwise lost, have
been preserved through having been quoted in other works. As
far as the compilers of the extant *fudoki* are concerned it is certain
only in the case of the *Izumo fudoki* that they were natives of the
province concerned. This may be what makes the contents of the
Izumo fudoki so special and distinctive. It has already been especially mentioned that the work's emphasis on the gods of the
Izumo clan, is in marked contrast to the *Kojiki* and the *Nihon shoki*
where the gods of the Yamato clan are treated as much more
important.

Provincial beliefs, different from the so-called myths of the
Kojiki and *Nihon shoki*, are not systematised in the *fudoki*. Even in
the same region contradictory tales appear, as is shown by the
Izumo fudoki's two stories of *Kunibiki* ('land-pulling', i.e. expand-
ing the province by the divine means of 'pulling' land to Izumo)
and *kuni yuzuri* ('surrendering the land'). The central character of
the first story is the god Yatsukamizuono-mikoto who, declaring that the province of Izumo is too small, casts a rope,
draws in land from various surrounding places and binds it to
Izumo. The process is repeated again and again until the province
is deemed big enough. However, the hero of the second story,
Ōnamochi-no-mikoto (Ōkuninushi), is named as 'The great god
who created the world'. In Izumo mythology it is not explicitly
clear which of these two created the land. The *Kojiki* attempted to
unite the gods of the Izumo line into one system by making
Yatsukamizuo the direct descendant of Susanoo in the fourth generation, but originally the two gods were not related, and even
within the Izumo clan itself we can judge that Yatsukamizuo and
Ōkuninushi were mutually independent from the fact that they
were 'born' in different places.

In the *Hitachi fudoki* there are three 'descent' myths. First in
order to subjugate the country of Mizuho, the 'great god of the
Heaven of Kashima' descended from the 'Plain of Heaven' and
later the same god, dressed in a white robe, descended to the
peak of Mt. Ōsaka. Second, the god Kamuhata-himeno-mikoto

made two descents respectively to Tsukushi Province and Hiuga, but later moved to the hill of Hikitsune in Mino Province. Third, the god Tachihayaono-mikoto descended to a pine tree at Matsuzawa in Hitachi Province, but later moved to a high peak at Kabire. The *Hitachi fudoki* was compiled by order of the central government some ten years after the completion of the *Kojiki* and it would not be surprising if there were evidence of some influence from the *Kojiki*. The first story, for example, is perhaps reminiscent of the *Kojiki*'s account of the descent of Takemikazuchi. However, the second story of Kamu-hata-hime does not feature among the descent myths of the *Kojiki*. Moreover, after Kamuhata-hime moved to Mino, Tateno-mikoto moved from Mino to Kuji and became the ancestor of the Nagahatabe, as the story in the *Hitachi fudoki* continues.

There is no mention of the relationship between Kamu-hata-hime and Tateno-mikoto, but the implication may be that the latter was a descendant of the former. If that hypothesis is correct, it can be imagined that the compilers of the *fudoki*, aware of the story current in the province that Tateno-mikoto (the ancestral deity of the Nagahatabe family) made a descent from heaven, connected this with Kamu-hata-hime and at the same time connected the two descent myths. Doubtless the substance of provincial belief was that the founder (of a family) descended from the skies to a mountain top. In the case of Tachihayao, there is no question at all of the royal family descending from deities.

The story goes that the god who descended from Heaven and lived in a pine tree brought a curse upon the people who lived close by and came to urinate and defecate near the tree. Thereupon they held a festival and requested the god to move to a mountain as he was being a nuisance to the neighbourhood. This he agreed to do. The story demonstrates that one of the purposes of a festival (in this case performed by specialists sent from the central government) was to deal with such divine curses. It also suggests both that there were innumerable examples of such gods as Tachihayao and that most of them were regarded as having descended from Heaven. Most of these gods who descended from Heaven down to the land as ancestral deities, or as the bringers of curses such as rain or hail, were swallowed up and lost through being absorbed into the unified mythological structure of the *Kojiki* and *Nihon shoki*. The accounts of the *fudoki* with regard to these gods help us to conjecture about the situation before the systematization of the mythological structure.

The *Hitachi fudoki* contains many secular legends and folk stories unrelated to the gods and they appear also in the *Izumo* and *Harima fudoki* mostly being told in the form of an account of how a particular place name originated. These tales contain virtually no Confucian or Buddhist influence, although a hint of Taoist influence may be seen in the story of Urashima which appears in the *Tango fudoki itsubun*. However, since, as what follows will show, the story of Urashima originated on the Asian mainland, this Taoist influence should not be overplayed.

In the *Harima fudoki*, there are stories of the conquest of the *Kuzu*. Among them is one which deals with how Takekashima-no-mikoto, ancestor of the founders of Naka, lures the *Kuzu* away from the fortress which they have been holding by dancing for seven days and seven nights, and then sends soldiers to kill them all. This story perhaps reflects the ruling authority which moved towards centralization after the Taika Reform. In the *Kojiki* and *Nihon shoki* also there are similar stories of legendary kings overcoming strong adversaries by such trickery.

However, stories of this kind of conquest mentioned above are exceptional, and the world of the legends and folk tales of the *fudoki* is filled with stories which, while often featuring gods in assumed human form, relate quarrels and reconciliations between human beings entirely unconnected with the gods and animals, such as snakes, white birds, deer, rabbits, sharks, etc. Typical incidents in these stories involve a snake born of a human woman growing up and turning into a thunderbolt; a white bird turning into a young girl; a goddess turning into a white bird; a deer and a rabbit having the gift of human speech and so forth. A typical story concerns the father of a girl eaten by a shark who in his wrath prays to the gods for vengeance, whereupon more than a hundred sharks surround the guilty one and bring it to the sea-shore. When the father kills the shark and cuts it open, the girl's leg comes out. Presumably, without the aid of the gods the father would have been unable to locate the shark.

In many other such stories the intervention of the gods is vital to the plot. However, the human elements of the story outlined above are those which are most striking and leave the deepest impression – the anger and grief of the father and the strong image of the girl's leg protruding from the belly of the shark. There is perhaps not to be found yet in these stories the thoroughgoing realism of the *Konjaku monogatari*, but at the same time they are in no sense disassociated from this world.

On the other hand, however, the various *fudoki* also contain some gentle and lyrical folk tales such as the story of 'Pine Grove at Unai Beach' which appears in the *Hitachi fudoki*. This runs as follows:

In ancient times there was a young man and a girl who were both highly sought after in their province – he for his handsome features and she for her beauty. From the hearsay passed on from village to village they both came to long for each other although they had not as yet set eyes on each other. By chance the two met on the night of an *utagaki* (a kind of party involving singing and courting) and exchanged poems. 'Fearing that they would be recognized', the couple fled the scene of the party and made for the sea-shore where they hid under a pine tree. So engrossed were they in their love for one another that they forgot that the night was passing until suddenly a cock crowed, a dog barked and it was dawn. 'Ashamed that people might see them', the couple turned into pine trees.

There are some obscurities in this story. For example, a man and a woman were in fact permitted to meet in this way on the night of an *utagaki*. Indeed, in the same *fudoki* the proverb is quoted, 'Unless you get a good match at a *Utagaki* party in Tsukuba mountain, you are not a woman'. How does this fit in with 'fear that they would be recognized' and 'shame that people might see them'? Doubtless some taboo was involved. However, the image of the two young lovers becoming pine trees on the sea-shore is full of tender emotion which is presented directly in a simple, apparently almost unstructured, story with no element of philosophy or psychology.

The story of Urashima which appears in the *Tango fudoki* (a work which no longer survives except in the form of extracts quoted in the *Shaku Nihongi* Vol. 12) is very different indeed. It runs as follows:

Urashima goes alone to sea to fish, catches a turtle and puts it in his boat; while he is asleep, the turtle turns into a beautiful woman. With the woman as his guide Urashima journeys to

Tokoyono-kuni, that is to say 'a great island in the depths of the sea' and lives there for three years. Eventually he decides that he wants to return to his home which he does, taking with him a *tamakushige* (equivalent to Pandora's Box). When he arrives home he finds that it is not three years which have passed but 300 and all the people he knew are long dead and gone. He misses the woman stroking the box, and then breaking the promise he gave to her, opens the box whereupon he ages 300 years in a moment and becomes aware that never again will he be able to meet the woman.

In this story the psychology of the hero is explored and the structure clearly adheres to certain rules. Moreover there is the meeting of the two worlds – the ordinary everyday world and the world beneath the waves – which differ from one another in terms of how quickly time passes in each. There is here an abstract concept, and it is that abstract thought which sets the tale of Urashima apart from other folk stories appearing in the *fudoki* and which is suggestive of a strong influence from mainland legends.

In the sense that the land beneath the waves visited by Urashima is represented as a happy island where the inhabitants live long without growing old, there is apparent influence from Taoism. However, there is more to it than that. The essential idea of the Urashima story itself – a mortal man returning from a land of 'wizardry' to his home only to find that so very many years have passed – occurs in Chinese *setsuwa* type tales. For example, in the story Liu Tieng and Yuan Chi, the two central characters visit Mt. T'ien-tai to obtain medicinal plants, lose their way, meet two girls, are guided by them to a land of 'wizardry', spend half a year of the greatest joy there and then finally return home only to find that ten generations have passed. Of course, the man who adapted this story and converted it into such an elaborate tale must have been an intellectual. The *fudoki* states that it is a record of regional legends and is no different from the narrative of Iyobe no Umakai no Muraji, the former governor of Tamba Province. Nevertheless, the reverse was probably true. That is, Umakai, who is said to have been conversant with mainland culture and to have participated in the framing of the Taihō Ritsuryō, first adapted the Chinese story and created from it the Urashima tale, and then the compilers of the *fudoki* took it up and connected it with a specific place in Japan. At any rate, the tale of Urashima was originally not a Japanese folk tale.

Despite the fact that both were written in Chinese and appeared in records compiled by command of the central government, the tales of the young couple who turned into pines and of Urashima, in their mutual contrast, also reflect the wider contrasts between the people at large in ancient Japan and the intelligentsia, between indigenous culture and mainland influences, between the everyday world and the 'other' world beneath the waves and between the world of the particular and the concrete and the world of the universal and abstract.

On the other hand there were the 'ancient ballads', a vague term which covers ballads included in the *Kojiki*, *Nihon shoki* and the *fudoki*, the 'music and dance' ballads typified by *kagura* and *saibara*, and ancient folk songs from the regions (also known as *fūzoku-uta*). The vagueness is occasioned by the fact that while we understand that the 'ballads' were chanted, we are not sure whether all the poems appearing in the *Kojiki* etc. were chanted, and although when we refer to 'ancient' we mean pre-eighth century, the date of origin of the 'music and dance' ballads is not known for certain. However, with the exception of the lyric poems composed by the compilers of the *Kojiki* and *Nihon shoki* (or the earlier works on which they were based) and inserted into stories, the great majority of 'ancient ballads' were chanted to the accompaniment of dancing on the occasion of court or folk festivals. It may be thought that most of them date from the fifth or sixth to the end of the seventh centuries.

The 'ancient ballads' in both form and content have a very pronounced distinctive flavour. The fact that while many of them were lacking in real form, there was a strong tendency towards the five- and seven-syllable line suggests that the '*tanka* form' (5-7-5-7-7) was highly regarded from a very early period. Rhymes were not systematically used, thus distinguishing the 'ancient ballads' from the rhymed forms of the ancient Chinese collections of folk ballads (such as the Shi-king). They differ, too, from the Okinawan ballad collection, the *Omorosōshi*, the ballads of which while lacking in definite form did not concentrate on the 5-7 syllable pattern as in the case of the 'ancient ballads'. (It is said that the ballads of the *Omorosōshi* were chanted between the twelfth and seventeenth centuries, the oldest of which can be traced back to the fifth or sixth centuries.)

A special characteristic of the content of the 'ancient ballads' is that while relating to gods, kings and peasants, the majority of them, at least as far as we can judge from the *Kojiki*, *Nihon shoki* and the *fudoki*, were love songs. That is to say, there was a strong tendency towards lyricism and an almost total absence of epic poetry. Moreover, apart from a few exceptions to be found in the *Nihon shoki*, they never touched on political subjects and there are very few war poems. Only one or two of the 1200 or so poems of the *Omorosōshi* are love songs and quite a large number of the poems of the *Shi-king* deal with politics and society, so here again the contents of the 'ancient ballads' are something set apart.

One of the oldest types of folk ballad derives from the previously mentioned ceremony of *utagaki* when the men and women of a village met, exchanged poems and enjoyed themselves. Four poems from the *Hitachi fudoki* were produced on such an occasion and two others refer to 'beach amusements' which probably implies something similar. The *Kojiki* contains about eight poems which may be judged as *utagaki* productions, making a total of fourteen poems altogether. Only one of these is completely lacking in form and six adhere to the *tanka* format (5-7-5-7-7). Thirteen of the fourteen at least approximate to the *tanka* format. However, these are only a few poems and to confirm that the *tanka* style format was widespread among the ancient ballads, it is necessary to examine the *saibara* and the *fuzoku-uta* also. The majority of these at first sight seem formless, but when one eliminates 'choruses' and refrains, it may be seen that the majority of them adhere closely enough to the *tanka* form to suggest that the use of this form as seen in the *utagaki* poems was quite general.

There is no reason to think that the *chōka* recorded in the *Kojiki* and *Nihon shoki* was an older form than that of the folk ballads. In the *chōka* form there was a preponderance of 5-7 syllable lines, but the number of syllables in a line was by no means standardized. With some *chōka* the last five lines corresponded to the 5-7-5-7-7 *tanka* form but were not separate in sense from the rest of the poem and did not form a separate poem in themselves. In fact, as far as we can tell, in the folk ballads written in ancient Japanese

there were poems completely without form, those in the pure
tanka form and others, such as the *fuzoku-uta* which fell midway
between the two extremes. Although it can only be conjecture
since there are no source materials to enable one to pursue the
hypothesis, it seems probable that they mark a point in the
development from formlessness to the *tanka*. At any rate, one
may think that the *tanka* and the *tanka* form motivation had their
origins among the people at large, and the intelligentsia, educated in long mainland poetic forms, came to write *chōka* in which
they still managed to preserve the rhythmic feeling of the popular
ballads.

Probably the *chōka* was a new form of poetry invented by the
intellectuals of the Asuka and Nara periods under the influence
of foreign culture. The *chōka* form began its development in the
ballads of the *Kojiki* and *Nihon shoki*, achieved its pinnacle of
attainment in the *Manyōshū* and virtually disappeared after the
time of the *Kokinshū*. In other words, the period when the influence of foreign culture was at its most marked, was the period in
which the *chōka* flourished best. It must be said that the *tanka*
form, however, was the most closely involved with the ordinary
people of ancient Japan, the oldest and longest-surviving form of
Japanese language lyric poetry, and, in fact, an ever-present part
of Japanese cultural tradition.

The previously mentioned fourteen *utagaki* poems were naturally related to love between man and woman. Among them there
are poems which can be categorized simply as laments for old age
or as pleas for constancy, but many of them directly speak of
spending a night in each other's company and sleeping together.
Six of the poems include the word 'neru' (or compounds of the
verb 'neru') used in this meaning. Here the relationship between
man and woman is not seen as something private and psychological, but collective and carnal. In an extreme case, the idea is
suggested that who one sleeps with is unimportant:

> The off-shore breezes
> Of Takashima bay.
> I long for a woman,
> And want to make love to her
> It doesn't matter if she's ugly,
> Nor does it matter if she's base.

> (Hitachi Fudoki)

Gods, agriculture, nature and rural customs all figure in the provincial folk songs, but the most frequent subject here again is emotions of the male-female relationship. Unlike the *utagaki* poems, these emotions are not confined to the group. Frequently, they are private emotions addressed as expressions of love towards a specific individual. Like the *utagaki* poems, they are carnal, sensual and poor in terms of psychological overtones. For example, unlike the *Omorosōshi* poems, the gods played no part in the folk songs and neither sorcery nor witchcraft figured at all prominently, although this of course does not mean that the people did not believe in taboos or in the gods making descents from Heaven to Earth. Rather it was because the centre of the emotional life of the people as manifested in the folk songs of ancient Japan was human relationships, not relationships with the gods or with nature.

These human relationships, particularly the male-female relationship and even more particularly the carnal and sensual presentation of that relationship, were taken up in the *chōka* and *tanka* of the *Kojiki* and *Nihon shoki*. For example, take the following lines from the song sung by Nunakaha-hime to the god Yachihoko (Ōkuninushi) which appears in the *Kojiki*:

> With your arms
> White as a rope of *taku* fibres,
> You will embrace
> My breast, alive with youth,
> Soft as the light snow;
> We shall embrace and entwine our bodies.
> Your jewel-like hands
> Will entwine with mine,
> And your legs outstretched,
> You will lie and sleep.

Almost the same lines were repeated in a *chōka* written by Suseribimeno-mikoto and addressed to Ōkuninushi. In other words the lyric poetry quoted above was not the presentation of private, individual emotions, but was linked to the collective and general world of folk ballads. The sensuality of the song is obviously apparent. Such sensuality rather reminds us of *Kālidasā* than Japanese lyrical poetry of later times. The achievement of the *Manyōshū* which was to come later was to standardize the *chōka* in form and to make lyric poetry in content a presentation of private and individual emotions. The poets of the *Manyōshū*, in place of carnality discovered and made a principal theme of nature which previously had featured only as incidental the lyric poetry of the 'ancient ballads'.

THE MANYŌSHŪ

The *Manyōshū* is the largest and oldest surviving collection of Japanese lyric poetry and was probably compiled in the second half of the eighth century. The compilers are unknown, but it seems that Ōtomono Yakamochi at least had a large hand in it.

There are about 4500 poems of which some 4200 are *waka*, some 260 *chōka*, and some 60 *sedōka*. The poems range in date of composition from the second half of the fifth century to the middle of the eighth century with the vast majority dating from the second half of the seventh to the first half of the eighth centuries. By content the poems can be divided into three categories: *zōka* (miscellaneous poems), dealing with travel, banquets, legends etc.; *sōmonka* (love poems), the vast majority of which deal with love between man and woman, but there are some which relate to the poet's feelings for his children, for his brothers and sisters; and *banka* (elegies). This mode of classification seems to have followed the divisions used for Chinese poetry.

The poems are written in what is known as *Manyōgana*, that is to say a system of recording the Japanese language with Chinese characters which are sometimes simply phonetic renderings of Japanese syllables and at other times have actual meaning (there are often differences of opinion among modern scholars as to how some words should be read).

Many of the earliest *Manyōshū* poems were written by Emperors, imperial princes and princesses. Among these are some which approximate to the ancient ballads in terms of both form (not to adhere to the 5-7-5-7-7 syllable pattern) and content (to be ceremonial and like folk songs). The very first poem by the Emperor Yūryaku on the 'Land of Yamato' is typical of this kind, but such examples are rare. However, the poems left by the Emperors and their close relatives in the late seventh century at about the time of the Jinshin Rebellion of 672 when they were closely involved in court power struggles are not of this type.

These poems were clearly expressions of private individual emotion which were written according to a settled format. For example, the brother of the Emperor Tenji, Prince Ōama (the future Emperor Temmu) one day approached Princess Nukata who once had been his wife and later married the Emperor Tenji and waved his sleeve as a signal, whereupon the Princess composed this poem:

> As they go through the fields of Murasaki,
> As they go through the hunting fields,
> Will not the field-watchers have seen it? –
> The waving of my lord's sleeves!
>
> (Vol. 1 poem 20)

The Prince replied with this poem:

> My love, delightful as the Murasaki flower;
> If I thought her hateful being the wife of another,
> Would I then still love her?
>
> (Vol. 1 poem 21)

That the elder brother had stolen the younger brother's wife and that she had a love affair with the younger brother again was not considered a taboo although this was undoubtedly a special circumstance. The special nature of the circumstances in this case was due not only to the position of the Princess Nukata, but to the strained political situation of the time. After the death of his elder brother, Prince Ōama attacked and killed his brother's son Prince Otomo and seized power in the Jinshin Rebellion. The relationship between Princess Nukata and the future Emperor Temmu was complicated from many angles and there is no doubt that this is reflected in their exchange of poems.

The struggle for power inevitably produced many tragic casualties. In 658 the Emperor Tenji condemned Prince Arima to death and in 686 the same fate befell Prince Ōtsu at the hands of the future Empress Jitō. Prince Arima when on the last journey he was to make in this life seems to have had still some slight hope of life:

> At Iwashiro I bind
> The branches of a shore pine.

If fortune favours me,
I may come back
And see the knot again.

(Vol. 2 poem 141)

Just before his death Prince Ōtsu paid a secret visit to his sister Princess Ōku at the Ise Shrine and the two poems composed by the Princess at their parting give the impression that she had some premonition her brother would soon be dead. However, here I quote the poem composed by Prince Ōtsu as he was about to die:

Today, taking my last sight of the mallards
Crying on the pond of Iware,
Must I vanish into the clouds!

(Vol. 3 poem 416)

In the *Kaifūsō* is a poem written, in Chinese, in similar circumstances:

The golden raven of the sun travels west
The beat of the drum sets my life towards its end
There are no guests, no host in the Underworld
Where this night I travel from my home.

Prince Ōtsu's poem, written in Japanese, speaks of taking a last look at the mallards on the pond, while the Chinese poem speaks of a man about to set his footsteps towards death, while lamenting the brevity of this life. Neither of the Princes seem to have given a thought to either Shinto gods or Buddhism. The hanging of Prince Arima was carried out about fifty years after the building of the Hōryūji (607) and the execution of Prince Ōtsu just after the building of the Yakushiji (684). Not only had Buddhism failed as yet to permeate to the people at large, it seems to have failed to make its presence felt even in the elegies composed by members of the aristocratic ruling class. There was no Buddha waiting for these men after death, at least to judge from their poems where they simply expressed the desire to live longer, a reluctance to leave this world and bewailed the brevity of life. However, we shall come to the elegies later.

In the second half of the seventh century, apart from the poets of the imperial family, there emerged a class of courtiers who practised poetry as a kind of profession. Kakinomoto no Hitomaro is, of course, the outstanding example of this kind of poet. Nothing is known of Hitomaro's life. The *Manyōshū* contains altogether more than 450 *waka* including 20 *chōka* written by him. These poems can be divided into two types: those written, so to speak, 'officially' in his capacity as a court poet when writing to a specific demand; and those poems which may be considered as private expressions of his own emotions.

His official poems include many eulogies and elegies and, particularly in his *chōka*, Hitomaro displayed unsurpassed craftsmanship. He made considerable use of *makura kotoba* ('pillow words') and *joshi* (introductory verses), excelled with refrain and *tsuiku* (parallel phrases) and with his rich, colourful and resonant vocabulary often achieved a kind of epic quality in his poetry. Take, for example, the following extract from one of his elegies

> So it may well be that grieving beyond measure,
> And moaning like a bird unmated,
> He seeks your grave each morn.
> I see him go, drooping like summer grass,
> Wander here and there like the evening-star,
> And waver as a ship wavers in the sea.
>
> (Vol. 2 poem 196)

This poem, of which only part appears here, was written on the occasion of the temporary enshrinement of the Princess Asuka and refers to the grief of the husband of the dead princess. It is given a kind of flow by the use of colourful vocabulary like 'bird unmated', 'summer grass', 'evening-star' etc. which all convey connecting ideas. It is worth noting that this association of ideas is often related to objects from the world of nature. *Makura kotoba* and *joshi* were in use before the time of Hitomaro, but no poet before or after him used them quite so effectively.

Hitomaro brought the *chōka* to the pinnacle of its achievement. Later, court poets of the eighth century, for example, such as Yamabeno Akahito, are commonly said to have imitated Hitomaro's *chōka* without achieving his success. One may think, however, that this served to demonstrate vividly that the *chōka* poetic form, for all Hitomaro's technical accomplishments with it, was suited neither to the Japanese language nor to the Japanese people. First, it did not regularize and make provision for rhyme (as in Chinese and European languages), for long and short vowels (as in Latin) or for undulating rhythms (as in English).

Technically, the *chōka* form is impoverished when compared with non-Japanese language poetic forms. Second, it confined itself to the eulogy wishing for the eternal reign of the Emperor and the evocation of the everyday world of nature. Occasionally one finds (as with vol. 2 poem 199) a *chōka* which while lamenting the death of a prince describes his valiant and mighty deeds in this life, but these are exceptional and are lacking in the epic richness one might expect. Third, in the *chōka* which Hitomaro wrote in his official capacity for ceremonial purposes, one finds no sign of the poet's own emotion or of lofty idealism. The 'great lords' of whom he writes in his elegies did not (as far as the poetry is concerned) serve an ideal; they *were* the ideal. To put this another way, the poems do not contain the ideals and values of the poet himself, but simply reflect those of the society group into which he was integrated. Under such circumstances, even with the talents of a Hitomaro, it was close to impossible to expand the *chōka* without degenerating into sheer monotony. Thus the 'long poems' (*chōka*) of Hitomaro may have been pre-eminently long as far as the history of Japanese language poetry is concerned, but in terms of the history of world poetry they were pre-eminently short. At any rate the *chōka* tradition virtually ended with the *Manyōshū*.

However, in the second type of Hitomaro's poetry, the private poetry, there is a pathos which still has the power to stir the modern reader. This is particularly true of some of the elegies – not the elegies written for the princes and princesses of the court, but the elegies written in grief for the death of his own wife. Here Hitomaro achieves astonishing quality as a lyric poet. There are two *chōka* on this theme each with two 'envoy' poems attached. The first *chōka* begins with words of regret that their time together was too short:

> Since in Karu lived my wife,
> I wished to be with her to my heart's content;
> But I could not visit her constantly
> Because of the many watching eyes –
> Men would know of our troth
> Had I sought her too often.
>
> (Vol. 2 poem 207)

The form of marriage in which the husband and wife lived in different places and the husband hesitated to visit the wife too often for fear of 'prying eyes' was a custom of seventh-century Japan. However, Hitomaro's expression of regret transcends time and place and can be understood by anyone. When the news was unexpectedly brought to Hitomaro that his wife was dead he did not know 'what to say' or 'what to do'. To ease his heart he went to the market place where his wife often used to go.

> And hoping to heal my grief
> Even a thousandth part,
> I journeyed to Karu and searched the market-place
> Where my wife was wont to go!
>
> There I stood and listened
> But no voice of her I heard,
> Though the birds sang in the Unebi Mountain;
> None passed by, who even looked like my wife.
> I could only call her name and wave my sleeve.
>
> (op. cit.)

Two *makura kotoba* are used in this extract, but all the other words simply and graphically serve to portray a man standing alone and still in the market place. Even after his wife was no longer there, life carried on as if nothing had happened. When he says that none of the passers-by looked like his wife it shows that their world and the poet's world were sundered. In Hitomaro's 'official' elegies his colourful language was not sufficient to stir the emotions, but in his own private elegy for his dead wife the situation was reversed and his strong human emotion gave profound meaning to the trivia of everyday life which he describes in restrained language.

This *chōka* was followed by a *hanka* or 'envoy' poem:

> In the autumn mountains
> The yellow leaves are so thick.
> Alas, how shall I seek my love
> Who has wandered away? –
> I know not the mountain track.
>
> (Vol. 2 poem 208)

It has already been mentioned that the two poems written by the Princes Arima and Ōtsu as they were about to die contained no reference to Buddhism. There is no trace of Buddhism either in this Hitomaro poem written in the seventh century for his dead wife. The second *chōka* tells of the tree which they looked at together, of the chamber where Hitomaro and his wife once lay together, of the son she bore him, and laments:

> Men tell me that my wife is
> In the mountains of Hagai –
> Thither I go,
> Toiling along the stony path;
> But it avails me not,
> For of my wife, as she lived in this world,
> I find not the faintest shadow.
>
> (Vol. 2 poem 210)

The 'mountains of Hagai' may refer to the place his wife was buried. Whether or not the poet expected to be able to meet his wife there, it is certain at least that he places no Buddhist connotation on her death.

One of the most famous court poets after Hitomaro was Yamabeno Akahito about whose life nothing is known. He not only wrote official poetry but is famous for his poems of scenic description. However, these poems which describe nature apart from human affairs were not an invention of Akahito and were written both by Hitomaro himself and his contemporary Takechino Kurohito. The scenery Hitomaro and Kurohito chose to depict was not lofty mountains, not desolate plains, not great oceans and not forests filled with wild beasts, but gentler places such as Kagu-yama, Murasaki fields, bays where boats passed to and fro between islands, and shallows where the cranes made their cries:

> As we row round the jutting beaches,
> Cranes call in flocks at every inlet
> Of the many-harboured lake of Ōmi.
>
> (Kurohito. Vol. 3 poem 273)

> From Nawa cove we see the distant isle;
> And rowing in the foreground is a ship.
> Whose ship? Perhaps some fisherman's.
>
> (Akahito. Vol. 3 poem 357)

These poems reveal no important differences and show that Akahito was not an original poet.

As one can see from their use of *makura kotoba*, the court poets of the *Manyōshū* were profoundly influenced by nature and both their love poems and their elegies reflect this. Because of love, cherry blossoms, birds, the wind and the moon seemed to have meaning to the poet; because of grief, mountains, rivers, grass and trees seemed to have life. Nature was always a reflection of human feelings; the reverse was never true. To be sure, these poets were deeply attached to and sensitive to nature and the changing seasons, but 'nature' was always interpreted in a very restricted way and there was a pronounced tendency to confine it to terms of highly conventionalized imagery. For example, there are many poems about the moon – a natural phenomenon – but few about the sun or the stars – just as much natural phenomena. The sea was somewhere small used by tiny boats and pleasure craft, not the mighty ocean over which the great ships to T'ang China sailed. Nature to them was not something vast and wild, but something small, gentle and intimate. The *Manyōshū* is in the main a collection of love poems, the poets of which entrusted their feelings to nature in this form.

Therefore in the poems of the *Manyōshū* there was bred a kind of undying love for nature which was entirely divorced from human love and the emotions of bereavement. This was true of Kurohito's poems and even more so of those of Akahito. Love is difficult to find, bereavement rare, but the affection for nature is constant and it is always possible to compose a poem of scenic description. Hitomaro was the author of 'official' poetry, but when the opportunity occurred he entrusted his own passions to his private poetry which was not written for public display. Akahito wrote even his private poetry as an official court poet, not necessarily waiting for bursts of emotion. Inevitably, therefore, he had to specialize in scenic description and he had to remain faithful to precedent. His great significance lies in that he was the first truly professional poet. This poet without originality discovered how to discover nothing. In other words, he was the master of cliché or stereotype. It is not in the least surprising that he was so revered by later generations of professional poets.

The *Manyōshū* contains many poems written by women and probably there have been few ages in the history of East or West when women in such numbers wrote lyric poetry. Some of the

accomplished women poets of the *Manyōshū* produced masterpieces. 'Women's literature' did not emerge suddenly and unexpectedly in the court literature of the Heian period. Already in the
age of the *Manyōshū*, women were playing an important role in
the development of native literature, and indeed it was only after
the thirteenth century and the development of the warrior ruling
class and their ethics (in particular Confucianism which stressed
the differences between men and women) that this role declined
and disappeared.

Feminine grace was an early ideal in Japan, but later, under the
influence of foreign culture, much greater emphasis was placed
on the quality of manliness. (Kamo Mabuchi wrote of the mascu-
linity of the *Manyōshū* and was fascinated by its contrast with the
essentially effeminate nature of the society of the Heian court. In
fact this was already well in evidence in the Nara period, but not
quite as fully developed.) The *Manyōshū* above anything else is a
collection of love poems and the female poets represented in it
certainly did not spare their talents in this direction.

Princess Nukata has already been mentioned. The Lady
Ōtomono Sakanoue was an eighth-century poetess who contributed many works to the *Manyōshū*. She was the aunt of Ōtomo
Yakamochi and is said to have exerted an enormous influence on
him. Her daughter was Yakamochi's wife. She wrote poems on a
very wide variety of themes including scenic description and
elegies, but the overwhelming majority are love poems. These
love poems are very revealing of the psychology of a woman in
love and at the same time are polished and rich in nuance. One of
her best poems is on the theme of a lover who does not keep an
assignation:

> Even if you say, 'I come',
> At times you will not come.
> Now you say: 'I will not come.'
> Why should I look for your coming–
> When you say you will not come!
>
> (Vol. 4 poem 527)

One can only say that this is a remarkable expression of the
psychology of someone kept waiting. One of her *chōka* is on a
similar theme of the woman who waits for a lover who does not
come and sends no tidings:

> . . . Truly men call us 'weak women'
> Crying like an infant . . .

(Vol. 4 poem 619)

The 'envoy' to this *chōka* reads:

> If from the beginning
> You had not made me trust you,
> Speaking of long, long years,
> Should I have known now
> Such sorrow as this?

(Vol. 4 poem 620)

In such psychological expressions as this there is an element of what almost amounts to analysis of human nature (moeurs) by French 'moralists'. So far had the Nara Court come.

However, to other female poets of the *Manyōshū* love was a matter of passion rather than psychology as in the case of Lady Kasa who wrote twenty-nine poems of love to Ōtomono Yakamochi:

> Oh how steadily I love you –
> You who awe me
> Like the thunderous waves
> That lash the sea-coast of Ise.

(Vol. 4 poem 600)

> As long as breath remains to me,
> Never shall I forget my love.
> Everyday my love will grow,
> Ever constant.

(Vol. 4 poem 595)

Nakatomino Yakamori and the Lady Sanuno Otokami exchanged sixty-three love poems when Yakamori was living in exile and the following are typical:

> O for a fire from heaven
> To haul, fold and burn up
> The long-stretched road you go! –

(Sanuno Otokami. Vol. 15 poem 3724)

> Within the bounds of heaven and earth
> None, none you can find
> Who loves you as I!

(Sanuno Otokami. Vol. 15 poem 3750)

A great many of the love poems of the *Manyōshū* rely on the imagery of cherry blossoms, birds, the wind and the moon, but the aristocratic women of the Nara court also knew how to present their passions in a direct form without the use of such imagery.

Where the love poems of the *Manyōshū* differed from the 'ancient ballads' and again from contemporary regional poetry was on one hand their sensitivity to the balance between love and the scenes of nature (even more pronounced in the period of the Heian court), and on the other hand their direct expressions of the passionate feelings encountered in love, while exploring the subtle, psychological nuances of love. This was not simply a world of sensualism and carnal passion, but one of subtle and delicate feeling. However, it was not a world of reveries, but of action and passion which were directed especially towards love. In such a world of love even the ruling class who were so enthusiastic for the culture imported from mainland Asia remained positively aware of the indigenous thought and feelings residing in their hearts and, in terms of emotions at least, these were thoroughly explored. The countries where Buddhism held sway were distant, but, in love, life was well worth living.

The relationship between man and woman which was the centre of the emotional life of the poets of the *Manyōshū* was explored not only in the *sōmonka*, but also in the *banka* or elegies. There were five types of elegy. First, the so to speak official or public elegy written in commemoration of the death of an Emperor or member of the imperial family. Second, there was the elegy written by either a husband or wife in mourning for the death of one or the other. In some cases a third person wrote such an elegy, imagining how the surviving husband (or wife) might feel. The majority of these poems, of course, were private elegies not for a public audience. Third, poets sometimes wrote an elegy for a complete stranger, when, for example, finding an abandoned corpse. These elegies too were usually private. Fourth, there is a very small number of what might be termed elegies written by men in the few moments before their death (by execution). Finally, there were elegies written mourning the death of some legendary character. Virtually all of the elegies of the *Manyōshū* fit into one or another of these categories, but it is curious that there are hardly any elegies written by a parent for its dead child or by a child for its dead mother or father. Moreover, since most of the elegies in the third category (elegies for strangers) described the grief of the husband or wife of the dead person and since the fourth category is so small, virtually all the 'private' elegies fall into the second category, at least in some sense.

Thus since the public or official elegies can be equated with any other poem written for ceremonial or other public purposes, it is perhaps reasonable to say that the majority of private elegies can be equated with love poems. To take this a stage further, except where they were written for specific ceremonial purposes, the elegies of the *Manyōshū* can be described as extensions of the love poems. In other words, they were none other than a rather specialized type of love poem.

Some of Hitomaro's elegies both public and private have already been quoted. Whether public or private, his elegies always took the form of laments on the part of the husband or wife left behind and were almost always related to thoughts of the loved-one as he or she was when still alive. For example, his elegy on the *Uneme* (a young girl serving at court, usually at the imperial table) from Tsu in the province of Kibi reflects on the transience of life and pictures the grief of the husband left behind (Vol. 2 poem 217); and his elegy on the dead body he discovers lying among the stones on the sea-shore at Sanuki (Vol. 2 poems 220–222) conjures up the image of the dead man's wife waiting for her husband to return. However, in exceptional cases the official elegies written by Hitomaro for Emperors or Princes sometimes mention the idea of their ascent into Heaven, as in the case of the elegy for Prince Takechi:

> Because of our lord who has gone
> To rule the Heavens above
> In what endless longing we live,
> Scarce heeding the days and months that pass!
>
> (Vol. 2 poem 200)

Nevertheless, such instances are rare and generally speaking the mainland idea of the spirit of the dead person ascending into Heaven does not appear. In other words, it is clear that there is hardly any trace of the influence of the Chinese interpretation of human fate after death. Moreover this applies not only to the elegies of Hitomaro himself but is supported by the general absence in the *Manyōshū* of elegies written by children for their dead parents. Again the Pure Land does not figure in Hitomaro's elegies. The dead person may go to some underworld place, but certainly not to a Buddhist realm. It is true that there are references to the transience of life, but these are made in relation to the life of a specific person and not on the nature of life in this world in general. In this sense there is a difference from the Buddhist concept of *mujō* or 'transience' which regards all life in this world as futile and emphasizes the next world (the Pure Land). However, the idea that 'life is fleeting' is in no way special to Buddhism and appears in the literature of East and West, ancient and modern. That seventh-century Japanese poets should have held this view too should not be taken to mean that they were under Buddhist influence.

With a few exceptions, the above mentioned characteristics of Hitomaro's elegies are to be found throughout the *Manyōshū* (the exceptions are principally to be found in the works of the eighth-century poets Yamanoueno Okura and Ōtomono Yakamochi and will be dealt with later). In general the elegies relate to either one or the other of the couple who was dead and dwell on what the person now dead was when still alive (the past of this world) and the grief of the partner left behind (the present of this world); scarcely ever do they mention the state of the person after death (the next world). When speaking of the person dead the central preoccupation of the elegies is with the shared experience the couple had of sleeping together and this highlights the relationship between the specific man and woman which was so vital to the world of the *Manyōshū*, whether one is discussing love poems or elegies.

The poets of the *Manyōshū* hardly ever touched on the questions of politics and society, which makes a very marked contrast to the poems of contemporary T'ang Chinese poets. On the one hand there was the Chinese poetry in which the authors showed acute concern for politics, while on the other hand there was the Japanese *waka* in which politics scarcely featured at all (here Yamanoueno Okura is again something of an exception). For all that, it is unimaginable that no one among the aristocrats and bureaucrats of the Nara court was concerned with politics. Probably the interest that existed there was different in nature from that of the T'ang Chinese poets which was bound up with their ideals, their whole sense of values and all aspects of character and so did appear as such in their poetry. For the *Manyo* poets, however, there was on the one hand the world of politics and power struggles, and on the other hand there was the world of *waka* poetry and cherry blossoms, birds, the moon and the wind – the world of love. Each was totally separate from the other. Nothing demonstrates this so vividly as the 145 poems (Vol. 15 poems 3578–722) composed by the Japanese envoys on their way to Shiragi (the Korean kingdom of Silla). About two-thirds of these are on the themes of thoughts of their wives left behind, the pain of parting and the anticipation of seeing them again. The remaining third are mainly scenic descriptions of places they visit on their journey and even here there are some ten poems on the theme of nostalgia for Nara. This deputation to Silla was a large-scale diplomatic expedition which set out in 736 and returned to Japan the following year. However, not one of the 145 poems composed by the envoys refers to the nature of their diplomatic mission. They may have composed other poems not included in the *Manyōshū*, but if they did and these did relate to political matters, then it seems that the compilers of the *Manyōshū* must have used some peculiar criteria not to have included any of them. At any rate the characteristic thought which was running through the *Manyōshū* as a principle was that the most important subject matter could not be anything but love between man and woman even for an envoy sent out by the government.

However, there were some exceptions among the aristocratic intellectuals of the eighth century who, under the influence of mainland culture, expanded the subject matter of lyric poetry and produced some very original works.

Ōtomono Tabito (665–731), after conquering a fierce tribe in Kyūshū at the behest of the Emperor, became Governor-General of the Dazaifu (the headquarters of the ancient government of Kyūshū) and died at the age of sixty-six a year after returning to Nara in 730. During his absence from Nara the Emperor Shōmu acceded to the throne, the Fujiwara family became very influential and the power of the Ōtomo family which had flourished so greatly in the sixth and seventh centuries swiftly waned. It is not difficult to imagine what violent dissatisfaction and impatience, he felt, as leader of the Ōtomo family, at being forced into the position of a regional governor. Representative examples of his feelings as presented in the *Manyōshū* are to be found in his '13 poems in praise of sake' (Vol. 3 poems 338–350).

The debt these poems owe to classical Chinese literature ('the great sage of old who gave *sake* the name of sage' – Vol. 3 poem 339; the thoughts on *sake* of the 'seven sages of the bamboo grove' – Vol. 3 poem 340; preferring to be a *sake jar* rather than a human being – Vol. 3 poem 343: all these having parallels in Chinese poetry) was noted early and pointed out by Aoki Masaji in his *Shina bungaku geijutsu-kō* of 1931. Moreover the expressions 'treasure without price' (Vol. 3 poem 345) and 'What should I care if in the next life I become a bird or a worm' (Vol. 3 poem 348) clearly derive from Buddhism and in other of Tabito's poems apart from those 'in praise of *sake*' there is clear evidence of Taoist thought.

The 'thirteen poems in praise of *sake*' could not have been written save under the direct influence of Chinese literature and yet it is difficult to imagine that his knowledge of Chinese literature would be enough to write a praise-of-*sake* poem.

> Far better, it seems, than uttering pompous words
> And looking wise,
> To drink *sake* and weep drunken tears.
>
> (Vol. 3 poem 341)

The expression 'drunken tears' recurs in three of the thirteen poems. This is not the *sake* of a Liu Ling or a Li Po and clearly here Tabito must have been expressing his own feelings of frustration and alienation. There was no custom in ancient Japan of expressing such feelings in lyric poetry. Even though Tabito's feelings arose from his personal situation, his mode of expression was only possible because he had a knowledge of Chinese literature.

> If I could but be happy in this life,
> What should I care if in the next
> I became a bird or a worm!
>
> (Vol. 3 poem 348)

The antithesis between 'this world' and 'the world to come' in this poem and the idea of changing form in different lives are clearly Buddhist, but not caring about the world to come and being content in this life only are equally clearly not Buddhist concepts. Perhaps this kind of Epicureanism was commonplace in aristocratic society of the seventh and eighth centuries. Yet no one apart from Tabito expressed it in such clear, general and abstract terms as an article of faith. This clear statement of 'Epicurean' philosophy by Tabito sharply distinguishes his poetry from virtually all that of contemporary court poets and places him much closer, for example, to Chinese poets of the late fourth century:

> Nobody knows where he goes after death
> It pleases me to live.

The Chinese poet T'ang Yuen-ming who wrote twenty poems on 'drinking *sake*' suggested in poems such as this that since he did not know what would happen to him after death he would enjoy his life according to the dictates of his heart.

There seem to have been many literary men grouped around Tabito in Kyūshū including poets represented in the *Manyōshū* such as Yamanoueno Okura, who served under Tabito as Governor of Chikuzen, and the priest Manzei who was in charge of the construction of the Kanzeonji temple in Kyūshū. We know this from the records of the poetry meeting of 730 held by Tabito while still Governor-General of the Dazaifu.

Thirty-two poets were present and the subject for composition was plum blossoms, although the majority of resultant poems were not different from the general run of Nara court poems on 'cherry blossoms, birds, the moon and the wind'. However, it might be said that this was the beginning of the poetry meetings which became so popular in the Heian period. An interesting feature is that they were not begun by the professional court poets – such as Yamabeno Akamito – but by aristocrats surrounding Tabito who, like Tabito, were living many miles away from Nara. It may be also that the custom of choosing a topic on which to compose was originated by this Kyūshū literary group.

Of course, the idea of holding poetry meetings was taken from China and that they began in Kyūshū was almost certainly related to the fact that Kyūshū was Japan's nearest point of contact with China. Moreover, these 'exiled' men of Nara living in the remote regions of Japan were doubtless brought together by their common recollections of Nara. Certainly, among

Tabito's work there are poems replete with nostalgia for Nara.

Yamanoueno Okura (660?–733?) was one of the most creative and original of the Kyūshū poets. Nothing is known of his origins, but an entry in the *Shoku Nihongi* records that in 701 he went to China as a member of an embassy. His position in that embassy was relatively minor. He returned to Japan three years later, became a member of the lower aristocracy in 714 and was made tutor to the Crown Prince in 721. This career progress was undoubtedly the result of Okura raising his position through his learning in Chinese matters. It is not known how this man of humble station acquired the learning necessary to join an official embassy in the first place, even in a minor capacity. His appointment as Governor of Chikuzen (*c*. 726) was made before the time Ōtomono Tabito became Governor-General of the Dazaifu. On Tabito's return to Nara in 730 the two men exchanged poems and later Okura became ill and died in 733. His illness may have been rheumatism and the cause of his death a weak heart.

Okura, who became proficient in Chinese composition during his years in China, was profoundly influenced by Confucianism and Buddhism. His poem 'an expostulation to a straying mind' (Vol. 5 poem 800) has a preface in Chinese in which he mentions the Three Principles (relations between ruler and subject, parent and child and husband and wife) and the Five Virtues (righteousness from the father, affection from the mother, kindness from the elder brother, modesty from the younger brother, and filial piety from the child) – clearly an influence from Confucian thought. His elegies for his dead wife (Vol. 5 poems 794–799) contain a preface written in Chinese replete with Buddhist terminology and suggesting that this world is not merely transient but sordid. Consequently he reaches the conclusion that since life is short, this life is a preparation for the life to come – a next-worldly philosophy which is the complete antithesis of the Tabito-like 'Epicurean' stance.

These poems are the only ones in the whole of the *Manyōshū* which so clearly reveal the underlying structure of Buddhist thought. However, how far Okura actually believed what he wrote is another question entirely. A careful examination of the preface to the elegies mentioned above tends to reveal that although Okura understood Buddhist thought, he was probably not capable of believing in it. Nevertheless, his understanding of both Confucianism and Buddhism was not shallow as his poems themselves prove.

Okura wrote his poems on subjects not dealt with by his contemporaries and seldom ever touched on again before the nineteenth century. First, he wrote about children and his wife as a mother of those children, as the following poems indicate:

> When I eat melon,
> I remember my children;
> When I eat chestnuts,
> Even more do I recall them.
> Whence did they come to me?
> Before my eyes they will linger,
> And I cannot sleep in peace.
>
> (Vol. 5 poem 802)

> I Okura, will leave now;
> My children may be crying,
> And that mother of theirs, too,
> May be waiting for me!
>
> (Vol. 3 poem 337)

The second poem has the title 'Leaving a banquet'. Later Japanese men not only did not write such poems, but also, from the Tokugawa period onwards, would have thought it shameful to leave a banquet for such a reason.

Second, he wrote on the wretchedness of old age. For example, his 'Elegy on the impermanence of human life' expressing the sorrow of getting grey-haired, wrinkle-faced and old without noticing contains the lines:

> . . . Before, with staffs at their waists,
> They totter along the road,
> Laughed at here, and hated there . . .
>
> (Vol. 5 poem 804)

This again is a subject not touched on by later anthologies of poetry.

Third, he wrote on poverty, the hardships inflicted by starvation, cold, and harsh taxation. This is particularly well depicted in his *chōka* 'A dialogue on poverty' (Vol. 5 poem 892), the contents of which are summed up by the 'envoy' poem which follows it:

Nothing but pain and shame in this world of men,
But I cannot fly away,
Wanting the wings of a bird.

(Vol. 5 poem 893)

Classical Chinese influence is evident in Okura's poems on old age and his poems on poverty too follow in the footsteps of a Chinese precedent *P'in-chia Fu* (Ode of a Poor Family) written by Tung Shih of the Tsin period. However it does not alter the basic originality of Okura. No other poet in the *Manyōshū* possessed his facility for sarcasm directed towards himself and a kind of black humour. For example, his *chōka* on poverty begins:

> On the night when the rain beats,
> Driven by the wind,
> On the night when the snow-flakes mingle
> With the sleety rain,
> I feel so helplessly cold.
> I nibble at a lump of salt,
> Sip the hot, oft-diluted dregs of *sake*;
> And coughing, snuffling,
> And stroking my scanty beard,
> I say in my pride,
> 'There's none worthy, save I!'

The intellectual distance he maintains from the subjects including himself allowed him to see what no other *Manyōshū* poet could, that is, children, old men and 'those who are poorer than me'; and this detachment became possible first of all through his training in foreign literature. Okura opened a new path in Japanese literature not because he imitated the mainland poetry but because through his study of Chinese literature he learned the art of revealing truth and maintaining detachment. In this way he expanded the horizons of native literature.

Ōtomono Yakamochi (717?–785) was a poet who spent his youth in Kyūshū and succeeded his father Tabito as head of the Ōtomo family. He served as Governor of Etchū (746–51) and in other provinces but lived a part of his life at the Nara court. His family received the worst end of some quarrel at court in 756 and thereafter Yakamochi seems to have enjoyed little political prominence. The last of the many Yakamochi poems contained in the *Manyōshū* – as has already been said, he was one of the compilers – was written in 759.

As far as Yakamochi's love poems are concerned, there is little individuality either in vocabulary or expression of emotion. There is no particular individuality either in his *chōka* or in three envoy poems (Vol. 18 poems 4094–7) where under the heading 'Congratulatory poems and envoys on the issuance of the Imperial Rescript regarding the production of gold in Michinoku' he took the opportunity, as representative of his family, to express loyalty to the Emperor.

His emphasis in these poems on the lineage of the Ōtomo family reinforces one's impression of his anachronistic view. For, the rise of his opponents, the Fujiwara family, in the court was no longer related to the matter of his ancestors' achievements. Even in his poem 'Admonition to his clansmen' (Vol. 20 poems 4465–7) composed in the crisis of his family in 756, Yakamochi had nothing to say other than expressing the loyalty and devotion of his forbears to the Emperor.

There are poems, written when he was ill, which contain hints of Buddhist thought, but these stop short at laments such as 'How brief is this lease of life' (Vol. 17 poem 3963) and '(This body of mine) is insubstantial as foam' (Vol. 20 poem 4470) and do not run to thoughts of aspiration for the after-life. There was some Buddhist influence to be sure, but Yakamochi, as with other poets, did not incline towards a Buddhist world view. Yakamochi's merit as a poet lies in his polished sentiments expressed towards the world of nature which within the framework of court *waka* opened the way towards the *Kokinshū* and even beyond to the *Shin kokinshū*.

> Through the little bamboo bush
> Close to my chamber,
> The wind blows faintly rustling
> In this evening dusk.
>
> (Vol. 19 poem 4291)

At this period the disillusioned aristocratic intellectual was already turning away from the passions of love towards the beauties of the sounds of nature.

> On this spring day with the sun shining brightly
> in the sky,
> How sad and lonely I feel
> As the skylarks soar on high.
>
> (Vol. 19 poem 4293)

Anybody would feel and write upon the sadness at seeing the setting sun in an autumn dusk. However, to feel some paradoxical sorrow and ennui in the midst of bright spring time listening to the song of a lark is an indication of the poet's utmost emotional refinement. This kind of poem would not have been possible without a considerable refinement having been achieved in the emotional lives of the aristocrats of the Nara court. Sadness is not dependent on a specific cause. The very existence of a poet is in itself a sadness and when, without resort to Confucianism or Buddhism, Yakamochi so thoroughly refined with such beauty the indigenous Japanese outlook on the world around them, he was early and clearly indicating the direction that court poetry was taking. The *mono no aware* of the Heian period was not far away.

The ruling aristocracy of the seventh century on one hand developed ceremonial *chōka* by standardizing the earlier collective ballads, and on the other hand produced lyric poetry as an expression of their own individual emotions. The *tanka* (*waka*) was the chief vehicle for the latter and the subject matter of such poems was mostly related to the longing for wives and lovers, expressed often in terms of the natural world surrounding the poets.

Already at this time the import of mainland culture was proceeding apace, but the influence of foreign philosophy did not permeate very deeply and was not manifested in lyric poetry. The representative poets of the eighth century described nature as something separate from man (as in the case of Yamabeno Akahito) or gave full expression to the psychology of love (as in the case of Lady Ōtomono Sakanoue) or explored all the delicate nuances of a refined world of the senses and emotions (as in the case of Ōtomono Yakamochi). The situation between the seventh and eighth centuries was unchanged, however, in that love remained the nucleus of lyric poetry, and in that the world view presented in the poems was thoroughly this-worldly. Also the poets followed the dictates of their emotions without the introduction of any kind of transcendental principle or value. In this sense eighth-century poetry remained within the framework of the seventh century and earlier tradition. Even in the Golden Age of Tempyō Buddhist art, next-worldly Buddhist philosophy did not capture the hearts and minds of the ruling aristocracy. Their training and education chiefly followed that of Chinese poets, but the Chinese literary trend of fondness for touching on political and social problems was hardly ever reflected either in the poetry of the *Kaifūsō* or the *Manyōshū*.

Thus the literature of the ruling classes from the seventh through the eighth centuries within the framework of the 'this-worldly' world view tended towards Epicureanism and within the framework of the short poetic form, while limiting subject matter to the scenes of the everyday world, showed tendencies towards the refinement of emotion.

However, there were exceptions and in the history of literature and philosophy exceptions are frequently important. There emerged among those taking part in the embassies to T'ang China a class of men, such as Abeno Nakamaro, who served as officials at the T'ang court and mixed with Chinese literary men. Again there were people like Yamanoueno Okura who became skilled in Chinese composition and who understood Confucianism and Buddhism and after returning to Japan had the talent to expand the vision of native lyric poetry and write special masterpieces. (Okura greatly enriched the *Manyōshū*, but it was not until the Tokugawa period that his contribution was properly valued. This serves to show just how far removed the viewpoint of Okura, nurtured under the influence of Chinese literature, was from that of his contemporaries.)

From then on, one continuing stream within the history of Japanese literature would run; an independent stream of masterpieces produced within each period by a small number of intellectuals responding to the 'challenges' of foreign culture.

What of the poetry of the people at large? Just as the 145 poems written by the envoys to Silla touched not at all on the diplomatic objectives of their mission, so the 80 or more poems written by the *sakimori* or 'frontier guards' taken from the Eastern provinces and sent to Kyūshū in the middle of the eighth century seldom touch on military matters. About a third of these poems (all of which are to be found in the twentieth volume of the *Manyōshū*) deal with the separation from wives and lovers; another third deal with the emotions felt at separation from mothers or parents (only in one case a father); and the remaining third simply deal with the duties of a frontier guard. Poems in this last category frequently lamented the fact of the author's conscription, and expressed his hatred against the conscriptive officers.

> How sad to see my weary fellow soldiers
> From so many different provinces
> Set sail from Naniwa!
>
> (Vol. 20 poem 4381)

> What ill fortune
> To be conscripted
> When I am ill in bed!
>
> (Vol. 20 poem 4382)

While one frontier guard expressed his grudge that it was quite inhuman to conscript a sick person, another composed a beautiful love poem missing his wife.

> Like a lily of Mt. Tsukuba,
> So lovely were you in my embrace at night
> So pretty in my day dreams, my love.
>
> (Vol. 20 poem 4369)

These were the cries uttered by the ordinary people who were sent from the Eastern provinces to Kyūshū to serve as frontier guards there for three years. The authors of these three poems were all rank and file.

However, there was a hierarchy of frontier guards. A squad was made up of ten soldiers and the 'Non-Commissioned Officer' in charge was known as a *Kachō*. Among the poems written by *Kachōs*, there can be found one as follows:

> I will not from to-day
> Turn back toward home –
> I who have set out to serve
> As Her Majesty's humble shield.
>
> (Vol. 20 poem 4373)

The people at large would never have said such a thing; nor would the members of the embassy sent to Silla, nor the aristocracy in general. It was only the class of minor leaders who could speak of serving their lord without regard to the risk to their own bodies. (It may not have been mere coincidence that over a thousand years later the militarists of the 1930s made use of this poem for propaganda purposes. The most fanatical supporters of the Emperor System were to be found among minor leaders such as small land-owners in rural villages, and small businessmen and factory owners in the cities and urban areas.)

The emotions and senses of the aristocratic bureaucracy living under the Ritsuryō system were substantially no different in their basic structure from those of the peasantry of the Eastern Provinces. This structure, indeed, was the structure of the indigenous world view held by the ruling class of Nara, despite its contact with mainland culture, and it was unswervingly supported, at least in the field of native language lyric poetry. For the people of the provinces who were virtually untouched by mainland culture it was the basis of their self-identification.

In this sense it is not only the poems of the frontier guards which are of relevance in the *Manyōshū*, but also the *Azuma-uta* (Poems from the Eastern Provinces) which were written by unknown provincials and which comprise Volume 14. The authorship of these 230 or so poems may have included members of the provincial ruling classes and travellers from Nara, but the vast majority were composed by provincial peasants and date mostly from the eighth century. They contain hardly any vocabulary indicative of an acquaintanceship with mainland culture, in particular with Buddhism. Consequently it is permissible to assume that the special characteristics of the *Azuma-uta* as a whole reflect the special characteristics, to a certain degree at least, of indigenous culture as it had been handed down to the peasantry of eighth-century Japan. Many of the things which we cannot learn from the poems of the frontier guards, which were written under special circumstances, we can learn from the *Azuma-uta*.

First, the focus of emotional life was the male-female relationship. This is clear from the fact that almost all of the 230 or so poems of *Azuma-uta* are love poems. In the official classification of the *Azuma-uta* 196 poems are designated love poems, with 42 'others'. However, the contents of many of these 'others' also touch on love. Of course the compilers of the *Manyōshū* may have selected only love poems, it may be thought, but to judge from other volumes we may be sure that if the *Azuma-uta* had included many elegies and miscellaneous poems, the compilers would not simply have discarded them. It is thus more logical to deduce that the majority of songs and poems in the regional tradition were related to love. The *Azuma-uta* contain hardly any poems on the theme of nature (at least nature divorced from human love) and in this respect differ from contemporary court poetry, particularly that of the professional poets. As has already been noted in the discussion of the 'ancient ballads' of the fifth and sixth centuries and earlier, the essence of indigenous Japanese thought was predominantly bound up with love rather than 'nature'.

The subject matter of Japanese literature began with a social phenomenon (the male-female relationship) and expanded to take in nature; not the reverse. The 'love of nature' which appears in lyric poetry was the result of the refinement of the sensitivities of city people. Only two Azuma-uta refer to death, one telling of how the author's love will never die even though the object of his love is dead, and the other regretting that the author has not had a chance to sleep with his love who is now dead. If the second of these is not classed as an elegy, then there are no elegies among the Azuma-uta. This elegy is not a lament for the dead person. Death was not a central preoccupation with the poets of the Azuma-uta who were thoroughly 'this-worldly' in their attitudes towards emotional life, the centre of which was the male-female relationship.

Second, popular beliefs, so far as they are manifested in the Azuma-uta were all concerned with achieving results (whether for good or ill) in this world, and, moreover, in the near future. Divination was one popular belief appearing in these poems, either by burning the shoulder blade of a deer (poems 3374, 3488) or by other methods; taboos were another, such as when offering the first of the year's harvest to the gods, not allowing the family to enter the house.

The names of the gods chronicled in the Kojiki and Nihon shoki do not appear in the Azuma-uta. The gods of the fudoki – at least a section of them – doubtless were an object of popular belief in the provinces, but it was thought that few of the ancestral deities, who descended from the Plain of Heaven, directly interfered in human affairs. In short, human society was an independent autonomous entity in which the influence of supernatural powers was minimal and whose order was bolstered by considerations of the series of practical benefits afforded by divination and taboos.

Third, the basic principle ordering human affairs seems to have been harmony within the group (especially the village community and the family). What we can learn of this from the Azuma-uta is confined to relationships between men and women, but generally speaking four kinds of obstacles stood in the way of a man and woman meeting and sleeping together.

One was the possibility of gossip at a man and woman being seen together (as has been mentioned previously in connection with the story of young boy and girl turning into pine trees in *Hitachi Fudoki* and with Hitomaro's elegy for his dead wife) and this features in several *Azuma-uta* (such as poems 3464, 3466 and 3490). The background reason for this is not clear, but presumably the fact that gossip or popular opinion was of such significance to the man and woman concerned strongly suggests that the male-female relationship was not independent of the community but was regarded as an essential element in the order of things. Order within the group was not an absolute, binding standard like the *giri* (conventional obligation) of the Tokugawa period. Nor were the emotions of love a purely individual, private property which did not preclude the possibility of a lovers' suicide. Not one of the *Azuma-uta* hints at the possibility of such lovers' suicide pacts and such poems are extremely rare in the whole of the *Manyōshū*, although there are exceptions. In the world of the people at large in the eighth century, even the love relationship between a man and a woman was an essential part of harmony within the group.

The second obstacle was the objection by the mother or the family of the couple involved (not one poem cites the father as an objector). The context here was probably a marriage where the husband lived apart from the wife and any children lived with the mother; this was probably the reason for the lack of the significance of the father's opinion. The weight attached to the mother's opinion suggests of course that the feeling of belonging to the group was very strong on the part of the children involved. It also clearly implies that no Confucian influence was at work, because if it had been, the father's opinion would have been paramount and the mother's would have counted for very little.

The third obstacle was if the woman were someone else's wife. Three of the *Azuma-uta* deal with this situation; two warning of the dangers of such a relationship (poems 3539 and 3541) and the third (3472) saying that it is like 'borrowing a neighbour's clothes' feeling no guilt. At any rate to have an affair with someone else's wife was not regarded as positively wicked. Again there are no

Confucian-type ethics involved in this, simply the feeling that in the interests of the harmony of the goup such a situation is best avoided.

The fourth obstacle to male-female relations was a physical nature, such as the absence of one of the parties or natural calamity. For example, there is a poem in which a man lamented that he would have stayed with his love longer if he had known that the river separating them would flood and become impossible to cross.

In short, the values which governed the passions of love were related to the stability, harmony and benefit of the group and there was no power, no god, no Buddha, and no Confucian moral principle which transcended the group. To put this another way, the ethical system to which the indigenous Japanese world view gave birth was centred not on transcendental values but on the group, and was governed by practical considerations.

Fourth, when one examines their concept of time one finds that the world of the people at large in the provinces was the world of the present *par excellence*. In the *Azuma-uta* there are no reflections on the past such as one finds in the work of the court poets represented in the *Kokinshū* and still less any speculation on the future such as is found in the *Shin Kokinshū*. In this culture people lived for the present.

> Worry not about the future, my love.
> The present is good enough for us.
>
> (poem 3410)

Moreover, in the *Azuma-uta* there are certain verbs which appear over and over again defining the relationship between man and woman. These verbs fall into two categories, one category relating to carnal aspects of love, the other to psychological aspects. The most common verb relating to the carnal aspect is *'neru'* (to sleep) which in about thirty poems appears in the sense of 'sleeping together'. There are also forty-five examples of the verb *himotoku* being used in the same meaning when accompanied by certain nouns. Examples of verbs relating to psychological aspects of love are *kanashi* ('to feel love for'), *kou* ('to love'), *omou* ('to think of') and so forth. One thing to be noted is that when these 'psychological' verbs are used they almost always take a direct object, directed to a specific person, and are not used in their abstract sense. Only three of the *Azuma-uta* (poems 3403, 3422 and 3491) use the word *koi* ('love') as a noun and *mono omou* ('to contemplate') is used only twice (poems 3443 and 3511).

The above verbs in both categories have in common that in all cases where they appear in the *Azuma-uta*, they are used in the present tense and are always used in relation to a specific person. Figuratively speaking, the world of the *Manyōshū* which provided the background to the *Azuma-uta* was a world of the 'present indicative'. (These people did not look into the future for a Pure Land or indeed a doom's day.) An individual's past was not a matter of importance in the present and the past of the community of the clan could be traced back only two or three generations before disappearing into the mists of mythology. For them there was no world to come and they were not interested in what had already happened in the past or what would happen in the future. The sole reality was the everyday world of here and now which could be directly experienced and which was the basis for practical deeds.

In the sense that the cardinal factor which most strongly affected the emotions in this everyday world was the relationship between man and woman and that the centre of that relationship was 'sleeping together', the world of the provincial peasantry in the eighth century may be said to have preserved the world of the 'ancient ballads'. However, the specific carnal expression and concrete physical descriptions of the female anatomy which appear in the 'ancient ballads' are missing from the *Azuma-uta*. It may be that here is emerging a special feature of Japanese culture in that later too, with the exception of certain Buddhist images executed in Indian style, no images or paintings of nudes were produced. (This strongly contrasts with the art of ancient Greece and medieval India and with the literature of India and the Arabic world where interest in the nude form was very strong. However, it does resemble a similar tendency in the literature of ancient China and in the sculpture and painting of all periods in China; so it may be more correct to say that lack of interest in the nude in art and literature is a Far Eastern rather than specifically Japanese phenomenon.)

There was a point of difference between the people at large as represented in the *Azuma-uta* and the contemporary Nara aristocracy in that the latter were greatly affected by mainland culture while the former were almost untouched by it, but, more basically, whereas within the framework of the indigenous world view there was already appearing in the aristocratic society a tendency towards the subtle refinement of sensibility, the people at large in the provinces continued to live directly in a world of action. However, this does not mean that the emotional life of the provincial 'peasant poets' was in any sense vulgar and lacking in subtle affection, delicacy or warmth.

> My hands so chapped from rice-pounding –
> Tonight again, he will hold them, sighing,
> My young lord of the mansion!
>
> (Vol. 14 poem 3459)

Here the workings of a woman's heart are admirably summarized in a way which could not be imagined of a court poet.

> My husband, come,
> If you long for me.
> I am waiting at the gate
> With all the willows trimmed.
>
> (Vol. 14 poem 3455)

The contents of the love poems from Nara and the Eastern provinces were not fundamentally different. In fact, the structure of the world view appearing in the whole of the *Manyōshū*, not just the love poems, was basically the same for the capital and the provinces, for the aristocratic bureaucracy and for the peasantry. It was the this-worldly, non-transcendental, everyday world of the present. Even contact with mainland culture, with the philosophies of Confucianism, Buddhism and Taoism did not change this structure, at least in the age of the *Manyōshū*. What was to happen in the future was the 'Japanization' of foreign culture through the vehicle of this kind of indigenous world view, the differentiation of its content and the refinement of the means of expressing it.

Chapter 2

The First Turning Point

The century spanning the establishment of Kyōto as capital in 794 and the discontinuation of the embassies to T'ang China in 894 was a period in which imported Chinese civilization was gradually digested and submitted to a native transformation. The results of this process had a decisive significance in shaping the subsequent development of Japanese culture and civilization. Of the patterns and tendencies which emerged in the ninth century in such fields as politics, economics, society, language and aesthetics, some were preserved to the end of the Heian period, others survived to the beginning or end of the Tokugawa period and some, particularly in the nature of politics and the written and spoken Japanese language, are still making their presence felt today.

It is true that we can trace back the origins of the basis of the world view adopted by Japanese culture in succeeding centuries to the Nara period, but within that framework most of the concrete manifestations of what is generally termed cultural tradition can be traced back to the ninth century only and no further. In other words, the history of Japanese culture can be broadly divided into two – the first being the period up to the end of the Nara period, and the second from the ninth century to the present day. The ninth century itself marks a turning point.

Looked at from a purely anthropological viewpoint, the ninth century was of no particular significance in the development of the Japanese race. If one considers it in terms of the development from the settled agricultural society of the Yayoi period (*c.* 200 B.C.–A.D. 200) to today's industrial society, the ninth century was not a watershed which has enormous significance. Perhaps one of the most typical examples of the importance of the ninth century as a turning point can be seen in terms of the Japanese language.

As scholars of ancient *kana-zukai* (the usage of the *kana* syllabary) such as, Hashimoto Shinkichi (1882–1945) have shown, the sound system of the Japanese language of the Nara period (in the Yamato region) had eight distinct vowel sounds and consonants which in some respects differ from those of today. It was during the ninth century that the vowels were cut to the present day five and the consonants changed to approximate more closely those of today. In other words the ninth century marks a period of substantial change and a turning point. The ninth century also represents the period in which there was a transformation of the Japanese writing system, for it was during this time that the *kana* system was devised and became increasingly used in preference to the phonetically based *mana* system of the Nara period. This invention of course led to the use of *kana-majiri* (mixed *kana* and Chinese characters) in the writing of literature, and although an obvious point, it is worth noting that the writing system used in today's newspapers fundamentally differed from that of the *Manyōshū* while the difference from that of the *Kokinshū*, compiled in 905, is much less marked.

Politically, the ninth century saw a marked native transformation of the Ritsuryō system which had been adopted earlier in imitation of the system used in T'ang China. When Fujiwarano Yoshifusa (804–72) became Regent (Sesshō) in 866 not only was he in the vanguard of a whole period of political control by regents, but also he laid the basis for the model Japanese political system in which formal power was held by the Emperor while real power was held by someone other than the Emperor. In other words, he helped to create a tradition in which power was not actually wielded by those who seemed to hold it.

This same tradition in fact persists in the political life of modern Japan, and even extends into a wide range of non-political areas and organizations. The methods by which the Fujiwara family attained power were twofold; the use of marriage politics and family relationships and the turning of the intrigues and power struggles among the aristocracy to their own advantage. This latter policy, of course, is by no means unique to Japan and even marriage politics has been widely applied in other countries. However, there are few societies in which marriage, politics and family connections have been exploited on such a massive scale as they were in Heian period Japan. It can be said, therefore, that some of the peculiar features in the nature of Japanese political power were evolved by the Fujiwara family in the ninth century.

It was likewise in the ninth century that the destruction of the *Ritsuryō* system was begun through the gradual passing of land into private ownership on an increasing scale. There were two causes of this phenomenon. One was the virtual disappearance of the *Handen-shūju* which was a system of allotting a certain unit of arable land to each farmer. The land was supposed to be returned to the government upon the death of the farmer. According to one authority, the disappearance of this system is described thus: 'The Handen-shūju system was enforced only every twenty to fifty years after the beginning of the Heian period, and by the tenth century it had disappeared altogether.' The implication of this statement is that during the ninth century more and more land was passing into private ownership. Indeed, this was the period which saw the rapid development of the land-owning farmer class who were to play such an important role in subsequent Japanese history. The second cause was the early development of the *shōen* or manorial system under which the private ownership of land gave enormous economic backing to the power of the imperial court, the aristocracy and the great Buddhist temples. It is hardly necessary to stress how long the power of these landowners was maintained, both centrally and in the regions, and it is clear that the ninth century marked the economic turning point between the *Ritsuryō* system of the Nara period on one hand and the fully developed *shōen* system on the other.

The Tendai and Shingon sects of Buddhism, which were to hold enormous power throughout the Heian period, made their first appearance in Japan in the ninth century. The Tendai Sect was founded in 805 by the monk Saichō (otherwise known as Dengyō Daishi, 767–822) who had spent the previous year studying in China. A year later the monk Kūkai (otherwise known as Kōbō Daishi, 774–835), who had been in China at the same time as Saichō, founded the Shingon Sect.

The essential feature of Tendai Buddhism is its all-embracing nature. Doctrinally based on the *Lotus Sutra* it also included such concepts as incantation, prayer, meditation and the *Nembutsu*, thus containing elements of esoteric Buddhism, Zen Buddhism, Pure Land Buddhism and even Shintoism through an interpretation of Shintoist deities as special forms of the Budda's incarnation.

While exhibiting such flexible and all-embracing qualities, the Tendai Sect also, particularly from the tenth century onwards, developed into a very strong force politically, economically and, later, even militarily. It also bred what might be called 'Buddhist scholasticism' within the ranks of its adherent monks. The Pure Land teachings of Genshin (942–1017), and the Kamakura period doctrines of such figures as Hōnen (1133–1212) and Nichiren (1222–82) all had their origins in Tendai Buddhism, and, indeed, all three of these monks at one time belonged to the Tendai Sect. Saichō himself did not produce any elaborate theoretical works, but it would be no exaggeration to say that the sect he founded decisively shaped the framework of Heian period thought.

Unlike Tendai, Shingon Buddhism is not all-embracing. It is a metaphysical sect which interprets the world in terms of the innumerable aspects of the Buddha Vairocana. Its ultimate goal is the concept of *Sokushin Jōbutsu* ('achieving Buddhahood in this life') which is attained by the practice of the 'Three Secrets', namely a secret programme concerning body, words and mind. The basic theory of this doctrine is set down and systematized in Kūkai's work *Jūjūshin-ron*. More will be said later of Kūkai and his works, but certainly after his time the Shingon Sect produced no theorists to compare with those of the Tendai Sect and achieved its popularity instead by the 'magic' power of its rituals.

However, during the ninth century at least there was no great doctrinal rift between Tendai and Shingon, particularly since at that period the esoteric elements within Tendai Buddhism were heavily emphasized. One remarkable feature they had in common was their emphasis on the concept of *Gensei riyaku* or 'profit in this life'. Where the interests of the monks of the early ninth century lay is clearly shown by Saichō's work *Kenkairon* which was written in 819 and which sought to establish Tendai as an independent sect in opposition to the ancient Nara Buddhist sects.

The *Kenkairon* is written in the form of a refutation of Tendai's critics who had asserted that if, as Saichō had said, 'Bodhisattvas' were truly Bodhisattvas there would be no such things as starvation, illness and all the calamities which afflict mankind. Saichō replies that even the Buddhas are unable to avert disasters when they are justified (i.e. when people bring them on their own heads), but when there is no such justification even the Bodhisattvas (of lower status than the Buddhas) are able to prevent the disaster. Since, however, it is not possible to know whether a particular disaster is justified or not, the inability to avert it is not proof of a failure on either Saichō's or the Tendai Sect's part.

What must be noted here is that through the performance of the correct services, it is expected to get the Bodhisattvas to intercede to prevent calamities such as drought, famine and fire, but not to get them to save souls after death; in other words, the opponents of Saichō and Saichō himself were focusing their debate on the power of Tendai monks *in this world*, and not the world beyond. It is significant that, on his return from China, it was Saichō's efficacious prayer for the recovery of the Emperor from a sickness which gained him permission to found the Tendai Sect in Japan. Kūkai too on several occasions is known to have prayed for rain in time of drought and been successful.

This kind of pursuit of worldly considerations extended not only to individual human questions such as sickness and natural or economic questions, but even to political matters such as the protection of the state. The Tendai and Shingon Sects each had two main aspects. On one hand they were monastic religions with temples in the mountains (Mt. Hiei in the case of Tendai, Mt. Kōya in the case of Shingon), while on the other hand both were state religions deeply involved in the affairs of the court. Moreover, since both were great landowners alongside the court and the aristocracy, it is not surprising that they should have concerned themselves with the preservation of social discipline and the machinery of ruling the country. Saichō taught that through the laws of the Buddha the country could be protected and he prayed that all the Buddhas together with Shinto deities would preserve Japan from harm.

It is interesting to note, however, that he prayed not only to the Buddhas, but also to the various 'gods' of Shintoism which is an indication of the flexible and all-embracing nature of Tendai Buddhism. Kūkai too was concerned with the protection of the state. When he moved from Kōyasan to the Tōji temple, he created there a seminary for holding prayers for the security of the country and the Jingoji temple was established by him for the same purpose. He also stated that to read the scriptures and to pray to the Buddhas for the protection of the state was a prime duty of both monks and nuns.

At roughly the same time as the Tendai and Shingon Sects were promulgating their doctrines of protecting the state, Buddhism was being vigorously persecuted on mainland Asia by the T'ang Chinese Emperor Wu-tsung. Throughout China in 845, Wu-tsung, under the influence of Taoism and the quest for the elixir of life, destroyed temples and Buddhist images and forced monks and nuns to apostatize.

The Japanese monk Ennin (794–864, later known as Jikaku Daishi) who was living in China at this time described the persecution in his diary *Nittō-guhō-junreikō-ki*. This work was the diary of Ennin's travels and since it contains dates it is a highly important historical document, supplementing histories of the time written by the Chinese themselves. However, it is much more than a historical document. It vividly depicts the difference in philosophical climate between China and Japan – a difference which was never a specific one in the mid-ninth century but has always been found ever since.

However foolish the Taoist quest for the elixir of life may have been, however much one realizes that the persecution of Buddhism was brought about by the historical accident of a Chinese Emperor who happened to believe in Taoism, the fact remains that in China during this period one philosophical system (Taoism) was in open conflict with another (Buddhism). It is generally known that in the Sung period the doctrine of the 'Three teachings (Buddhism, Taoism and Confucianism) in harmony' was propounded and gained favour, but the 845 persecution of Buddhism demonstrates that in China at least different philosophical systems could be seen as mutually exclusive and that this exclusivity was not necessarily to be broken down by non-philosophical considerations.

This period, in which Japanese Buddhism had an inseparable relationship with the power of the state, also saw the emergence of the Tendai Sect whose most characteristic feature was its compromising nature; it tried to assimilate into its own system all imported foreign and indigenous thoughts and beliefs. In China there could be a life-and-death struggle between two philosophies, in Japan there could not; in China there could be profound antagonism between the state and a philosophy, in Japan there could not. This profound antithesis is encapsulated in the writings of the Japanese Tendai monk Ennin which cover the years 838–47.

Ennin wrote his diary in Chinese but was never trapped into Chinese literary embellishments. Although he saw pain and impossibly tragic events, himself experiencing hardships which baffle all description, he was an impartial observer who recorded accurately what he saw without resorting to emotional outbursts and never deviating from a matter-of-fact style.

For example, after he records that the Emperor poisoned the devout Buddhist Empress dowager, then tried to get his own beautiful mother to marry him, was refused and so shot her to death, Ennin adds no comments of his own on the matter (historically there is some doubt about this disastrous happening). Also, after he tried hard to return to Japan in spite of the oppression and suffering, he was finally able to meet envoys from Japan. He, however, just writes down the fact that he was able to see the envoys, and he describes the official letter they carried. He does not express any emotional reaction.

Strangely, he was not involved in the ideological battle on the mainland at all, but just observed and described what was going on around him in a sober and matter-of-fact way, no matter in what situation he was. In that sense, he was first and foremost a Japanese, and secondly an extraordinary prose artist with few equals in Japanese literary tradition from the author of *Konjaku-monogatari* to *Saikaku*.

When he returned to Japan, Ennin put the knowledge he had gained in China to use to assist with the management and organization of the Tendai Sect as it developed in the tenth century. The Buddhist purges in China were no more than a vague dream to him. In the first place, throughout the whole history of Japan, there have been quite a lot of Japanese who, after returning from abroad have concentrated their activities on unifying and protecting the nation using the ideas gained abroad.

In 894 the embassies to T'ang China were discontinued and thereafter in Japan the all-embracing doctrines of Tendai Buddhism continued to develop without serious conflict with other systems of thought.

One of the distinctive features of the ninth century in social terms was the way that the bureaucratic intelligentsia began to form itself into groups. One such group emerged from the politically ruined aristocracy following the Fujiwara family's success in gaining power for itself exclusively. A typical member of this group was Kino Tsurayuki, one of the compilers of the *Kokinshū* and author of the *Tosa Nikki*, whose family in this way had become removed from the centre of power.

A second group was made up of those people who came not from aristocratic families, but from relatively humble Confucian scholar backgrounds and who had reached the top ranks of the bureaucratic system. A typical example of this group was Sugawara Michizane who came from generations of Confucianists and rose to become Minister of the Right. Tsurayuki wrote in Japanese making free use of the *kana* syllabary, while Michizane wrote poetry using the classical Chinese language.

We shall return later to this phenomenon, but the ninth-century establishment of a literary intelligentsia typified by such men as Tsurayuki and Michizane marks a turning point in regard to the subsequent development of Japanese literature. Nothing more vividly demonstrates the beginnings of a split between the political and economic rulers of Japan and the country's literary and cultural creators – a split which widened with the passage of time and which still prevails today.

Then there is the question of aesthetic values. As we shall say in more detail later there is a world of difference between the *Manyōshū* and the *Kokinshū* both in terms of the social backgrounds of the poets and in the classification, form, vocabulary and style of the poems contained in these two anthologies. Yet there is virtually no such difference between the *Kokinshū* and the later Imperial anthologies.

It is a logical deduction, therefore, that the system of prevailing aesthetic values changed markedly between the time of composition of the *Manyōshū* and the *Kokinshū* and hardly at all between the composition of the *Kokinshū* and at least the end of the Heian period. Heian period aesthetics of which the *Kokinshū* is an integral part exerted a profound influence on the aesthetics of later ages. That is not all, however. The age in which most of the *Kokinshū* poems were written corresponds to the age in which the earliest forms of Japanese literary theory were born, Kūkai'

Bunkyō-hifu-ron (written between 810 and 820) being the first such theoretical work in Japanese history. In other words, in the establishment of aesthetic values which came to shape decisively the development of Japanese literature, we see the first consciousness of aesthetic values *per se*. This may be thought of as one of the stages of the native transformation of imported continental culture.

It is noticeable, for example, in Shingon Buddhist statuary that there is a world of difference between the images made in the middle of the eighth century which conform to T'ang models and those made in the early and middle ninth century which are very different and show signs of native inspiration. However, whether this also is part of the native transformation of continental culture is difficult to judge, since there are also marked differences between Buddhist images made in the ninth century and made in the later Heian period.

THE JŪJŪSHIN-RON AND THE NIHON RYŌIKI

Kūkai was not only founder of the Shingon Sect, a performer of services for the protection of the country, a performer of rain-making ceremonies and a builder of temples; he also devised systems of irrigation and founded schools for the education of the ordinary people. According to the *Shōryōshū* (828) in which he describes these schools there were both priest and lay teachers and not only Buddhism, but also the Chinese classics were taught. Education in these schools seems to have been available to everybody – 'irrespective of rank, and without discriminating the poor from the rich'. Indeed, Kūkai was a man of outstanding enterprise. He was also famed as a calligrapher and was skilled in the composition of Chinese poetry, testimony to the latter being the inclusion of his work in the Imperial anthology *Keikokushū* (827). In the previously mentioned *Shōryōshū*, a collection of Kūkai's prose and poetry edited by his disciple Shinzei (800–60), more than one hundred items of both poetry and prose are contained. This poetry is in the style of Chinese poetry of the Six Dynasties period and is regarded as being among the finest Chinese poetry ever written by a Japanese. His work not only demonstrates complete mastery of the highly ornate Chinese style, but also shows evidence of his highly individualistic taste. One of the poems is *Yu-sien-ku* (Days in the Wizards' Land), others are the farewell poems quoting legends and on such subjects as the joy of successful praying for rain, the views seen from Mt. Kōya and a Buddhist view of death. He also wrote many prose pieces on various occasions such as articles dedicated to the Emperor, and letters. Through his calligraphy and poetry, Kūkai came to enjoy a close relationship with another celebrated poet and calligrapher of the day, the Emperor Saga.

Kūkai's aptitude as a philosopher is clearly shown in an early work which he wrote at the age of only twenty-four, the *Sango-shiiki*. This was written in 797. There appear six imaginary characters – a man, his prodigal son, nephew and three guests whom the man has invited so that they might convert his nephew by expressions of their own views. It takes the form of a dialectical debate between three people representing Confucianism, Taoism and Buddhism. The three characters and their arguments are described in elegant style, in imitation of the *Monzen* with many quotations from Buddhist and Chinese classics.

The Confucianist speaks first and explains the Confucian teachings on loyalty and filial piety to admonish the prodigal man; the Taoist speaks of the elixir of life to impress the others including the Confucianist, and finally the Buddhist preaches the doctrines of Buddhism and ends up by converting the others. The work adds up to a kind of apologia for the Buddhist teachings, but it should be admitted that the highly ornate prose style does not seem to fit its theme. To have written such a work at the age of twenty-four shows Kūkai to have been a man of exceptional talents.

There is nothing particularly creative or original about his summary of the three teachings, but nevertheless from the viewpoint of the history of philosophy in Japan, the *Sango-shiiki* has enormous significance. It demonstrates that in the early ninth century in Japan there was the literary and philosophical capacity of presenting matter-of-fact accounts of three teachings, comparing and contrasting their relative strengths and weaknesses and thus providing a point of view from which all the different ideologies could be interpreted.

Here, the criteria of comparison may be arbitrary, criticism of each system may be shallow, and the internal relationships be-

tween the three teachings, due to the work's ornate style, may
not be very clear, yet the *Sangō-shiiki* sufficiently demonstrates
that Kūkai's Buddhism was not only a belief based on his own
experiences but a standpoint which he had chosen intellectually.
This is a completely different dimension from such practical
matters as 'rain-making' and protection of the state. It is here for
the first time that native Japanese thought encountered Buddhism as the basis for structuring a world view, or at least the pages
of the *Sangō-shiiki* seem to provide the first tangible evidence of
such a development.

Thirty years later in 830, towards the end of his life, Kūkai
wrote the *Jūjūshin-ron*, a work in ten chapters. In this work Kūkai
summarized in an ontologically structured world view various
doctrines ranging from the worldly, through the philosophies of
India, both Buddhist and non-Buddhist, to the specific doctrines
of Shingon Buddhism, and laid down ten stages of spiritual
development.

The first stage is that of the 'confused heart' in which man does
not know good from evil and does not believe in cause and effect.
For him there is no distinction between the moon reflected in the
water and the true moon and he just lives in a state of lust and
desire and craving. Kūkai recognizes two non-Buddhist views of
this condition, the first that all things have their origin in Heaven
and are governed by Heaven, and the second (the teaching of
Lao-tse and Chuang-tse) that all things simply exist and there is
no creator. Kūkai refutes the first of these by saying that if it were
true there would only be happiness and no suffering in the
world, and that if Heaven created all things, who created
Heaven? He refutes the second view by stating it is simply not
true since men have built boats, houses and so forth and have
thus transformed nature.

In the second stage, which Kūkai equates with Confucianism,
there is an awakening of moral values and men form moral codes
and precepts governing human relationships (such as prohibit-
ing killing, stealing, obscenity, indecent talk and drinking).
However, in this stage there is no belief in Buddhism.

In the third stage (the first on the path towards Buddhism) men
not only maintain the moral precepts, but also fear Hell and
desire to be born into Paradise. Kūkai lists sixteen different non-
Buddhist philosophies equivalent to this view and three different

worlds (the world of desires, the world of senses, and the world without senses).

All these first three stages are essentially non-Buddhist and correspond to the teachings of various Indian and Chinese philosophical teachings, while the remaining seven stages each correspond to a particular school or type of Buddhism.

The fourth stage is the first teaching of Hinayana (Lesser Vehicle) Buddhism in which it is taught that the self is non-substantial and only the world manifested through the senses and experience is substantial. It is to this level of awareness that the *Śrāvaka* attains.

The fifth stage is the second teaching of the Lesser Vehicle in which it is taught that both the self and the world are non-substantial. In this stage the root of *Karma* is exterminated, the cause of ignorance (avidyā) is eliminated, the impermanence of everything is realized, and the individual attains *Nirvana*. However, because that individual lacks 'Great Compassion', he is unable to help others on the path towards enlightenment. This is the stage of the *Pratyeka-Buddha*.

The sixth stage is represented by the teaching of the Hossō Sect of Mahayana (Greater Vehicle) Buddhism and corresponds to the first Mahayana doctrine. In this stage it is taught that the world is non-substantial and only the mind exists. 'All three worlds are nothing but mind.' 'Swearing to save all people equally', 'for the sake of people in the world of the senses', 'the way of the Bodhisattva' is followed. This is the stage of the Bodhisattva.

The seventh stage is represented by the teaching of the Sanron Sect in which both the world and the mind are non-substantial. 'All things are void; the void is all things.' 'Life-death is Nirvana; all worries are enlightenment.' Therefore, 'it is not necessary to give up all worries in order to attain Nirvana.' As world and mind alike are regarded as non-substantial, there is no particular emphasis on the non-substantiality of self. 'Thus, in giving up non-self, the mind is completely free, realizing that the mind in itself has no origin.' This is one of the innumerable aspects of the Buddha Vairocana.

The eighth stage is represented by the teachings of the Tendai Sect in which the world and the mind are one and the same. 'The world is wisdom; wisdom is the world.' 'To know one's own mind as to know the reality of the world' is enlightenment.

The ninth stage is represented by the teachings of the Kegon Sect in which the mind and the Buddha are one and the same thing. 'The mind and the Buddha are not different.' Eternity is perceived as an instant; one is considered as the many. All things are there by circumstance and have no original nature. 'Ultimately, no original nature of mind exists' – this sums up the doctrine of the Kegon sect.

The tenth and ultimate stage is represented by the teaching of the Shingon Sect wherein a 'mystic, sublime state of mind' is recognized. One reaches an awareness of the innermost depths of one's own mind by realizing the immeasurability of mind, body, wisdom, being and non-being. Its ontological structure is not shown clearly. This may be because it implies a mystical absolute which goes beyond all structural analysis. This Shingon doctrine is not a product of the Buddhas and is considered to be unchangeable whether Vairocana appears or not.

These ten stages of the *Jūjūshin-ron* indicate organized steps for the attainment of Buddhist enlightenment, culminating in the mysteries of Shingon. In those stages are summarized the doctrines of non-Buddhist Indian philosophies, Hinayana Buddhism and the major schools of Mahayana Buddhism. The different doctrines are presented not in chronological order but in logical order in terms of each doctrine's ontological arguments, i.e. how each defines the relationship between being and non-being, world and mind, and subjectivity and objectivity. In other words, the grouping of each argument and each sect is in accordance with theoretical and not historical considerations.

In the *Jūjūshin-ron* there is not the ornate style that one finds in the *Sangō-shiiki*, but in simple and lucid prose Kūkai unravels the complexities of extremely abstract systems of ideas. The subject matter may not appeal to the taste of the modern reader, but that is no doubt due to the passage of a thousand years since it was written. That the beauty of its ordered structure, however, can still be appreciated even today is due to the fact that it has a kind of universal quality which transcends time. From an historical viewpoint, the *Jūjūshin-ron*, written some 300 years after the introduction of Buddhism to Japan, stands as one of the most splendid examples of an 'architecture of ideas' ever produced by a Japanese. Alternatively, it might be said that in the comprehensiveness and internal coherence of the *Jūjūshin-ron*, the 'systematic mind' was asserting itself for the first time in Japan. These are the reasons for the epoch-making quality of Kūkai and his major work.

Kūkai was also a great scholar of literature and teacher. Among his works are the *Bunkyō-hifu-ron* (*c.* 810) and the *Bumpitsu-ganshin-shō* (820 – a summary of the previous work) in which, through his extensive reading of the works of poetic theory of the Six Dynasties and T'ang dynasty periods, he systematized the rules for the composition of poetry. The richness of his source material may be judged from the fact that he quotes many poems which no longer survive today and are known only through his having quoted them. Such a wide-ranging coverage of poetical theory was not even produced in T'ang China. His standards for selection or rejection of source material are made clear in his preface to the *Bunkyō-hifu-ron;*

> I examined the rules of prosody offered by different authors and compared them to find their similarities and points of difference. Volumes were many; essential points few. Different names were often used to mean the same thing which complicated matters. Following an incurable habit of mine, I applied the knife, cut out repetitions and kept one word for one thing.

The Bunkyō-hifu-ron could have been written only by the kind of mind capable of producing *Jūjūshin-ron*. Systematically, he begins with an explanation of four tones (of Mandarin Chinese), proceeds to a discussion of harmony of tones, analyses poetic forms, provides detailed descriptions of technical devices used in poetry and then goes on to deal with the 'diseases' afflicting poetry (i.e. styles and forms of presentation which should be avoided in the composition of poetry). Each different subject for discussion is presented methodically with examples.

It has already been said that no such wide ranging systematization of poetic method was ever produced in China, and the same remark applies equally to the history of Western poetic theory from Horace in the sixties B.C. to Boileau in the seventeenth century. Treatises on *waka* poetry which of course began to be written for the first time in Japan in the Heian period very often imitated the *Bunkyō-hifu-ron* and on occasion plagiarized it. When discussion of the native poetic form managed to escape from the influence of Kūkai's monumental work, it never achieved the same degree of systematization.

In the first half of the ninth century, through the works of the Shingon monk Kūkai, Japanese Buddhism reached the pinnacle of intellectual standards (though there was not necessarily any marked originality in religious terms). However, the audience for Kūkai's works, written in Chinese, was limited and the works themselves in content reflected very little of indigenous Japanese thought. Kūkai's religious activities (protection of the state, praying for rain, his general welding of the temples of the Shingon sect to court power) marked a period in the 'Japanization' of Buddhism, while his philosophical thought denied the 'Japanization' of Buddhism and his next-worldly world view overcame the indigenous world view. In all these senses he was an epoch-making figure.

There is the question of how the indigenous world view which was shared alike by the intellectuals and people at large of the period related to the acceptance of Buddhism. The *Nihon ryōiki*, compiled in the early ninth century by the monk Keikai of the Yakushiji temple, gives a remarkable picture of the relationship between the two. Nothing at all is known of Keikai's biography. The text of the *Nihon ryōiki* was written in *Hentai Kambun*, that is to say Chinese with reading marks inserted to enable a Japanese to reconstruct the sentence according to the grammar of the Japanese language. The work is in three volumes and consists of a collection of strange and wonderful stories, following Chinese precedents, illustrating the working of the theory of 'reward according to deed' in Japan. As Keikai's preface indicates, the sources for the stories included provincial legends and Chinese literature, especially the *Ming-pao chi*, compiled by Tong Lin in the mid-seventh century, and the *Chin-kang pan-jo-ching chi-yen chi*, compiled by Meng Hsien-chung in 718 (the latter includes many of the stories contained in the former). However, of the 111 stories in the *Nihon ryōiki*, only nine can be said to have derived from the *Ming-pao chi* and only ten per cent of the whole collection are of Chinese origin.

For whom did Keikai compile the *Nihon ryōki*? Since the number of people who could read *Hentai Kambun* was small, it could not have been intended for a popular audience. At the same time the relationship between the stories and Buddhism was too superficial for the work to have been much use to Buddhist monks for their own purposes. Not one of the stories touches the heart of Buddhist philosophy and therefore it is only possible to see it as a vehicle for the education of the masses.

It seems probable therefore that the *Nihon ryōiki* was compiled as a collection of source materials to be used by monks when offering sermons to the people at large. It may even have been a collection of stories which Keikai himself had used for such purposes. If it can be thought that although the direct readership of the *Nihon ryōiki* was monks, the contents were designed not for monks but for a popular audience, then it can be imagined that the work not only reflected the thoughts of its compiler but to some extent the tastes and points of view of its audience.

The shortest of the stories runs to only a hundred characters and even the longest does not exceed some ten pages. The plots are frequently very simple. There are stories which, usually relating to the merit possessed by individual monks or the scriptures, tell of the unhappiness resulting from evil deeds, and there are also not a few which, while almost totally unrelated to 'reward according to deed', arrive at a Buddhist connotation and interpretation just in the last few lines. For example, there is the story of the two strong women (Vol. 2 story 4) which runs as follows.

A strong woman who lived in the province of Mino made her living by attacking and robbing travelling merchants. There was another woman of slight build who was also very strong. She went to test her strength against the woman thief. When the woman thief got up and was about to beat her, 'she seized both of the thief's hands in one of her own hands and with her other hand grabbed a *Kuma kazura* vine whip and gave the thief a single lash. Flesh stuck to the whip. She then grabbed another whip and beat the thief one more time. Again flesh stuck to the whip. She gave her ten lashes with ten whips and flesh stuck to them all.' Then the thief gave in and after that never stole again. The people of the region were pleased. Here, at the end of the story is the interpretation, 'Such people of strength continue and never disappear from the world, you should truly realize that the causes of great strength are in previous lives and such strength can be effected in our own time'.

In other words the relationship between the content and interpretation of the story is tenuous. Doubtless the story of the two strong women was a folk tale which originally had no connection with Buddhism and Keikai heard it, added an arbitrary interpretation and converted it into a Buddhist moral tale. This frequent divergence between content and Buddhist interpretation in the tales of the *Nihon ryōiki* is indicative of the fact that provincial folk tradition was completely unrelated to Buddhism. In other words, in the folklore itself, there were many wondrous events; but there were no moralistic explanations of the cause and effect of these miraculous happenings. What the people believed in was the existence of the strong women, not the source of their strength nor the events of their previous lives.

What gave liveliness to Keikai's writing and gave force to his narratives were the plots of his stories rather than his Buddhist interpretations, and his portrayals of details even more than the plots themselves. In the case of the story of the strong women, the interpretation was that the existence of persons of strength in any age is dependent on the laws of cause and effect. The plot was that at one specific time there were two strong women and one overcame the other. (The plot of the story does not suffice to show that persons of strength exist in all ages.) This story describes a concrete, physical scene in detail in which the flesh of the thief stuck to the whips. (This detail is completely unnecessary to the plot development.)

The special appeal of the *Nihon ryōiki* rests not in the interpretation and plots of the stories, but in the concise, accurate and vivid description of detail. How was it that Keikai, whose conscious intention was devoted to the interpretation – he specifically says this in his preface – so to speak *unconsciously* managed to impart colour to his stories through his portrayal of detail? One possible explanation is that before he wrote down the *Nihon ryōiki*, he tried his stories out on his audiences until he was able to judge exactly what the tastes of those audiences were. However, if he had not concentrated his attention on the details of the present world of the senses (as opposed to concentration on the management of abstract Buddhist philosophical ideas and next-worldly philosophy) he would not have been able to satisfy the demands of his audience in such a vivid manner as he did. In other words, Keikai had direct contact with his audience and that had the effect, perhaps contrary to his own will, of liberating the world view of the masses which also lay dormant within Keikai himself.

The nature of the Buddhist philosophy to be found in the *Nihon ryōiki* can be gauged from the following story (Vol. 2 story 25).

A sick woman prepared a feast for a demon who had been sent (to claim her spirit) by the King of Hell. The demon had come running and was tired, so he was overjoyed to partake of the feast. By way of paying his debt to her, the demon selected another woman living in the same village with an identical name and instead killed her and took her back with him to Hell. The King of Hell saw through the deception and ordered the demon to go back and bring him the first woman. However, the substitute woman when the possibility arose of her being returned to life saw that her body had already been burned and there was thus nowhere for her spirit to inhabit. When she returned to Hell to complain of this state of affairs, the King of Hell said that since the body of the first woman had not yet been cremated, the spirit of the substitute woman could take that to live in. Thus the spirit of the substitute woman entered the body of the first woman and she was restored to life. When the substitute woman in her new body said that she wished to return to her own house, the parents of the first woman were stupefied. When she returned to her own house, her own parents (not recognizing her in her new body) said that their daughter's body had been cremated. Finally, she explained to both sets of parents exactly what had happened and what the King of Hell had decided, whereupon all concerned agreed to abide by his decree. The moral of the tale was that there is some merit to be gained by offering bribes to demons. If you have something to offer at all, it would be better for you to use it as a bribe.

Doubtless, even Hell was an extension of this world. The suggestion to offer a bribe to a demon bespeaks what Japanese people should do as so-called 'economic animals' in later ages. Hell, the demon and the King of Hell are in this story no more than part of the stage-setting, so to speak. Similar stories with Buddhist-derived settings but with no real relation to Buddhist philosophy are scattered throughout the Nihon ryōiki.

When one compares the nine stories in the Nihon ryōiki which derive from the Ming-pao chi, one finds in them certain specific tendencies. The plots of the Ming-pao chi stories are simply told and are sparing of detail, seeking to make their point through the structure of the story, so to speak. In the Nihon ryōiki the basic plots of the Ming-pao chi tales are followed, but details are added which do not necessarily serve to explain the plots more fully.

The descriptions of those details are precise, lively and often picturesque. When compared with Chinese originals there is no room for doubt that there is a remarkably strong tendency in the Japanese mind for a taste for detail in isolation, a tendency away from the general towards the specific and a tendency away from abstract ideas towards concrete facts.

Thus the world of the *Nihon ryōiki* was one in which indigenous thought tried to dismember, disperse, and give decorative effect to Buddhism rather than Japanize it. All of the ninth-century Japanese mind can be thought of as lying somewhere between the two extremes represented by the *Jūjūshin-ron* and the *Nihon ryōiki*.

LITERATURE OF THE INTELLECTUALS

At the beginning of the ninth century three anthologies of 'Chinese' poetry were compiled in quick succession by imperial command: the *Ryōunshū* (*c.* 814), the *Bunka shūreishū* (818) and the *Keikokushū* (827). These respectively contained 91, 143 and about 900 (of which 210 survive) poems in Chinese. The first two of these were virtually the same size as the Nara period anthology of Chinese poems, the *Kaifūsō*, and only the *Keikokushū* was larger. The *Keikokushū* contains prose as well as poetry and of particular interest in this respect are the specimen examination papers for promotion within the bureaucracy and some of the candidates' answers.

Compared with the *Kaifūsō* where five-graphs-to-the-line poems predominated, throughout the three imperial anthologies there are very many poems with seven graphs to the line and there are also many more long poems in excess of twenty lines. This was probably due to the fact that between the eighth and the ninth centuries the Japanese developed considerably greater facility in wielding the techniques required by poetry in a foreign language. However, the subject matter of the imperial anthology poems did not substantially change. A large number of poems continued to deal with excursions and banquets and mainland legends and landscapes also figured prominently.

The *Bunka shūreishū*, in addition to such poems, included a category designated as 'love poems'. However, these comprised only eleven of the total of 143 poems in the anthology and the majority of them were written from the standpoint of a Chinese woman from Ch'ang-an telling of her 'loneliness in her bed'. They were in no way related to the authors' own loves.

When one considers the fact that from the time of the *Kojiki* onwards through the *Manyōshū* the overwhelming number of Japanese lyric poems had been related to the love relationship between man and woman, it should still be said that early ninth-century Japanese poets who wrote in Chinese and who were beginning to become adept at Chinese poetic technique had still not reached the point where they could use the language skilfully enough to present their own emotions. The three imperial anthologies indicate how far the Japanese had progressed in the art of writing poetry in Chinese, but it was not until the late ninth or early tenth century that they became sufficiently accomplished to use the Chinese language in poetry to express true emotions, particularly in the case of Sugawara Michizane. The development from writing Chinese poetry as an exercise to using it as a meaningful lyric form took place in the span of the ninth century.

The two major poets of the three anthologies were the close friends Kūkai and the Emperor Saga (786–842). The small number of poems contributed by members of the Fujiwara family (only one Fujiwara is represented) indicates that their position was not as strong as it was later to become and the numerous poems contributed by members of the imperial family perhaps suggests that specialization in scholarship and the arts had not as yet progressed very far. This situation too changed during the course of the ninth century in that the Fujiwara family gradually began to monopolize power and specialization in the arts became widespread. The reason why the *taisaku* (examination papers and answers) of the Nara period were included in the *Keikokushū* was that there was at the time the work was compiled a heightened interest in the contents of examination papers for candidates wishing to advance within the bureaucracy.

The *taisaku* were made up of questions and answers. Typical questions asked candidates to compare the creation theories of Confucianism and Buddhism, or posed problems such as 'Confucianism causes the country to flourish while Buddhism and Taoism bring good fortune, but which is the more righteous?', or 'which is of more importance, loyalty or filial piety?'. Most of the

answers to these questions, relying heavily on rhetoric, seem not
to have made logic their prime aim. Taking, for example, the
question about loyalty and filial piety, some candidates replied
that loyalty was more important and others said that if one has
the quality of filial piety then one is of necessity also loyal and so
did not actually state which should take precedence in the event
of an actual conflict between loyalty and filial piety. It is difficult
to draw firm conclusions from the mere 26 *taisaku* which have
survived, but it seems reasonable to think that the compilers who
included these examination papers in the *Keikokushū* were much
more interested in style and fine rhetoric than in the thoughts
expressed.

The most revered title accorded to lay scholars was that of
Monjō hakase or 'Doctor of Letters'. The Sugawara family,
together with the Ōe family, produced many scholars who
earned this exalted title, and were famed for their scholarship.
Originally the Sugawaras were not aristocracy but a family of
craftsmen specializing in the making of pottery who adopted the
name Sugawara in the eighth century. The head of the second
generation of the Sugawara family, Sugawara Kiyotada, received
the title *Monjō hakase*, sailed to China in 804 on the same ship as
Saichō, and participated in the compilation of the *Bunka shūreishū*
and the *Keikokushū*.

His third son, Sugawara Yoshinushi, went to China in 838 in
the role of scholar as part of an embassy, and his fourth son,
Sugawara Koreyoshi, like his father received the title of *Monjō
hakase* and rose to the position of participating in government.
Sugawara Michizane (845–903) was the son of Koreyoshi. He
again was honoured with the title of *Monjō hakase*, was selected
for the great embassy to T'ang China of 894 (in fact the ship never
sailed and from that time forward the embassies were discontinued), became *Udaijin* (Minister of the Right) in 899, and later,
in 901, was overthrown in a court intrigue and exiled to Kyushu.
His poetry and prose can be found in the two collections, the
Kanke bunsō(900) and the *Kanke kōshū* (903). As we shall see later,
Michizane was the great master poet in number and quality of the
poems of the early Heian period.

The activities of the Sugawara family from Kiyotada to
Michizane demonstrate well the situation in the ninth century
where it was becoming increasingly possible for intellectuals of

non-aristocratic birth to achieve advancement through talent and learning even in society outside that of the great Buddhist temples. However, as the Fujiwara family began to monopolize power it seems to have become impossible, even with the patronage of the imperial family, for such men to rise to the highest ranks unless they were themselves members of the Fujiwara family.

In the middle of the ninth century the Ki family which had enjoyed considerable political influence since the Nara period quickly lost that influence and power through the pressure exerted by the Fujiwaras. From the family's political ruin arose many members who made their way through scholarship and specialization in the arts, beginning with Kino Haseo (845–912) who studied under Sugawara Michizane and became one of the best poets writing in Chinese of the late ninth century. His son, Kino Yoshimochi, contributed a preface in Chinese to the first imperial anthology of *waka* poetry, the *Kokinshū*, compiled in 905. Kino Okimichi became a master of *gagaku* and his nephew Kino Aritsune also advanced his career in the field of music. Kino Tsurayuki (?–945) was a grandson of Okimichi. He was one of the compilers of the *Kokinshū*, wrote a Japanese preface to that anthology which was a paraphrase of its Chinese preface, and after serving as Governor of Tosa from 931 to 934 wrote the *Tosa nikki*. He was past the age of seventy, in 941, when he finally rose to the Junior Fifth Rank, Upper Grade but his position in the aristocracy was not high.

However, as we shall see later, he contributed more poems (451) to the imperial *waka* anthologies than any other single poet, he was the representative *waka* poet of the ninth century, and exerted enormous influence on later generations of poets. Tsurayuki's younger cousin, Kino Tomonori, was one of the best poets represented in the *Kokinshū*, was one of the compilers of that anthology, and his son, Kino Tokibumi, was one of the compilers of the *Gosenshū* (951).

Unlike the Sugawara family which raised its status in the bureaucracy through its activities in the arts, the Ki family turned to the arts after the failure of its aspirations in politics. If we call the former an ascending type intellectual, the latter can be called a descending one. Intellectual society in ninth-century Japan was a mixture of both these types.

The most notable representatives of these two patterns in intellectual society were, respectively, Sugawara Michizane and Kino Tsurayuki. The gaining of advancement in the bureaucracy through activity in intellectual fields demanded skill in the Chinese language and so Sugawara Michizane wrote in Chinese – indeed, had to write in Chinese. Kino Tsurayuki, with his unfortunate aristocratic background, probably had no aspirations towards promotion of the type sought by Sugawara and did not hesitate to concentrate on writing lyrical poetry in his mother tongue, using the new transcription system in the Japanese language, *kana*.

The contents of Michizane's poetry and prose was either directly related to public affairs or at the least set against the background of public affairs. The previously mentioned *Kanke bunsō* was one of three works (*the Kanke sandaishū*) which he compiled personally and submitted to the Emperor. Apart from his preface to the *Kokinshū* all of Tsurayuki's poetry and prose was essentially private. In the *Tosa nikki*, far from Michizane's attitude of submitting his works to the Emperor, Tsurayuki disguised his identity and opened his famous diary with the words: 'Diaries, I am told, are things written by men, but I am trying my hand to see what a woman can accomplish.' And in the last line he went even so far as to write that it would be better to discard it immediately. The light humour which appears here and there in the *Tosa nikki* was mostly directed towards the diary itself. Michizane was a tragic hero but Tsurayuki seems to have been the kind of man who was capable of laughing at himself.

This is not to say, however, that there was no point of contact between the world of Michizane and the world of Tsurayuki and the *Kokinshū*. As we have already seen, Kino Yoshimochi, who was the son of Michizane's close friend Kino Haseo, wrote the Chinese (*Mana*) preface to the *Kokinshū*. The *Mana* preface took the general theory of its opening statement from the 'Preface on Major Principle' of the Shi-king and Tsurayuki's *Kana* preface followed the sense of the *Mana* preface. According to the 'Preface on Major Principle' of the Shi-king, the definition of Chinese poetry is as follows. Poetry comes from human intent. Human intent is in one's heart. When it blossoms into words, it produces poetry.

The *Mana* preface to the *Kokinshū* defines *waka* poetry as follows. Japanese verse is something which takes root in the soil of one's heart and blossoms forth in a forest of words.

The opening line of the *Kana* preface reads 'The poetry of *Yamato-uta* has sprung from the hearts of the people as seeds to grow into myriads of words.'

There is here clearly a connecting thread and Michizane's world of Chinese poetry and Tsurayuki's world of *waka* poetry were not in pursuit of completely separate objectives. There was more to it than that. Take for example Michizane's four-line poem on 'an autumn evening':

> The autumn moon shines like a mirror
> Without clearing up the crime
> The wind is like a sword
> That does not sever sadness
> All that I have seen or heard
> Makes me shudder
> This fall is my own fall.
>
> (*Kanke Kōshū*, poem 485)

One of the poems which Kino Tsurayuki selected to appear in the *Kokinshū* (poem 193 by Ōeno Chisato) reads as follows:

> The pathos of the autumn moon
> Is not for me alone,
> And yet, I wonder,
> Who feels as I?

The former poem was an expression of a man who was exiled on a false charge, while the latter was 'Composed at the *Uta-awase* party held at Prince Koresada's'. Despite the difference in the circumstances in which these poems were written and despite the fact that one is in Chinese and the other in Japanese, there was clearly much in common between the poetical view-point of these two contemporaries. However, the *Kaifūsō* and the *Man-yōshū* did not have this in common. There was enormous mainland influence in the poetry of intellectuals such as Ōtomono Tabito and Yamanoueno Okura, but the Chinese poetry of the *Kaifūsō* did not go beyond simple imitation of Six Dynasties Chinese models and, with very few exceptions, did not present the emotions and sensitivities of their authors. This was also true in the case of the early ninth-century imperial anthologies of Chinese poetry.

There was no ground on which the contemporary and common nature of the poet's feelings and sensitivity could be a matter of importance.

Through the ninth century the situation gradually changed until a man such as Sugawara Michizane, skilful in his use of the Chinese language, could write not of the emotions of a beautiful woman living in the city of Ch'ang-an which he had never seen, but of his own grudges and discontent arising from his own frustrations. Like the Sugawara family, the Ōe family was a family of scholars and when Chisato began a poem with a line like 'The pathos of the autumn moon', he may have been writing under the influence of Chinese poetry. However what is more important than this is that in Michizane's four-line poem on 'an autumn evening' was truly an example of the author's self-expression.

Therefore it would not be strange that the two 'selves' living in the same age and same society should leave their imprints in common in their self-expressions, that is, in their poetry whether it was written in Chinese or in Japanese.

In contrast to the *Kokinshū* which in its range of subject matter was far more limited than the *Manyoshū*, the *Kanke bunsō* and the *Kanke kōshū* greatly expanded the world of lyric poetry. First, apart from Yamanoueno Okura's 'dialogue on poverty' treating of the hunger and cold afflicting the people, it is only in the collections of Michizane that any poet of the entire Heian period touched on the same subject. For example, Michizane's group of eight-line, five-graphs-to-the-line poems, each of which begin with 'To whom does the cold winter visit first' (*Kanke bunsō* Vol. 3 poems 200–209), comprise ten poems on the general theme of the hardships of cold weather, the poems respectively dealing with 'a runaway peasant', 'a vagrant', 'an old man who has lost his wife', 'an orphan child', 'a gardener', 'a pack-horse driver', 'a sailor', 'a fisherman', 'a salt seller' and 'a woodcutter'. In these poems he speaks not only of the sufferings of cold, but of other factors which affected the people at large in an adverse way, such as infertile land, heavy taxation, sickness, the perils of wind and waves, and the dangers of losing one's job. Other poems in the *Kanke kōshū* on such themes as robbers, wicked tradesmen and rapacious officials were again outside the traditional subject matter of both Chinese and *waka* poetry in Japan.

Second, Michizane not infrequently referred to court plots and intrigues in his poetry. In one poem he stated that even the footprints of an ox were a pitfall set for him; in another two lines he said he was afraid that he would fall dead in the street before he could achieve his ideals for the state. Poems which, regarding politics and individual fate as being closely related, expressed either anger or grief at political policies were frequent in classical Chinese tradition, notably in the case of the poet Tu Fu, but before Michizane had hardly ever featured in Japanese poetic tradition. In this sense, Michizane was probably the first Japanese poet to come close to the poetic world of mainland Asia. Third, Chinese poetry which touched on Buddhism had already appeared, as in the category of the ten poems on Buddhism, which were included in the *Bunka shūreishū*. However, these ten poems in some cases were simple depictions of scenes at Buddhist temples, in other cases he eulogized the merit of specific monks, and in still other cases spoke of transmigration of the soul, but all were Buddhist in only very general terms and none related to the sincere religious aspirations of their authors. As we have already seen, even though *waka* poetry from the time of the *Manyōshū* onwards on rare occasions made use of Buddhist vocabulary, in sentiment they seldom went beyond such trite observations as 'life is fleeting'. However, Sugawara Michizane, who was sacrificed to the court intrigues of the Fujiwara's, saw his family scattered and he himself demoted from the post of Minister of the Right to exile in Kyūshū, and wrote poems as a desperate cry 'de profundis' and resorted to Kwannon; he wrote of Buddhism in a way no Japanese poet had ever written before him. Take, for example, the following poem:

> We are pursued by sickness
> Until we arrive at senility
> We are chased by sadness
> Until we go into exile
> There's no place where we can hide from death
> Recite the name of Kwannon one time.

(Kanke kōshū, poem 513)

Here, 'Kwannon' may not have been written just figuratively.

With Kūkai at the beginning of the ninth century, philosophical aspects of Buddhism became part of Japanese thought. With

Michizane at the end of the ninth century, religious aspects of Buddhism for the first time became a subject for lyric poetry. Fourth, another new subject to be discovered in the poetry of Michizane was the life and career of the poet himself. For example, take the poem 'Seeing in the Mirror' in the *Kanke bunsō* (Vol. 4 poem 254) where Michizane seeing his white beard in the mirror, feeling that the fire in his heart is still burning and that his will is as strong as that in his youth, realizes that the springtime of his life is gone never to return. Yet many love poems had reflected on the violent passions the poet had felt at a moment in his life, but did not contain reflections on that life as a whole.

Questioning the pattern and meaning of life as a whole was a habit of the poets of China, but was not customary among Japanese poets. When Michizane wrote this poem, he was not merely imitating Chinese precedent (the individuality of the poem is too strong for that to be a possibility), but he was approaching the Chinese style of examining one's attitudes towards life.

When this ambitious forty-four-year-old intellectual wrote, 'Even though the position of Senior Fifth Rank is high, even though the income of 2000 koku is rarely received', he must have regarded such status relatively, with a certain distance or perspective. Such an attitude, however, could not have been acquired without the awareness of the meaning of his whole life and career. His clear presentation of that awareness in a poem was something new and very important in the history of Japanese literature.

In the two anthologies *Kanke bunsō* and *Kanke kōshū* were collected about 550 of Michizane's poems. The best of these were probably the 'One Hundred Couplets on my Thoughts'. These were written after his exile from Kyōto to Kyūshū and treat at length of many things including scenes along the road he travelled, his thoughts on life, Buddhism and his nostalgia for home, his recollections of Kyōto, his despair and his deepest feelings. For example, when describing his journey, he vividly depicts his nausea at seeing the curious passers-by coming over to look at him, crowding all over the street, as soon as his carriage stopped. This very concrete portrayal sums up his wretched condition. Speaking of his fall from power, he likens it to a towering tree being bent by the force of the wind and says that the society in which he lived was not one in which it was possible for a man to live out his days in honesty and integrity. On the condition of his exile, he wrote the following lines:

> I wrote down what came to my mind
> I composed poems, which I then burn.

He said he did such things over and over again. He had no poet friends to meet. All of the poems in *Kanke kōshū* are said to have been written and collected by the poet all alone in despair in exile, and left posthumously with his close friend Kino Haseo.

What he wrote he burned and yet even as it burned, wrote more; writing seemed to be a waste of effort and yet still he wrote. Thus one of the greatest masterpieces of Japanese lyric poetry was written. In broadness of subject matter, in the vividness of description, and especially in the intensity of the bitter cry from his innermost heart, the poetry of the *Kanke kōshū*, particularly the hundred poems on 'my thoughts' were never surpassed in Japanese poetry either before or after.

Sugawara Michizane while he was at the post of Minister of the Right expressed his desire to resign three times, perhaps because the poet within him could not compromise with the plots and intrigues of court life. From the tone in which he submitted his resignations (cf. *Kanke bunsō*, poems 629–631), it seems possible that he had some presentiment of the dark fate awaiting him. Be that as it may, three times his resignation was refused.

We shall come to Kino Tsurayuki as a poet in discussing the *Kokinshū*, but, as we have already seen, his major work as a prose artist was the *Tosa nikki*, written in *kana*. The *Tosa nikki* is a travel diary covering the fifty-five day journey which Tsurayuki made from Tosa (he left Tosa in the 12th month of 934 after giving up his post of *Kokushi* there) by sea to Kyōto (arriving in the 2nd month of 935). He records various events relating to his journey such as his fear of storms and pirates, the words and actions of his fellow passengers, his attachment to his little daughter who had died while he was in his post, and his yearning for Kyōto. He also included fifty-seven *waka* poems which are presented as being the work of various people he met on the way (although actually, of course, written by himself).

About a hundred years earlier Ennin (Jikaku Daishi) had written the travel diary *Nittō-guhō-junrei-kōki*. Conscious of his official responsibilities, Ennin had been a cool and detached observer who described in detail the social customs and so forth that he encountered. In this respect, the *Tosa nikki* is poor by comparison. It has nothing to say about the author's official responsibilities, and although the ship during its journey stopped at many harbours there is hardly any record of the society and customs of the provincial people Tsurayuki must have encountered. Unlike Ennin, Tsurayuki's interests did not transcend the ordinary, everyday events of life and his sphere of observation merely encompassed the people aboard his ship. When he finally returned to his home in Kyōto, he found that his house was in a sorry state:

'The heart of the person to whom we had entrusted the house must have gone to ruin, too.' And he reflected 'In the five or six years that we were away, centuries seem to have passed here.' Also, he lamented, 'Innumerable feelings press upon me and among them the dearest are thoughts of the girl who was born in this house. It is impossible to say how broken-hearted I am that she has not returned with us.'

This is a surprising reduction in scale of the world of the *Nittō-guhō-junrei-kōki* as an example of diary literature, and as a record of a contemporary journey it is dwarfed by the richness of experience to be found in Michizane's 'One Hundred Couplets on my Thoughts'.

However, in the *Tosa nikki* Kino Tsurayuki achieved some things not accomplished by either Ennin or Michizane. First, he wrote in *kana* prose, and, second, the narrative style contains a blend of poems on personal things related to the author and humour. In these two respects, the *Tosa nikki* had considerable significance as a pioneering work. In the Heian period nothing like the *Nittō-guhō-junrei-kōki* ever appeared again and the complex tensions of Michizane's 'hundred couplets' were never repeated. However, the *Tosa nikki* was the forerunner of many *kana* diaries including the mid-tenth-century *Kagerō nikki*, the early eleventh-century *Murasaki Shikibu nikki* and *Sarashina nikki*, and the twelfth-century *Sanukino suke nikki* and the diary-form novel the *Izumi Shikibu nikki*. But there was more to it than that. The tendency to interweave poetry with a personal narrative in *non*-diary literary forms was carried on in the *uta monogatari* genre of fiction of which the *Ise monogatari* is typical. Moreover, the tendency to include humour was echoed in the *haibun* literature of the

Tokugawa period. These two features of the *Tosa nikki* were undoubtedly the reason why so much has been written about it in the history of Japan's literature and so little about the diary of Ennin and the 'One Hundred Couplets on my Thoughts' of Michizane.

Although he did not match Ennin as an observer of 'externals' (social customs etc.) and did not match Michizane as a seeker after internal truths, the author of the *Tosa nikki* was more profoundly than either bound up with the indigenous Japanese world view—the world of everyday experience, its private characteristics and its unstructured temporal progression. Indeed, the literature of this ruined aristocrat of the ninth century seems to have presaged the 300 years of the so-called 'female' culture, diary literature, *uta monogatari* and *emakimono* of the tenth to twelfth centuries.

However, it was not only the *Tosa nikki* which was a forerunner of the *monogatari* fiction of the golden age of the Fujiwara's. There were two prose works written in *kana* – one remarkable for the richness of its world of the imagination and the structure of its stories, the other for its polished changes of scene and psychological narrative – which far and away excelled the *Tosa nikki*. These were, respectively, the *Taketori monogatari* and the *Ise monogatari*. We do not know precisely when they were written, but although there are several theories, the consensus of scholarly opinion places them at some time between the end of the ninth and beginning of the tenth centuries. If this is true, then the probability is that their authors were late-ninth-century intellectuals perhaps the contemporaries of Michizane and Tsurayuki.

The basic plot of the *Taketori monogatari* concerns an old bamboo cutter who finds a tiny girl in a bamboo plant. Within the short span of three months the three-inch girl grows into a beautiful princess (Kaguya-hime) whose hand in marriage is sought by various suitors. She sets each of them an impossible task which they all fail. Eventually, the girl who is a daughter of the moon-people and who has been set inside the stem of a bamboo for some transgression, is reclaimed by her own race and ascends into the skies. Numerous stories of this type existed in Japanese folk tradition and there is little room for doubt that the author of the *Taketori monogatari* drew on at least one or two of them for his plot. Precisely what he added to the basic material of his story is clear from the special features presented by the finished work.

First, it is written in *Kana-majiri* prose and there is influence from mainland literature (including Buddhist scriptures) in the vocabulary. Some scholars have also pointed out special features in the way some of the Chinese characters are read which could imply that the author was familiar with classical Chinese literature.

Second, the structure of the story is extremely logical, beginning with the miraculous 'birth' of Kaguya-hime, following with the quests of the various suitors for her hand and ending with a truly dramatic climax. There are five suitors – two princes and three noblemen – who, as mentioned above, are set impossible tasks in which they are bound to fail (to find the Buddha's stone bowl, to bring back a branch of a tree in the Taoist land of immortals, to obtain the unburnable hide of a fire mouse, to take one of the five jades around the dragon's neck, to bring back a *Koyasugai* sea-shell from a swallow's nest on a precipitous cliff). The first prince produces a fake stone bowl, which deception Kaguya-hime immediately detects; the second prince has a branch made out of gold and silver, but is betrayed by the craftsman he has commissioned when he comes to collect payment; the first nobleman is himself deceived by a merchant and given a fake hide; the second nobleman sets out to sea in search of a dragon, but has to abandon his plans because of a storm; and the third nobleman falls from a great height as he plunges his hand into a swallow's nest (only to find the swallows' droppings) and faints. Five failures – all different. The fact that no particular type of failure is repeated indicates careful calculation on the part of the author. After the failure of the five suitors, the Emperor himself seeks the hand of Kaguya-hime, but she refuses him with 'I'm not particularly moved by the Imperial summons'.

The Emperor then seeks to enlist the help of the old bamboo cutter by offering him an official post, but he too is unable to persuade his adopted daughter. Thus all suits for Kaguya-hime fail and she returns to the skies. No later Heian period *monogatari* work was structured to so good an effect, so concisely told or so dramatic as the *Taketori monogatari*. Indeed, it is a rare exception within the whole history of Japanese literature.

Partial detail is not described solely for its own interest, but is placed within context, and while being related to the whole, is also related within a necessary and sufficient range. This attitude, this kind of logical, abstract attitude could only be gained through assimilation of Chinese culture by the ninth-century intelligentsia (from Kūkai to Michizane). It probably could not have appeared as an expression of the indigenous thought (from Keikai to Tsurayuki). In other words, the author of the *Taketori monogatari* was not only able to read Chinese, but was thoroughly conversant with the Chinese classics.

Third, the plot itself may have been pure fantasy, but the details are vivid, the settings are sharply observed and there is unsparing insight into human psychology. For example, the first prince's plausible description of the Paradise he had never seen; the story of how one of the noblemen forsook his wives to set to sea in search of a dragon that he might win Kaguya-hime's hand, and when he had failed and run home after encountering a storm, his wives laughed at him and mocked him; another nobleman climbed to the roof to search the inside of a swallow's nest, and fell to the ground with a handful of excrement. He was knocked unconscious, doused with water and finally recovered.

In those scenes bitterness and even traces of ridicule against aristocratic society can be detected. At the same time the author did not overlook the weakness of character of the humble bamboo cutter who was prepared to try to inveigle his adopted daughter into a marriage she did not want when the Emperor offered him an official post in the bureaucracy. This may suggest that the author of the *Taketori monogatari* was not an aristocrat by birth, but a member of the 'specialist' intelligentsia. There can be no doubt at all, however, about his literary talent which is apparent from the way he blended an imaginary tale in a fanciful setting with sharp and perceptive observation of reality.

Buddhist vocabulary can be found in the *Taketori monogatari*, but there is no firm evidence to suggest that the author subscribed to Buddhist philosophy. The early eleventh-century *Genji monogatari* contains the statement that the *Taketori monogatari* was the ancestor of the *monogatari* genre. If true, then from the very beginning the *monogatari* was very much secular and worldly – typical of the Heian period.

The *Ise monogatari* (author and date of writing unknown) comprises 143 passages. The shortest consists of no more than a single *waka* poem with a line or two of introduction, while the longest approximates to a short story with prose narrative and *waka* poetry intermixed. In other words, apart from the fact that each passage contains at least one *waka* poem, there is no unity of form (altogether there are 209 poems of which about a third also appear in the *Kokinshū*). There is no real chronological order to the passages and the settings are very varied (ranging from Kyōto, through rather vague 'country' scenes and specific geographical locations). There is no single central character who links all 143 passages, different passages figuring different characters who do not necessarily relate to those going before or after. In contrast to the author of the *Taketori monogatari*, the author of the *Ise monogatari* – assuming that there was one author – did not trouble to aim for a unified structure, but instead made up his work from many pieces each according to its particular interest.

However, the *Ise monogatari* is not entirely without a central theme in that many of the stories are related to the amorous encounters of Ariwarano Narihira. Quite frequently stories begin with the clause 'once there was a man' in which Narihira is 'the man', and sometimes he is mentioned more directly, as in passage 65 which contains the words 'a man called Ariwara' (or 'a man of the Ariwara family'). Poems which in the *Ise monogatari* appear as the work of 'the man' are included in the *Kokinshū* as the work of Ariwara Narihira (there are, however, exceptions where the *Kokinshū* ascribes them to someone completely different).

There was an actual historical character named Ariwarano Narihira (825–880) who is described in the *Sandai jitsuroku* (901) as having been the fifth son of an imperial prince, and as having achieved the rank of Lieutenant-General in the Right Imperial Guard. He was apparently famous for his good looks, loose morals and skill in the composition of *waka* poetry. Probably he was one of the Tsurayuki type of intellectuals of the time and wrote all (or at least most) of the poems ascribed to Narihira in the *Kokinshū*. Doubtless the author of the *Ise monogatari* used these poems as his principal source material in depicting the life of the legendary Narihira.

Ariwarano Narihira, the hero of the *Ise monogatari*, was the prototype of the 'Don Juan' characters in Japanese fiction (Genji,

Yonosuke etc.) and is very special in that not only did he have relations with numerous women, but also seems not to have recognized any taboos where women were concerned in either a secular or religious sense. Take, for example, the stories where 'a courtier from the Ariwara family' had an affair with the Empress (65) and where 'the man' seduced the Ise Virgin Priestess (69). In the first story the Emperor, discovering the liaison, banished the young courtier from Kyōto and confined the lady to a room in the palace, but every night the courtier returned from his place of exile and played the flute outside the lady's room, mourning the fact that they could no longer meet. The significant point in this story is that nowhere is there any indication of moral taboos (at one point in the story the youth prays to the gods of Shintoism and Buddhism to remove his passion from him, but this is not for moral reasons, but because he fears that this affair will lead him to his own ruin).

In the second story a man is sent to the province of Ise as an Imperial Huntsman and has an affair with the Virgin Priestess. At one time such an occurrence would surely have invoked Shinto religious taboos, but although the man expresses great distress that the two will not be able to meet again after his return to Kyōto, there is no indication on either his part or hers of regret, fear, unease or guilt at what has happened between them. Everywhere that Narihira goes there is a joyful sexual relationship between him and a woman. It seems as if he has no defence to Shinto, Buddhist or Confucian morals and is hardly subject at all even to social pressures. He may have been indeed the ideal of the author of the *Ise monogatari*, and if so, that ideal had no relationship at all with the prevailing mainland ideological background and could only have been possible within the framework of the indigenous world view. Probably, the historical significance of the *Ise monogatari* is that it was the first expression of being conscious of traditional hedonism concentrating on the male-female relationship as an actual individual ideal.

The stories of the male-female relationships told in the *Ise monogatari* are short, but encompass a very wide range of circumstances and settings ranging from the tale of a boy who 'died' of a broken heart (14) to the story of a man's deep emotions at parting from his wife after a marriage of forty years; from the tale of the lady who was eaten by a demon after eloping with a man (6) to the

story of the complicated psychological background to a relationship between a licentious man and lustful woman (139).

There are other stories which in complexity of plot and effectiveness as short stories compare with the tale of the courtier and
the tale of the Ise Priestess. There is the tale of the man and wife
living in a remote country region (24). One day the man set out for
the capital to try to enter the service of an aristocratic house and
did not return home for three years. One night, just as the wife
who had become weary with waiting was about to sleep with
another man for the first time, her husband returned and
knocked at the door. The woman confessed the situation. The
husband was about to leave when his wife recited a poem which
contained the line 'my heart has always inclined towards you'.
The husband left all the same and the wife chased after him, but
she was unable to catch him up and eventually died of exhaus-
tion.

Then there is the tale of the young boy and girl in the country
who played together when children and fell in love when they
grew older. After they had been married for some years, the man
took to visiting another woman, but since his wife was apparently so undisturbed by this, he begun to suspect her too of
having a lover. One day he pretended to set out to visit his own
lover, but in reality concealed himself near his home to await
developments, only to hear his wife recite a poem which made
clear her deep love for him. Thereupon, he gave up going to his
lover and she for her part, deeply in love with him, composed
poems expressing her feelings for him. As he was moved by it, he
promised to visit her, but he never went to her again (23).

Again, there is the tale of an old woman who desired to meet a
man who would love her (63). She could not speak openly of this
so she pretended to have a dream which she recounted to her
three sons. Two of them just ignored her desire, but the third, the
youngest, realized the implication behind his mother's dream
and thought that he would try to arrange for her to meet Ariwara
Narihira. One day he met Narihira on a hunting expedition and
told him the story. Moved by pity Narihira went to the woman
and slept with her, but did not return again. Eventually, the old
woman went to Narihira's house and peeped in whereupon he
seemed to go to see her. The woman hurried back ahead of him
and greeted him. 'The man was moved to pity and slept with her

that night.' The story ends with 'Most people in this world think of the person whom they love and ignore those whom they don't love. However, Narihira had a heart that would not differentiate loving from not loving.'

Probably, the author of the *Ise monogatari* first composed the poems, then expanded the introductions to each poem. He must have imagined the conditions under which the poems were composed, created more than one hundred episodes, and collected them together into a single volume. The variety of circumstances within *Ise monogatari* was the earliest preview of the state of refinement that could be achieved within the realm of the prose tale by an attitude which concentrated on daily life and male-female relationships in particular. This attitude was possible because of the existence of a firm, traditional indigenous world view which did not allow the interference of extraordinary elements.

Thus, in the late ninth and early tenth centuries (as far as we can tell) there were two works – the *Taketori monogatari* and the *Ise monogatari* – which were completely contrasting. Both surpassed the *Tosa nikki*, the former in its compact structure, the latter in its subtle, psychological exploration of multi-faceted situations. It has already been said that the *Taketori monogatari* was the work of an intellectual on the pattern of Sugawara Michizane, the *Ise monogatari* of an intellectual on the pattern of Kino Tsurayuki. When the two different patterns came together the result was the two greatest works of Heian period prose literature – the *Genji monogatari* and the *Konjaku monogatari*.

THE AESTHETICS OF THE KOKINSHŪ

The significance of the ninth century as a turning point is most vividly apparent in the field of *waka* and the transformation of aesthetic awareness through *waka*. What happened can best and most easily be understood by comparing the *Manyōshū* and the *Kokinshū*. The *Manyōshū* was a collection of *waka* poetry principally written in the late seventh and first half of the eighth centuries (the latest date of any poem is 759), while the *Kokinshū* (compiled in 905) was a collection of *waka* poetry principally written in the ninth century.

The *Manyōshū* was not compiled by imperial command. The

three anthologies compiled by imperial command in the early ninth century (the *Ryōunshū*, the *Bunka shūreishū* and the *Keikokushū*) were all collections of Chinese language poetry which excluded *waka*. The appearance about a century later of the *Kokinshū* – the first imperial anthology of *waka* poetry – indicates that in the intervening period *waka* had established itself as a legitimate part of 'official' literature. Of course, the idea of an 'official' literature was imported from China. Therefore, the earliest imperial anthologies were concentrated on Chinese language poetry and prose (excluding native language lyric poetry) and examinations for promotion within the bureaucracy were designed to test competence in Chinese and not the ability to express oneself in the native language of Japan. This is not to say that after the ninth century Chinese language poetry and prose were ignored as constituents of the training and education of the intellectual classes, but recognition of *waka* as a legitimate part of such training added a new dimension. The vital significance of this development is reflected in the introductions (one in Chinese by Kino Yoshimochi, one in Japanese by Kino Tsurayuki) to the *Kokinshū* where it is asserted that it is the *waka* and not the Chinese language poem written by a Japanese which is the true Japanese counterpart of the *shi* poem so revered in China. It was probably no coincidence that the idea was accepted through the compilation of the *Kokinshū* at about the same time that the embassies to T'ang China were discontinued.

Unlike the *Manyōshū*, the *Kokinshū* included poems which were the products of *uta-awase*. *Uta-awase*, which began at this period, were basically a kind of contest in *waka* poetry in which the poems were all composed on one particular theme and then were compared and judged to see which was the best. These contests became an integral part of later culture, representing the complete integration of *waka* into Japanese culture. The judgement of the excellence of a *waka* poem had to be based on certain objective criteria besides the tastes of the judge of the contest and, naturally enough, the popularity of *uta-awase* could lead to development in the field of *karon* (treatises on *waka*). Kūkai's *Bunkyō-hifu-ron* has already been mentioned in this connection. According to later sources (for example, the early twelfth-century *Toshiyori Zuinō*), the *Kisenshiki* and other similar *karon* were produced, it seems, before the time of the *Kokinshū*. Throughout the

Heian period not one theoretical work on *monogatari* fiction was written, while *karon* were written in ever-increasing numbers – an indication that *waka* had become integrated into culture to a very high degree while *monogatari* only to a very limited extent.

One of the most marked contrasts between the *Manyōshū* and the *Kokinshū* lay in the social origins of the poets represented. The authorship of the *Manyōshū* poems ranged from Emperors to peasants from the Eastern provinces, from aristocrats to conscripted soldiers. Among key poets, in the mid-seventh century there were many aristocrats, in the late seventh century aristocrats and official court poets, and in the eighth century quite a number of intellectuals and anonymous members of the people at large as well. However, in the case of the *Kokinshū* (which contains 1100 poems), about a third of the total was contributed by 'yomihito shirazu' ('Unknown authors') and to judge from their vocabulary and content, few, if any, of these were written by the provincial peasantry.

Unlike the *Manyōshū*, the world of the *Kokinshū* was closed and confined to the court aristocracy. Of the poets who wrote from within this closed aristocratic society, certain features emerge. First, of the 1100 poems, only fifteen were written by members of the imperial family (represented here are one Emperor, one Empress and six Imperial Princes – eight individuals in all). Authors identified as contributing to the *Kokinshū* numbered 127. Second, of the aristocrats who contributed few were members of the highest rank; most of the important authors from these spheres coming from the lower aristocracy, the Buddhist priesthood or the circle of court ladies. Particularly noticeable in this respect is that the four compilers of the *Kokinshū* (Kino Tsurayuki, Ōshikōchino Mitsune, Kino Tomonori and Mibuno Tadamine), who between them contributed about a fifth of the total number of poems, were all of them low-ranking aristocrats. Kino Tsurayuki never rose beyond the fifth rank and Kino Tomonori was of the fifth rank at the time of the *Kokinshū*'s compilation. The biographies of the other two compilers are obscure, but according to the *kana* preface they were low-ranking officials in the bureaucracy. None of them ranked anywhere near Ōtomono Yakamochi who played such a large part in the compilation of the *Manyōshū*. The compilation of the *Kokinshū* was indisputably the work of intellectuals of the Kino Tsurayuki type.

Later Heian period literature, both lyric poetry and prose novels, was likewise the work of men and women of the lower aristocracy intellectuals, the point being that such people were close enough to the centre to be able to describe and depict very well the life of the court and yet far enough removed from the centre of power to escape being involved in court power struggles.

The success of *waka* in achieving separate status as a link in the chain of aristocratic court culture, and the recognition of its legitimacy were of course related both to the Japanization of its mode of presentation and its unified form. The presentation of the Japanese language entirely through Chinese characters as seen in the *Manyōshū* was replaced in the *Kokinshū* by a *kana* presentation (albeit with an admixture of several Chinese characters). The importance of this in terms of how much easier it was to read goes without saying. Moreover, the principal poetic forms to be found in the *Manyōshū* were the *tanka* (*waka*), the *chōka* and the *sedōka*, but in the 1100 poems of the *Kokinshū* there are only ten *chōka* or *sedōka*. Later imperial anthologies also in this respect followed not the *Manyōshū* but the *Kokinshū*.

The *tanka* is much less difficult than the *chōka* to write and much easier to extemporize. That *uta-awase* became so popular in the aristocratic society of the Heian period and that exchanging of *waka* poems became such a normal part of the love relationship between man and woman was due to the adoption in the ninth century of the *tanka* as virtually the sole form of lyric poetry and the diffusion of the *kana* presentation.

The ideological background to lyric poetry (especially the relationship with Buddhism does not seem to have changed fundamentally in the period of the *Kokinshū*. Buddhist thought in the eighth century when the *Kokubunji* were established and the Tōdaiji Daibutsu was built left virtually no mark on the poetry of the *Manyōshū*. Buddhist concern with the next world was hardly at all reflected in the poetry of the *Kokinshū* either and there was virtually no influence from the 'contemplation of non-being', developed initially by Kukai and refined by the monks of Hieizan.

> Is this a world of dreams or reality?
> I do not know.
> It may be or may not be.
>
> (Vol. 18 poem 942)

This poem is the sole exception. Of course, there are other poems which seem to have been influenced by Buddhism, but no more than one in a hundred. Even those there are confine themselves to thought such as life is like a dream and so forth and these same thoughts could have been written whether the authors knew of Buddhism or not. Ariwarano Narihira's (poem 861) is one of the most inspiring of this type:

> Though I had heard that someday
> I would have to walk this fateful road
> Never did I think that day would come so soon.

Of course, here there is no Buddhist connotation. In the sense that anthologies of Japanese lyric poetry were thoroughly this-worldly even in an age when Buddhism was the national religion of Japan, when Buddhist art had reached its highest point, and Buddhist philosophy was at its most refined, there was no great difference between the *Manyōshū* and the *Kokinshū*.

Major differences there were, however, in the subject matter of lyric poetry, in the constituents of 'love' (a major shared theme), attitudes towards time and in the extent of refinement of feelings. In short, there was a major difference between the *Manyōshū* and the *Kokinshū* in terms of literary aesthetics.

A general idea of subject matter can be gained from the system of classification of poems and the number of the poems which were placed into each category. The overwhelming majority of *Manyōshū* poems were love poems or were at least about the male-female relationship. In the whole of the *Manyōshū* there are only two examples of a division of poems under the heading of the four seasons ('Miscellaneous poems on the four seasons', and 'Love poems from the four seasons', in Vol. 8 and Vol. 10 respectively). Moreover, the 'Love poems from the four seasons' are basically love poems treated through seasonal imagery while the 'Miscellaneous poems on the four seasons' are in most cases also related to love.

However, of the twenty volumes of the *Kokinshū*, six are devoted to seasonal poems and five to love poems, the former coming first in the anthology. In number the poems in each category are roughly the same (360 love poems, 342 seasonal poems). Among the seasonal poems there are those which are basically love poems treated in terms of seasonal imagery, but unlike the *Manyōshū*, the majority have nothing to do with love and speak of the emotions inspired by the changing seasons. For example, take Kino Tsurayuki's 'spring' poem:

> Spring has come
> And soon its breezes will melt
> The water now frozen
> In which in summer we dipped our sleeves.
>
> (Vol. 1 poem 2)

Such poems, rare in the *Manyōshū*, are typical of the *Kokinshū*. Thus the aesthetics of the *Kokinshū*, which attached as much weight to poems of seasonal description as to love poems, were clearly different from those of the *Manyōshū*. The famous Japanese feeling for the seasons which would lead to the seasonal theme in haiku poetry began here as probably did also what is often known as the Japanese love for nature.

We have already seen that the 'ancient ballads' transmitted in the *Kojiki* and the *Nihon shoki* concentrated on matters to do with human affairs – particularly the male-female relationship – and hardly ever mentioned 'nature'. We have also seen how the poets of the *Manyōshū*, while describing nature in so far as it affected human concerns, were not concerned with the oceans, high mountains or forests infested by wild beasts. This was the condition up to the middle of the eighth century. The poets of the *Kokinshū* did not 'discover' a new nature. It was simply that the *Kokinshū* poets began to compose poems about flowers and birds and the wind and the moon for their own aesthetic values independent of thoughts of love – the same flowers, birds, wind, and moon to which the *Manyōshū* poets entrusted their love. This tendency had previously appeared in the works of the *Manyō* period professional poet Yamabeno Akahito. The ordinary activities of a professional poet were simply incompatible with the sole use of the extraordinary emotion of love as an artistic impulse.

The majority of *Kokinshū* poets, typified by the four compilers, were intellectuals who to a greater or lesser degree specialized in *waka* poetry. To this was added the *uta-awase* and other social occasions for the composition of *waka*. It was thus only natural that the approach of Akahito should be inherited, expanded and strengthened. Moreover, this process was an internal development of court and aristocratic society which was much more fully developed itself than in the Nara period. Akahito travelled widely and at least observed nature with his own eyes, but in the *Tosa nikki*, Kino Tsurayuki was simply full of longing and yearning for Kyōto and did not pay any attention to the natural surroundings along his route. He seems not to have seen the blue sea, the morning sun, the high mountains surrounded by rainy haze or the wide plains devastated by raging snow storms. We should be careful about using the phrase 'the Japanese love of nature' as it is. At least, we cannot pretend Tsurayuki really loved nature. What he loved was the spring waters and cherry blossoms of the capital, the spring rains and mists of Kyōto, and the maple leaves and winds of Mt. Tatsuta in autumn. Only six varieties of flower figure in his poems of spring and autumn – the cherry blossom, the plum blossom, the *yamabuki* (a wild yellow rose), the *ominaeshi*, the *fujibakama*, and the chrysanthemum – and only two varieties of bird – the *uguisu* (nightingale) and the *hototogisu* (cuckoo).

It cannot truly be thought that Tsurayuki loved either cherry blossoms or birds, but what then was it that he did love? Perhaps it was not 'nature' itself – perhaps it was just the words themselves. It was not the *hototogisu* as a bird that he loved, but the word *hototogisu*; not the thing itself, but the name of the thing. One entire volume of the *Kokinshū* (Vol. 10) is given over to poems making verbal play on 'the names of things' (*mono no na*). Moreover, Tsurayuki was by no means exceptional among the poets of the *Kokinshū* – indeed as one of the compilers and author of more poems than any other single author, he was the representative poet of the *Kokinshū*. There were quite a few *Manyōshū* poets, besides Akahito, who wrote travel poems. Many *Kokinshū* poets apart from Tsurayuki who wrote poems about travel scenery did not have any true interest in the subject. In the whole of the *Kokinshū* there are only 16 travel poems – far fewer than the 47 *mono no na* poems. Nonetheless it was this the first imperial anthology of *waka* poetry which set the pattern of the 'Japanese feeling for the four seasons' and the 'Japanese love of nature'.

Thus the age of the *uta-makura* (a place with poetical associations) was born. In *uta-makura* a 'Japanese' tendency was interestingly expressed; that is, the interest in the natural surroundings was pointed not to the scenic beauty itself but primarily to the 'names' of the places which had appeared over and over again in *waka* poetry. Therefore, poets of the Heian period described in their poems the natural beauties of *uta-makura* which they themselves had never seen (for example, the autumn winds at the Shirakawa Barrier) and painters depicted scenes which they had never visited – famous places, such as the 'eight sights' of Japan which they had never seen. This so-called 'love of nature' traced its origins not to the *Manyōshū* but to the *Kokinshū*.

Ranking with nature as a theme for lyric poetry in the *Kokinshū*, and perhaps surpassing it, was again 'love', but the nature and essence of that love had changed from *Manyōshū* times. The typical *Manyōshū* love poem took the form of an expression of love by a specific individual (most usually the author) for a specific individual. The verb 'to love' was a transitive verb which required a specific direct object. The meaning of the verb 'to love' was that the consciousness of the speaker was directed to an external object, or to go one step further, acted on that external object. In the *Manyōshū* that action was frequently expressed in the desire 'to embrace', 'to sleep with', or 'to get into bed with' the other party.

One might say that the special characteristic of love in the *Manyōshū* was that it was active, directed towards the specific, implied concrete physical relations. However, in the *Kokinshū* the verb *kou* ('to love') was usually replaced by the verb *mono-omou* which was hardly used at all in the *Manyōshū* and which has the meaning of being deep in contemplation. *Omou* is, of course, used actively with the direct object *mono*, but the *mono-omou* compound is used as an intransitive verb. Its use in the love poems of the *Kokinshū* implies not so much an interest in a specific objective beyond the author, but the author's reflection on his own condition. There is a transference here from love as a concrete act to love as a state of mind, from the world of a transitive verb to the world of an intransitive verb.

The direct expression of 'sleeping together' which is found so often in the *Manyōshū* is entirely absent from the *Kokinshū*. Poems dealing with 'sleeping together' were exceptionally rare. There are only a few poems which imply the sexual act, but in this context such direct verbs as *ineru* ('sleeping together') are avoided and the act is hinted at rather than explicitly stated. For example, the poem which is given in the *Ise monogatari* as the work of the Ise

Priestess after her encounter with Narihira appears in the *Kokinshū* as an anonymous poem:

> Did my lord come to me or did I go to him?
> I scarcely know.
> Was it a dream or a reality?
> Was I asleep or awake?
>
> (Vol. 12 poem 645)

The dream imagery used in such a context occurs many times in the *Kokinshū*, as in the following two poems of Onono Komachi:

> Yearning for him I slept in sadness
> And saw him in a dream.
> Had I known it was a dream
> I never would have woken with the dawn.
>
> (Vol. 12 poem 552)

> My soul will go as often as I like
> To my lover in a dream,
> Because no one will blame me there.
>
> (Vol. 13 poem 657)

Poem 658 (also by Onono Komachi) contains the idea that even though she saw the man many times in her dreams, to see him in person even at a glance would be much better. However, such poems are exceptional.

The characteristic tendency in the *Kokinshū* is an emphasis on thinking of a lover rather than meeting and sleeping together, and rather than that, on the state of *mono-omou* (contemplation) which culminates in a dream. The less the actual active approach toward the other is present either spiritually or physically, the less the distinction between dream and reality. In the *Kokinshū*, for the first time in Japanese history, the 'dream lover' entered into the stage.

Another great difference between the *Manyōshū* and the *Kokinshū* is related to attitudes towards time. The *Manyōshū* speaks not of the memories of the past, but of the emotions of the present. In the *Kokinshū* for the first time (at least as a general norm) there appears the expression of a complex psychology which saw the past and the present as inter-related. We have already seen the presence of past, present and future concepts in Kino

Tsurayuki's 'spring' poem quoted earlier. Another poem of similar type was written by Ariwarano Narihira:

> It is not the moon of old
> Nor has the spring become the spring of old
> Only I am still the same.
>
> (Vol. 15 poem 747)

Here, the changes of the circumstances are constrasted with
the poet's identity. The intention of the poem is to stress the
passage of time.

And again, Onono Komachi's poem:

> The cherry flowers have faded
> Here in the reign of mortality,
> Here in the weary rain.
>
> (Vol. 2 poem 113)

Here, the passage of time during which it rained incessantly and
the cherry blossom faded and the long span of time during which
the poet lived are metaphorically overlapped.

The sharp perception of time and experience offered by these
two poems could probably not have been envisaged in the Nara
period.

The objects of interest to the aristocratic poets who seldom
ventured outside Kyōto became ever narrower and correspondingly their perceptions of the subleties of the objects within their
limited vision became ever sharper. When he visited his native
place after a long while, Kino Tsurayuki noted that the scent of
the blossoms was just the same as it had always been (Vol. 1
poem 42); he remembered the owner of the house where he had
stayed when he noticed the scent of *fujibakama* blossom (Vol. 4
poem 240). One anonymous poet compared the sweet-smell of
the mandarin orange flower in May with the scent of his old
lover's sleeves (Vol. 3 poem 139). Poets, like Fujiwarano Toshiyuki,
who could sense the coming of the autumn season by the sound
of the wind, were sensitive to sounds, too. One unknown poet
(Vol. 3 poem 159) even compared this year's cuckoo song with
that of last year. This refined perception, this sensitivity to the
passage of time and the subtle aesthetics which were founded on
them matured in aristocratic society within the framework of the
indigenous world view (and only within that framework) reach-

ing a level of consciousness which never permeated to the Shingon or Tendai sects of Buddhism. Once in being, it became the fulcrum of culture for more than 300 years.

Thus the tradition of the *Kokinshū* was the tradition itself of the aristocratic culture of the Heian period, and it was that culture which provided the means of self-identification for the aristocracy when at the beginning of the thirteenth century political power passed into the hands of the warrior classes.

Then they created the *Shin kokinshū* (1205) and were filled with enthusiasm for the *Kokin denju*. As will be seen later the *Shin kokinshū* imitated the *Kokinshū* in terms of classification of poetry. The *kokin denju* was a custom in which a master initiated a particular pupil in matters not generally known relating to the extremely detailed *minutiae* of the subject matter of the *Kokinshū* (for example, the names of all the birds and all the plants mentioned in the poems of the *Kokinshū*). This practice is said to have begun in 1138 when Fujiwarano Mototoshi gave instruction on these matters to Fujiwarano Toshinari. The reason why the *Kokin denju* was so important for the poets despite its appalling triviality, was probably that it was linked with qualifications for the compilers of imperial anthologies (cultural authority) and also linked with economic interests (authorized land holdings).

Secret transmission became widespread in many art forms after the end of the Heian period, but the *Kokin denju* was the prototype of this tradition. Even when in the first half of the eighteenth century Tominaga Nakamoto said (comparing the cultures of India, China and Japan) that a special characteristic of Japanese culture was the way that 'things were hidden', he was only trying to indicate this. The phenomenon characteristic of Japanese culture, the practice of secret transmission, can probably be traced back to the *Kokinshū*.

In fact the pattern of aesthetic receptivity which was formulated in the ninth century not only continued through the Heian period, but was maintained even after the political ruin of the aristocracy. It influenced *Nō* and *renga*, *kabuki* and *haiku* and is still making its presence felt today, whereas the aesthetic patterns developed in the eighth century and before have virtually no influence on the modern age.

Chapter 3

The Age of the *Genji monogatari* and the *Konjaku monogatari*

THE FIRST PERIOD OF THE CLOSED COUNTRY

The ruling classes of Nara period Japan were overwhelmed by the new culture imported from the Asian mainland. During the ninth century what been imported underwent a native transformation and new Japanese patterns emerged in politics, economics, language, art and aesthetics. During the tenth and eleventh centuries these patterns became confirmed and continued in operation until the end of the twelfth century. In the meantime there was hardly any communication with the Asian mainland and the island country of Japan became completely isolated from the rest of Asia. This 300 year period of isolation constitutes what might be termed the first period of the 'closed country' and it was no less significant than the more famous second period of the 'closed country' which lasted from the beginning of the seventeenth to the middle of the nineteenth centuries.

What happened in Japan during this period of isolation was that the aristocratic ruling class fused elements of foreign and native culture and created an internally coherent, independent, individualistic cultural system which has been known by various names such as 'Heian Court Culture' and 'Ōchō Culture'. The special features of this cultural system applied to all aspects of society ranging from political structure through economics, religious beliefs, arts and crafts, and the lifestyles of the Japanese people. At the same time, the culture imported from mainland Asia, Buddhism in particular, began to permeate to the ordinary people with the result that Buddhism itself was transformed in the process.

Through the medium of Buddhism as it underwent this native

transformation, the Buddhist ruling classes and the non-Buddhist ordinary people were drawn together, and through the medium of a literature written in much 'Japanized' Chinese (i.e. *Kambun*, which in turn influenced native Japanese style), the two sections of the ruling classes – those adhering to foreign cultural patterns and those adhering to indigenous cultural patterns – were also drawn together.

The power structure during this 300 year period can be divided into two types; during the tenth and eleventh centuries there was rule by the Regents and from the end of the eleventh to the twelfth centuries there was *Insei* (Retired Emperor) rule. The Regents broke down the systematized framework of the *Ritsuryō* system and while retaining the formal dignity of the position of the Emperor, created instead a system under which power was held exclusively by the Fujiwara family. The Retired Emperors created a separate power structure in which an abdicated Emperor held a power parallel to that of the reigning Emperor and the Fujiwara government, a kind of two-tier system. In fact, the establishment of the *Insei* system reflects the great dissatisfaction of those elements within the ruling class which had been excluded from power by the Fujiwara monopoly. These dissatisfied elements comprised those members of the aristocracy who were not related to either the imperial family or the Fujiwara family, the middle and lower aristocracy which had come into being under the *Ritsuryō* system (primarily local officials) and the village heads and warrior classes in the provinces.

Without doubt the most notable feature of the period from an economic viewpoint was the *shōen* or manorial system. In the sense that these huge private estates continued to develop on an ever-increasing scale, there was no difference between the rule by the Regents and the rule by the Retired Emperors. The *shōen* were the reason why the Retired Emperors were in favour of a return to the *Ritsuryō* system and why they were unable to organize the middle and lower aristocracy into opposing the Fujiwaras. Needless to say *Insei* power, which was by nature aristocratic, concentrated at the Retired Emperor's court, and economically based on absentee Landownership, was not in a position to mobilize the non-aristocratic local powers such as the village heads and warriors in different provinces.

The tendency towards the centralization of political and

economic power which began to emerge among the nobility from the ninth century onwards had the effect of strengthening the barrier between the imperial family and the Fujiwara, between the higher and the middle and lower aristocracy and between the centralized aristocracy and the village heads and warrior classes. Thus the *Ritsuryō* system which had been transformed by the end of the tenth century crumbled towards final destruction under the rule of the Retired Emperors in the twelfth century.

However, the establishment of Fujiwara power which was brought about through intermarriage with the imperial family until it was almost impossible to distinguish between the two had the effect of creating a period of stability which lasted at least 200 years. The closely knit, exclusivist society of the aristocracy centred on the imperial court in Kyōto brought about a period of extreme importance in the history of Japan and Japanese culture.

In religion, art, literature and way of life, this society institutionalized and formalized its culture into a surprisingly durable entity. Japan at this time was a 'closed country', isolated from the Asian mainland, but even more important, the court aristocracy itself formed another 'closed country' within Japan itself and even within that aristocracy there was another 'closed country' made up of members of the female aristocracy. It was in such conditions that the process of the native transformation of continental culture continued, alongside the integration of artistic activities into court life.

What was the life of the ordinary people of this period like? In works such as the *Makura no sōshi* and the *Genji monogatari* we have a clear picture of the life of the court aristocracy, but obviously the life of the majority of Japanese people was very different. As Hara Katsurō wrote in his *Nihon chūsei-shi* in 1906: 'The excessive wastefulness and extravagance of the court was a burden on the weakened and impoverished peasantry. . . . In dire straits, many of them were forced to sell their homes and fields and move to another province. In this way fathers and sons drifted apart and husbands were lost to their wives.'

Magical elements of the Buddhist religion, allied to indigenous Shinto beliefs began to permeate to the ordinary people. On the other hand, they were living with the strength and will to attempt to extricate themselves from their predicament by their own efforts. Their pragmatic attitudes and this-worldly philosophy is

shown, for example, by many of the stories included in the
Konjaku monogatari. The transformation of the people by Buddhism and of Buddhism by the people were two different things.
What happened in Japan in the period spanning from the tenth
century to the end of the twelfth century was not the former, but
the latter – the transformation, so to speak, of Buddhism through
popularization.

One of the most remarkable characteristics of Heian period
Buddhism lay in its emphasis on prayer and incantations. The
effect of prayer and incantation on such matters as weather,
politics, childbirth and sickness from the ninth century onwards,
or rather the belief in its efficacy, is a phenomenon which ran
right through the Heian period. Since it was believed that sickness, for example, was caused by the possession of evil spirits,
there were many cases of Buddhist prayers and incantations
being used to exorcise those spirits. There are several examples of
this to be found in the *Genji monogatari*. There are also cases of
some future catastrophe or unhappiness being forecast by the
divination masters and of Buddhist monks being called in to say
prayers to avert the disaster.

The divination masters based their prophecies on the *I-ching* or
Book of Changes and since they were mostly drawn from the Taoist
tradition, their principles differed fundamentally from those of
the Buddhists. Nevertheless we find them working together
because the Fujiwara family with no real adherence at the pro-
foundest level to either teaching, were interested solely in the
possible practical benefits of both. We have already seen how
from the Nara period and before this emphasis on the magical
side of Buddhism arose from indigenous concern with practical
matters of this life. However, during the Heian period two new
facets were added to the situation with the advent of the *Honji
suijaku* theory and the Jōdo sect of Buddhism.

The *Honji suijaku* theory was not simply an attempt to reconcile
Buddhism and Shintoism, but was rather an attempt to explain
the Shinto *kami* or 'gods' in Buddhist terms and to fuse Buddhism
and Shintoism into one entity. According to Tsuji Zennosuke in
his *Nihon Bukkyō-shi* (Vol. 1) published in 1944, three separate
stages in this process can be identified, namely the stage in which
kami were regarded as part of mankind saved by the Buddha;
then the stage in which the various *kami* were called Bodhisattvas

without specifying which Bodhisattva was related to which *kami*, and finally the stage in which *kami* were regarded as actual incarnations or manifestations of particular Buddhas and Bodhisattvas.

Written evidence of the second of these three stages can be traced back as early as 783, but it was from the tenth century onwards that the theory became widely accepted, whereas the third stage (the theory in its most developed form) appears for the first time in the late eleventh or early twelfth century when Hachiman was identified with Amida and was fully accepted by the end of the Heian period. This union of two beliefs was accomplished without either being overthrown by the other and indeed it survived until the Meiji period when the two were forcibly separated.

However, the system cannot be characterized as wholly Buddhist or wholly Shinto. It is certainly true that a society which saw nothing to wonder at in the unification of the native gods and the deities of Buddhism, already had a strong motivation towards the creation of an eternally coherent culture. This motivation was nurtured not by the all-embracing doctrines of Tendai Buddhism, (if that had been so the Buddhist system would undoubtedly have swallowed up Shintoism) but by the internal coherence of the social reality. The union of the two systems of Buddhism and Shintoism took place on the basis of the unified, coherent culture of the closed aristocratic society. In other words, neither *Kami* nor Buddha transcended the reality of the nobility's daily life.

The doctrines of Pure Land Buddhism which had their origin in China during the Six Dynasties period and which reached great popularity in the T'ang dynasty were given increasing prominence within the Tendai Sect after the tenth century and became widely known by the Japanese aristocracy. There are three main elements at the root of Pure Land (Jōdo) teaching; first, weariness of this world and fear of hell; second, the desire to be reborn in the Western Paradise after death; and, third, reliance on Amida Buddha to fulfil his original vow (that all men believing in him and calling on his name shall be reborn into the Western Paradise). In other words, Jōdo teaching in its denial of 'profit in this life', its quest for life after death and its stress on the transcendental nature of Amida, is the complete anthithesis of magical 'worldly' Buddhism. When there is no concern for prosperity in this life and simply an obsession with the world to come, prayers for rain or for recovery from illness become very much secondary. Since Amida was transcendental and his vow would be fulfilled, there was no need in Jōdo thinking to take any consideration of the Shinto gods or to desire any merging between Shintoism and Buddhism. There is then the question of how the Heian period aristocracy reacted to these teachings.

To those members of the aristocracy who had been ruined by Fujiwara monopoly of power and to the middle and lower aristocratic bureaucrats under the *Ritsuryō* system which had been destroyed economically by the *shōen* system, there was perhaps every reason to feel dissatisfied with this world. For example, in his work *Chiteiki* (Chronicle of the Residence), Yoshishige Yasutane (d. 997) says that he has no desire to achieve success in this world 'by bending the knee and currying favour with the powers that be', and that he is 'not at all attached to the contemporary world', where 'teachers forever pick disciples' and 'friends take advantage of each other'. Thus he built a house in the capital, with a small hall in the West featuring an image of Amida, a library in the East, and a humble dwelling in the North to house his wife and family. In the mornings he did his official duties and then returned home and visited the Western hall to pray to Amida and read the *Lotus Sutra*. After he had eaten, he went to the library and drank in the ancient wisdom from books to his heart's content.

Yoshishige's 'Western hall' is undoubtedly a place to which he went as a result of weariness with this world. There was certainly no reason why the upper echelons of the Fujiwara family should have shared this outlook, but such men often turned to Jōdo teachings for different reasons. The Fujiwara family built halls devoted to *Amida* and decorated them with fine sculptures and splendid paintings. The Phoenix Hall (Hōō-dō) in the Byōdō-in, built in the mid-eleventh century and one of the finest surviving examples of Jōdo inspired art, has a huge seated image of Amida. The wall paintings surrounding it are now much deteriorated, but one can gain a good idea of their original brilliance by looking at other examples of the period in, for example, the Kōyasan temples.

The man responsible for building the Phoenix Hall was none other than the courtier Fujiwarano Yorimichi (992–1074). Among the Emperors and princes of China who enjoyed this present life there were several who engaged in the Taoist quest for the elixir of life. By contrast, it seems that the Fujiwaras, instead of seeking to extend the pleasures and splendours of this life into infinity sought to bring the Jōdo Western Paradise into this world. The scriptures of Jōdo Buddhism may have assisted in this since they portray the Western Paradise in graphic detail. The author of the *Eiga monogatari* in describing Fujiwara Michinaga's Hōjōji (since destroyed by fire) wrote, '(the temple) looked unreal, unutterably beautiful and dignified just like the Pure Land . . .', a view at complete variance with that of Yoshishige Yasutane. In other words, some came to the doctrines of Jōdo Buddhism through weariness with this world and others through love of it.

There is the question of how Tendai Sect monks taught Jōdo doctrines. One of the most popular Tendai practices was the system of meditation known as *Jōgyō-zammai* which was especially favoured by Ennin after his return from T'ang China. In the *Jōgyō-zammai* a monk spent a ninety-day period without rest repeating the name of Amida Buddha continuously and meditating on him. Although Ennin did not say that this form of meditation was in any way superior to other practices such as the *Hokke-zammai* (meditation on the *Lotus Sutra*), after him meditation on Amida and the invocation of his name (the *Nembutsu*) became gradually more popular among Tendai monks until it became dominant under the patriarch Eshin Sōzu (941–1017), better known as Genshin. The *Ōjōyōshū* or 'Essentials of getting to Paradise' compiled by Genshin was written in 985 and is the representative work of Jōdo teaching within the Tendai Sect. In three volumes and ten chapters, the *Ōjōyōshū* is written in Chinese and is filled with quotations from the scriptures and narrative explanations.

The first volume of the *Ōjōyōshū* begins with a summary of the various categories of Hell, including graphic descriptions, and then proceeds to an account of human life in this world. Three aspects to human life are recognized – 'impurity', 'suffering' and 'transience'. Under the heading of 'impurity' Genshin begins with a surprisingly accurate account of human anatomy and then goes on to talk about the decay and corruption of the body after death. Under the heading of 'suffering' Genshin distinguishes between the inner sufferings which afflict the human being in the form of the 'four hundred and four diseases' and the external sufferings of imprisonment, cold and heat, hunger and thirst, and wind and rain. Finally, in the first volume, Genshin speaks at length about the transience of human life; 'to rise inevitably means to fall; to meet inevitably means to part'. It is difficult enough to achieve birth as a man and even one so born does not necessarily hear of Buddhist teachings. Therefore, Genshin argues a man who is acquainted with Buddhism should try to liberate himself from the endless cycle of death and rebirth.

In the second volume Genshin describes Amida and his followers appearing to a dying man and indicates ten advantages of rebirth in the Pure Land, giving in the process a detailed description of the Pure Land itself. Among these advantages he counts not only a man's own place in the Pure Land, but also his ability to lead others along the same path. He closes this section by posing the question that if there are ten Pure Lands in ten different directions, why then should one meditate only on the Pure Land in the West? Quoting the scriptures, he answers this by stating that it was the Buddha's commandment, in the first place to concentrate on one Pure Land. Why that one should be the Western Pure Land, however, Genshin says simply that it is the Buddha's will that it should be so and passes his own understanding. He can do nothing but have faith. The problem here, of course, is the ultimate reasons for the Amida cult and for the widespread aspiration for the Pure Land in the West, in other words for the Pure Land doctrine as a whole. Since that problem was incapable of solution by arguments genuinely based on the scriptures, nor perhaps by any form of rational argument, it appears that (in Genshin's own words): 'Just believing, without reason, is all'.

In the third volume, the longest, Genshin approaches the subject of how one is born into the Pure Land. It is impossible to go into the full details of this here, but the following two points should be made. In Tendai doctrine a variety of different meditation practices are taught. Genshin's branch of Tendai Buddhism, in placing heavy emphasis on the practice of *Nembutsu*, was at marked variance with previous Tendai teaching from Ennin to Ryōgen. Secondly Genshin never really made it satisfactorily clear whether it was more important to meditate on Amida or to call on his name in the *Nembutsu* incantation. In this sense his teaching diverges from that of the later monk Hōnen (1133–1212) who taught very firmly that the *Nembutsu* was the more important.

In the *Yokawa hōgo*, written after the *Ōjōyōshū*, Genshin also preached the importance of incantation: 'even in the presence of impure thoughts, even with a weak belief, you should intensify your aspiration (for the Pure Land) and constantly call on Amida's name'. This sounds much like Hōnen's words in *Ichimai Kishōmon*: 'To be reborn in the Pure Land, all we can do is call on Amida's name, firmly believing that we undoubtedly will go to the Pure Land as a result.' The meanings are the same, but the emphases are different. In Genshin's view, one should intensify one's aspiration for the Pure Land, while in Hōnen's view the sole emphasis is placed on absolute belief. This difference in emphasis reflects, even in the same framework of the Pure Land doctrine, a fundamental contrast between Genshin's religion and Hōnen's, and, beyond that, between Heian Buddhism which was set against the background of a stable society, and Kamukura Buddhism which was born against a background of great social change.

The *Ōjōyōshū* was written some 150 years after Kūkai's *Jūjūshin-ron*. As a theorist Genshin in some respects does not match Kūkai, for although the works of both men are alike in that they draw heavily on Chinese translations of the Buddhist scriptures to prove their points, there is no doubt that the *Jūjūshin-ron* is much more clearly and logically expressed (in the *Ōjōyōshū* for example, the same words are often used with different meanings). However, in its graphic and colourful depictions of Hell and the Western Paradise the *Ōjōyōshū* is the more interesting and superior work; many artists of the Heian court drew on it for inspiration and many aristocrats clearly enjoyed reading it. It is almost certain that none of the readers of the *Jūjūshin-ron* were lay men while the *Ōjōyōshū* was, as it were, 'bedside reading' for some sections of the aristocracy. Herein lies a great difference.

At the beginning of the tenth century there were monks such as Kūya Shōnin outside the Tendai Sect itself who wandered round the countryside begging their living, repeating the *Nembutsu*. They fasted, meditated on the Bodhisattva Kannon, drove off robbers by repeating the *Nembutsu* and beat off snakes with their staffs. The miraculous deeds of such monks figured prominently in collections of folk tales from the *Nihon ryōiki* to the *Konjaku monogatari*. In fact their only real connection with the doctrines of Jōdo Buddhism taught within the Tendai Sect was the *Nembutsu*.

One might well term such monks as members of the 'Nembutsu Sect', but members of a Jōdo sect they were certainly not. The audience to which they preached were not solely concerned with whether they were to be reborn into the Western Paradise after death, but with what was going to happen to them in this life. After the time of Kūya Shōnin many holy men known by such names as Shōnin, Hijiri and Shami, appeared and were active throughout the Heian period but always outside the formal religious groups. Their activities were frequently magical and shamanistic, and were the means of spreading Buddhism to the ordinary people without fundamentally changing the world view of the ordinary people, but moulding Buddhism into the framework of their world view.

Of course, the aristocracy and the ordinary people were not completely separated one from the other, but although their fundamental approaches were different these two groups had this at least in common that they did not attempt to deny the reality of this life. The common people's acceptance of this world stemmed from the obvious conviction that at least it was better than Hell, while the aristocracy accepted this life in the belief that it was already rather like Paradise. It was no more than a small section of the middle and lower aristocracy who were able to accept easily the notion taught by Genshin that one could be reborn into the Western Paradise through repetition of the *Nembutsu* while believing in Amida's original vow. For the bulk of the higher aristocracy believing as they did that the Western Paradise was already here, so to speak, such concepts held no attraction.

We have already looked briefly at how the Jōdo beliefs of the aristocracy were reflected in art. However, Heian aristocratic society produced not only religious art but excelled in secular forms such as *waka* poetry, paintings skillfully executed on folding screens and painted illustrations to picture scrolls of *monogatari* fiction written in the *kana* syllabary – in other words they created the new painting style known as *Yamato-e*. The Japanese turned from the Chinese style in painting both in terms of subject matter and technique and created something intrinsically Japanese. From the early ninth century they produced painted *uta-e* and these were soon followed by *monogatari-e*, painted novel scrolls. By the middle of the eleventh century the new *Yamato-e* style of painting was in full flood.

INSTITUTIONALIZATION OF LITERATURE

The special characteristic of the closed Heian aristocratic literature lay in its institutionalization of traditional literary activity. This phenomenon was at its most marked in *waka* poetry. Apart from strictly ceremonial motives the writing of *waka* for amusement and as a means of developing love relationships between men and women had already become part of the daily life of the Heian aristocracy by the early ninth century, a point which is illustrated by many of the *monogatari* novels of the Heian period. The ability to compose and appreciate *waka* in fact was a *sine qua non* for success in Heian society and was often useful for extricating oneself from difficult circumstances. The enormous social force of *waka* poetry is seen to good effect in the two imitations of the imperial anthologies of *waka* and poetry contests which became prevalent from the tenth century onwards.

The earliest of the imperial anthologies was the *Kokinshū* compiled in 905 and the last, the twenty-first in all, was the *Shin zoku kokinshū* compiled in 1439. In other words this special form of poetry anthology continued to be produced over a period lasting more than 500 years. Virtually all the poems included were in the *waka* form and their predominant subject matter was love and the four seasons, such things as religion, philosophy and politics figuring hardly at all. The authors were mostly members of the Heian aristocracy or at least belonged to the court society and since they seldom ventured outside that immediate circle, their poems followed standards laid down in the *Kokinshū* as being the earliest work in the genre. Vocabulary, grammar and stylistic presentation all followed *Kokinshū* modes. In other words, the tradition of court lyric poetry was established in the *Kokinshū* and was supported and continued in the later imperial anthologies.

In the works of the very late Heian period poets such as appear in the *Senzaishū* (compiled in 1189) and the *Shin kokinshū* (1206),

however, there are signs of the strain engendered by the precari-
ous political situation. Of this we shall speak later. In the pre-
Senzaishū anthologies (the *Gosenshū*, the *Shūishū*, the *Goshūishū*,
the *Kinyōshū* and the *Shikashū*);, there is virtually no sign of
individuality: it is extremely difficult to tell from style and content
where a poem comes from. These anthologies were edited and
compiled in one of two ways. The *Gosenshū* (which was variously
edited and used poems by authors already represented in the
Kokinshū – compiled in the mid-tenth century), the *Shūishū* (compiled by Fujiwarano Kintō in the late tenth century) and the *Shikashū*
(compiled by Fujiwarano Akisuke in the mid-twelfth century) were
all collections of poems not contemporary with the period of
compilation. The *Goshūishū* (compiled by Fujiwarano Michitoshi
in 1086) and the *Kinyōshū* (compiled by Minamotono Toshiyori
between 1124 and 1127), however, were collections of more or less
contemporary poetry. It goes without saying that the former type
of anthology exhibits virtually no stylistic advance on the *Kokinshū* and introduces hardly any new subject matter for poems. The
more the poems were institutionalized, the less original they
became. The poems were clearly devised as a means of preserv-
ing court culture.

Fujiwarano Kintō in a work entitled *Waka kuhon*, written at the
end of the tenth century, divided *waka* into nine categories of
excellence, illustrating each category with two poems, usually
chosen from the *Kokinshū*. Of the ten poems chosen to illustrate
the first five categories of excellence, all are poems of scenic
description, and there are three such poems even in the second
four categories of excellence together with three love poems, one
on old age and one on the sorrow of this world. This represents a
considerable change of emphasis on the part of the aristocracy in
their attitude towards *waka* since the *Kokinshū* itself, compiled a
century earlier, lays heavy emphasis on love poems. Fujiwarano
Kintō's two ideal poems (that is to say the two he places in the
first category of excellence) are taken respectively from the first
book of the *Shūishū* (a poem by Mibuno Tadamine), and from the
ninth book of the *Kokinshū* (a poem of unknown authorship).
They are as follows:

> Today is the first day of spring.
> How hazy Mt. Yoshino must look this morning.

> In the morning mist
> Crossing Akashi bay
> I think of a boat
> Passing behind an island.

The scene evoked in the first poem is Mt. Yoshino and in the second the bay of Akashi. The operative 'scenic' words in both are 'haze' and 'mist' respectively. Therefore we can assume that since these poems were chosen as the most outstanding ever written up to this period, then it was these locations and these scenic descriptions which appealed most to the aristocracy of the day. It seems that their taste in nature was not represented, for example, by the raging waves of the Pacific Ocean beating against the mountainous shores of Japan. Even with the majority of love poems favoured by the aristocracy at this period, the same feeling of faintness and mistiness prevails and there is none of the sexual passion of the 'ancient ballads' or the *Manyōshū*.

There are exceptions to this general rule, notably in the poems written by the women of the court, as, for example, those contained in the eleventh-century *Goshūishū* by poets such as Izumi Shikibu and others whose biographies are obscure in the extreme. Take, for example, the following two poems by Izumi Shikibu from that anthology:

> I lie with my hair dishevelled,
> But I do not even notice
> As I long for the man who caressed it.

> To make another memory
> For my after-life,
> How I wish I could see him once more!

Here there is none of the trivial scenic descriptions so favoured and idealized by Fujiwarano Kintō and others of his type. Instead, these are poems written with a compelling urgency of feeling which show the poet's strong individuality and which successfully cross the barriers of time. One finds many other poems written by women which explore the psychology of relationships between men and women.

If one seeks originality in *waka* poetry written after the time of the *Kokinshū*, one almost invariably finds it in the poems composed by women and there was perhaps none greater than Izumi

Shikibu. However, the Heian court did not value originality but tradition. At least, to the thoroughly institutionalized world of *waka* poetry it was the men and not the women who were the final arbiters of what values were to be most highly prized. For instance, not one of the imperial anthologies was edited and compiled by a woman and not one woman is known among the legions of authors who wrote works on *waka* theory.

Waka was an integral part of court culture and the centre of that court culture was masculine, although of course it is often said that the men were effeminate (this, however, is rather hard to define).

That authors such as Izumi Shikibu were able to emerge was not due to the institutionalization of literature, but was despite of it; it was not because women were at the centre of court culture, but because they were not. In an age when men were able to secure advancement through their proficiency as poets, women strove to use poetry as a means of self-expression, it being impossible for them to secure such advancement anyway. It is significant, perhaps, in this respect that the biographies of female poets of the period are so obscure.

Uta-awase or 'poetry contests' in which groups of poets composed poems to be judged by some specific individual added a new dimension to *waka* poetry. In an *uta-awase* the poets were given a particular theme on which to compose and it was the judgements given in such contests which gave rise to the appearance of works on *waka* theory which in turn could be used as vehicles of judgement.

The earliest *uta-awase* of which the records are still extant was that held on the thirteenth day of the third month, 913. For this occasion we know the poems composed, who won and the reason for the victory. It perhaps comes as no surprise that regardless of whether his work was truly the best, the Emperor emerged as victor in the contest. In another contest held in 960 where the judge was Fujiwarano Saneyori, the questions of 'sentiment' and 'choice of words' were brought into the judgement and the fact that it was possible to make objective decisions about such basically subjective matters was probably due to precedents afforded in the *Kokinshū*. Inevitably, if such extremely conservative modes of judgement had been broken down, the decision of the judge would have become purely arbitrary. In other words, *uta-awase* were undoubtedly used or at least had the effect of being used to establish tradition. Since there was such a strong inherent tendency in the Heian court to perpetuate itself, *uta-awase* came into being and since they were practised on such a flourishing scale, the strict adherence of the Heian aristocracy to formalized tradition in poetry was itself reinforced.

Despite this the judgements given at *uta-awase* were quite subjective and arbitrary. In the cases where there were two judges their opinions were often sharply divided. An example of this is provided by the contest which took place in 1118 where Minamotono Toshiyori (d. 1125) and Fujiwarano Mototoshi (d. 1142) were the judges. The essential arbitrariness of decisions on the quality of individual poems is shown by an examination of Minamotono Toshiyori's theoretical work.

Toshiyori zuino (written in 1124 and printed in Sasaki Nobutsuna's *Nihon kagaku taikei vol. 1*) is filled with the most detailed discussion of the aesthetics of *waka* making apparently objective points about why one word is better than another, why one sentiment is more profound than another and so forth. In reality, of course, this is a completely subjective statement. Consequently, at the contests which required the evaluation of specific poems, arguments on concrete terms were more useful than theoretical arguments. For example, at a contest, the expression 'constantly burning smoke at the Muro islands' in a certain poem was criticized on the ground that what looked like smoke on the islands was actually not from a fire but simply mist. This sort of down-to-earth realistic approach to poetry was quite common in contest judgements but never appeared in *waka* theory. Although *uta-awase* undoubtedly gave birth to works on *waka* theory, the theoretical works were not always of use in making decisions in contests. In this connection the following two points are to be noted.

Even though theoretical works were not necessarily of use in making judgements at contests, they did serve to reinforce the authority of the judges. The fact that there was a theory of *waka* poetry enabled the judge to assert himself and preserve his authority and dignity in the world of *waka*. Secondly, poets who were inept at *waka* theory themselves, despite the differences in approach to theory and in individual antagonisms between theorists, were at least in common in their positive attitudes and intensive interests in concrete facts, as indicated by the *uta-awase* judgements. This kind of desire to hold on to some positive notion shared by others is a connecting thread which runs through not only Heian aristocratic society but through the history of the Japanese people as a whole. Indeed the same thread can be seen pervading the literatures of the different social classes – in the poetry contest of the Heian aristocracy and the folk stories of popular origin found in the *Konjaku monogatari* – of which more will be said later.

The institutionalization of literature with regard to poetry and prose written in the Chinese language was already well established by the ninth century onwards. We have already discussed the enthusiasm for writing in Chinese which stemmed from the adoption of Chinese governmental institutions culminating in such great literary figures writing in Chinese as Sugawara Michizane. In the writing of poetry in Chinese no figure emerged to surpass Michizane, but the aristocratic tradition of writing literature in Chinese continued after his time. A notable example is provided by the Honchō monzui compiled in the mid-eleventh century by Fujiwarano Akihira (989–1066). This work was modelled on the example of the Chinese *T'ang-wen-ts'ui* (written in 1011) and in its system of arrangement imitated the celebrated *Monzen*. The Honchō monzui contains more than four hundred and twenty pieces of poetry and prose written in Chinese, the work of about seventy authors from the ninth century on. In them one can detect some new developments which were not apparent in ninth-century anthologies of similar type such as the *Ryōunshū*.

For the first time in history there appeared in an official anthology criticism of society under the Fujiwara family rule. A typical case was 'Chiteiki' by Yoshishige Yasutane. Some essays by authors such as Prince Kaneakira (914–87) and Minamotono Shitagō (911–83) were in the same vein. Criticism of contemporary aristocratic social customs was hardly ever made in *waka* poetry and very seldom in *monogatari* fiction. It was only when they wrote in Chinese, indeed following continental precedents, that the writers of Japan made comments on society at large. The comments they made, however, were not of the type made by the poets of T'ang China. In China from very early on it was the custom to criticize men in power and political policies, for example, Ch'ū Yuan. It was also quite normal for writers to display a distaste for political society and to extol the virtues of a quiet country life. For example, T'ung Yuen-ming. Among T'ang poets, Tu Fu was like Ch'ū Yuan; Li Po was in the same vein as T'ung Yuen-ming.

The social criticism of the *Honchō monzui* is clearly far removed from that made by Ch'ū Yuan and Tu Fu and is much closer to that of T'ung Yuen-ming and Li Po. One of the most popular Chinese poets among the Heian aristocracy was Po Chü-i. The poems of Li Po and Tu Fu, particularly the latter, seem hardly ever to have been read. In other words, from their own choice the Japanese opted for one particular tradition of Chinese literature (not the one most popular in China itself) and when it came to social criticism, they rejected concern with political society, as practised by many of the T'ang poets, in favour of an attitude which was basically escapist.

The social criticism of works such as the *Honchō monzui* was not specific to particular individuals or policies, but was aimed broadly at political society as a whole. It confined itself to general issues raised by court power struggles and was certainly not concerned at all with the true condition of society outside the court – with the exception of Sugawara Michizane. Its general conclusion was the virtue of withdrawing from public life and the sublimation of life.

To Yoshishige Yasutane private life was bound up with the worship of Amida and the study of ancient wisdom; to Prince Kaneakira it was the freedom to lead a solitary existence, enjoying the occasional visits of monks. Later, to Kamono Chōmei it lay in the quiet pursuit of Buddhism, poetry and music, and still later to Matsuo Bashō it was the way of *haiku*. In Japan at all periods it was one of the ideals of the writer to escape from the cities into the tranquillity of the mountains and one may cite Yoshishige's *Chiteiki* as a notable example of the expression of this kind of escape from society.

However, the basis of Yoshishige's escapism lay in his criticisms of aristocratic society, whereas Kamono Chōmei was writing in a period when that society was already decaying and Bashō and other Edo period *haiku* poets scarcely mention contemporary society at all. This is one of the paradoxes of Japanese literary history. Although Japanese literature under Chinese influence broadened its horizons and inherited literary forms erected on the foundations of those broadened horizons, gradually it narrowed and restricted its field of vision. Interest in society as a whole is much less evident in Bashō's work than it is in Yoshishige's work written centuries earlier. The *Honchō monzui* itself contains elements of this diminution of social vision for in it, for the first time, social criticism justifies non-participation in society.

The second characteristic of the *Honchō monzui* is that it contains several pieces of what we today would call pornography, for example the *Danjo kon'in fu* and the *Tettsuiden*. The former was written by Ōeno Asatsuna (886–957). The Ōe family produced many writers and Asatsuna himself contributed forty-four pieces to the *Honchō monzui*. The *Tettsuiden* is of unknown authorship, although there is a theory that it was written by Fujiwarano Akihira, the compiler of the *Honchō monzui*.

'Danjo kon'in fu' first describes the sentimental attractions, then proceeds to a detailed account of sexual intercourse. 'Tettsuiden' is a burlesque description of the penis in the formalized style of short biography of a man of Confucian virtues, whose different names all suggest the male sexual organ. 'Tettsui (Ironhammer), alias Strawhat, or *mara* (penis), is a man from the hairy country between thighs', so begins the 'Tettsuiden'. For a while he hides himself under the cover of trousers. A Lord often calls on him, but he doesn't stand up. He becomes greater in his seclusion. Finally he goes out from his hiding place to serve at the Red Gate (vagina), and receives special favour of his Lord.' The life of Tettsui excels in 'the art of intercourse', which 'even the Six Confucian Classics never explained, and even great Confucian teachers never told'.

The T'ang novel *Yūsenkutsu* (*Yu-hsien-k'u*) also contains specific sexual descriptions in contrast with Heian period *waka* and *monogatari* which contain none. Thus the subject matter of the *Danjo kon'in-fu* and the *Tettsuiden* was clearly derived from China. The Heian period aristocratic intelligentsia, like their ninth-century counterparts, wrote about different subjects according to whether they were using the Chinese language or native Japanese. Just as the social criticism which was written only in Chinese and never in Japanese differed fundamentally from Chinese prototypes, so sexual matters, also only written of in Chinese and never in Japanese, already displayed differences from their prototypes in the way they were treated. To begin with, in China the

Yūsenkutsu was an independent work, not part of an anthology. Second, sexual descriptions were included in novels, not in prose non-fiction. Naturally enough, Japanese who specialized in the study of ancient Chinese prose writing in the manner of their way of life and their feelings were far removed from the Chinese. As a result, they may have felt it necessary to write of their innermost private lives in prose rather than fiction.

Perhaps the emergence of pornography in prose and Chinese-style poetry was one aspect of the process of the native transformation of the Chinese language as a literary vehicle. The third of the new developments indicated in the *Honchō monzui* is that there are many instances where the authors of poetry written in Chinese were also famous as *waka* poets. From the time of the *Kaifūsō* and the *Manyōshū* to that of the *Kokinshū* and the *Kanke bunsō* there were a few such writers who were equally at home with either poetic form. In fact Kino Tsurayuki wrote a piece in Chinese entitled *Shinsen waka-jo* and Michizane was the author of many famous *waka* poems.

Nevertheless, up to the end of the ninth century, there was a clear division between those writers such as Tsurayuki who wrote principally in Japanese and those such as Michizane who excelled at writing in Chinese, and it is easy to identify these two parallel traditions. In the tenth century this situation began to change and there was more interplay between the two traditions as in the case of Minamotono Shitagō. His eight poems and twenty-four pieces of prose are contained in the *Honchō monzui*, and his *waka* poetry is contained in the private anthology *Minamotono Shitagō-shū*. The significance of this is that Shitagō was adept at both forms, and that in him the Tsurayuki and Michizane tradition merged.

Thus, since during the tenth century and afterwards the writing of prose in Chinese underwent a gradual process of 'Japanization' and since *waka* poetry became more and more integrated into the daily lives of the Heian aristocracy, it was inevitable that literature written in Chinese and literature written in Japanese would at some point discover common ground. Minamotono Shitagō was by no means unique. He was followed by Fujiwarano Kintō (966–1041) and Ōeno Masafusa (1041–1111), both of whom were adept in native as well as Chinese learning. The two volumes of *Wakan Rōei-shū* compiled by Fujiwarano Kintō at the beginning of the eleventh century is a representative example of this general trend.

The *Wakan Rōei-shū* is an anthology of 588 poems written in Chinese and 216 *waka* poems, with the two mixed and not in separate sections. The enormous significance of this can be seen by making a comparison with the *Kaifūsō* which contains not a single *waka* poem and the *Manyōshū* which contains only four Chinese poems. The rule of separation of poems in Japanese and Chinese had always been respected by all anthologies before the *Wakan Rōei-shū*. This anthology did not only combine both types of poems for the first time, but also for that purpose 'Japanized' poems in Chinese. Japanization took place in the following ways:

First, the *Wakan Rōei-shū* took a few lines out of the context of the original Chinese poems, in most cases two lines of seven words each. For example two lines from Po Chü-i's long elegy on T'ang Emperor and his mistress run:

> Around the pavilion in the evening fire-worms fly, his reveries are sad;
> The lamps in the autumn continue to burn, he cannot sleep.

This is a part of the emperor's long lamentation over his dead mistress. But out of the context it can also be read as *waka*, which simply describes a somewhat sad autumnal scene, by a word-by-word translation from Chinese into Japanese.

In the period of the *Manyōshū* Japanese long poems were produced under the influence of Chinese poetry; in the time of *Wakan Rōei-shū*, one might say that the Japanese came to read Japanese short poems in 'Japanized' Chinese poetry. Second, the way of reading Chinese poems changed, gradually shifting from reading more or less in the Chinese way to a special Japanese way of reading Chinese texts, a kind of word-by-word translation (*kundoku*). Needless to say that this helped much in identifying Chinese verses with *waka*. Third, Chinese verses as treated in the *Wakan Rōei-shū* were in close relationship with music and painting. In the tenth century at least some of the Chinese poems included in the *Wakan Rōei-shū* were sung to the accompaniment of melodies. Also in the same century some screen paintings consisted of Japanese style pictures with *waka* in one section, and Chinese style pictures with Chinese verses in another. Thus

Chinese verses out of the context of the original poems, read in the Japanese way, went together with the music and paintings, exactly as in the case of *waka*, and were gradually integrated into the whole system of Heian aristocratic culture.

Of the 588 Chinese pieces in the *Wakan Rōei-shū*, 354 were written by Japanese (for example, 44 are by Sugawara Fumitoki, 38 by Sugawara Michizane, 30 by Ōeno Asatsuna, 30 by Minamotono Shitagō and 22 by Kino Haseo) while 234 are by Chinese authors. Of this 234 no less than 139 were written by Po Chü-i who far outstrips his nearest rival Yuan Chen who wrote only 11. Not a single poem comes from either of the great Chinese poetic traditions of Li Po and Tu Fu. It is clear that the choice of pieces to include made by Fujiwarano Kintō was not only far removed from the taste of modern readers, but also from that of contemporary Chinese. In other words, Japanese taste in Chinese poetry was in itself a thing apart. As regards Kintō's choice of *waka* poetry, Tsurayuki is the most represented author with twenty-six poems and he is followed by Mitsune with twelve poems. It is not clear on what basis the Chinese poems were selected, but as far as can be judged he took no account at all of contemporary Chinese taste and simply selected from works by Japanese authors and from Po Chü-i poems he decided were most suitable matches for the *waka* of Tsurayuki and Mitsune.

As regards the system of arrangement and classification of poems, *Kokinshū* models were adhered to. The poems of the first volume are arranged under the seasonal headings of spring, summer, autumn and winter with further sub-divisions such as 'early spring', 'nightingales', 'plum blossoms', and 'willows'. The second volume, deviates from *Kokinshū* patterns, there being, for example, only one small section on 'love', one of the major *Kokinshū* categories, and this is a reflection of the difference in subject matter between Chinese and *waka* poetry.

Despite the differences between the climates of China and that of the Kyōto area, it is interesting to see that enough poems on seasonal subjects could be taken from the literature of both traditions to make up at least one volume adhering to *Kokinshū* patterns.

THE WORLD OF THE NOVEL

The representative work of prose fiction written in the tenth century by court intellectuals who had begun to Japanize Chinese poetry and prose and treat it on a par with *waka*, was the *Utsuho monogatari*, the longest and richest of the pre-Genji *kana monogatari*. In this case, within the framework of its institutionalization, Heian court literature, in contrast to the imperial *waka* anthologies with their rigid adherence to tradition, produced something that was without doubt original.

The aristocratic intellectuals of the tenth century (and later) who wrote lyric poetry in both Chinese and Japanese likewise used both languages in prose writing. We have already looked at prose writing in Chinese as typified by the *Honchō monzui*. Diaries written in 'Japanized' Chinese (known as *hentai Kambun*), such as Fujiwarano Michinaga's *Midō kampaku-ki*, Fujiwarano Sanesuke's *Shōyūki* and Fujiwarano Yukinari's *Gonki*, are valued by historians as source material for the post 887 period (the last of the six 'official' histories of Japan concluded its coverage in 887), but these works were principally designed as records of court events and ceremonial and matters relating to *yūsoku kojitsu* (court etiquette etc.), indicating next to nothing of the authors' thoughts and feelings.

In the late tenth century, however, several epoch-making works in pure Japanese prose were written of which two have survived to the present: the *Ochikubo monogatari* and the *Utsuho monogatari*. Their authors are unknown, but it may be imagined that they were intellectuals well-versed in both Japanese and Chinese language like Fujiwarano Kintō. The significance of these works lies in the fact that they were both novels which more or less realistically depict the everyday life of the Japanese aristocracy. Neither in China nor in Japan was there any precedent for such works, and the claim has been made for the *Utsuho monogatari* that it was the world's first full-length novel.

The *Ochikubo monogatari* is the story of the Lady Ochikubo who is cruelly treated by her wicked stepmother, the tale being recounted in the third person with extensive use both of dialogue and 'letters'. The *Ochikubo monogatari* is just one of many novels on the wicked stepmother theme written before the time of the

Genji monogatari (early eleventh century). It was in the court society of the tenth century that this type of fiction evolved in which the details of the everyday lives of the characters and the psychological relationships between them were treated in realistic fashion without resort to the 'extraordinary' and the supernatural. Such fiction did not appear in France until the seventeenth century and in England until the eighteenth century.

Since it is customary to speak of the fiction produced from the eighteenth century onwards in England describing the everyday realities of secular life as 'the modern novels', then the *Ochikubo monogatari* perhaps corresponds to Japan's 'modern novel'. The next world philosophy of the *Ōjōyōshū* did not extend to the world of the novel, nor did it exert any influence on it. It was indigenous Japanese thought that was so strongly linked with everyday reality and so strongly resisted efforts to transcend the everyday world in both values and concrete action. The *Ochikubo monogatari* may be regarded as yet another manifestation of that indigenous thought. However, there was more to it than that.

The story of Lady Ochikubo is not a fragmented collection of pieces relating to an individual (like the *Tosa nikki*, for example), but was written as a continuous whole with an ordered and structured pattern of development. The first portion of the story details the cruel treatment received by the Lady at the hands of her stepmother; the second portion deals with how her lover Ukonno Shoshō plots and carries out revenge against her family, after rescuing her from her wicked stepmother's house. Revenge and punishment. Thereafter, both the Lady Ochikubo and her more and more successful husband live happily every after. Interwoven with this main theme is a skilfully executed sub-plot describing the progression of a love affair between Lady Ochikubo's maidservant Akogi and her husband's attendant Tachihagi.

The *Ochikubo monogatari* has order and structure in the true sense, and, short stories apart, no other work of fiction extant today produced in the Heian period is so tightly structured, with the possible exception of the *Taketori monogatari*. However, the *Taketori monogatari* is something very special indeed. It seems to have been written in the ninth century, but its economically written narrative, and its compact and rational structure place it apart not only from the Heian period *monogatari* in general, but

also from all other Japanese novels known today. It gives the
feeling that it was alien to the indigenous Japanese spirit.

The *Ochikubo monogatari* is not so tightly constructed as *Taketori
monogatari*. If we consider that the author of the *Taketori monogatari* began from a concept of the entire story and applied himself
in the particular sections, then the author of the *Ochikubo monogatari* began from a concern and interest in particular sections and
compiled these into an entire story. The quality of the way this
was done cannot be explained entirely in terms of the influence of
the *Taketori monogatari*, for although that work was widely known
among the court aristocracy, if its influence alone was sufficient
to produce an orderly structure in other works of fiction one
would expect to find other similar examples apart from the
Ochikubo monogatari itself.

In my view the basis for the ordered structure of the *Ochikubo
monogatari* was provided by the moral code of the author which is
manifested in his idealization of the central characters and the
clear distinction between the Good and the Evil. The Evil has no
redeeming features; the Good has no weaknesses; Evil is
punished; Good is rewarded. This is a device used in fiction to
emphasize contrasting moral values and is not necessarily related
to Buddhist doctrines of cause and effect. In Buddhist teaching
the deed (or 'cause') in a previous existence is manifested in the
present life and deeds in the present determine effect in the next
life.

In the *Ochikubo monogatari* cause and the fulfilment of effect are
both confined to a relatively short period in the present life and
there is no intervention in the lives of the central characters by
such deities as Kannon and Jizō (who, however, did frequently
appear in Buddhist *setsuwa* tales). The author's idealization of the
central characters lies in the Lady Ochikubo's forbearance in
enduring her stepmother's cruelty, in her gentleness in not desiring revenge, in her skills in the management of household affairs,
in calligraphy and *waka* poetry. The centrepoint of the idealization is revealed in the devotion between husband and wife – a
state which is eulogized, particularly in the last section. The idea
of a happy monogamous husband and wife relationship is an
unusual one in the court literature of the Heian period. For the
typical male hero of the fiction of the period and slightly later is represented by Narihira in the *Ise monogatari*, by Heichū in the *Heichū*

monogatari and by Genji in the *Genji monogatari*. The idealization of the male hero Shōshō, of the *Ochikubo monogatari*, is a world apart from that of these famous 'Don Juan' type lovers such as Narihira, Heichū, Genji. The author of the *Ochikubo monogatari*, probably under the influence of Confucianism, offered a moral ideal applicable to only a small minority in this period and it may be imagined that he was a great deal keener to emphasize his viewpoint in this respect than most contemporary writers. Hence the novel as a whole had to be unified and structured around this moralistic standpoint.

The *Utsuho* (or *Utsubo*) *monogatari* is a long novel about three fifths the length of the *Genji monogatari* itself and a novel of such magnitude had never appeared previously in China, Japan, or perhaps anywhere else in the world. The author is unknown and the date of writing is likewise unknown, but one leading scholar has suggested that it was written in the late tenth century some time after 952 and before 965. It would probably be true to say that the Japanese invented the long novel as a literary form with this work, although it is not easy to explain the reasons for the discovery. However, since nowhere in the world was there in the tenth century a society like that of the Heian court aristocracy which was producing imaginative tales against the background of the realities of everyday life, it seems natural enough that if anyone should devise the long (full-length) novel at such an early date, then it should have been the Japanese.

The structure of the *Utsuho monogatari*, the world's first full-length novel, lacked the internal coherence of the later *Genji monogatari*, comprising as it did a number of mutually independent sections. That is not to say, however, that the novel has no unifying thread. This connecting thread is the wondrous music of the *koto* and the master player Nakatada. The novel begins with the discovery of a miraculous *koto* by Toshikage who brings it to Japan where it is transmitted through various generations of his family, the central character throughout being Toshikage's grandson Fujiwarano Nakatada and ends with the miracle the music has worked. In the course of the novel there are many incidents told which are unrelated to the *koto*, to music or to Nakatada himself, but it is certain that the author envisaged the work as a whole entity and not as a collection of short stories.

The story can largely speaking be divided into four sections.

The first (*Toshikage*) tells of a character named Toshikage who sets out by ship for China as an envoy. The ship is caught in a storm and drifts to an unidentified country called Hashi where Toshi-kage comes into possession of a heavenly *koto* which he learns to play very skilfully and receives the blessing of the Buddha. Toshikage teaches the instrument to his daughter and later dies. Toshikage's daughter bears a son (Nakatada) to the future Minis-ter of the Right, Kanemasa, but their relationship is broken up and she takes her son to live with her in a great hollow tree (the 'Utsuho' of the title) in the mountain north of Kyōtō where she teaches him all she knows of the art of playing the *koto*. Nakatada for his part displays an almost superhuman filial piety towards his impoverished mother. The supernatural power of the Koto music is related to Buddhism, but Nakatada's devotion to his mother is clearly a reflection of Confucian thought.

The second part of the novel deals with the quest for the hand in marriage of Atemiya, the fabulously beautiful daughter of the Minister of the Left, Masayori. In this respect the *Utsuho mono-gatari* was continuing the tradition of the *Taketori monogatari*. There are sixteen suitors among whom there is an almost com-plete lack of mutual relationship. The two most important among them, Nakatada and the Crown Prince, are exceptional. In the end the Crown Prince triumphs over Nakatada and wins Atemiya's hand. What is left at the end of the courtship story is the complex family relationships between Atemiya, the Crown Prince and Nakatada who becomes betrothed to the Emperor's daughter. There are three other characters who are extremely vividly portrayed. The first is a talented official of the bureaucracy named *Miharu Takamoto*; the second is a man named Kamunabi Tanematsu who is of the rural gentry and not himself a suitor but the maternal grandfather of one of the suitors; and the third is Prince Kanzuke and people around him.

The *Utsuho monogatari* vividly portrays the action and sur-roundings of these three types of characters – the efficient official, the gentry, and the aristocrat – but Heian period novels after the *Genji monogatari* never touch upon the first two types.

Miharu Takamoto, 'Governor of six provinces', is portrayed as a man who 'perfectly administered six provinces, and accumu-lated a vast private fortune'. In other words, he accumulated his private fortune not through improper conduct but through diligence and frugality. He is shown as a wise and talented official who is 'of resolute heart and attentive to administrative business' and who 'pacifies violent soldiers and wild beasts alike'. On the other hand, Miharu appears as a very frugal man with no wife, no personal attendants and with a carriage so mean that people laugh at it as it passes through the streets of the capital. When it was suggested one day that he build a new lavish palace like that of Masayori by opening one of his treasuries, he replied as follows:

> How vain! The Minister built the lavish palace on his vast estate to let the suitors to his daughter gather together only to waste what he has earned. The master of the palace cannot be compared with the beauty of the palace. A wiser man should save what he has earned, and taking advantage of this wealth, engage in trade. Even though I'm living in such a shabby house, I have never put people in distress. People who live a lavish life do harm to the public and put them in distress.

This is not merely a criticism of wasteful use of titles. It is also clearly linked with the concept of investment rather than personal consumption of wealth. There was no character like Miharu Takamoto who could convey such a sophisticated concept of human economic activity in Japanese literary works until the *chōnin* novels of Saikaku appeared in the late seventeenth century. But after his wife ran away from him, Miharu Takamoto lamented: 'If you are in public service, you cannot do without attendants and servants. From now on, I'll cultivate the land with only one or two hired hands.' Then he resigned his post as Minister and moved to Mino Province. Here we can glimpse the character of a man whose spirit was capable of regarding his own personal power and wealth in relative terms.

The thoughts of Tanematsu, a member of a powerful family from Kii Province, are not so clearly described as those of Miharu, but his residence and business interests are described in great detail. On an estate surrounded by a hedge he has 160 storehouses, twenty horses, fifteen oxen, ten falcons and more than a hundred men to do the business and see to the running of the estate. Besides agriculture, Tanematsu's workers make *sake*, do carpentry jobs, smithying, dyeing textiles and so forth. The author of the *Utsuho monogatari* seems to have paid close attention to what was happening in Japan outside the capital and to the collapse of the central authority of the *Ritsuryō* system as it worked in the economic sphere. It goes without saying, of course, that these matters were beyond the horizons and scope of the female writers of the court.

In order to win the hand of Atemiya, Prince Kanzuke discusses his problems with a monk who addresses him as follows: 'If you make offerings of sacred fire and streamers to the million deities and the thousand Buddhas, each deity and each Buddha will exert himself in your favour. Even Heavenly beings will descend to you.'

Here both the Buddha and the Shinto deities are treated on an equal footing and as no more than tools to be used to win the hand of Atemiya. Moreover, the monk tries to make use of Prince Kanzuke to collect donations for his temple and plans to squeeze all he can out of him. The Prince for his part sets an ambush for Atemiya and her entourage as they journey to a temple in Higashiyama and tries to seize her by force. In this he succeeds, but because of a clever stratagem on the part of Atemiya who had previously judged what might happen, the Prince captures not the real Atemiya but a substitute. Not only is this incident told very graphically, but it is of profound interest in that it gives an eloquent illustration of exactly what the Buddha and the Shinto gods meant to the majority of the aristocracy at this period. This is in complete contrast to the kind of Buddhism which is associated in the novel with the miraculous *koto* and it is most likely that the author was aware of both the 'next-worldly' elements of Buddhism newly introduced by the *Ōjōyōshū* and the 'this-worldly' fusion of Buddhism and Shintoism in the indigenous world view.

The third section of *Utsuho monogatari* deals with the power struggle at court over whether the child of Atemiya or the child of Nashitsubo (the Crown Prince's other wife) will become the next Crown Prince. The Crown Prince himself and the Minister of the Left (Masayori) favour Atemiya's child, while the Empress (the wife of Emperor Suzaku) favours Nashitsubo's child. She tries to enlist to her cause the Minister of the Right (Kanemasa), the Minister-President (Tadamasa) and Nakatada, but they, on account of the power of the Minister of the Left and their relationships with his daughters, are non-committal in their replies, saying that they will wait for the Emperor's decision, excusing themselves on account of their blood relationships with the Minister of the Left and so forth. In the end the low-key reaction of all of them, including Nakatada, in refusing to look beyond this question of their relationships, prompts the Empress to sigh: 'There isn't a single wise one among them; they're all like girls.'

When it comes to a power struggle the miraculous powers of Nakatada which have formed such an important part of the novel all the way through do not appear and he is portrayed as just a court politician like all the rest of them. The only exception in this is the Emperor Suzaku. When his wife, the Empress, complains to him about the vacillation of his Ministers, Suzaku says:

> It is the duty of the Minister of the Left and the Lord Nakatada to administer the country. The great lord Tadamasa is a good man, but has no ability. It is bad for a man of no ability to work for the stability of the world. The great lord Kanemasa seems wise in attitude, but he is a little too fond of women. Such a man is not to be relied on. Both of them are talented, wise, and serious, but especially so in Nakatada's case.

It was only Suzaku who considered the talents of these men as human politicians apart from their various marriage relationships and looked at the matter of who should be the next Crown Prince from the viewpoint of the political influences it would engender. This kind of politically-minded person appears only here in the whole of the novel and is almost entirely absent from subsequent *monogatari* fiction.

The fourth section of the *Utsuho monogatari* returns to the matter of music. Nakatada builds a high tower where he and his mother then teach the *koto* to his daughter. When her instruction ends, the people of the court gather together and then his mother plays the secretly transmitted *koto*. Thunder crashes miraculously, the ground trembles and the waters of the ponds rise up. The long novel is thus held together from beginning to end by the music of the *koto* transmitted from Heaven through Toshikage, his daughter, Nakatada, and finally Nakatada's daughter, Inumiya.

Thus two contrasting aspects of the *Utsuho monogatari* may be discerned. First, there is the contrast between new and old forms. The long novel was a new form of literature while that part of the plot which dealt with the suitors for the hand of Atemiya imitated a form in literature which had been well known since the time of the *Taketori monogatari*. Further, although the *Utsuho monogatari* is shorter than the *Genji monogatari*, it contains many more *waka* poems. This reflects the true state of a society into which literature, *waka* poetry in particular, had been thoroughly institutionalized, but at the same time, it also implies the continuation of the tradition of the old form of the *uta monogatari*, dating from the *Ise monogatari* onwards.

Secondly, in the setting of the aristocratic court society we find an open aspect and a closed aspect towards the outside. The former is typified by the broadening of horizons into the sphere of economic activity in the descriptions of Tanematsu's residence and the latter is typified by the marriages, conceptions and births among the ruling classes in closed aristocratic society. The world which created Emperors, Crown Princes, Retired Emperors, Minister-Presidents, Ministers of the Left, Ministers of the Right, Generals, Councillors, Chamberlains etc. was one of the small groups closely knit by complex blood ties and marriage relationships. (The unity of these small groups must have been strengthened by the high degree to which polygamous and consanguineous marriages were allowed.) Class structure within the group was essentially defined in terms of blood relationships rather than in terms of the talent, industry and loyalty individuals displayed as politicians or administrators. Consequently childbirth was an important event. Therefore, it is natural in the context that the biggest power struggle described in the *Utsuho monogatari* should centre on the question of which child of the two wives would become the Crown Prince. Of course, the novel is not based on historical fact, but as far as the extremely closed nature of the ruling class tied together blood relationships is concerned, it does admirably reflect the truth of the power monopoly held in the tenth (and eleventh) century by the ruling clique of Imperial and Fujiwara family.

Third, in philosophical terms there is the contrast between realism and idealism. The realistic aspect of the novel is represented by the sharp perceptions of the trivia of the everyday life of the aristocracy (which are to be found everywhere in the book), by the character and attitudes of Miharu Takamoto, by the actions of Prince Kanzuke, by the vivid description of Tanematsu's estate, and by the political conceptions which emerge through the words of Emperor Suzaku. Here we have perception of humanity and society as they actually were – perception free from any idealization, superstition, or ideology. The idealistic aspect of the novel, sometimes indeed close to fantasy, is shown in the author's emphasis on and idealization of artistic, moral and aesthetic values – the miraculous *koto* which is described with free use of Buddhist vocabulary, the extremely exaggerated filial piety shown by Nakatada to his mother, following Confucian values, and the eulogization of the wit and beauty of Atemiya. There is no doubt that the realistic aspect of the novel stemmed from the indigenous world view, and the idealistic aspect from foreign ideology (Buddhism and Confucianism).

If we understand the *Wakan rōeishū* as uniting in lyric poetry indigenous culture and foreign culture submitted to indigenous transformation, then we may regard the *Utsuho monogatari* as a manifestation of the world of the *Wakan rōeishū* in prose. To put this another way, the strands of Sino-Japanese culture represented in the late ninth century by intellectuals on the pattern of Ki no Tsurayuki and Sugawara Michizane were, in the tenth century, gradually drawn together and met in the *Wakan rōeishū* (in lyric poetry) and in the *Utsuho monogatari* (in prose fiction).

It is not permissible to see the *Utsuho monogatari* with its dual nature as simply a stage on the road towards the *Genji monogatari*. Certainly, it did prepare the way for *Genji* in certain senses – in its format as a long novel, in its setting against the background of closed court society, and in its idealization of art (Genji himself was a virtuoso on the flute), humanity and aesthetics. However, it was not the *Genji monogatari* but the *Konjaku monogatari* which took up and more thoroughly explored the other aspect of *Utsuho monogatari* – the way it looked outside the closed circles of court society and its sharp and unsparing observations, largely free from the influence of foreign thought systems, of the realities of everyday life. On the one hand, *Genji* was a novel which, making use of the framework of 'Japanized' foreign thought, refined indigenous receptivity within an extremely closed environment. On the other hand, the *Konjaku monogatari* explored the world of commonsense reality against the background of the indigenous world view through the medium of the people at large of the times.

If we see the Heian period as an age of contrast between the *Genji monogatari* and the *Konjaku monogatari*, then we can view the Muromachi period as an age of contrast between *Nō* and *Kyōgen*. Then we should probably mark the *Utsuho monogatari* as the source of these dualities and its two-fold nature reflected the dual contrast of the culture of the times – the social contrast between aristocracy and the people at large, and the philosophical contrast between foreign thought and the indigenous world view.

WOMEN'S DIARIES

It was in the tenth century, particularly the second half of the tenth century, (when male intellectuals were beginning to write prose novels) that female members of the aristocracy who did not write in Chinese and specialized in the *waka* started to write diaries in Japanese prose. First came the *Kagerō nikki*, then in the late tenth or early eleventh centuries the *Makura no sōshi* and the *Murasaki Shikibu nikki*, then in the mid-eleventh century the *Sarashina nikki*, then in the late eleventh century the *Jōjin Ajari no Haha-shū* and finally at the beginning of the twelfth century the *Sanuki no suke no nikki* – these being the most important of the now extant diaries written by women in the Heian period.

These diaries – often, though not invariably – were records, usually with dates, of the day-to-day lives of their authors, the things they saw and heard, and their emotions and impressions. In this sense they differed from novels and from chronicles and historical stories which departed from events actually experienced by their authors. The *Izumi Shikibu nikki* is perhaps best considered as a novel. It is not known for certain when it was written and the author could have been male or female, so it is not numbered among the Heian period diaries written by women. The *Makura no sōshi*, despite the fact that it does not contain the word 'diary' (*nikki*) in its title, should certainly be regarded as a diary.

In that these diaries, while describing everyday events, were written in Japanese (principally *kana*) and contained *waka* poems, they followed the precedent of the *Tosa nikki*. In not one case is the date of composition established beyond dispute and the dates of the authors' births and deaths are uncertain. From this we may

judge the essentially private character of these diaries written by
women – in marked contrast to the 'official' diaries written by
men in Chinese or *Kambun*. The author of the *Kagerō nikki* (which
was written c. 974–78) is not known by name except for the fact that
she was the daughter of Fujiwarano Tomoyasu and the mother of
Fujiwarano Michitsuna (955–1010). Her father, Tomoyasu, was a
provincial governor. The *Makura no sōshi* (late tenth or early
eleventh century) was written by the lady Sei Shōnagon, whose
real name is not known. Her father, Kiyowarano Motosuke, was
Governor of Higo and a distinguished poet who contributed
more than a hundred poems to various imperial anthologies. She
herself was born about 960 and served as lady-in-waiting to the
Empress Teishi from about 993 to 1000. The author of the
Murasaki Shikibu nikki (also, of course, the author of the *Genji
monogatari*) likewise is not known by her real name and also
served as a lady-in-waiting to the Empress Shōshi (from 1005 to
about 1007). Her diary was written c. 1008–1010. Her father was
Fujiwarano Tametoki who late in life served as Governor of Echizen
and who wrote poetry in Chinese. The author of the *Sarashina
nikki* (written over some forty years from the early to mid-
eleventh century) was the daughter of Fujiwarano Takasue (973–
c. 1036) and her real name is unknown. Takasue was a minor
provincial official. Not much is known about the author of the
Jōjin Ajari no haha-shū (c. 1071–3) beyond the fact that she was
the mother of the Buddhist priest Jōjin. It is said that the author
of the *Sanuki no suke no nikki* (c. 1107–08) was Fujiwara Nagako who
served as lady-in-waiting to the Emperor Horikawa (reigned
1086–1107). Of these six women, four (the exceptions are Sei
Shōnagon and the mother of Jōjin) were related. The author of
the *Sarashina nikki* was a niece of the author of the *Kagerō nikki* and
the author of the *Sanuki no suke no nikki*, assuming it was Fujiwara
Nagako, was her great grand-daughter and Murasaki Shikibu
was a daughter of her distant relative.

Three facts emerge from the above. First, this kind of diary
which was prevalent in the 200 years spanning the mid-tenth to
mid-twelfth centuries was written by women who belonged to
the middle-ranking aristocracy mostly, provincial governors.
Second, many of them were related and belonged to families
which also produced male poets writing in either Japanese or
Chinese. Third, it is known, that the best of them attended at

court in service as high ranking court ladies-in-waiting (nyōbō) who had their own separate apartments. That the works of these female writers of the Heian court have come to be known rather vaguely as nyōbō bungaku ('court lady literature') is not far from being inaccurate. Originally, female authors were not necessarily nyōbō ('court ladies' i.e. ladies in direct service of the court) and still less was their literature representative of the whole of Heian court literature. However, it is difficult to find any other example either in Japan or elsewhere of women playing such a great role in the literature of a given period and the question is how did it come about?

The position of these women was first that they were part of the ruling circles and thus cut off from the outside world, and, second, that they were completely excluded from power itself. In the first respect they were more or less like the aristocracy in general in that they were thoroughly integrated into the closed aristocratic groups. However, the male aristocracy, through their administrative duties, came into contact with the outside world and were exposed to relationships between their own groups and those outside them in administrative terms. In other words, the world of Japan, in this context was totally in their hands and they must have been conscious of that fact.

The position of the female aristocracy was very different. While they entered court in the position of 'court lady', they did not participate in administration and had no contact with the outside world. Their world did not extend beyond the boundaries of the court and did not truly extend beyond the female society of that court. Truly, in the female literature of the Heian court as it has come down to us today, no character of humble station appears and there are no descriptions of political and social conditions in the provinces. There are none of the depictions of the regions such as appear in the Utsuho monogatari and the mass of the people with their life-styles and feelings such as are described in the Konjaku monogatari were completely beyond their field of vision. In terms of the closed nature of the groups to which they belonged and their high level of integration into them, if the society of the court ladies was not an actual parody of aristocratic society in general, then it was at least an extremely exaggerated form of it.

Secondly – the fact of their complete removal from power – the position of the female aristocracy was again very different from their male counterparts. Under the power monopoly of the Fujiwara family there were certainly limits to how far members of the middle and lower aristocracy could rise. However, since power was an attribute of the well-ordered class structure, within those limits advancement was possible and as existing source materials indicate, it would not be going too far to suggest that such advancement was an obsessional interest for members of the middle and lower aristocracy. However, for women the question of advancement and promotion simply did not arise. Since the road to participation in the machinery of power of court society was completely closed to them while living within it (or very close to it) there is no doubt that they were in the ideal position to act as observers of the life of that court. Since they had no power to change the world, they observed and interpreted it.

It was chiefly Pure Land Buddhism which provided the philosophical background of the female aristocracy. It is true that in the *Makura no sōshi* Pure Land teachings and Buddhism in general are treated only as a part of social custom. For example, at one point Sei Shōnagon writes: 'My favourite temples are Tsubosaka, Kasagi, and Hōrin' (chap. 208). 'My favourite Sutras are the Lotus Sutra and the Kegon Sutra . . .' Then she ennumerates several names of Sutras which she highly appreciates. However, there seems no philosophical connection between the temples she mentions and the Sutras.

In her brief list of 'Things That are Near Though Distant' she includes 'Paradise', her meaning being that when one meditates on Amida even the far distant Western Paradise is close at hand. However it is extremely dubious whether to Sei Shōnagon this was anything more than clever rhetoric. Under the same heading she also lists 'Relations between a man and a woman' while in the preceding list 'Things That are Distant Though Near' (166) she includes 'Relations between members of a family who do not love one another'.

It seems that it was in this kind of perception of the realities of everyday life that Sei Shōnagon could show herself at her best. Certainly, the *Makura no sōshi* provides no evidence that Sei Shōnagon's Buddhism was anything but shallow. However, in the case of the *Murasaki Shikibu nikki* the situation is rather different. In the so-called 'letter section', Murasaki Shikibu touches on the jealousy shown of her scholarship by another lady at court and says:

> Everything in this world is a trouble . . . No matter what others say, I shall kneel before Amida-Butsu and recite the scriptures. When my mind has become free of the troubles of this world, I shall spare no efforts to become a 'saint' (*hijiri*). . . . Many things have happened to me in this life to make me think I committed some wickedness in my previous existence, and everything saddens me.

The idea of having committed some bad deed in a previous life which transfers its effects to the present life and that the only hope of an afterlife in Paradise rests with reliance on Amida is very clearly derived from the teachings of the Jōdo sect. This is not simply a conventional expression of belief in Buddhism; rather, to Murasaki Shikibu, Buddhism provided a framework which made her consider the troubles of this world in relative terms. One should perhaps beware of taking what she says too literally, but at the very least the Pure Land world view was a means for providing some distance and detachment, in Murasaki Shikibu's case, between observer and what was observed. However, her Buddhism was, when all is said and done, not strong enough to enable her to break away from the aristocratic court society in which she lived and become a nun, and the same could be said of the author of the *Sarashina nikki* who so delighted in reading the *Genji monogatari*.

It may be thought that to at least a section of the female aristocracy of this period, Buddhism was too weak to break down their integration into their social group, but was strong enough to give them intellectual and psychological distance from the world in which they lived. What enabled Murasaki Shikibu to progress so much further in her writing than Sei Shōnagon was probably not unconnected with the teachings of Pure Land Buddhism. Thus, there is no doubt that the social conditions and philosophical circumstances of the middle-ranking female aristocracy enhance each other. In other words, the integration into the closed group was perpetuated because philosophical convictions were too weak to break it down, while at the same time a combination of separation from power and the teachings of Pure Land Buddhism provided the observer with the necessary objectivity in attitude towards the group.

But of course all the sharp observers were not authors. For an author's work to become accepted both mode of expression and conventions were vital factors and in the aristocratic society of this period these were provided by the previously mentioned institutionalization of literature. Moreover, the institutionalization of literature had a kind of dual structure which was tied to the special characteristic of Japanese literature that it made use of two languages. Works of a public or official character were presented in Chinese and works of a private nature in Japanese.

We have already seen how from the tenth century onwards there was a tendency towards compromise in the field of lyric poetry in the serious consideration which was given both to the native *waka* and 'Japanized' Chinese poetry, as typically seen in the *Wakan rōeishu*. However, in the field of prose writing the compromise was much more limited. Moreover, not only was there a division between official works being written in Chinese and private works written in Japanese, but also between men and women in their uses of the two languages. The *Murasaki Shikibu nikki* tells eloquently of this situation. For example, Murasaki Shikibu speaks of court ladies seeing her reading works in Chinese gossiping about her and saying: 'In ancient times it was only men who made it their business to read such books.'

On another occasion she tells of how the Empress had requested her to teach her about the works of Po Chü-i and how both of them had had to practise this in secret for fear of people at court finding out. Equally, it had to be a secret hobby for men to write diaries and novels in *kana*, while for women it could be quite open and part of their work. Educated women wrote about their private lives because they were excluded from public life.

We do not know how many ladies there were at court at any given time, although it is said that the Empress or the wife to the Crown Prince had some thirty to forty attendants. It may be thought that the ladies of court formed a separate group within aristocratic society, that their numbers did not exceed a few hundred and that most of them were well acquainted. Writers and readers (or audience) were part of that same small group. Thus the creator of a literary work and its readership were very close – to put this in an exaggerated form one might say that the writer *was* the reader. Certainly the reader was a potential writer. This claustrophobic proximity was certainly not unique to the Heian court (most court literature has displayed a similar tendency as, for example, in French court literature of the seventeenth century), but it probably never elsewhere reached the same extremes as it did in the female world to which Sei Shōnagon and Murasaki Shikibu belonged.

Such were the circumstances under which the female aristocracy wrote their *waka* poetry, novels and diaries. However, although many of the writers of original *waka* poetry were women, the overwhelming majority of famous *waka* poets were men. The greatest masterpiece of *monogatari* fiction (the *Genji monogatari*) was written by a woman, but the majority of court novels of the Heian period were composed by men. It is only diaries written in Japanese prose that, as far as we know today, were exclusively the domain of women.

In content, female diaries were basically of two types. The first type concentrated on one subject of particular interest to the writer – the tale of the unhappy relationship with her husband in the case of the author of the *Kagerō nikki*; the story of the author's painful separation from her son after he has left her to become a priest in the case of *Jojin Ajari no Haha-shū*. Although members of the aristocracy, the women who wrote this first type of diary were not court ladies in the sense that they were not personal attendants at court. The second type of diary did not have any particular unifying theme apart from the trivia of everyday life at court. These diaries – of which the *Makura no sōshi*, the *Murasaki Shikibu nikki* and the *Sanuki no suke no nikki* are typical – were written by ladies in direct service of the court.

The *Sarashina nikki* which is a collection of reminiscences written describing the life of its author over a forty year period and with a kind of unity in its own way, probably belongs specifically to neither category. In 1309 the author of the *Sarashina nikki* entered court service, but gave it up almost immediately. All of the diaries mentioned above share their essentially private nature in common. And specifically with type one its emphasis is on introspective aspects of the authors' private experiences, and specifically with type two on its keen observation of the private events of everyday life. In terms of originality as a literary work, the *Kagerō nikki* stands out and as an expression of the world view of a typical member of the female aristocracy at that period, surpasses both the *Makura no sōshi* and the *Murasaki Shikibu nikki*.

The originality of the three volumed *Kagerō nikki* lies in its discovery of the 'I-novel' type psychology. It was the psychology of a woman who was a daughter of a provincial governor and was married to the great lord Fujiwarano Kaneie (929–90) and who in the circumstances of unmatched ranks of their background gave birth to and brought up her son Michitsuna. She kept waiting for her husband who many times neglected her, she was by turns jealous, angry, resigned and, ultimately, feeling her old age, concentrated all her interest and devotion on her by then grown up son, Michitsuna. Kaneie once stopped coming to her and she found a letter he had written to another woman. On another occasion Kaneie went out one evening saying that he had business at court and when she checked up on his whereabouts, she found that in fact he had gone to see another woman. Afterwards, even when Kaneie came to her, she could not feel any intimacy towards him, but just when she thought that their marriage was truly finished, another letter would arrive from him. Her house lay on his route to the palace and the passage of his carriage at night brought her grief:

> I did not want to hear, but . . . unable to sleep . . . I would listen for the approach of his carriage.

Meanwhile, the other woman with whom Kaneie had a liaison became pregnant and she could hear the carriage taking her to her confinement pass by her door.

> I was beside myself and did not know what to say. I heard those who had seen them pass talk about it afterwards, 'That's cruel. He could have chosen any other road.' All I could think was how much I wanted to die.

But she could not die and their relationship continued; after the child was born Kaneie gave up visiting the woman and this made her happy. When she came to know that the child in fact was not his own, she gained consolation by imagining to herself how greatly disappointed Kaneie would be because he had made such a fuss without knowing the truth.

> I had thought I would have to keep lamenting more and more over my neglected state, but now, I really feel relieved.

Once, she thought of breaking up their relationship.

I wonder whether I should break up this long relationship. Or, should I resign myself however hard it might be to forebear everything, persuading myself that it is my destiny?

However, when he happened to visit her after a long absence he was seized with a sudden illness and had to be carried to his palace. She was concerned and wrote down in her diary: 'My anxiety is more than I can put into words.' And after that she 'sent two or three letters to him even in a single day'.

All these examples are taken only from the first volume of the *Kagerō nikki*, but it can be seen from them what a fine picture the work gives of the working of the mind of a woman in the male-female relationship in all its delicate nuances. No work before the *Kagerō nikki* gave such a sophisticated description of this kind of psychology, and, with the exception of the *Genji monogatari*, no later work was to rival it. If we regard the *Utsuho monogatari* as opening up the prospect of the long novel, then the *Kagerō nikki* was the first psychological novel with its exhaustive exploration of all the subtle, psychological nuances of the private life and emotions of its author. The only thing left to Murasaki Shikibu was to combine the two in one novel, the *Genji monogatari*.

The *Makura no sōshi* and the *Murasaki Shikibu nikki* seem never to weary of describing the trivia of court life. For example, Sei Shōnagon tells of a foolish episode in detail, viz. that the Emperor Ichijō's beloved, pet cat – he actually promoted this cat to the fifth rank – was one day attacked by a dog, as a result of which the dog was punished.

In the *Murasaki Shikibu nikki* there is the author's account in microscopic detail of events surrounding the Empress' giving birth. Whether the Empress had a son or daughter was of course of great importance to the ruling group at court and thus this matter was not in itself trivial. However, Murasaki Shikibu's obsession with the colours of the dresses of the court ladies as they passed to and fro was carrying concern for trivia to excess. Running through the whole account there is no real theme other than the author's desire to eulogize the court and the Empress whom she served. The consequence of this is that evidence of a structure defined in terms of relationship with theme (such as is found in the *Ochikubo monogatari*) is noticeable only by its absence. The Japanese style concern for allowing parts to stand independently from the whole simply for their own interest is most thoroughly and typically manifested in these two diaries.

These fragmentary passages, amounting in the case of the *Makura no sōshi* to a kind of collection of aphorisms, indicate considerable rhetorical skills and sharp observation of customs and conventions. More than that, in their treatment of the scenes and events of the four seasons and so forth, they reveal the extreme refinement of the author's aesthetic sensibilities. The *Murasaki Shikibu nikki* contains no aphorisms and no rhetorical flourishes attempting to condense the impression of an instant into a line or two. However, her thumbnail sketches of her colleagues and people who entered the female court world including Sei Shōnagon, are graphic and testify to her profound and acute perception of human nature.

In the writings of Sei Shōnagon and Murasaki Shikibu there was no criticism of the social order of the court and scarcely any concern about the majority of Japan's non-aristocratic population. However, whereas Sei Shōnagon did not hold back in her praising of the powerful in society, Murasaki Shikibu, as has already been observed, managed to maintain intellectual distance between herself and those around her through the medium of her belief in Pure Land teachings.

The aesthetics of the *Kokinshū* were institutionalized into court society from the tenth century onwards. The female diarists of the Heian court in their closed group, while accepting these aesthetics in their entirety, studied their own sensitivities and concentrated their attention on subtleties and details. By skilful disposition of a comparatively limited vocabulary they refined their own distinctive style of rhetoric. Because they lived in a world where everyone was acquainted, they wrote about the life of that world and created a special form of literature for a situation in which the writer to all intents and purposes was the reader and the reader could identify himself with the characters. However, this did not mean that there was none among them capable of writing a work which would transcend that particular time and place, for, indeed, it was one of their number who wrote the *Genji monogatari*.

THE GENJI MONOGATARI

The *Genji monogatari*, the first long novel (in fifty-four chapters) after *Utsuho monogatari*, was written by the Lady Murasaki Shikibu early in the eleventh century, although the precise date of composition is unknown and the authorship of at least part of the book is disputed.

The bulk of the novel (the first forty chapters) deals broadly speaking with the career and, in particular, amorous adventures at court of the idealized hero of the tale, the 'Shining' Prince Genji. It begins with a love affair between Genji and his step-mother Lady Fujitsubo ('Wakamurasaki') and ends with adultery between his wife Onna San-no-miya and Kashiwagi ('Wakana') and the death of Genji's other wife Murasaki ('Minori'), in the interim Genji's promotion at court, his exile ('Suma', 'Akashi') and return are described. His affairs with a long series of different ladies, quite apart from his two wives, are treated as separate episodes and amount almost to independent short stories within the main theme of the novel. The final thirteen chapters follow the fortunes of the characters surviving after Genji's abrupt death, though his death itself was not described in the novel, centring on the 'triangle' relationship between Kaoru (the illegitimate child of Genji's wife and Kashiwagi, the son of Genji's best friend, Tō no Chūjō), Prince Niou (Genji's grandson) and the beautiful girl Ukifune. This almost amounts to a separate novel.

In the sense that the *Genji monogatari* contains episodes which are only tenuously connected, it rather resembles the *Utsuho monogatari*, but although this feature is very pronounced in the earlier parts of Genji's story, the structure becomes much tighter in dealing with the second half of Genji's life and the events following his death. Compared with the hero (Nakatada) of the *Utsuho monogatari*, Prince Genji is a much more prominent character who provides the novel's coherence. Therefore, by comparison with *Utsuho monogatari*, the *Genji monogatari* is not merely longer but is structurally more developed.

Moreover, there are no supernatural elements in the Genji story. Magical Buddhist ceremonies are described, but only because they were part of the reality of court society in Heian period Japan. In nature the 'magical' element of the *Genji mono-gatari* is very different from the kind of miraculous events caused by *Koto* music which are so important to the theme of the *Utsuho monogatari*. In the sense that it concentrates on description of the everyday life of the aristocracy, the *Genji monogatari* is, in fact, rather closer to the *Ochikubo monogatari*. Certainly, the amount of idealization accorded to Prince Genji is considerable, but he is idealized as a man and this is very different from the idealization of the hero of the *Utsuho monogatari* who is treated almost as a god born into human form.

As in the case of the *Ochikubo monogatari*, the idealization of Genji is in no way related to the supernatural world, but whereas the hero and heroine of the *Ochikubo monogatari* were idealized for their Confucian moral virtues, Genji is idealized aesthetically and emotionally – for his good looks, his talent in the arts and his captivating power as a lover. Morally speaking he was at times guilty – his affair with the Empress was hardly desirable, to say the least – and, he suffered accordingly.

In both form and content the *Genji monogatari* was the heir of the *Utsuho monogatari* and the *Ochikubo monogatari*, but it was more fully developed than either. This development lay in the direction of total concentration on everyday life and refinement of the senses, to which was added the psychological introspection of the *Kagerō nikki*. This last feature emerges even in Murasaki Shikibu's literary style.

The narrative of the *Genji monogatari* is made up from the author's objective descriptions, the words and poems of the characters of the novel, and records of what they were thinking. However, these basic ingredients are not always sharply differentiated and quite frequently are mixed up in one sentence or paragraph. Thus, often the subject changes even within a sentence and sometimes this is not specifically stated so that the reader has to judge the subject from the context.

With such a literary style, the thoughts and impressions of the author self-identifying with the hero and the thoughts and impressions of the hero himself can be extremely close together. It is a style which, despite the inclusion of many stories amounting to almost independent entities and an ever changing *dramatis personae*, gives a strong feeling of the author's presence. This provides continuity to the novel as a whole and creates a kind of intimacy, rather as if the tale were being told as gossip.

Another special feature of the style of the *Genji monogatari* is the constant repetition of a comparatively limited range of vocabulary, indicating both the narrowness of the world of the novel and the tendency to convey suggestions indirectly or by hints rather than explicitly. Both the above-mentioned features of Murasaki Shikibu's style heighten the effectiveness of the description of the psychological relationships between characters. The reader was able to direct his attention onto the characters and how their minds were working, without being distracted by a wealth of detail concerning the complex world in which they lived.

It goes without saying that these stylistic features made the *Genji monogatari* very difficult to interpret by later generations of readers, but it should not be thought that contemporary readers had any such problem. Murasaki Shikibu wrote her novel for the limited number of aristocrats and court ladies who lived in the same world as she did and with whom in most cases she was even personally acquainted. There can be no doubt they were thoroughly familiar with the background which provided the setting for the novel, that they probably had a fair idea of the identity of the actual people on whom the characters of the novel were modelled, and that they perfectly understood the subtle nuances of the limited vocabulary.

Of course, Murasaki Shikibu omitted the subject of sentences because this is permitted by Japanese grammar and perhaps because what she was saying was perfectly clear to her readers anyway. A long novel which needed scholars to interpret who was saying what would not have been popular. The style of the *Genji monogatari* succeeded only under the conditions of an extremely small and closed society into which author, readers and the characters of the novel alike were thoroughly integrated where one (although by no means all) of the possibilities of the Japanese language could be explored to the uttermost.

Buddhism provided the philosophical background to the *Genji monogatari*. Naturally, the influence of Confucian morality can also be detected, but it is by no means as noticeable as in the case of the *Ochikubo monogatari* and very sparse indeed compared with the *Utsuho monogatari*, except the filial piety of Nakatada. The career advancement of the characters is described, but power struggles at court are hardly mentioned and still less is there any indication of influence of Confucian political philosophy. There are two aspects to the role played by Buddhism – first, the anticipation of the magical efficacy of Buddhist ceremonies performed in this world, and, second, the desire for salvation in the next world. The first of these stems from traditional, conventionalized and institutionalized practices from earlier court society, and the second from the influence of Pure Land Buddhist beliefs as summarized in the Ōjōyōshū.

'This-wordly' Buddhism is typically manifested in the prayers and incantations repeated over and over again with the purpose of ensuring recovery from illness, safe delivery in childbirth and exorcising the 'demons'. These prayers and incantations involved numerous monks and impressive ceremonial to the point where it may even have been that the magnificence of the ritual was an end in itself. For example, when describing in detail the prayers which were recited by many priests for Murasaki (Genji's wife) when she fell sorely ill, the author writes: 'As it was the tenth of the third month, the cherry blossoms were in full bloom . . . It seemed precisely like the land of the Buddhas.'

This line puts one very much in mind of the viewpoint of the author of the Eiga monogatari who equated the magnificence of this world with Paradise. Taking the tonsure and secluding oneself into a temple was frequently practised by both men and women as a convenient means of escaping from the problems of this world and seems to have been a kind of institutionalized form of 'retirement'.

Of the ten women with whom Genji was deeply involved two met untimely deaths, five became nuns, one wished to become a nun but was not allowed to do so; only two (apart from those who died suddenly) did not become nuns. However, since the ultimate ends of these two women are not described in the novel, they too may well have entered a temple. It is easy to believe that in this age becoming a nun at a certain time in their life was part of the custom of the female aristocracy.

On the other hand, however, there are passages which indicate the author's belief in 'next-worldly' Buddhism. For example, the word sukuse (karma or 'fate') is frequently used when explaining the inevitability of a character's destiny (a fate which cannot be avoided). Since *sukuse* is a concept used to explain present effect in terms of the 'cause' of a previous existence, naturally it must also imply that the deed of the present will bring reward or retribution in a future existence. This is the principle on which the Pure Land Sect's 'desire for the after-life' is based. In these terms, the act of becoming a nun is not a question of convention, but of aspiration for the next world. That Murasaki Shikibu apparently believed that the desire to become a nun in this sense was a vital attribute of the ideal human being is clearly shown by the fact that her most idealized character (Murasaki) expressed such a desire. Unlike Fujitsubo who became pregnant after her adulterous affair, Murasaki had not encountered problems difficult to solve in the context of this (secular) life. That she expressed the desire to become a nun was not because she had a pressing reason to do so, but because, from the author's viewpoint, she was an ideal character.

Murasaki Shikibu's Buddhist ideals may also be judged from her description of the 'High Priest of Yogawa', said to have been modelled on Genshin. This monk, overcoming the opposition of his disciples, saved Ukifune when she tried to commit suicide and fainted, and caused her to become a nun. When his disciples said that it was a fuss to leave their mountain (Hieizan) and damaging to their master's reputation in the world when only one woman was involved, the monk replied that even though it was the life of only one woman, 'The Buddha will surely save her'. As for his reputation in the world, that did not matter to him. He said, 'Now I'm already over sixty, it doesn't matter to me if people criticize me for that'. ('Tenarai') Ukifune, for her part, captivated by two men and attempting suicide, had ample reason for desiring the Pure Land, while the monk, in persuading her to become a nun, had a force which was derived from his transcendental beliefs.

In his own attitudes towards Buddhism, Prince Genji was divided between these two aspects. After the death of his beloved wife Murasaki, he 'kept desiring the afterlife earnestly'. This is not merely a conventional expression and clearly at this point Genji was profoundly concerned with the next world. However, unlike the case of the 'High Priest of Yogawa' who did not care about his worldly reputation, Genji's interest in the next world was not strong enough to enable him to transcend such worldly concerns as his reputation in this world. Almost in the same breath as expressing his desire to enter holy orders, he wondered what people might think of his motives for doing so. Readers will not witness their hero becoming a priest. Genji's attitude here corresponds to Murasaki Shikibu's own as expressed in the *Murasaki Shikibu nikki*. She herself was clearly identifying not with the 'High Priest of Yogawa', but with Genji.

The Buddhism of the *Genji monogatari* went beyond simple convention and formed an integral part, at least, of the author's field of vision, probably being a major reason for the objectivity of her observations and descriptions. Here, Buddhism is an inherent part of the structure of the whole novel giving it a cause and effect order as can be seen from the fact that the novel begins and ends with two adulterous love affairs. The novel's obsession with the portrayal of the *minutiae* of everyday life was a direct manifestation of the 'this-worldly' nature of the indigenous world view, while the maintenance of structure and order throughout such a long tale was a reflection of the comprehensive discipline of the Buddhist world view. In this sense one might say that the *Genji monogatari* was a work born of a Buddhism which had undergone native transformation.

However, the most lasting impression left by the *Genji monogatari* has nothing to do with Buddhist philosophy, the Buddhist interpretation of fate as typified by the concept of *sukuse*, or even the idealized characterization of the beautiful men and women who people the novel. The psychological relationships between the men and women who come and go in the pages of the novel are skilfully told and have considerable charm, but they are not what provide the hallmark of the novel. What is it then which only the *Genji monogatari* has and sustains throughout its fifty-four chapters? In my view it is an awareness of the reality of the passage of time; a feeling for the reality of time as something which cannot help but make all the activities and emotions of human beings relative. The *Genji monogatari* is a presentation of the emotional condition of human beings conscious that they tread this earth but once: 'Life is not long, but make the most of it even if only one or two days are left.' ('Tenarai') What is expressed here is the mortality of man as well as eternity caught within 'only one or two days'.

With the exception of the last thirteen chapters, the *Genji monogatari* can be read as the biography of its hero. We have already seen how the life of Genji – his birth, upbringing, his loves, his exile, his promotion, and, in old age, his desire for the afterlife – is a connecting thread running throughout the novel. We have already seen also how through the literary style of the book the author is always with us and provides continuity despite the inclusion of many independent anecdotes and stories. However, it is not solely these two factors which provide the sense of the reality of time in the *Genji monogatari*.

In the course of the *Genji monogatari* the natural and social environment change and the various characters (not only Genji) change. Sensitivities to the changes in the four seasons nourished since the age of *Kokinshū* are clearly apparent and many events (mostly trivial events) are closely related to shifts in human emotions occasioned by the changes of the seasons. For example, Genji's exile to Suma begins at the end of the third month 'when the days are long', and when he has become a little more settled there, 'the rainy season comes' and he thinks of the women of the capital, his endless memories of the women over-lapping and harmonizing remarkably with the never-ending rain. There are innumerable similar examples of emotions and natural conditions being attuned in this way. The social background is provided by the court where changes are denoted by the accession of different Emperors. The novel covers the reigns of four Emperors and the rule of three Regents and one of these summons Genji from Akashi back to the capital. Almost overnight the position of Genji and his family at court is changed completely.

Many other characters, both men and women, also follow their own 'destinies' from childhood to adulthood and reveal their personalities in the process. As a child the beautiful Murasaki is put into the care of Genji, then when she grows up she marries him, falls ill and eventually dies tended by Genji. She is a character who represents a unifying thread in the novel from the very beginning. Then there is the undying love which Fujitsubo has for Genji even after she has become a nun. Again there is the boy Kaoru who grows up after Genji's death and plays a leading role in the final thirteen chapters. In all these instances one feels an acute awareness of the passage of long periods of time.

However, the course of time is clearly accentuated not only by the world changing even as it continues, but also by the different reactions of the characters when, after the passage of years, they are confronted by similar circumstances to those they had previously experienced.

Murasaki Shikibu displayed truly great skill in constantly resurrecting situations resembling each other with which to face her characters. This is one of her characteristic methods of dealing with time, as is typically represented by the two adulterous affairs; one is Genji's affair with Fujitsubo and the other is that of his wife Onna Sanno Miya with Kashiwagi. As a result of the first of these affairs Fujitsubo suffers and becomes a nun, but Genji himself does not feel any particular remorse or responsibility. On the contrary, even when Fujitsubo's child becomes Emperor and he himself as a father of the Emperor rises to the state of ex-emperor and lives in great splendour, he does not feel any doubt whether it is right or not. Therefore, when his own wife commits adultery, it does not have the effect on him of being a retribution for his own transgression. The re-occurrence of similar circumstances is not a matter of cause and effect, but gives the impression of a change of Genji's role within those circumstances and makes the reader sharply aware of the fact that it is the passage of time which has brought about that change in role.

The second method which Murasaki Shikibu uses to bring home the passage of time is her emphasis on the influence of the past on the present. Impressions of characters from the past are overlapped with the impressions of present characters and operate in a special way on any given character. For example, the reason Emperor Kiritsubo loves Fujitsubo is that she reminds him of his dead wife, Lady Kiritsubo. Genji was captivated by Murasaki because she reminded him of Fujitsubo. The reason he was attracted by Tamakazuna was that she was a living image of her mother Yūgao who died an untimely death. Kaoru loved Uji no Ōigimi and when he met her step-sister Ukifune who put him in mind of her, he came to love Ukifune. In the case of these men, they found in one woman what they had loved in another, with echoes of the love past mingling with the anticipation of the love to start. Thus, by overlapping the past, present and future into the emotion of one moment, the author demonstrates the flow of time vividly.

By skilful use of such fictional devices, Murasaki Shikibu succeeded in conveying the intensity of time. The truth about humanity which the *Genji monogatari* reveals to us is not the destiny, nor the transiency of human life but the passage of time which is so ordinary and at the same time so fundamental a condition to all of us. To present or to reveal this truth indeed demanded a long novel.

HEIAN FICTION AFTER THE GENJI MONOGATARI

There were two aspects to the *Genji monogatari*. First, there was the realism of its setting in close touch with the everyday life of the Heian period aristocracy. Here there was nothing miraculous or contrived. Second, there was its purely fictitious aspect as a romantic novel peopled by embellished and idealized characters. Here the keynote of the narrative was the highly refined emotions and sensibilities of the characters where violent human conduct, strong will and clear characterization are hardly present at all.

For 200 years after the *Genji monogatari*, the literature of the Heian aristocracy was characterized by these two aspects, by the alignment of fact and fantasy. The realistic aspect was at its most pronounced in the *rekishi monogatari* or 'historical tales', the representative works of this genre being the *Eiga monogatari* and the *Ōkagami*. The fantasy aspect was exaggerated in a group of romantic novels in which was created a completely unreal world divorced from everyday life. Principal surviving works of this type range from long novels such as the *Sagoromo monogatari*, the *Yowa no nezame*, the *Hamamatsu Chūnagon monogatari* and the *Torikaebaya monogatari*, to collections of short tales such as the *Tsutsumi Chūnagon monogatari* and various short *uta monogatari*.

The *Eiga monogatari* (author unknown) is a work in forty volumes, the first thirty of which are said to have been written in the first half of the eleventh century and the remaining ten in the second half of that century. It is written with *kana* and in chronological order covers such matters as the genealogies of the imperial family and the Fujiwara family from the time of the 'Six Histories' onwards, annual festivals, customs and so forth interspersed with anecdotes relating to numerous people and accounts of their characters, their looks etc. The central character is Fujiwara Michinaga (966–1027) and great attention is paid to the autocratic power of the Fujiwara family gained through its marriage relationships with the imperial family, and to eulogizing, in particular, the power of Michinaga himself. There is of course no criticism of autocracy, and none directed towards the figure of Michinaga. People outside the court and the aristocracy are hardly ever mentioned. Events are recorded in chronological sequence, but without any attempt to delve into cause and effect relationships – in other words there is no sense of historical development. This, together with the numerous errors in fact which have been pointed out by scholars, make it unreliable as a historical source. As a work of literature, though, the *Eiga monogatari* is far inferior to the *Genji monogatari* in terms of insight into human character and psychology, but its prose style has considerable graphic power and its pictorial descriptions of court spectacle are impressive. Buddhism is represented as a conventional custom which has become completely systematized. 'As many buildings of the temple were constructed so they gave an impression of the Pure Land.' (Vol. 18)

This reflects a rather distorted influence from Genshin's *Ōjōyōshū*. In the case of Genshin first came a weariness with the impurity of this world which was followed by a hunger for the Pure Land. Here in *Eiga monogatari*, however, the author regarded pure what Genshin had despised as impure. Their points of origin were directly opposed to each other. Schematically speaking, dissemination of the profit-seeking, this-worldly Buddhism made it necessary for the Pure Land Buddhism to arise as an answer to the question of life and death. When that Pure Land Buddhism became popular in aristocratic society, there was a complete turnabout from this world to the vision of the other shore. Then, looking from the perspective of the other shore to this world provided a platform for a religion which in fact affirmed this world and regarded it as the Pure Land.

The exceptional nature of the Buddhism of the author of the *Genji monogatari* in this sense has already been touched on. The Buddhism of the author of the *Eiga monogatari* was more typical – aristocratic society was not integrated into Buddhism but Buddhism into aristocratic society. If even Buddhism could not transcend society, there was nothing at all which could transcend the closed group, not even historical time flow. Consequently, whereas the *Genji monogatari* has a structured sense of the passage of time, in the *Eiga monogatari* time is unstructured with no beginning and no end. In the strictest sense of the word the first section of the *Eiga monogatari* (the first thirty volumes) does not end, but is brought to a close purely coincidentally by the death of the autocrat who has been the object of all the praise and veneration.

The *Ōkagami* (six volumes – author unknown) was probably written in the second half of the eleventh century, although some scholars favour the early twelfth century. It takes largely the same subject matter as the *Eiga monogatari*, but dispenses with chronology and adopts a basically biographical approach. It begins with biographical-style accounts of the reigns of fourteen Emperors and Retired Emperors (from Montoku to Go-Ichijō), followed by accounts of twenty different Ministers of the Fujiwara family. More weight is given to this second section and Michinaga plays the role of central character. Again Michinaga is fulsomely praised and there is hardly any criticism of him, but the nature of the praise is very different from that of the *Eiga monogatari*. Here there is no idealization of Michinaga as a handsome, refined man of profound sensitivity; instead he is portrayed as a shrewd political tactician capable of wielding both the whip and the carrot, as a man of action full of resolution – a man with something vulgar about his character. Of course, as in the case of the *Eiga monogatari*, admiration is expressed for his good fortune and success, for his magnificence and power. However, this is not where the originality of the *Ōkagami* lies. It lies in the vivid and graphic depictions of the action and will and crude violence of an aristocrat in Heian period Japan who had once been portrayed in the *Utsuho monogatari* but had disappeared from literature after the *Genji monogatari*. The Michinaga of the *Ōkagami* was an artful and ruthless manoeuverer as numerous different incidents show; for example, he forced the Crown Prince to resign in order to replace him with his own grandson (Volume 2 – 'Morotada'); the instance when, hearing a rumour that the Crown Princess (Michinaga's sister) was pregnant after a secret liaison, he went to the girl and twisted her breasts until the milk flowed in order to test the truth of the rumour (Volume 4 – 'Kaneie').

This Michinaga at times acted just like a detestable villain laying a bet. This is the story of a Michinaga who 'of the whole court had the best appearance and behaviour'. Therefore, it is quite understandable that other figures of the same clan as his were depicted in extreme miserliness, pettiness, drunkenness, and seeking marriage for the sake of wealth. A son of a highly ranking family abandoned all other things and suddenly decided to become a monk; we have a minister who, on his death bed, declared that he wondered whether he could meet his drinking companions in Paradise in response to somebody's suggestion to recite *Nembutsu*.

The *Ōkagami* shows the aristocracy in a light completely different from the portrayals of them which neither *Genji monogatari*, the *Eiga monogatari* nor any 'women's literature' in general could have written. The *Ōkagami* did not enlarge the world of court society, as depicted in the *Genji monogatari*, in social terms, but in its descriptions of the people who lived in that world it treated the aspects which the *Genji monogatari* had ignored, and by doing so, it intensified the reality of the world.

So much for the *rekishi monogatari* of the period, but what were the novelists accomplishing?

About thirty novels pre-dating the *Genji monogatari* and about sixty novels of the Heian period post-dating it have not survived to the present day and are known only by their titles. Thus it is only about ten per cent of the total output that we can still read today. Moreover, in not one of the novels previously cited is the date of composition precisely known. Scholarly opinion is agreed only that the *Sagoromo monogatari*, the *Hamamatsu Chūnagon monogatari* and the *Yowa no nezame* were written in the second half of the eleventh century and that the *Torikaebaya monogatari* and most of the stories of the *Tsutsumi Chūnagon monogatari* were written in the period spanning the late twelfth to early thirteenth centuries. (There is one minor exception to this in that it *is* known for certain that one story in the *Tsutsumi Chūnagon monogatari* was written by an unknown court lady called Ko Shikibu in 1055.)

As far as authorship is concerned there are quite good reasons for thinking that the *Sagoromo monogatari* was written by a lady-in-waiting of a daughter of the Emperor, and the *Hamamatsu Chūnagon monogatari* by the daughter of Sugawara Takasue (who also wrote the *Sarashina nikki*). Nothing at all is known about the authorship of the *Yowa no nezame*, the *Torikaebaya monogatari* and the majority of the tales in the *Tsutsumi Chūnagon monogatari*. Therefore, it is difficult to trace the vicissitudes of the novel accurately in the post-*Genji* era. However, when one compares the *Genji monogatari*, this group of novels from the late eleventh century and works probably composed in the late twelfth century, some kind of pattern of development can be distinguished. Four principal features can be identified.

First, there were those novels which imitated the *Genji monogatari*. Extant novels from the late eleventh century may be regarded as traditional not only in the general sense that they were romantic novels set against the background of the imperial court and aristocracy, but also in the sense that they imitated the specific kind of human relationships portrayed in *Genji* and the story structure of *Genji*. This tendency can be detected even in the *Yowa no nezame* which has not survived in its complete form, but in the case of the *Sagoromo monogatari*, several characters remind us of those of *Genji* such as Fujitsubo, Genji, Yūgao, Aoi, and Murasaki. In the case of the *Hamamatsu Chūnagon monogatari* too the plot echoes the relationship between Kaoru and Uji no Ōigimi as told in *Genji*. Even the relationship between the hero and the T'ang Empress reminds one of the adulterous affair between Genji and Fujitsubo.

This direct influence from the *Genji monogatari* is not evident in the *Torikaebaya monogatari* and the *Tsutsumi Chūnagon monogatari*, probably because the setting against the background of aristocratic society in the last days of the rule of the cloistered Emperors (Insei) is far removed from the age of *Genji* – the golden age of Fujiwara power. In this later period the *Insei* system had led to a twofold division of the ruling powers within the court and the society of the aristocracy was beginning to be threatened by forces outside the court (the great Buddhist temples, the warrior classes and the provincial gentry).

The basic style and form of the culture of the Heian aristocracy (magical and secular rituals, institutionalized literature and fine art, and life style in the closed society) had not altered by the end of the twelfth century, but the centripetal tendencies (typically manifested by the *Eiga monogatari* and the *Ōkagami*) of that culture were gradually being lost and the optimism of the 'this world equals the court equals the Pure Land' view was giving way to the pessimism of the *mappō*. Consequently, to perpetuate the *Genji monogatari*-like world could no longer be the sole interest of authors of fiction.

Second, the realism which typified the *Genji monogatari* was lost, and there was extreme emphasis on imaginative elements within the novel. There were two aspects to this – first, the tendency towards the creation of fantastic and abnormal situations, and, second, there was a tendency to simplify the structure of the story, often to the point of making it symmetrical. In the *Sagoromo monogatari*, whenever the hero plays his *yokobue* (flute) an envoy comes down from the Heavens which is reminiscent of the miraculous stories of the *koto* found in the *Utsuho monogatari* and far removed from the everyday world of the *Genji monogatari*. The *Yowa no nezame* is not supernatural in plot, but there are elements in the story which are highly fanciful and fabulous. However, the *Hamamatsu Chūnagon monogatari* is totally divorced from reality and was turned by its author into a nonsensical 'dream tale'. Its setting encompasses both China and Japan and the plot runs as follows. The T'ang Empress was a woman born from a liaison between a Japanese woman and the T'ang envoy to Japan. Her third son was a reincarnation of the hero, Hamamatsu Chūnagon's dead father. The Empress died to be reborn in Heaven; then was reborn again as a daughter of the hero's step-sister. The hero got the information of the rebirth in a dream.

Against this absurd background a relationship is described which bears a very close resemblance to that between Kaoru and Uji no Ōigimi or between Genji and Fujitsubo, but the subtle and delicate psychological nuances to be found in the *Genji monogatari* are missing. It is difficult, not to say impossible, to imagine the psychology of a hero when he met a young Chinese who was his father reborn. This is why the hero's filial piety towards his father, is pushed to the fore in the novel, following traditional Confucian morality instead of the psychological 'shades'. Again, for example, unlike the case of Fujitsubo, the description of the love of the Empress who can be reborn freely never goes beyond the commonplace, ordinary interpretation. Just because a human being cannot be reborn, he falls in love, and goes through all the complex emotions of being in love. There was certainly a close relationship in the case of the *Genji monogatari* between its realism and its refinement as a psychological novel.

When the realistic background was discarded, inevitably the

charm of the exploration of the characters' psychologies was discarded with it. The characters of the *Hamamatsu Chūnagon monogatari*, placed in such weird and unrealistic situations, became mere puppets for the author to manipulate arbitrarily. Such tendencies appeared also in the schematization of the stories' structure in such novels. A typical example of this is where a character pledges himself to a different woman from the one he had really wanted to by mistake. This kind of mistaken identity appears in at least two of the *Tsutsumi Chūnagon monogatari* tales. In one story there is confusion of identity between a girl and her grandmother who is a nun and in the other two young gentlemen confuse the identities of two sisters with whom they are having affairs.

This second story reveals a typical symmetry of structure. In this kind of tale the central characters have no inner selves of their own but are mere counters to be pushed wherever the author desires. However, in the case of the *Tsutsumi Chūnagon monogatari* there are frequently humorous results and many of the stories are close to parody. The story of the *Torikaebaya monogatari* is also symmetrical. A man has two wives, one of whom bears him a son, the other a daughter. The son is effeminate and marries as a woman, while the daughter is masculine and has a successful career as a man. So the son is married to a man and the daughter serves the Crown Princess disguised as a man. Then the prime minister who is a libertine enters on the scene and becomes involved, and so the story develops. The characters of the leading figures do not emerge clearly. The description of their psychological reactions is commonplace and bears no originality. Instead, there are perverted sexual scenes in the unreal situation of this story.

In all, in the second half of the tenth century the aristocratic society of the Heian court discovered the long-novel form through the *Utsuho monogatari*, everyday realism through the *Ochikubo monogatari* and introspective psychology through the *Kagerō nikki*. After these three elements had been welded into one through the vehicle of the *Genji monogatari* in the early eleventh century, from the second half of the eleventh century to the end of the twelfth century, no important new discoveries were added and the world of the novel went into decline. However, there were exceptions in the elements of humour and sexual perversion found in some of the post-Genji fiction of the *monogatari* genre.

Third, there was the parody of the *monogatari*. As we can guess that there must have been many stories imitating the *Genji monogatari*, it is also probable that many parodies of it may have been written to judge from the few extant examples found in the *Tsutsumi Chūnagon monogatari*.

The situation is similar to that of Europe where stories of chivalry and knight errantry were popular in the Medieval Age. Then *Don Quixote* was written as a parody of them. Of course, in scale and scope the short stories of the *Tsutsumi Chūnagon monogatari* fall far short of this famous novel of sixteenth-century Spain, but just as one finds a kind of realism apparent in *Don Quixote* not found in other novels of knight errantry, so in the *Tsutsumi Chūnagon monogatari* too one finds a type of character which did not emerge in any of the other *monogatari* of the Heian court. Take, for example, the story of the 'Young lady who loved insects'. Because beautiful butterflies developed from hairy caterpillars, she became fond of caterpillars, and refused to take any care of her personal appearance saying that all the artificialities of man were to be avoided. When her parents said that this eccentric love for caterpillars would be injurious to her reputation in the world, she replied that she did not care what people thought of her and that 'all things will have meaning only when you inquire into them and see their outcome'. When a man sent her a poem half in jest in which he expressed the feeling that it would be embarrassing for a man to have a wife who collected caterpillars, the lady replied: 'When one perceives anything thoroughly, there is nothing to be ashamed of. In this world of dreams who lives long enough to see that this is evil or to think that that is good?'

The 'world of dreams' of course, suggests a Buddhist viewpoint. However, no such expressions can be drawn directly from such Buddhist viewpoints as 'all the artificialities of man were to be avoided'. Rather, the opinion of the character is that one should look at origins rather than outcomes and that the criteria for beauty and ugliness or good and bad are nothing but convention. All the characters of *monogatari* fiction live according to their *emotions*, but only the 'Young lady who loved insects' lives consistent to her *opinion*. Not only is this kind of character not found elsewhere in Heian court *monogatari*, it is extremely rare in the whole history of Japanese literature. Probably therefore the *Tsutsumi Chūnagon monogatari* went beyond simple parody and at times revealed some essential truths about the human condition.

Finally, there was the movement away from love to sexuality. Love in the *Genji monogatari* is above all related to psychology and emotion and its physiological and carnal aspects are hardly ever depicted. When allusion to the sexual act was necessary, it was approached in a roundabout way. Take, for example, the question of pregnancy and childbirth. Since power at court was to a large extent founded on marriage relationships, who was bearing whose child was a matter of importance to the whole social order of things, and considerable attention is paid to the questions of pregnancy and childbirth not only in the *Genji monogatari*, but also in the *Eiga monogatari* and the *Ōkagami*. The case of Fujitsubo is typical of the *Genji monogatari*'s approach to this. 'Indeed, she did not feel well, which was not usual. In secret, she was wondering why.' This indicates pregnancy. Slightly later it says: 'In her third month, it became noticeable', and this is as close to a direct reference to pregnancy as the author of the *Genji monogatari* comes. In the late eleventh century *Sagoromo monogatari* and *Yowa no nezame* reference is made to 'darkened nipples'. In the late twelfth century *Torikaebaya monogatari*, the woman who has risen to become *Chūnagon* while pretending to be a man and her 'wife' both become pregnant by the same man, and detailed physiological descriptions are given of the suspension of the menstrual cycle, nausea and so forth. Thus, even by examining the single question of pregnancy we can see that there had been a movement away from the indirect approach towards the direct; away from the emotions of love towards the sexual aspects; away from the psychological towards the physiological. There was also a movement away from heterosexuality towards either direct homosexuality or in the extreme, transvestite relationships where characters are disguised as a man or a woman. One can probably say, at least, as far as we can judge from the *kana monogatari*, that the attitudes of the Heian court aristocracy towards the male-female relationship had gradually moved in a certain direction.

The system of rule by Retired Emperor (*Insei*) brought about a split in aristocratic power, and the *shōen* (large private estates) of the *Insei* period brought about the economic collapse of the *Rit-*

suryō system. The optimism of the teachings of the Pure Land Sect began to shift into the pessimism of the *mappō* philosophy and outside aristocratic society forces antagonistic to aristocratic rule were growing. Because their society was closed, homogeneous and elaborately organized in its sensitivities, the aristocratic class itself was not even capable of realizing what was happening, let alone taking effective counter-measures. In short, their power and culture were declining towards their eventual destruction. Thus there was no tragic literature, but instead a literature based on abnormal events happening in a fantasy world, and sexual stimulus. After the same kind of stimulus is repeated over and over at a same level of intensity, the physical and psychological responses to it gradually weaken.

There were only two ways to maintain the strength of those responses. One was to change the type of stimuli, the other to increase the intensity of the stimuli. Since there was no scope left within aristocratic culture for the former which was characterized by its cultural homogeneity and internal coherence, it was natural that the latter course be adopted. This was what happened between the *Genji monogatari* and the *Torikaebaya monogatari*. In this sense the direction of the development of the Heian court *monogatari* followed logical necessity.

THE WORLD OF THE KONJAKU MONOGATARI

The *Genji monogatari* in depicting the life of aristocratic society at court idealized its emotions and sensitivities, and the *Ōkagami*, depicting the same society, often included sharp perceptions of the realities in everyday life in that society. Both concentrated on the court at Kyōto and the question remains of what life was like beyond the Kyōto court and what kind of beliefs were current. What stories were there among the provincial nobility, the warrior classes, farmers and fishermen, artisans and merchants and so forth? This was a world of which the literature of the Heian court had nothing to say and which was described only by the *Konjaku monogatari*. Of all the sixty provinces in Japan at that period the names of only three (Iki, Tsushima and Iwami) are not mentioned in the *Konjaku monogatari*, and not only the imperial family, the aristocracy, monks and scholars, but people of nearly every other social class figure as characters in the stories.

The *Konjaku monogatari* is in thirty-one volumes and is thought to have been written early in the twelfth century, probably around 1120. Volumes 8, 18 and 21 have been lost. The compiler is unknown. Altogether the collection contains around 1000 stories which are divided into three parts – India, China and Japan. All the stories in the first part (*Tenjiku* – India) relate to Buddhism and range from traditional tales of the life of the Buddha, through stories of the Buddha's disciples and other types of Buddhist anecdote. This part covers Volumes 1–5. The first two volumes of the second part (Vols. 6, 7) begin with tales of Buddhist tradition and the next two volumes include stories relating to filial piety. The remainder of the work is devoted to Japanese tales, Volumes 12–20 consisting of stories explaining the teachings of Buddhism, and Volumes 22–31 of more general secular tales. In other words, the classification of the three parts is extremely logical, according to the route of historical transmission of Buddhism; each part starts with Buddhist tales and proceeds to more secular stories; and stories concerning Buddhism are arranged in an order which runs from the principles to more peripheral episodes.

It is clear that such a structure reflects a purpose of the compiler and it may be imagined that the collection was made by a monk from one of the great Buddhist temples as source materials for 'sermons'. Since the stories are fragmentary, cover many different sects, are not devoted purely to theoretical and doctrinal matters and include non-Buddhist tales, it is difficult to believe that the work was compiled for monks. However, it is certain that the vast majority of Buddhists (outside the priesthood) would have been unable to read the *Konjaku monogatari* which contains many Chinese characters. Consequently, the obvious conclusion is that the collection was designed for Buddhist monks to read out loud to popular audiences.

The method adopted by the compiler to achieve his objectives was to search thoroughly through both Buddhist and non-Buddhist materials and select stories most suitable for the edification of that popular audience. It seems likely that probably all of the tales in the first two sections were free translations of stories from scripture and classical literature including such works as the *Fa yuan chu lin*, the *Ming-pao chi* and the *Ta hsi yü chi t'ang*.

Source material was also provided by Japanese works, ranging from the *Nihon ryōiki* to the *Jizō Bosatsu reigenki* (date of compilation unknown, but belonging to the early eleventh century). Take, for example, two stories about turtles repaying kindness. One (Vol. 9 no. 13) is faithful to a story which appeared in the Chinese work *Ming-pao chi*, while the other (Vol. 19. no. 30) completely adheres to a story found in the *Nihon ryōiki*. However, the compiler added to the section of Japanese tales stories which he had heard himself.

There is a coherence in the stylistic characteristics of the *Konjaku monogatari* which argues strongly for the hypothesis that its compilation was the work of one man. Many Chinese characters are used in combination with the *katakana* syllabary. The vocabulary owes much to both Chinese and Japanese and there are many onomatopoeic words, with colloquialisms being frequently used in conversational passages. There are relatively few adjectives, but the use of numerous nouns and verbs is accomplished, the end product being stylistically both simple and graphic. The style is perhaps better suited to the portrayal of action and movement rather than that of subtle human emotion and feelings.

Basically, three major Buddhist-derived themes may be perceived in the *Konjaku monogatari* stories. First, the miraculous powers of the Buddha, celebrated Buddhist monks, pagodas, Buddhist images and the scriptures (particularly the *Lotus Sutra*). Some stories relate to the manifestation of various Buddhas and Bodhisattvas in different forms, especially in the case of Kannon. Second, the consequences of the evil deeds of humans. In some cases these consequences are portrayed as manifesting themselves in a future existence where, for example, the transgressor descends into hell or is reborn as an animal. In other cases, the consequences are realized in this life by, for example, the evildoer being killed or deformed in some way. Third, the consequences of good deeds of humans. As with evil deeds, the rewards for doing good are sometimes manifested in a future existence (entering Paradise after death, for example) sometimes in this world (for example, the saving of the person's life, his resuscitation even after death, the poor man acquiring riches, the sick man being cured, the ugly person becoming beautiful, or the do-gooder being rewarded with kingship and so forth). Perhaps the four most common rewards for doing good are entry into Paradise, escape from some great peril, resuscitation after death and the acquisition of riches.

It was the Tendai Sect of Buddhism which particularly revered the *Lotus Sutra* and it goes without saying that the idea of entry into Paradise after death represents the influence of Pure Land teachings. Shingon Esoteric influence also may be detected in some episodes such as those of great monks who became live Buddhas. One might say, therefore, that the Buddhism of the *Konjaku monogatari* is firmly based on the teachings of the two major sects of Heian period Japan (Tendai and Shingon) with very strong influence from the Amida cult of Pure Land Buddhism which became very popular from the end of the tenth century. The consequences of good and evil deeds are explained in terms of Buddhist teaching on cause and effect, but there are far more stories about reward for good deeds than about retribution for wickedness. In this sense, unlike the Kamakura Buddhism to come, the Buddhism of the *Konjaku monogatari* was positive rather than negative in its attitudes towards human life, optimistic rather than pessimistic. In the whole work there are very few stories about descent into hell. As far as entry into Paradise is concerned, there are no stories on this theme in the India section, several in the Chinese section and a great many (particularly in Vol. 15) in the Japanese section. This suggests that the otherworldly aspect of the Buddhism of the *Konjaku monogatari* was almost completely under the influence of post-*Ōjōyōshū* Japanese Pure Land Buddhism. However, there are far too many stories on the theme of 'profit in this life' to allow us to regard the *Konjaku monogatari* as in any real sense a Pure Land Buddhist text.

As indicated above, the majority of stories of this type are related to escape from perils, the dead being brought back to life and the acquisition of riches. Making a comparison of the occurrence of these stories in the different sections of the *Konjaku monogatari*, it emerges, naturally enough, that there are many more of them in the much lengthier Japanese section than in either the Indian or Chinese sections. Stories relating to escape from peril and the acquisition of riches are very infrequent in the Chinese section. There are hardly any stories relating to bringing a person back to life in the Indian section and there are approximately the same number in both the Chinese and Japanese sections. This strongly suggests that the idea of bringing the dead back to life was basically Chinese. Doubtless, to the mass of the Japanese people in the first half of the twelfth century the prospect of living longer and in material comfort had more appeal than entering Paradise. Therefore, among the stories which the compiler of the *Konjaku monogatari* intentionally selected to act as a kind of propaganda for Buddhism, there were as a *result* many which told of living longer and gaining riches by following the Buddha's law. His *intention* may well have been to emphasize the other-worldly nature of Buddhism. Not despite this, but indeed because of this, the *result* that most of the stories are 'this-worldly' may be thought probably to have been a faithful reflection of the attitudes of the ordinary people who heard the stories.

Certainly, the ordered grouping of the stories is a reflection of the Buddhist intent of the compiler, but among the various individual tales are many which do not relate to Buddhism at all. For example, the *Konjaku monogatari* tells the tale of the strong women (Vol. 23 no. 17) which is also to be found in the *Nihon ryōiki* and which has been described earlier in this book. As was mentioned at that time, the compiler of the *Nihon ryōiki* added an arbitrary Buddhist interpretation and stated that the strength of the women was the result of their deeds in a previous life. The *Konjaku monogatari* on the other hand tells stories unrelated to Buddhism simply as they stand without adding any further explanations. The stories demonstrate that the author/compiler (and indirectly probably his audience also) had a strong interest in the human world and do not indicate any kind of philosophy beyond that interest.

Thus there are many stories in the *Konjaku monogatari* which we may assume derived from folk tradition and of course these would have been unrelated to Buddhism. For example, there is the tale of the man who, after having been spat upon by a demon, became invisible and whose voice could not be heard (Vol. 16 no. 32). Instead of trying to take advantage of this situation the man was simply annoyed. Thus far the tale was purely traditional and the conclusion in which the man became visible again after following instructions given him by a monk who appeared in a dream, was probably a later addition. The original folk part of the story is very imaginative and graphic.

The stories were not only frequently divorced from Buddhism, but on occasion were even severely iconoclastic. For example, there is the tale of the hermit-wizard of Kume who when flying around in the sky one day caught sight of the bare white flesh of the legs of a woman. Not only did he fall from the sky and marry the woman, but even worked as a wood cutter to gather the material necessary to build a palace. Hearing that he had once been a wizard, an official asked why he could not have transported the materials through the air. The hermit said that he had forgotten the arts of wizardry, but would try what prayer could achieve. Thereupon he prayed for seven days and seven nights until on the morning of the eighth day to the sound of thunder he transported all the timber at one go to the capital. There is a kind of comedy flavour to this story (Vol. 11 no. 6) and in conveying the idea of a man, once a wizard, working at cutting lumber, the author seems to have been expressing iconoclastic attitudes.

Another story (Vol. 20 no. 13) tells of a monk who goes into seclusion in the mountains and walks around holding a copy of the *Lotus Sutra*. He suggests to a hunter that since every night he is favoured with a visitation by the Bodhisattva Fugen, they should pray to him together. The hunter does as the monk suggests and finally sees a white Bodhisattva mounted on a white elephant. The monk is deeply moved and prays fervently, but the hunter is suspicious and thinks to himself that remarkably little effort has been needed to get the Bodhisattva to appear. Thinking to make sure that something else has not assumed the form of the Bodhisattva, while the monk's head is bent in prayer he shoots an arrow into the Bodhisattva's breast. The next morning he goes to the spot where the Bodhisattva had stood and finds a trail of blood which he follows until eventually he finds a huge wild boar lying dead, having been shot through with an arrow. In the end the discovery that the Bodhisattva was in reality a wild boar in an assumed form was not made by a pious monk who was not intelligent but by a sinful hunter who was wise enough.

The wisdom of the hunter was not religious or ethical but practical and his mind was shrewd, commonsensical and logical. Probably (in the mind of the author) such qualities were not found in the ladies of the court, but frequently in hunters. A typical story of iconoclasm in its extreme form can be seen in the tale of the man who prevented a sacrifice (Vol. 26 no. 8). The man was an itinerant Buddhist priest who one day received hospitality from a village in the mountains of Hida, became a lover of the only daughter of the family and got married. Discovering that the woman was about to be sacrificed to the gods, the priest decided to take her place and was duly sent out into the mountains by the villagers, but, unknown to them, took with him a sword. When he was in the mountains a monkey appeared who tried to kill and eat him as the sacrifice, but the priest took out his sword, slew the monkey and bound its body. Then he burnt down the shrine of the monkey god and took the bound body of the monkey with him back to the village. When he set the body of the monkey before the villagers, they were very frightened and said, 'This man treats even a god like this. He will certainly kill us and eat us.' The priest showed the bound monkey to the villagers and declared, 'It is quite appalling of you to call this a god and to have offered up two persons a year to it. This is nothing but a monkey which you may chain, domesticate, and control. It was extremely stupid of you to have sacrificed live human beings every year without realizing the truth.'

Thereafter the people gave up the practice of sacrificing to the monkey god and the monk became chief of the village. This monk displayed two different types of courage. The first kind – to go out alone into the mountains in face of great danger armed only with a sword – is not uncommon in Japanese literature, but the second kind – the courage to doubt traditional authority when one has not personally ascertained its validity – is rare indeed. However, the courage of the hunter who shot an arrow into a Bodhisattva and of a monk who defied similarly the anger of the gods may be thought to represent one aspect of the culture of the people at large in Japan.

One might say that such an iconoclastic attitude was transmitted to the Kyōgen plays, later to comic *haiku* and satirical short poems of the Tokugawa period, and even in the late nineteenth century to Fukuzawa Yukichi who tested the validity of a house god by stepping on its shrine deliberately. Of course, the people were foolish as the monk in the story above described them, but concealed within them was the courage to see through folly and rise above it.

It has already been touched on that court literature after the *Genji monogatari* moved away from the psychology of love between man and woman towards sexual perversion. The sexual world of the *Konjaku monogatari* was not perverted although it was explicit. There was a tendency towards a direct interest in the sexual organs when male-female relationships were being described whoever was involved – whether Empress, monk, female aristocrat, doctor, servant or even snakes and other animals. This was in part, perhaps, a reflection of popular folk belief in fetishes and also, in part, a reflection of the daily lives of people who were by no means averse to using crude and vulgar expressions.

Either way, in the *Konjaku monogatari* there is a kind of egalitarianism in sexual attitudes. In this category there are some stories which are humorous and some which are weird. For example, there is the story (Vol. 24 no. 8) of the beautiful woman who comes to the house of a famous physician to seek a cure for a boil in the region of her sexual organs. The doctor immediately took a fancy to the woman, but she said she would have nothing to do with him until after she was cured. She did not give him her name. As the cure progressed the doctor's anticipation grew. However, when the cure was complete one day the woman just vanished without trace. At this the doctor was greatly vexed and became an object of mirth among his disciples. Compared to the witty overtones of this story, the episode of the priest Zōga is bizarre and vulgar. The priest was called to perform the tonsure ritual for the Emperor's mother who was becoming a nun. After the ritual, he came out of the palace and declared in the presence of many courtiers, 'I don't see why I was called for such an intimate occasion. Perhaps she may have heard of the size of my penis.'

The height of pornography is reached in the tale (Vol. 20 no. 7) of the Lady of Some dono (Fujiwarano Akiko, concubine of the Emperor Montoku) and the 'noble sage' from Kongō mountain. The lady has for some time been praying without success for a cure from a sickness until it is effected by the sage whom she meets. At the same time the sage conceives a great passion for the lady, creeps into her room and rapes the lady whereupon he is discovered and captured by a physician. Later the sage becomes a demon, drives the lady mad and then has intercourse with her. The ladies of the court tremble in fear at this, but the lady herself when it is all over is calm. Because of this the Emperor summons monks to exorcize the demon and for about three months after-

wards the demon makes no appearance until one day the
Emperor visits the lady's apartments and complains tearfully.
Then the demon appears and enters her bedroom and she follows
it. The Emperor could do nothing. After a while the demon came
out of the room. Ministers and noblemen were frightened to see
it.

> Then the lady reappeared following the demon. They made love right
> in front of the Emperor and everyone else present. It was so ugly an act
> that it cannot possibly be described. She performed it without any
> restraint at all. When the demon arose, she also stood up and went back
> into her room. The Emperor felt that there was nothing that could be
> done and collapsed in tears.

The compiler of the *Konjaku monogatari* was not a commoner.
He, however, tried to present the world of the people at large
with a concern for his general audience. The remarkable difference between him and the authors of *monogatari* fiction after the
Genji monogatari, including Murasaki Shikibu herself, who
described the court life and court people for the court audience
lies in the fact that in narrating physical and sexual scenes, the
former recognized no taboos at all, while the latter did. In the
Heian period sex had a dual nature and this dual nature was
closely tied to the social structure of the rulers and the ruled of
Japan.

The world of characters in the *Konjaku monogatari* was also a
world of actions. Take, for example, the story of the man who,
with his wife, tried to cross Ōeyama. They met up with a robber
to whom the man gave his bow in exchange for a sword, whereupon the robber threatened the man with the bow, took back his
sword, tied the man to a tree and raped his wife in front of his
eyes (Vol. 29 no. 23). This story was psychologically treated later
by Akutagawa Ryūnosuke in his story *Yabu no naka* and by
Kurosawa in his film *Rashōmon* in such a way that the three main
characters – the robber, the woman, and the man – tell three
different versions of the same event leaving the reader (or the
audience) unable to figure out which version is true, which
reminds us of Pirandello's approach in his play, *Right You Are, If
You Think So*.

The original story is told simply and after recording the words
of the woman who is in utter disgust with her husband once the

robber has fled concludes bluntly with the sentiment that a man who ventures into the mountains and allows himself to have his bow taken from him is indeed a fool. This is by way of a practical observation and no attempt is made to examine the emotional psychology of the characters involved or ethical values. In order to carry on living, one's judgement of situations must be sound and one's reactions swift. A world in which a fool's a fool and there's no help for it is clearly reflected in this tale.

However, the world of action is most typically represented by the stories in Vol. 25 which deal mostly with warriors. The characters portrayed here are not simply men of action but embody splendidly the value systems of the early warrior classes. For example, there is the tale (Vol. 25 no. 4) where Tairano Koremochi visits the governor of Kazusa – his father Tairano Kanetada. While the son who had journeyed from afar was meeting with his father, four or five members of his bodyguard were lined up in the front garden in full armour. Kanetada pointed out to one of his own retainers that the leader of Koremochi's bodyguard some years earlier had slain that retainer's father. Therefore, the retainer, who was a young man, contrived to kill the leader of the bodyguard as he slept in vengeance for his father. When he learned of this Koremochi wanted the retainer punished, but Kanetada defended him and said how could he be blamed for such a filial act and to this Koremochi assented. Thus here the *Konjaku monogatari* gives a foretaste of the image of the warrior as he was later depicted in the *Heike monogatari*. In another story (Vol. 25 no. 9) 2000 warriors led by Minamotono Yorinobu, governor of Hitachi, engage with 3000 warriors under Tairano Koremoto at a crossing on the river Tone. In this tale the author's descriptions of the warriors trying to come at each other and dismounting from their horses as they try to cross the river, in their graphic power put one very much in mind of the *Heike monogatari*. Probably the greatness of the *Konjaku monogatari* does not lie solely in its close observation and detailed description of things as they were at the time it was compiled. It managed somehow even to see things that were to come in the near future. To this author/compiler (and to him alone) of the early twelfth century the gates of that great age of change – the Kamakura period -- were already opening.

Chapter 4

The Second Turning Point

COURT AND BAKUFU – THE DUAL GOVERNMENT OF THE
KAMAKURA PERIOD (1185–1333)

The system of rule by Retired Emperor (*Insei*) which came into
operation in the late eleventh century may be regarded as a
retaliatory reaction on the part of the Japanese Emperors against
the power of the Fujiwara family. The reaction developed to the
point where, in the late twelfth century, the Retired Emperor
Go-Shirakawa while pretending to act as guardian to the
Emperor sought to take over the reins of real power for himself by
means of a *coup d'état* which resulted in a series of civil wars
known to historians as the Hōgen and Heiji wars. On the other
hand the leaders of the military classes who had played a prominent part in the *coup d'état* replaced the Fujiwara family and
immediately found themselves next to the centre of political
power, as is evidenced by the appointment of the warrior Tairano
Kiyomori to the post of Minister-President in 1167.

Not many years after this the Taira family of which Kiyomori
was the head found itself embroiled in yet another power struggle with the Minamoto clan which finally resulted in the destruction of Taira power in the great sea battle of Dannoura in 1185.
The civil wars between the Taira and the Minamoto are known as
the *Gempei* wars and the principal difference between this conflict
and the earlier Hōgen and Heiji wars lay only in the scale of forces
involved – tens of thousands in the *Gempei* wars as opposed to
only a few hundreds in the previous disturbances.

Another important difference was that in the *Gempei* wars for
the first time in Japanese history the provincial warrior groups
were fully mobilized and also the leaders of both sides were not
Kyōto aristocrats. Minamotono Yoritomo, leader of the Minamoto

clan, succeeded where Tairano Kiyomori failed in that instead of attempting to construct the framework of his power within the existing rule-by-aristocracy system, he created a regime of military dictatorship in Kamakura which was known as the Kamakura Bakufu. The new military rule (starting with Yoritomo and later taken over by the Hōjō family made the provincial warrior groups (the *gokenin* retainers), who had supported him in the Gempei wars, the bulwark of the Bakufu's military power and, deriving his economic strength from the great manorial estates (*shōen*) confiscated from the Taira's, proceeded to make new laws based on *samurai* codes. He also wrested away from the Bakufu almost all administrative control (Shugo and Jitō) relating to military affairs, taxation and policing. Thus this period marked the end of the power of the Japanese aristocracy who had ruled Japan from Kyōto since the ninth century.

However, the aristocracy were not in all respects supplanted by the new military power and from the very beginning Yoritomo himself adopted an attitude of compromise towards the Kyōto court. While sharply opposed to the old order by authorizing the private ownership of the land of the provincial gentry some of whom were warriors, he soon must have discovered some of its advantages particularly in the economic sphere, deriving, as has already been said, much of the Bakufu's wealth from the court manorial system. Moreover, both in order to legitimatize himself as the new ruling power of Japan and to maintain his dignity as such, he was forced to cultivate the support of the imperial court.

The necessity for legalizing his position was clearly shown by his need after seizing power to purge various disputing claimants to his position, including two of his own brothers, and to put down several insurrections. Despite the fact that power had firmly passed into the hands of the military classes, if Yoritomo and his own heirs were to be maintained as wielders of that power, it was necessary to have his position and rights confirmed by the Emperor (or Retired Emperor) himself in Kyōto.

It was the court which gave Yoritomo the title of *Shōgun* and when, after Yoritomo's death, the Hōjō family took over control of the Bakufu, they chose to exercise their power in the nominal role of Regent (*Shikken*) rather than make any attempt to become the nominal *Shōgun* who was still appointed by the court. Nor did they take over the title of *Shōgun* conferred on Yoritomo. Thus both Emperor and *Shōgun* remained as symbolic figureheads under the Hōjō 'Regency' and this phenomenon of maintaining figureheads while real power is exercised elsewhere is a noteworthy feature of Japanese political tradition.

However, in the thirteenth century the relationship between Kyōto and Kamakura was not that of an absolute division of roles, the former the source of ritual dignity and prestige, the latter the source of real power. Even though the military government of Kamakura may have wished to see just such a relationship, the Kyōto court strove to take maximum advantage of the essential weakness of the Kamakura Bakufu's position – its need to rely on the court for the maintenance of its dignity, authority and prestige. The aristocracy and the great Buddhist temples with the court in the centre retained many of their estates, found ways round the administrative power of Kamakura, maintained two legal systems, one aristocratic and the other military, and even on occasion had the ability to mobilize military forces of their own. In other words, two governments, one in Kyōto and one in Kamakura, were both functioning at the same time and the whole Kamakura period was an age of dual rule.

The two governments each had facets which made up for weaknesses in the other. Yoritomo derived the legitimacy of his rule from the court, while the Retired Emperor Go-Shirakawa used *samurai* warriors as well as aristocratic bureaucracy to support him and the aristocrat Fujiwara (Kujō) Kanezane maintained his power at court through the co-operation of Yoritomo. This was one example of mutual dependence.

Another connecting feature was the common dependence of the unproductive aristocracy and the equally unproductive military classes on the produce of the peasantry to supply the necessities of life. Also both these centralized governments had to keep in check the independent tendencies of provincial power groups. In some respects a symbiotic relationship developed, but at the same time the tension between Kyōto and Kamakura held the potential for military conflict. Although the Kamakura administration felt obliged to curb the defiance of Kyōto in answer to the demands of its own supporters (especially those of the *Gokenin*), the imperial court made use of dissensions among the various warrior groups to aspire towards a policy of 'divide and rule'. The behaviour of the Retired Emperor Go-Shirakawa immediately after the establishment of the Kamakura Bakufu provides a typical example of the Kyōto attitude towards Kamakura. Go-Shirakawa used Yoritomo to drive away Yoritomo's own cousin Kiso Yoshinaka (1154–84) who had occupied Kyōto after a successful pursuit of fleeing Taira supporters. When Yoritomo himself became the leading power in the land, Go-Shirakawa commanded Yoritomo's brother Minamotono Yoshitsune (1159–89) to vanquish this too-powerful figure. Almost immediately, however, he saw that things would not go the way he hoped and so revoked the command and appointed Yoritomo as *Shōgun*. In this way the court sought to undermine the Bakufu by turning the quarrels among its leaders to their advantage and this imperial policy of watching for opportunities to recover lost ground was a constant factor throughout the thirteenth century until the collapse of the Bakufu in 1333.

After Yoritomo's death, the Retired Emperor Go-Toba (1180–1239) raised an army which in 1221 unsuccessfully fought against the forces of the Bakufu, resulting in Go-Toba's exile, and just over a hundred years later in 1331 Emperor Go-Daigo (1288–1339), perceiving the decline of the Hōjō Regents, took the opportunity to mobilize anti-Bakufu *samurai* into a revolt which although initially unsuccessful ended in the Imperial Restoration of 1334. During the period before the temporarily successful Kemmu Restoration of 1334, again and again plans were made to overthrow the Kamakura government and time after time they failed. For all that, they clearly underline the state of strain which existed between the Kyōto and Kamakura governments throughout this age. The repeated failures also demonstrated the fact that social conditions under which the aristocratic type of power of the Heian period could recover no longer existed. This was inevitable because of the increasing economic power of the resident-land-owner-warrior group which developed in the thirteenth century through increased productivity of the land (assisted by improved irrigation techniques, land reclamation programmes and so forth) and culminated in the emergence of a fully-formed feudal system in the Muromachi period as the organizational capability of the land-owner-warrior group became more developed.

In other words, the dual rule system was *stable* as far as the division of roles between formal authority and substantial power is concerned. However, if we consider all efforts to unify those roles, then the system could be said to be quite vulnerable. The overthrow of the Kamakura government in the end was not because of imperial plots and machinations, but because there was an increased tendency towards independence on the part of the land-owner-warrior group which resulted in hostilities and antagonisms among various factions within this group. The truth of this land-owner-warrior dominance is nowhere shown more clearly than in the fact that the Imperial Restoration of 1334 lasted no more than two years. The genius who organized the military classes opposed to the *Gokenin* was not the Emperor Go-Daigo, but the Kantō land-owning warrior Ashikaga Takauji (1305–1358).

In general, how did the absentee land-owning Kyōto aristocracy react to the dual government situation? It seems that their central concern was with securing, through the influence of those with power at court, the revenues from their *shōen* estates. For example, the *Meigetsu-ki* (the diary written by the courtier Fujiwarano Teika (1162–1241)) is famous for the poet's bold phrase concerning the Gempei War, 'warriors' banners and armour are no concern of mine'. This may seem to be evidence of the poet's art-for-art's sake attitude. However, in reality, it is full of passages relating to matters of promotion and advancement within the court. On the other hand, the provincial warriors concentrated all their deliberations on the choice of which leader they would serve. The question became one of which military leader would be most advantageous to serve, and how to assure the levies from his manor. For example, the warrior Yuasa Muneshige from the Province of Kii served Tairano Kiyomori during the Heiji war. He adopted a neutral stance at the beginning of the *Gempei* wars, but later he gave his allegiance to Tairano Shigemori's son and with more than five hundred followers attacked the forces of the Minamoto clan. Realizing eventually there was no future in this he gave up his allegiance to the Tairas. When Minamotono Yoshitsune rebelled against his brother Yoritomo, most of the Kii provincial warriors took Yoshitsune's side. Yuasa Muneshige however, refused to have anything to do with it, thereby winning Yoritomo's confidence.

For aristocrat and warrior alike survival in that age of civil war and dual rule was a problematical and difficult art and consequently there were many who gave their undivided attention simply to living through such troubled times. This was an age of machinations and intrigues and through them individual personalities began to emerge.

KAMAKURA BUDDHISM

While the collapse which followed the decay of the rule by aristocracy system produced apprehension in many individual aristocrats who had depended on the system, at the same time it undoubtedly meant a degree of liberation from the system into which they were totally integrated. There was a phenomenal rise in a kind of 'individualism' among the land-owning-warrior classes who had achieved power from outside aristocratic society. (In this sense, the case of the peasantry who continued to live in communal village society was different. They were hardly affected by the collapse of the aristocratic regime.) The idealogical expression of unease stemming from the decay of the old order was manifested in the philosophical concept of mappō ('the last days of the Buddha's law'). A new kind of Buddhism offering individual salvation became the spiritual mainstay of those who had now lost anything temporal on which to rely. The mappō concept stemmed from the belief that after the Buddha's death there would be a period of the True Law (Shōhō), followed by a period of Imitative Law (Zōhō) and finally of the mappō. According to this theory, after the middle of the twelfth century began the mappō period in which it became impossible to achieve salvation in this world.

The new Buddhism with its promise of individual salvation was of necessity concerned with the 'next world'. The Zen Sect which continued not to recognize the 'next world' substituted for the Pure Land of the new popular Buddhism an absolute world which transcended distinction between life and death and 'this world' and the 'next world'. Nevertheless the 'Kamakura Buddhism' of the thirteenth century was diametrically opposed to the Buddhism of the Heian period with its emphasis on seeking this-worldly profit and magical practices and firmly concentrated its attention on the next world and transcendentalism. The great significance of this development lay in the destruction of the practical everyday realism which hitherto had dominated the indigenous Japanese world view.

For the first and perhaps the last time in Japanese history in the thirteenth century values transcending everyday reality became the nucleus of Japanese thought. Other transcendental ideologies which later appeared in Japan such as Catholicism of the late sixteenth century, the Confucianism of the early eighteenth century, the Protestantism of Uchimura Kanzō, in the nineteenth century and the Marxism of the twentieth century were none of them the ruling philosophical ideologies of their age. In that sense, they are essentially different from Kamakura Buddhism.

Metaphorically speaking, Kamakura Buddhism was like a wedge deeply struck into the indigenous world view of Japan which had lasted for several centuries. To see how it developed and how widely its influence spread is to consider the central problem of 'medieval' culture, provided we may apply the term 'medieval' to the whole span of time between the Kamakura and Muromachi periods.

The Jōdo Shinshū or True Pure Land Sect was founded by Shinran (1173–1262) who inherited and developed the teachings of Hōnen (1133–1212). In many respects the relationship between the Jōdo Shinshū sect and Heian (particularly Tendai) Buddhism was rather akin to that between Protestantism and the Catholic Church in sixteenth century Europe. The Lotus Sect founded by Nichiren (1222–82) also, in that it proceeded from the base of an absolute faith to tackle social problems and took a religious state as its ideal, occupied a somewhat similar position to Calvinism in European Christianity.

We have already seen how the Pure Land teachings of Genshin were accepted for their secular benefits by the Heian period aristocracy, but in the teachings of Hōnen and Shinran there was no room for such a compromise. With them Pure Land doctrines became a completely 'next world' faith and defying the strong pressures of the established Buddhist sects and secular political authority as they then existed, spread their influence widely to the lower grade *samurai* and the upper peasantry in the provinces. Nichiren too, different from the case of Heian Buddhism again defying the pressures of the Establishment, gained most of his followers in the provinces.

Of the newly established Buddhist sects which arose at this time it was the Zen Sect which was the first to establish strong ties with Japan's military rulers. Dōgen (1200–53) introduced the Sōtō branch of Zen from Sung China and the Sung Chinese monks Rankei Dōryū (1213–78) and Mugaku Sogen (1225–86) introduced the Rinzai branch of Zen. Later the Ashikaga family were converted to belief in Rinzai Zen and the Bakufu established separate groups of 'Gozan' temples of Rinzai denomination in both Kamakura and Kyōto. Zen teachings came to provide a new ideology for the military rulers of Japan.

However, even though the political 'revolution' was accompanied by ideological reforms, this did not necessarily mean that the classes controlling literature and art were supplanted. The old and new forms of Buddhism were reflections in a dual religious system of the dual government system, but it was not possible to reflect that dual government system also in a dual cultural structure. The aristocracy and the Buddhist priesthood continued to monopolize scholarship, literature and the prestige of the arts and the new military classes were left trailing in their wake; even the *Shōgun* Manamotono Sanetomo was not an exception. One might say that the most distinctive feature of thirteenth-century Japanese culture was the response of the aristocracy, having lost political power, to new alien circumstances.

The first response of the aristocracy to their changed position was in a number of *waka* poems lamenting the lost power and glory of the court society of the Heian period, as seen in such collections as the *Kenreimon'in ukyōno daibu-shū*. The second response was in the increase of 'recluse' literature written by those who travelled into secluded parts of Japan in an attempt to escape from the decay of the old order, this kind of literature being typically represented by the poetry of Saigyō and the *Hōjōki* of Kamono Chōmei. (While neither Saigyō nor Kamo were members of the aristocracy, in their poetry they lived in the world of the aristocracy. In the sense that the destruction of aristocratic society meant the destruction of the world to which they belonged, their position was no different from that of the true aristocracy.)

Thirdly, the termination of aristocratic rule brought about a tendency in which a part of the nobility, who separated culture from the social system, became more sharply aware of cultural values than when they were integrated into society. They

developed a consciousness of cultural and aesthetic values completely distinct from political and religious values, it seeming
almost as if the defence of culture and cultural values had become
the whole *raison d'être* for an aristocracy which had lost all political
aspiration. Under such circumstances were the theoretical works
on *waka* of Fujiwarano Teika written and a devotion to art by the
poets of the *Shin Kokinshū* emerged.

The fourth response lay in a renewed awareness of history. The
end of one ruling system opened up for consideration a whole
host of alternative types of ruling system. Such consideration
immediately may have led to questioning how such systems
would begin and how they might end. To answer these questions
meant not only to record events of the past chronologically as a
kind of random sequence, but also to accept history in terms of
causal relationships and to interpret it as a development in a
certain direction. It was against such a background that the
epoch-making history book, the *Gukanshō*, was written by the
chief priest of the Tendai Sect, Jien.

As has been indicated previously, few literary works were
written by *samurai*. With the exception of the *Kinkaishū waka*
anthology written by Teika's pupil Minamotono Sanetomo, the
military classes' literary works which might be regarded as masterpieces were perhaps in the area of letters and proclaimed
laws such as the *Jōei shikimoku*, written in a combination of
Chinese and Japanese languages the style of which has special
strength.

However, the fact that the classes who produced literature in
the Kamakura period did not substantially change does not mean
a lack of expansion in readership. We have already examined
some of the works written by aristocrats for aristocrats, but there
were two types of literature written by aristocrats and monks
aimed at people outside aristocratic society, principally *samurai*
and perhaps even a much wider audience. The first of these, as
we have already seen in examining the *Konjaku monogatari*, were
the *setsuwa* tales which were collected and written down for the
purpose of propounding Buddhist teachings in a popular form
for a wide audience. Of the many such works produced in the
Kamakura period, the *Shasekishū* is representative. The second
type was that genre of literature known as *Katarimono*, stories
such as the *Heike monogatari* (the *Gempei* wars were a popular

theme in this type of literature) which were recited to the accompaniment of *biwa* music. Even though aristocrats and monks were the authors of such works, the contents were far removed from those of literary works written by aristocrats for aristocrats since they were written for a more general audience. Books of the first half of the twelfth century such as the *Konjaku monogatari* did no more than note the customs, codes and values of the warrior classes, but the *Heike monogatari*, written a hundred years later in the thirteenth century, presents a far more vivid picture of warrior society.

Thus the culture which characterizes the thirteenth century (which I have called the second turning-point) can be explained in terms of the following three points: the rise of the new Buddhism and its relationship with new social classes; the aristocratic response to their exclusion from a warrior-dominated society; and the expansion of the audience for literature (both in terms of readers and listeners to orally told stories) and presentation in literature of the worlds of the *samurai* and people at large. Naturally, this aspect of Japanese culture in the thirteenth century cannot be considered without regard to influence from China. However, the political 'revolution' came from within Japan itself and the development of new facets to religion and culture likewise originated spontaneously in Japan. If the invading Mongol armies of 1274 and 1281 had succeeded in occupying Kyūshū, the situation within Japan might have changed, but violent storms and the geographical position of Japan frustrated all attempts at invasion.

THE REFORM OF BUDDHISM

The Mahayana strain of Indian Buddhism was transmitted to China where two entirely new sects of Buddhism developed – the Pure Land (Ching-t'u) and Zen (Chan) Sects. We have already seen how the doctrines of Pure Land Buddhism, particularly through Genshin's *Ōjōyōshū*, influenced the Heian aristocracy and later we shall see how the monk Eisai (1141–1215) introduced Zen Buddhism from China at the end of the Heian period. However, it was in the thirteenth century that both these Sects underwent a revival in Japan, Pure Land Buddhism making considerable development independent of its Chinese parent and Zen inspiring some of the greatest masterpieces of Buddhist doctrinal writing ever produced in the Japanese language.

The main period of Pure Land development began with Hōnen (1133–1212). The focal points of Pure Land doctrine in the post *Ōjōyōshū* period were the desire to be reborn after death into the Western Paradise, the concentration on belief in Amida Buddha (the three main Pure Land scriptures – the *Kammuryōju-kyō*, the *Muryōju-kyō* and the *Amida-kyō* all centered on Amida), and the emphasis on the *Nembutsu* as a means of achieving rebirth into the Western Paradise. All these facets of Pure Land teaching originated within Tendai Buddhism and were accepted by the aristocracy in general. The more the aristocracy welcomed it, the less the-other-worldliness of Pure Land Buddhism was absorbed. They had a tendency to regard this world as a paradise rather than to have the aspiration for the Western Paradise which resulted from refutation of this world. They were not convinced of the absolute nature of Amida (they believed that the Pure Land practitioner could aid his chances of rebirth in the Western Paradise through various traditional devices such as memorial services and the building of temples), and thought of the *Nembutsu* as only one, although the easiest and most convenient, method of ensuring salvation. Hōnen, born into a rich and powerful family in Mimasaka Province, went to study on Hieizan after his father's death where he mastered all the teachings of Pure Land Buddhism and established the-other-worldliness of Pure Land Buddhism, the absoluteness of Amida and the importance of the recitation of Amida's name.

The crisis facing the rule-by-aristocracy system was already apparent at the time of the Gempei civil wars. As his father, an official of the Ritsuryō system, was killed by the caretaker of a manor, we may say that Hōnen himself directly experienced the fundamental contradiction in the late Heian society, namely the *Ritsuryō* system versus the development of manorial estates. The step from feeling the sordid miseries of this life to seeking the joys of the Western Paradise was but a short one to take and a consequent conviction that religion should be concerned with that future world is not to be wondered at. It was believed by Pure Land Buddhists that Amida was absolute and that salvation was to be achieved by relying on his power. A principal difference in

Pure Land teaching from that of Tendai and Shingon Buddhists who thought that salvation should be achieved by 'self-helping' religious practices and devotions was that Amida's great compassion extending to all mankind made the path to salvation an easy one.

All these things were taught by Hōnen, but his single great and original contribution to Pure Land thought was his doctrine that the Nembutsu was not just one practice among many for achieving rebirth in the Western Paradise but only the best one, rendering all other religious devotions unnecessary. Amida had made his 'original vow' and it was only in the Nembutsu that the believer drew close to Amida. The essence of Hōnen's teaching was that salvation was assured by the constant invocation of the words 'Namu Amida-butsu' (i.e. the Nembutsu) and this was something which every individual could practise without the need to resort to temple ceremonies and services. It was a simple and direct religious expression valid for all men and women. What we should note here is that the transcendental nature of the object of the faith (Amida) and a tendency to internalize the faith (recitation) had already appeared. We will later see how these aspects were brought to completion by Shinran.

Hōnen presented these ideas in his work Senchaku hongan nembutsu-shū (1198) which propounded his arguments through the medium of quotations from the three basic sutras of Pure Land Buddhism and Chinese Pure Land texts compared and explained. This book, written in Chinese, opened with the words 'Namu Amida-butsu' and the rest of the work went on to explain its meaning in a tightly-organized structure. The principle which formed the nub of Hōnen's arguments was none other than the 'senchaku' or 'choice' appearing in the title of the book, a reference to Amida's 'choice' of all the good elements and shunning of all evil among many of Buddha's realms when constructing the Western Paradise. Also Amida 'chose' the Nembutsu and the Nembutsu alone of all Buddhist practices as the supreme means of entering the Western Paradise. In other words, from the whole complex array of Buddhist practices and doctrines Amida chose the Western Paradise and the Nembutsu as the supreme concepts. However, to understand why Amida chose them one cannot help but rely on Hōnen's own view point. To answer this question Hōnen says in the Senchaku-shū 'Amida's intentions are beyond our understanding'. But after this he fell into conjecture; first that the name of Amida itself contains all virtues, second that as it is easy to recite Amida's name and difficult to practice other disciplines, we should choose the easy way so that everybody can be saved equally. It should be said immediately that all of this is dependent on Hōnen's own concept of and interpretation of the nature of Amida, and it is really Hōnen himself who is making the 'choice'.

It was not only aristocrats such as Kujō Kanezane of the men of influence in Japan at that period who accepted the *Nembutsu* not as an easy expedient but as the supreme practice, but also warriors such as Kumagai Naozane (d. 1208). Hōnen himself never ventured far from Kyōto until he was exiled to Tosa Province (1207), but through the activities of his disciples, his teachings on the *Nembutsu* which were widely followed in Kyōto itself showed signs of spreading to the provinces. This evoked a reaction from the traditional church establishment. After the downfall of Kanezane and the death of Yoritomo who, through Kanezane's influence, had been sympathetic towards Hōnen, several temples, notably the Kōfukuji, pressed the Kyōto government to ban the *Nembutsu*. In this they were successful. In 1206 two of Hōnen's disciples were executed and in 1207 Hōnen and Shinran were expelled from the priesthood and banished respectively to Tosa and Echigo. Meanwhile the monk Myōe (1173–1232) wrote in 1212 a refutation of the *Senchaku hongan nembutsu-shū* from the Kegon standpoint under the title *Saijaron* and Jien (1155–1225) made disparaging observations on the movement in his *Gukanshō*.

Ironically enough, oppression of the Buddhism of Hōnen and Shinran by the Kōfukuji Temple (representing the religious establishment) and aristocratic power helped to strenghten the ideology that all living creatures should equally enter the Western Paradise after death and expelling the priesthood helped Shinran's concept of lay Buddhism to flourish.

The *Ichimai Kishōmon* (Pledge on one page) was written by Hōnen in his last year in 1212. It says

> Practice and enlightenment in Pure Land Buddhism can be found in this one sheet of paper. There is no other mind at all. . . . One who believes in reciting Amida's name, even though he may have completely mastered the doctrines of his time, should consider himself as

an illiterate man, or regard himself to be the same as an ignorant nun. He should recite the name of Amida without thinking of anything else and without acting as if he knows anything at all.

The 'easy practice' of the Nembutsu was not only considered as the best practice, but was developed under circumstances in which scholarship was monopolized by the Hieizan monks, into a kind of anti-intellectualism, possibly even with an anti-cultural overtone.

It is said that Shinran was born the son of a member of the lower aristocracy named Hino Arinori. While accepting the basic the other-worldly tenets of Hōnen's teachings, Shinran carried his master's ideas much further. He taught that since Amida was absolute, salvation depended on his will to save rather than on the will of a person to be saved. If this idea is carried to the extreme, even the Nembutsu becomes a form of 'self-help', so the salvation is not brought about only by the Nembutsu. The relationship between Amida (the saver) and mankind (those to be saved) was nothing but that of the latter believing in the former and Amida's intervention on behalf of the people. It was Amida himself who would decide who was to be saved. However, since it is impossible to gauge the will of an absolute being, salvation from the human viewpoint became something that was predetermined. What remained to the human being ultimately was only the faith itself which did not always guarantee salvation. In this sense the development of thought from Hōnen to Shinran was from the absolute practice of the Nembutsu to faith and faith alone in Amida. In other words the transcendental nature of Amida was advanced a step and with reliance now placed on the absolute power of Amida to aid mankind, the internal nature of Pure Land faith also advanced to the extreme. Shinran's work Kyōgyō shinshō (written some time prior to 1224) instead of opening with 'Namu Amida-butsu', places most emphasis on the concept of ekō ('transference of merit') which is Shinran's equivalent to Hōnen's key theme of 'choice'.

In Shinran's system of thought the concept of Ekō is taken to mean that all things stem from Amida. The thought of Shinran is also well expressed both in the numerous letters he wrote which have survived to this day and the Tannishō, a collection of the sayings of Shinran compiled in the late thirteenth century by his disciple Yuien. What is repeatedly emphasized in both is that salvation is dependent on Amida's vow to save and not on good works undertaken by human beings to achieve this end.

> You don't have to think that you cannot be saved because you are a man of ill-deeds. Instead, you should think nobody is perfectly good (with his worldly desires). However, you should not think that you can be saved because you are a man of good deeds. You cannot be reborn in the true paradise only by self-effort.
>
> (a letter in the *Mattōshō*)

However, a man who relies on self-effort (a man of good deeds) does not depend on Amida as much as a man of ill-deeds who has no other way open to him. Therefore, if this idea is carried to the extreme, a man of ill deeds has more probability of being saved than a man of good deeds. Hence: 'Even a good man is reborn in the Pure Land, and how much more so a wicked man.' (*Tannishō*) In other words, 'The true intention of Amida's vow is to save a wicked man, who depends on Amida. This attitude is the most important cause for salvation.' (ibid.)

Thus far in Shinran's thinking, there is a close resemblance to Christian teaching. The Christian belief that salvation depends on the will of a personalized almighty being is at least in one aspect in accord with the idea of relying on the absolute and the dependence on 'other power' for salvation. The dependence on 'other power' leads to the same idea as Charles Péguy said, 'Sinners are the centre of Christianity'. However, Amida is different from the Christian God as he intends to save all human beings and does not punish anybody. It goes without saying that a 'wicked man' in Buddhism is not identical with the Christian 'sinner'. However, religious genius such as Shinran and Péguy tried to define the relationship between the transcendental being and humanity and there are similarities in their conclusions with regard to verbal expression and the very structure of philosophy.

Towards the end of Shinran's life his pupil and son Zenran went to the Kantō region to spread his teaching as follows: 'The doctrines that I have heard are the only truth. All the *Nembutsu*'s you usually recite are in vain.'

What Zenran meant by 'the doctrines that I heard' is not clear today. The Kantō region was the centre of Shinshū religious activity and the by then old Shinran, living in retirement in Kyōto, asked his son's intention by letters, while he tried to explain his doctrines to his pupils who were perturbed by Zen-ran's activities. It seems likely that Zenran's interpretation of these doctrines were heretical and in the end Shinran broke off relations with his son because of this. He even lamented that the 'faith' was failing in the Kantō region because of his son's activities, rendering all the missionary efforts to no avail, and to Shinran this was the greatest crisis that could happen in his whole religious life. In the *Tannishō* are recorded the words he had to say probably at that time to those who came to Kyōto from the Kantō area to hear the real intention of Shinran:

> I am entirely ignorant as to whether the *Nembutsu* is really the cause of rebirth in the Pure Land, or whether it is the deed meant for hell. I should never regret even if I were to go to hell by being deceived by Hōnen Shōnin. The reason is that if I were so constituted as to become Buddha by performing some deeds of merit, went to hell by reciting the *Nembutsu* instead, then, I might regret that I was deceived. But I am the one who is incapable of observing any deeds of merit, and for that reason, my ultimate abode is no other than hell itself. If the original Vow of Amida were true, the teaching of Shakyamuni could not be untrue; . . . if the teaching of Hōnen were true, how could it be possible for me, Shinran, to utter untruth?

This line of argument runs parallel to Pascal's 'bet' – 'if I believe in God and there is a God, I shall go to heaven; if there is no God there is neither heaven nor hell. If I do not believe in God and there is a God, I shall go to hell; if there is no God there is neither heaven nor hell. Therefore, if one does not know whether or not God exists, it is better to believe that he does exist.' (*Pensées*). The view which acknowledges the transcendental nature of an absolute being does not permit the questioning of the will of that being. Therefore apologetics must follow the line of reasoning taken by Pascal's 'bet'.

The development of Pure Land thought from Hōnen to Shin-ran bears some resemblance to sixteenth century European reli-gious reform and the Jansenist movement in the Catholic Church in the seventeenth century; first in the emphasis on the transcen-dental nature of the absolute being accompanied by an inward-turning of faith and the consequent reliance on 'other power'; second, on the turning directly towards scriptures or Holy Bible as the sole basis of its doctrine; third, in the reaction against the highly abstract scholastics of, in one case, the old Buddhism and in the other the Catholic Church – a kind of anti-intellectualism; fourth, on seeking for support from the peasantry and people at large – they were sometimes against authority, but not always – as opposed to the great temples and churches so closely allied to secular authority.

In two important respects, however, the religion of Shinran differed from European Protestantism. First, whereas Protestantism formulated a new set of ethical values through the medium of its beliefs, the Jōdo Shinshū did not. While the two beliefs resembled each other on purely religious grounds (the making relative of existing values through the faith in the absolute being), culturally, in terms of returning from the absolute back to historical society to establish a new set of values, the former was completely different from the latter. Since in Shinshū teaching, salvation was unrelated to good or evil deeds, the individual was left in the position of not knowing at all what deeds he should perform while living in this world. One's attitude towards Amida was a religious question, while one's attitude towards one's fellow men was an ethical question, and the problem existed of relating these two questions.

There seem to have been many practitioners of the *Nembutsu* who interpreted 'a good opportunity for salvation of a man of ill-deeds' as that everybody could do anything, hence, alcohol and meat consumption, licentious relations with men and women. Then Shinran said, 'I've never told you that you could do (willingly) wrong things because it does not have to do with salvation'. This is also related to what he has to say of the shintoistic *kami* in the same letter: 'The person who believes in the *Nembutsu* should not abandon the *kami* of heaven and earth.'

However, Shinran offers no definition of what is 'wrong', nor does he offer any explanation of why one must not abandon the *kami* of heaven and earth. These statements might have been motivated by strategic considerations in order to avoid repression by the authorities. The situation is completely different from that of sixteenth century Europe. Protestantism established new social values in this world after it had negated social conventions through absolute faith, while Pure Land Buddhism failed to produce new ethical values even after it had relativized the old ones at a religious level. Secondly, Protestantism and the Jōdo Shinshū greatly differed from each other in terms of their subsequent roles in history. Protestantism played a positive part in the development of capitalist society, while it may well be thought that Jōdo Shinshū did not play an important part as the ideological background (in any social reforms). It is difficult to know in detail which classes were reached by the teachings of Jōdo Shinshū, but it is certain that while Hōnen stayed in Kyōto until his exile to Tosa, Shinran's teaching penetrated mainly in Kantō region and that Shinran's doctrines were supported by many upper and lower grade *samurai*, merchants and peasants. However, there is no indication of any positive relationship between devotion to Amida and *Bushidō* (in the way that such a relationship existed between Zen and *Bushidō*), and no indication of any positive effect of Jōdo teaching on the structure of merchant morality (in the way that later *Shingaku* teaching was to have just such an effect). The effects as far as the peasants were concerned are an open question, but it is certain that Shinran's doctrines in no way represented their class ideology.

Shinran was not the only one in the thirteenth century to take up the ideas of the Jōdo Sect of Hōnen. The monk Ippen (1239–89) was another. Born the son of a *samurai* in Iyo Province, Ippen became a monk at an early age and went to Kyūshū where he studied the doctrines of the Jōdo Sect under a disciple of Hōnen. Later he gave up holy orders for a time, but after a while once again became a monk, went to the Zenkōji temple in 1271 and devoted his latter years to journeying round the country preaching the *Nembutsu*.

Ippen's activities in the way he visited Shintō shrines on his journeys, originated the so-called 'dancing *Nembutsu*' and in the very fact of his unceasing travelling were very different from those of Hōnen and also of Shinran (Ippen in fact started a sect known as the Jishū). However, as is shown in the collections of his sayings later compiled by his pupils – the *Ippen shōnin goroku* (2 volumes) and the *Banshū hōgoshū* – his concept of the *Nembutsu* was closer to that of Hōnen rather than Shinran and did not include new ideas of his own. Nevertheless, what we find reflected here are words which could not possibly have been uttered unless one has grasped the essentials of Hōnen's beliefs and lived them oneself.

Ippen taught that 'the *Nembutsu* practitioner should abandon all thoughts of "wisdom and folly, good and evil, riches and poverty, fear of hell, desire for paradise, and the enlightenments sought by other Buddhist sects", and concentrate entirely on the *Nembutsu*'. Later in the same work (*Ippen shōnin goroku*) are recorded his words:

> When one repeats the *Nembutsu* over and over again, there is no Buddha and no self, no sense of reasoning; good and evil and the boundaries between them merge into the Pure Land; . . . we seek nothing, we dislike nothing, all living creatures, mountains, rivers, grass and trees, the sighing of the wind in the trees, the waves pounding the shores are all *Nembutsu*.

Here Ippen is describing a state of trance, but Ippen's use of the natural rhythm of the Japanese language has few equals in prose writing. His belief that everybody should consider himself as a fool and recite the *Nembutsu* is exactly in accord with Hōnen's view as expressed in the *Ichimai kishōmon*. However, when it comes to describing the psychological state of a person practising the *Nembutsu*, Ippen's sonorous words seem to surpass Hōnen's statements in *Senchaku Hongan Nembutsu shu*. It is said that when Ippen was on his death bed, his disciples told him that a purple cloud appeared over the place producing a sign as a portent of the high priest's death. He scoffed at this saying, 'Well, then, I'm not going to die now after all; such a thing would not possibly happen at the moment of real death.'

A similar figure before Ippen's time was the monk Kūya (903–72) and much later, in the Edo period, came Enkū and Mokujiki. All these men were close to the common people and may be thought to have been a personification of a popular and distinctly Japanese brand of Buddhism. Probably their worlds were not entirely unrelated to the aesthetics of Saigyō and Bashō, nor to the frantic ephemeral enthusiasm of the 'dancing *Nembutsu*' of later times, but we have little grounds on which to base a judgement. However, it can be said that the Jōdo Sect, founded by Hōnen, developed theoretically through Shinran and was brought to the hearts of the ordinary people through Ippen. After the collapse of a system of a culture, the Kamakura period obviously needed to support itself spiritually through a transcendental faith.

Doctrinally speaking, both Hōnen and Shinran were in sharp conflict with the old Buddhism and inevitably provoked antagonism on the part of the great temples. Nichiren (1222–82), however, despite the fact that again doctrinally speaking he was in almost total accord with the teachings of the Tendai Sect, came into conflict both with other sects and secular authority on account of his aggressive individualism. Schematically speaking, as far as doctrine is concerned, Nichiren was opposed to the teachings of the new 'Kamakura Buddhism' from his old Buddhist standpoint while at the same time in terms of actual practice he had his own views which were in opposition to those of the old Buddhism.

His doctrinal viewpoint is expressed in the *Kanshin honzon-shō*, written in Chinese in 1273. The starting point and cardinal principle of his teaching is the concept of *ichinen sanzen* as expressed in the *Mo-ho chih-kuan* (*Maka shikan*), a work written by the Tendai Chinese monk Chih-i. The essence of this teaching is that the whole universe (the *sanzen* or 'three thousand' worlds) exists in the heart of each man and that if each individual (contemplates profoundly) he will be able to understand the universe. In the *Kanshin honzon-shō*, Nichiren, taking the *Hokkekyō* or *Lotus Sutra* as his supreme authority, quotes some rather arbitrary chosen passages from this *sutra* and makes some dogmatic statements concerning religious belief on the basis of them. This attitude philosophically implies ipsism and suggests the absolute religious authority of the *Lotus Sutra* as interpreted by Nichiren. In the *Senjishō* (written *c*. 1275) where Nichiren expounds a rather '*mappō*'-istic view, he draws together the two elements of his religious beliefs and the cardinal principle on which the beliefs are based. The year 1275 was the year following the first Mongol invasion of Japan and some six years before the second invasion of 1281.

Nichiren declared himself to be 'the greatest man in Japan', 'the pillar of the Japanese nation' and eventually even boasted that he was a Bodhisattva come down to earth to save Japan from her troubles in the period of *mappō*. He was born the son of a fisherman in Awa province and later wrote of himself:

> I came into this world as a person of poor and humble origins, from a family of pariahs. Since my heart believed in the *Lotus Sutra*, I was not afraid even of Brahma or Indra. The body is animal. Thus my heart is the highest and my body is the lowest. This is why the fool despises me.

> (*Sado-onsho*)

This was the reason he was persecuted. The *Lotus Sutra* tells of people who were persecuted for their belief: 'Nobody has ever defended the *Lotus Sutra* as strongly and had so many enemies in this country as Nichiren.' (*Senjishū*)

Therefore Nichiren considered himself to be the greatest practitioner of the *Lotus Sutra* in India, China or Japan.

However, since Nichiren had made the *Lotus Sutra* an absolute concept it was a logical step to believe that the *sutra* transcended secular authority. Even the Emperor or a general couldn't be spared if he made mistakes. 'When a bad king destroys the good law and when unrighteous monks help him destroy men of wisdom, the man who possesses a lion's heart will without fail became a Buddha. Such is the case with Nichiren, myself.' This formed the basis of Nichiren's attitude towards authority.

In the *Risshō ankokuron* (1260) Nichiren attempted to express his views on the government of Japan in the form of a memorial to the authorities. In essence this work said that : first, the disasters, natural and man-made, afflicting Japan were due to the popularity of heretical Buddhist sects such as the the Pure Land Sect and because the authorities were ignoring their harmful activities; second, that such sects should be banned and Nichiren's own Lotus Sect made the 'true religion'; and third, that if Nichiren's policies were not implemented and he was persecuted, more disasters would befall Japan. What is noteworthy here is not Nichiren's dogmatism and over-statement, but his attitude towards state authority, an attitude very rare in Japanese history. He says that the law (the *Lotus Sutra*) transcends all secular authority and therefore the state should serve that law and not the law serve the state.

The doctrinal differences between Tendai Buddhism and Nichiren's teachings are trifling and amount to no more than technicalities, but Nichiren is completely at odds with Tendai in his view of the relationship between the state and Buddhism. In the view of the old Buddhism, including Tendai, Buddhism filled the role of protector of the state, but according to Nichiren the state should serve Buddhism.

In Nichiren's teachings the *Lotus Sutra* corresponds in its absolute nature to the Amida of Hōnen and Shinran, and also, as we shall see later, the 'enlightenment' (*satori*) of Dōgen. These are common features in the thirteenth century reform of Buddhism, but in two basic respects Nichiren's attitude differed from those of the others. First, his beliefs were constructed within the doctrinal framework of the old Buddhism and, second, unlike any other religious leader of the time, he confronted directly the problems of the relationship between state and religion.

However, even Nichiren did not establish a new set of principles and ethical codes governing human relationships. After Nichiren's death, his sect fragmented and displayed tendencies, as in the case of the Jōdo Shinshū after Shinran, to become involved with worldly and *Gensei riyaku* concerns. In a sense Nichiren drove a wedge into the indigenous Japanese world view, but in spite of that, indigenous thought as a whole was not transformed.

Nichiren had a kind of genius as a prose writer, his work displaying a fiery nature and spirit. In Nichiren's writing, particularly his letters, Japanese prose as a polemical medium reached standards seldom surpassed.

ZEN

The practice of composing mind and body through quiet meditation was followed in India from ancient times. The practice was absorbed into Buddhism where *Zen* (*dhyāna* in Sanskrit, i.e. meditation) became one of the six basic practices undertaken by a *Mahayana* monk. One sect in China – the Chan or (in Japanese) Zen Sect – emphasized this practice and made it the basis of its religious activity. The Chan Sect in China originated in the T'ang period and reached its highest point of development in the Sung period.

It is said that Zen was imported to Japan in the late twelfth century by the monk Eisai (1145–1215), but since Eisai's sect placed emphasis on meditation within the context of comprehensive Tendai doctrine as a whole it did not come into sharp conflict with the old Buddhism in the same way as did the sects of Hōnen and Shinran, nor did it seek on practical grounds to reject the teachings of other sects as did Nichiren. Eisai's principal work, the *Kōzen gokokuron* (1198), was an explanation of the author's individual viewpoint written in response to denounciations of the Zen sect, but nevertheless in it he emphasized the importance of maintaining the traditional Buddhist Precepts and spoke of Zen as serving a part in the 'protection of the nation'.

This rigid adherence to the Precepts and emphasis on the role of religion in protecting the state had been an important aspect of Tendai Buddhism as practised on Hieizan ever since the time of Saichō's introduction of the Sect. Also the temples (the Kenninji and the Jufukuji) established by Eisai in Kyōto and Kamakura did not seek to exclude the teachings of other sects and the doctrines of both Tendai and Shingon Buddhism were taught there as well as those of Zen. Eisai made two visits to China, the second from 1187 to 1191, and the Zen doctrines he learned there in the great Chinese Chan temples were, when introduced to Japan, no more than a new addition to the framework of Heian period Buddhism. The 'new addition' found its support from the upper echelons of warrior society in such people as Hōjō Masako (1157–1225), wife of Minamotono Yoritomo and Shōgun Yoriie.

The Tendai Sect at this period, with its tradition of association with the imperial court in Kyōto, began to emphasize the concepts of Zen which had become so popular in mainland Asia, and at the same time developed close ties with the new Kamakura government. This was in part an adaptation by the old Buddhism to new social conditions and also in part a reform within the old Buddhism in response to the general religious reform of the period. That it was possible for the Tendai Sect to adapt itself in this way was due to the all-embracing nature of Tendai doctrine which contained Zen elements (*Shikan*-meditation in Tendai terminology) within itself as well as many others.

However, Tendai's doctrinal flexibility did not necessarily imply flexibility in the matter of church policy. Hieizan, through the court, exerted pressure even on Eisai. On the other hand the leaders of the military classes were undoubtedly seeking some new ideology to separate them from the nobility and give them their own independent identity. They warmly invited monks from Sung China to visit Japan and supported Japanese monks who wished to study in China. The Zen Sect which began in Japan as an 'old Buddhist' adaptation to new conditions was soon influenced by Sung Chinese Zen Buddhism and eventually established itself as an independent sect in its own right, breaking down the framework of its origins in old Buddhism.

The man who perhaps transferred the purest brand of Chinese

Zen Buddhism to Japan was the monk Dōgen (1200–53) who went to China with Myōzen (1184–1225), a disciple of Eisai, and achieved enlightenment under the Zen master Ju-ching (1163–1228). Unlike Eisai, Dōgen refused to compromise either with secular authority or with other Japanese Buddhist sects.

Dōgen's father was Kogano Michichika, a Minister of the Imperial Court, and his mother was the daughter of the Regent Fujiwarano Motofusa (1140–1230). His father died when Dōgen was only three and his mother when he was eight years old, so the boy was brought up by his grandfather Motofusa until taking holy orders at the age of fourteen. We do not know his motive for becoming a monk. On one hand he had, through his powerful and influential background, the opportunity for advancement within the aristocracy, while on the other he may have been reacting to the shock of his mother's death and felt a natural antipathy towards the life of intrigue which the aristocracy led in these troubled times. His decision to become a monk inevitably meant giving up any ideas of the worldly success which his background promised.

Dōgen was a stern critic both of himself and others and his attitude of lofty reserve together with his nobility of character may have been related to some idea of *noblesse oblige* stemming from his aristocratic upbringing. He maintained his uncompromising attitude towards the court, the great temples and the Bakufu even when pressures from Hieizan forced him to retire to Echizen in 1243 and his ability to do so may have stemmed from the same strength of character which had enabled him voluntarily to give up all the opportunities for advancement open to him. His thought transcended any culture and nationality. In the *Shōbō genzō* he wrote: 'Japan is a far distant country; the hearts of its people are steeped in folly.' In a passage from the later work *Shōbō genzō zuimonki* he is recorded as saying: 'Even at the temples of Sung dynasty China, among the hundreds of thousands of disciples of one master, only one or two had attained true enlightenment.'

Dōgen's Buddhism transcended the history and culture of both China and Japan and in this sense his standpoint resembles that of Nichiren who boasted that he was the greatest practitioner of the *Lotus Sutra* in Japan and regarded himself as better than any other priest in either Japan or China. However, Nichiren discussed national policies as great and important matters and called himself the 'pillar' of the Japanese nation, while Dōgen regarded such things as mere trivialities compared with the vital question of attaining enlightenment. Nichiren hated the secular authorities of his day, but Dōgen despised them. Nichiren, the fisherman's son, used his transcendental beliefs as a weapon with which to wage war on secular authority. But on the other hand Dōgen, scion of the Imperial family, according to their custom of ignoring the masses withdrew into the mountains and by intellectual means refined his own type of transcendental thought.

Dōgen was the author of many works, but the structure of his philosophy is summarized in the *Bendōwa* (1231) and fully expounded and developed in his principal work, the *Shōbō genzō* which he wrote in almost a hundred chapters over a period of years spanning from 1233 to the end of his life. In addition, his disciple Ejō (1198–1280) collected some of Dōgen's lectures to his disciples between 1234 and 1238 and edited them in simplified form in the *Shōbō genzō zuimonki*.

The *Shōbō genzō* is one of the prose masterpieces of thirteenth-century Japan. That it was not written in Chinese in accordance with the conventions of the time was not because of Dōgen's desire to make the work easily understandable to the mass of people (Mujū composed the *Shasekishū* in Japanese for precisely this reason), nor was it for 'nationalistic' reasons (the intellectuals of the Kamakura period made no connection between the national language and nationalism as such, unlike the eighteenth-century National Learning Scholars (*Kokugakusha*). Even the intensely nationalistic Nichiren wrote much of this theoretical work in Chinese. In the *Zuimonki* Dōgen is recorded as saying: 'Whether my writing is stylistically good or bad, it is important in the Buddhist way to write down the arguments as they come to mind regardless of whether or not posterity considers it bad writing.'

The author's purpose in writing was not for the benefit of his readers but for the sake of the Way, and the essence of prose to Dōgen was to write down his argument just as he thought it. The reason Dōgen, who had lived for four years in China, chose the Japanese language as the means to achieve this end was not that he was less skilled in Chinese than Shinran or Nichiren, but that he knew the language too well. He made no pretence to the concept: 'The state of enlightenment cannot be conveyed by words.'

His purpose was to attempt to describe the Zen experience in objective terms, the experience itself not being enough. The immediacy of the experience was best described in Japanese while objective discussion was best suited by Chinese. It is the tension between these two elements that produced in the *Shōbō genzō* a style remarkable in its force. In the *Shōbō genzō* Dōgen began with the following lines: 'When all phenomena appear to be Buddhist truth, we have false enlightenment, religious practices, life, death, Buddhas and people. When there are no phenomena within me, there is no enlightenment, no Buddhas, no people, no life, no death.'

The two 'when's' refer to the same moment of enlightenment. The outlooks of the world in diversity and in unity are inseparable and are perceived as such through enlightenment. This is a clear laconic presentation of the main theme of this chapter: two contradictory appearances of the truth. This abstract statement is followed by a concrete explanation through quotations from the *Sutra* and examples from various epistles. In other words, the chapter is not constructed on the basis of deductive reasoning. Rather, he takes different approaches to one single central theme through explanations at different levels of abstraction. Like this example, every chapter of *Shōbō genzō* does not use deduction and is not particularly comprehensive.

Kūkai, as revealed in his work *Jūjūshin-ron*, had a deductive and wide-ranging mind with a talent for abstract thought within an orderly framework, while Dōgen, as seen in the *Shōbō genzō*, was non-deductive and possessed a remarkable ability for swiftly changing from the abstract to the concrete and back again to the abstract in his thinking. Kūkai, writing in the ninth century, had a remarkable command of a foreign language (Chinese) which he used to great effect, while Dōgen in the thirteenth century opened up a whole new world through his polished use of the possibilities of the Japanese language which he had discovered through the medium of Chinese. An example of Dōgen's coupling of the abstract with the concrete follows: 'But, despite all, flowers we love fall, and weeds we hate grow.'

The form of this coupling derives from Chinese poetry, but the way of using it is Dōgen's own, stemming from the device of putting in every day sentiments amidst highly abstract discourse on the phenomenal world. The flowers and the weeds are objects of concrete images which bear abstract meanings. In other words, in the Kamakura period new elements were added to Japanese prose writing which had not been accomplished either by the Chinese prose of the *Ōjōyōshū* nor the Japanese prose of the *Genji monogatari*.

One of the essential characteristics of Dōgen's religion was that it was the first in Japan to place the concept of meditation (*zazen*) at the centre of the Buddhist 'Way', regarding it as the only practice to be undertaken.

> You don't need burning incense, prayer, recitation of the Buddha's name, confession, or reading scripture at all. Just sit in order to achieve the state of disappearance of the self.
>
> *(Bendōwa)*

Here, what is called the disappearance of the self is enlightenment. Sitting in meditation is the sole practice here, and is different from Eisai who argued for all the practices of the three disciplines, that is, Tendai, Esoteric, and Zen Buddhism. According to Dōgen, if one does not concentrate on one thing, one cannot achieve anything, and enlightenment and sitting in meditation are inseparable.

> As enlightenment is conditioned by practice, there is no end to enlightenment. As this practice is supported by enlightenment, there is no beginning to practice.
>
> *(Bendōwa)*

> The Buddha's great way is to always follow the supreme process which goes from determination and practice to enlightenment, an uninterrupted process just like a circle.
>
> *(Shōbō genzō, 'Gyōji')*

Even after achieving enlightenment, sitting in meditation is required constantly. *Nembutsu* (recitation) can be practised by lay believers, while constant sitting in meditation can be practised only by those who become priests and abandon all else. Here may lie the difference between Pure Land Buddhism, which was for the masses, and Zen, which was for the élite.

A second special characteristic was that Dōgen did not regard his Zen as yet another Buddhist standpoint, but as the true law of the Buddha transmitted through generations.

According to Dōgen, all the Zen masters in every generation practised 'Zazen' (sitting in meditation), constantly, and so the term 'Zen Sect' was made by rather ignorant laymen who merely observed the masters' practices.

If one regards the 'practice-enlightenment unity' as the core of Buddhism itself, then the sects which expound other practices are essentially non-Buddhist. Dōgen's denouncements of other sects of Buddhism, the Pure Land and Nembutsu Sects in particular, were extremely harsh. In the Bendōwa he wrote: 'To recite the Nembutsu just by moving the mouth is like frogs in the fields in spring croaking day and night.'

Again since Zazen is Buddhism and is the true practice which transcends time and space, the problem of whether or not it is suitable to the Mappō ceases to exist. In fact Dōgen did not even recognize the concept of the 'periods of the Buddha's law' – Shōhō, Zōhō and Mappō. 'In the true teachings of Mahayana, there is nothing to be seen concerning "True Law" or "Last Days of the Buddha's Law."' (Bendōwa) It was through generations of transmission from master to disciple that the true teachings of the Buddha came down to the present and the method of instruction from master to pupil placed special value on 'man to man transmission'. This was something which had always been emphasized by Zen masters and was not peculiar to Dōgen. It had two basic aspects. The first was the attitude that a truth which is beyond words must be directly imbibed from a personal confrontation between master and disciple where words are not used. The second was the traditionalistic view that after everything had been dissolved in the experience of absolute enlightenment (satori) it was necessary to follow the precedents laid down by earlier masters when seeking order in the relative world.

The third special characteristic lay in the understanding of the meaning of enlightenment (satori). Theoretically, two stages in this process were recognized. The first was the transition from transcending the individual self to reach the non-individual consciousness, and the second, to experience in this non-individual consciousness disappearance of all distinctions concerning variety of all phenomena as well as being and non-being, nature and appearance, and eternity and temporality.

Thus all ontological problems vanish. The indestructibility of the spirit after death is no more than a misguided belief. 'Body and soul are one.' 'Nature and appearance are inseparable.' If you take the point of view of eternity, then body and soul are both eternal. If you look at things from the angle of temporality, nature and appearance are both temporary. Thus, distinction between being and non-being is nothing but a difference in point of view.

Thus *satori* is a matter of direct experience and an awareness of the ultimate reality. That experience comprised the world rather than the world containing the experience and since problems concerning existence were all part of that experience, *satori* transcended existence. Inevitably, therefore, *satori*, both in practice and in intention, transcended all values and historical society.

Consequently, a fourth characteristic of Dōgen's religion was its absolute nature transcending all worldly considerations. *Satori* is not concerned with home, love and loyalty, family or wisdom and folly. It is realized in a state in which one has broken all these ties. Since *Zazen* was a constant practice, it was even more important than missionary work. For example, there is the story in the *Zuimonki* concerning Myōzen's visit to Sung China. Myōzen went to China for enlightenment leaving his old master on his death-bed. Dōgen considered Myōzen's attitude as a true approach to enlightenment. Twice he refused the purple robe (symbol of the highest rank in the priesthood) offered him by the Emperor. The third time he accepted it but wouldn't wear it. He steadfastly refused all invitations to go to Kamakura, preferring to remain in the Eiheiji temple in Echizen. It is quite clear from these episodes the enormous importance Dōgen attached to *Zazen*.

The next special characteristic lies in the questions of good and evil. We have already seen that neither Shinran nor Nichiren propounded any new system of ethical values and it was the same with Dōgen. However, in Dōgen's case one might say that his attitude was far more rigidly traditionalistic than that of the other Kamakura Buddhist sects. As *satori* relativized any existing values, it could not serve as the basis for a system of specific values, Dōgen said that it was only natural that through the process of *Zazen* one should come to abhor evil. However, at another point he also suggests that as society differs what is good is not always the same. 'What I think is good and what the people regard as good are not necessarily the same.' (*Zuimonki*) In other words no one can see the distinction between good and evil as the basis for a system of ethical values. Dōgen no doubt thought that one should overcome such relative considerations as ethical values and this was the reason for his rigorously traditionalistic approach.

His traditionalism was based on following, first, the traditions and conventions of the Zen temple institution of China and following, second, the teachings of the *Lotus Sutra* as being the most basic Buddhist scripture. The tradition of Zen temples in regard to the way a monk should live (what he should wear, eat, etc.) was exceptionally concrete and rigid. In 1246 Dōgen issued similar regulations for the Eiheiji based on these old rules of conduct and in the *Shōbō genzō* even had something to say about such an apparently trivial matter as washing one's face. On the one hand there is an extremely internal world of enlightenment and on the other there is an exceptionally external rigor. And between them a great effort is required to internalize the external factor and to externalize the internal factor.

However, these were rules governing the lives of monks and were not designed for laymen. The *Lotus Sutra*, however, is very specific about distinctions between good and evil regardless of whether one is monk or layman. Dōgen's view that the *Lotus Sutra* was 'the king of Sutras' was traditional to Tendai Buddhism and this was extremely basic to general judgements about good and evil.

It has already been noted that the concept of there being 'a good opportunity for salvation of a man of ill-deeds' may also be a basic concept in Christianity. Shinran, however, was greatly concerned about spiritual matters and hardly at all concerned with human values. Dōgen's turning to historical precedent over practical matters while at the same time stressing the absolute nature of *satori* in religious matters corresponds in its structure to the traditionalism of the Catholic Church with its own emphasis on the doctrines of the church outweighing matters related to individual subjectivity.

> I will follow what the master-priests of earlier times said and did whether it is good or evil.
>
> (*Zuimonki*)

If one were only to follow Buddhism and the precedents set by the old masters' then one's behaviour would naturally follow ethical value.
(ibid.)

The expression 'good or evil' in the former quotation demonstrates the difficulty in establishing the theoretical basis for ethical value; while the expression 'one naturally follows ethical value' in the latter quotation indicates an attempt to re-establish the objectivity of ethical value by relying on tradition.

Dōgen's Zen in the transcendental nature of its religious experience (as also in the case of Shinran and Nichiren's teachings) and in its conservative attitude towards culture and ethics shares the common feature of Kamakura Buddhism. While resembling the religious reform movement of sixteenth-century Europe in religious terms, in regard to the development of ethical values it was completely unlike its European counterpart. The Jōdo Shinshū, the Nichirenshū and the Zenshū became institutionalized and popularized in the Muromachi period and in the process, particularly in the case of Zen, came to fulfil a decisive cultural role. By the time that happened the warrior classes had fully developed not a 'bourgeois' society, but a feudal society.

THE ARISTOCRATIC RESPONSE

The aristocracy reacted in two basic ways to the military power of Kamakura. The first, as we have already seen, was to seize every opportunity to set in motion plots aimed at resurrecting the old system. The unsuccessful Jōkyū uprising of 1221, led by the Retired Emperor Go-Toba (1180–1239), was a typical example of this reaction. The second reaction is well illustrated by the policy of Fujiwarano Kanezane (1149–1207) and his close relationship with Yoritomo; Kanezane's policy being to preserve the autonomy of Kyōto by compromise with Kamakura and to maintain for the aristocracy as many as possible of the special privileges, especially 'shōen', they had enjoyed under the old system. Many individual aristocrats adopted this second attitude as a means of self-preservation.

The general conditions of the time in this respect are well revealed by the Meigetsuki, a diary covering the thirty-six years of the period 1180 to 1235, written in Japanese-flavoured Chinese prose by Fujiwarano Teika (1162–1241) who served the Kujō family to which Kanezane belonged. Judging from the *Meigetsuki*, Teika's main interests seemed to be *waka* poetry, advancement within the bureaucracy and the preservation of his *shōen*. Later we shall come to Teika's poetry, but the means he adopted to achieve his other two aims was to make maximum use of individual contacts made with the rulers of Kamakura through the power and influence of the Kujō family (after their power waned, he tried to approach their opponents) and other prominent aristocratic families.

For example, in response to a request from the Shōgun Minamotono Sanetomo (1192–1219), Teika sent him a manuscript copy of the *Manyōshū* and was thereby able to enlist the aid of Sanetomo in resolving a dispute concerning his estates. Also to strengthen the position of his son Tameie (1198–1273) he arranged for him a marriage with the daughter of a powerful Kantō *gokenin* family. Whatever attitude the aristocracy might have taken towards Kamakura, whether they tried to plot against it or to compromise with it, they must have had a sense of cultural supremacy.

Since *waka* poetry was institutionalized and was the pivot around which that culture had revolved, the aristocracy at the beginning of the Kamakura period at the transitional period between the regimes was obliged to cling to this poetic form with special tenacity. Typical examples of this were the Retired Emperor Go-Toba and Fujiwarano Teika. Go-Toba ordered the compilation of the *Shin kokin waka-shū* and in 1201 organized an Imperial Bureau of Waka Poetry prior to embarking on his attempt to topple the Kamakura government politically. It was Fujiwarano Teika, author of numerous poems and works on the theory of poetry such as *Kindai shūka*, who was made one of the compilers of the *Shin kokinshū*.

The theory of *waka* poetry had been evolving since early in the Heian period. It classified *waka* poems in a manner similar to Chinese poetics, and recommended a list of practices improper in poetry as a basis for judgement in poetry contests. The institutionalization of *waka* and efforts to establish objective values in *waka* had developed hand-in-hand. However, after the time of Teika's father (Fujiwarano Shunzei (1114–1204) compiler of the *Senzaishū* and author of the theoretical work *Korai fūteishō*).

waka theory in the Kamakura period, particularly through the efforts of Teika himself, escaped from the direct influence of the theory of Chinese (*shi*) poetry and went beyond simple outlines of form and improper practices to assert new aesthetic values. An awareness of purely literary values distinct from other values developed, resulting in an extension of the methodology of the creative process, already established in the Heian period. When the regime which had controlled the institutionalization of *waka* collapsed, there developed a consciousness of poetry as having a value which transcended any regime and this was directly presented in the works of theory written in the Kamakura period.

There were two aspects to the contents of such works. First came the assertion of aesthetic values expressed in such words as *yūgen* and *ushin*. *Yūgen* implied an indescribable subtle feeling or emotion to be read, as it were, between the lines and suggested by the usage of words (Shunzei and Chōmei). *Ushin* seems to have been applied to refined tasteful expression or that of graceful scenes (Teika and Go-Toba). Since, however, neither of these terms was rigidly defined in *waka* theory and there were various ways of looking even at a poem supposed to possess these qualities, it is perhaps impossible to be certain of their meanings in the strictest sense. There is, therefore, not a great deal of sense in charting their historical development. The important point, however, is not what these values were in precise terms, but the fact that thirteenth-century Japanese aristocracy emphasized a special set of aesthetic values as one of their responses to their exclusion from warrior society. Nevertheless, these values which can be deduced only vaguely from works on *waka* theory are mirrored in most of the poems of the *Shin kokinshū* which we shall come to later.

The second aspect to *waka* theory was its traditionalism in discussing the stream of Imperial anthologies beginning with the *Manyōshū* through the *Kokinshū* onwards. When traditional society was in the process of collapse, there developed an awareness of cultural tradition and both Shunzei and his son Teika, while describing this tradition attempted to place themselves within it. In terms of the composition of poetry itself, this corresponds to the *honkadori* poems which were new poems composed on the basis of some famous poem from earlier times, presenting a different meaning and atmosphere from that of the original poem, but having a reverberatory effect towards the original. (In Western literature the *Waste Land* of the American-born but naturalized British T. S. Eliot may be seen as a parallel and in China poets of the Sung dynasty also used the similar practice of taking quotations from the classics and putting them into their poems.)

On the other hand, in the traditionalism in the theory of *waka* poems, there could be found an attitude which not only ennumerated and described poems of the past chronologically but also tried to discern a certain direction of development in style even though it was in a limited range of *waka*. Here, the embryo of a new historical awareness may be seen in terms of growth from a mere chronology to a history of development. In this sense works of poetical theory, in particular the *Kindai shūka*, were not perhaps totally unrelated to historical works such as the *Gukanshō*.

The *Shin kokin waka-shū* (or *Shin kokinshū*) is a work in twenty volumes containing 1978 *waka* poems selected by Minamotono Michitomo, Fujiwarano Ariie, Fujiwarano Teika, Fujiwarano Ietaka, Fujiwarano Masatsune and the Priest Jakuren at the command of the Retired Emperor Go-Toba. The classification of the poems basically follows that of the *kokinshū* except that two categories in the *Kokinshū*, 'Poems on Things' and 'Poems from Imperial Ceremonies', are excluded and replaced by 'Shinto poems' and 'Buddhist poems'.

There are, however, other more important differences. To begin with, in the *Shin kokinshū*, there are hardly any of the anonymous poems which appear in such numbers in the *Kokinshū* and most of the poets represented are more or less contemporary with the date of compilation, an indication that in the *Shin kokinshū* an attempt was made to assert the new poetic trends of the times. Moreover, the standard-bearers of the new trend were 'professional', specialist poets. The age of the institutionalization of *waka* was at an end and the age of professionalism and specialization had begun.

However, this was not yet the age of the literature of individualism and the poets did not have the prime aim of presenting their own personality in their poems, but the attitude that anonymous poems could not be considered as authentic poems and the close association of poet and poem were for the first time firmly estab-

lished. To put this another way, one might say that after the
collapse of the society into which poets from the time of the
Kokinshū had been thoroughly integrated, literature became not a
necessary part of social activity but a subjective individual enterprise. A second major difference lies in the fact that whereas of
the eight major poets (contributing more than ten poems each) of
the *Kokinshū*, only two were women, of the thirty-one major
poets of the *Shin kokinshū*, eleven were women. This doubtless
meant the official recognition of feminine literature throughout
the Heian period.

Towards the end of his life Fujiwarano Teika had the fifty-four
chapters of the *Genji monogatari* copied and wrote about it in his
diary (entry for the sixteenth day of the second month, 1225) as
follows: 'Even though it is an embellished fictional work, it was
created by a genius. And so we must value it very highly.'

He does not speak of even the *Genji monogatari* as the representative masterpiece of Heian period literature, but says that since it
is the expression of a great literary talent it cannot be dismissed
on condition that it is 'an embellished fictional work'. *Monogatari*,
he appears to have thought, were stories written for women by
women and, with certain exceptions, no more than 'embellished
fictional works'. Therefore in the Heian period although there
were numerous theoretical works on *waka* poetry, there were
none on *monogatari* fiction and even female poets themselves did
not write on *waka* theory. Against this background we must
consider the significance of the fact that a third of the poets of an
imperial anthology such as the *Shin kokinshū* were women. It was
perhaps not until the editors of *Shin kokinshū* looked back all
through Heian court culture that they became aware of the existence of 'female literature'. A third difference lies in the fact that
poems of the *honkadori* type, mentioned above, did not appear at
all in the *Kokinshū*. The *honka* of the *Shin kokinshū* were taken from
the *Kokinshū*, the classical anthology which of course was not
'classical' at the time it was compiled, any more than the *Manyōshū* was 'classical' when viewed from the standpoint of Kino
Tsurayuki. One of the technical features of the *Shin kokinshū* is
that in a poem there are many short breaks or pauses, and endings
with a substantive. Doubtless the intention behind this was to
produce as wide as possible a variety of images in the limited
thirty-one syllables available. For example,

The floating bridge of
my spring night dreams
has collapsed.
The sky with trailing clouds
parted by a mountain peak.
(Fujiwarano Teika, Vol. 1 of the *Shin kokinshū*)

This is not a *honkadori*, but the floating 'bridge of dreams' is taken from the *Genji monogatari* and the image of the clouds drifting apart is a subtle expression of the sweet sorrow of lovers parting.

If I should live through these days,
I shall have memories to enjoy;
for now with deep regret I think of
days gone by when I was sad.
(Fujiwarano Kiyosuke, Vol. 18)

There is anticipation that the view of the present will change in the future just as the view of the past at that time has changed now. There is no play on words in this poem, but the complex relationship between past, present and future is skilfully condensed into the thirty-one syllables.

As the smoke rises from the brushwood fire
in the evening, I cough and am reminded
of the unforgettable fires of death.
(Retired Emperor Go-Toba, Vol. 8)

Almost every word in this poem has a double meaning and it is possible to interpret it either as a lament or as a love poem. Borrowings from the classics, the condensing of complex meaning into a few words and the extensive use of *kakekotoba* are all features of the *Shin kokinshū* in general and, in particular, of the poems of Teika himself.

Apart from the previously mentioned works of *waka* theory and the Meigetsuki, a collection of Teika's poetry was compiled under the title *Shūi gusō*. His copying and collation work on the *Genji monogatari* has already been mentioned and in addition to this his interest extended to other Heian period *monogatari* fiction and diary literature.

According to the *Go-Toba-in Onkuden* which is said to have been written while the Retired Emperor was exiled to Oki Island in his last years, Teika seemed to be arrogant at least as far as his attitude towards *waka* was concerned – 'He acted as if he was the only man in the world. Simply too calculated.' As has been previously mentioned, he took whatever means were available to be promoted in rank and office and to preserve his estate. On the other hand Go-Toba himself was the author not only of a work on *waka* theory, the *Go-Toba-in Onkuden*, but of a collection of poems compiled under the title of *Go-Toba-in goshu*.

Go-Toba himself seems to have been a capricious tyrant whose court was nonetheless always the scene of the utmost gaiety with many aristocrats and Shirabyōshi courtesans. His ineptitude and reactionary thinking as a politician is well demonstrated by his numerous plots against the Bakufu culminating in the disastrous failure of the Jōkyū rebellion. For all that, his talents as a poet are undeniable.

The question remains of the relationship between the poets of the *Shin kokinshū*, such as Teika and Go-Toba, and Kamakura Buddhism. The priest Jien (1155–1225), younger brother of Kujō Kanezane and a capable poet was the abbot of a Tendai temple (the Enryakuji) so, naturally, as we have seen, was highly critical of the *Nembutsu* sects in his historical work *Gukanshō*. However, Kanezane himself was well-disposed towards these sects. Teika too, who was in the service of the Kujō family and became involved with Jien through the medium of poetry, was just as critical of Hōnen and his followers as Jien. He made a copy of the *Makashikan*, a Tendai book of meditation. The words *mappō* and *mujō* (transience) constantly occur in Teika's diary *Meigetsu-ki*, but it is difficult to judge the extent of his belief and we know nothing of the religious attitudes of Go-Toba. It seems most likely that both men, while being adherents of the old Buddhism, were basically not very concerned with religious problems.

The final volume of the *Shin kokinshū* comprises sixty-three poems classified under the general heading 'Buddhist poems' of which twenty-four were written by poets who were alive in 1200, in other words little more than 1% of the whole *Shin kokinshū*. Of these twenty-four poems eight are by Jien written in praise of the *Lotus Sutra* and the remaining sixteen are mostly concerned with the Western Paradise and the coming of Amida. These factors cannot be found in the *Kokinshū*, but in *Shin kokinshū* we can see the influence of Pure Land teachings as they had affected and permeated aristocratic society since the time of the *Ōjōyōshū*.

However, when we look at the 100 poems which comprise volume eight ('Elegies'), we find that there is no mention at all of either Amida or the Western Paradise. Since these poems are elegies, most were composed in lament of someone's death. However, even though the poet was a Pure Land Buddhist, if he did not think of the Western Paradise nor mention Amida in the face of somebody's death, his faith in the Pure Land Buddhism must have been essentially different from that of Shinran or Hōnen. The poets of the *Shin kokinshū* writing on this subject lament the premature departure of the deceased from this world, sympathize with the loneliness of those left behind, present memories of the dead person and speak about his appearing in dreams and the transience of this world, but never mention the other world. It represents precisely the same attitude towards death on the part of the lyric poet which had prevailed in both the *Manyōshū* and the *Kokinshū*. The 'Pure Land' teachings as they appear in the twentieth volume of the *Shin kokinshū* in the poems written by Jakuren, Shunzei and Saigyō (1118–90) are conventional observations rather than the expression of positive beliefs.

Although the new Kamakura Buddhism did not exert any direct influence on the *Shin kokinshū*, this is not to say that there was no relationship between them. The teachings of the Jōdo and Jōdo Shinshū sects found their support among people at large in the provinces (we have already seen that a noble such as Kujō Kanezane was sympathetic towards Hōnen, but this was a rare case), and the teachings of Zen Buddhism among the warrior class.

The people who wrote and compiled the *Shin kokinshū* were court nobles, members of the Kyōto aristocracy. There is thus no direct influence of the new Buddhism on the poetry, but there is a similarity between both as products of their times in that while Kamakura Buddhism individualized religion ('protection of the country' replaced by salvation of the individual; the personal practices of *Nembutsu* and *Zazen* replacing the great temples), the *Shin kokinshū* individualized literature (few anonymous poems; poetry no longer practised as a necessity of life in court society, but as the individual expression of people more or less excluded from society).

While Kamakura Buddhism was at war with the Buddhism of the ancient temples of the Heian period, the aesthetics of the *Shin kokinshū* warred with the flavour of the new warrior-created society. Just as Shinran found support and followers in the provinces, the aesthetics of the *Shin kokinshū* made converts among the warrior classes, notably Saigyō and Sanetomo.

Saigyō, whose secular name was Satō Norikiyo, was born into a *samurai* family and after entering the priesthood in 1140 when still a young man, he travelled widely in Japan. The *Sanka-shū* (date of compilation unknown), the principal collection of his poetry, contains 1552 poems of which several were later included in the *Shin kokinshū*. Stylistically, Saigyō avoided the elaborate technique of Teika and his poems are simple and direct, often stemming from his own emotions and experiences.

> I cannot control
> My desire to go wondering,
> But shall I do what I want
> No matter what happens?
>
> How mutable our life!
> I long to live a thousand years,
> But time elapses like a short, short dream.

The feeling that one cannot control one's self and so one should do as one likes no matter what happens is neither that of *Yūgen* nor *Ushin*. The phrase to 'live a thousand years' probably suggests his longing for perpetual days of love. The author substitutes a special kind of emotional force deriving from his own experience for the elaborate *Shin kokinshū* device of borrowing from the classics.

Most of Saigyō's poems, however, rely on such conventional themes as seasons and cherry blossom, birds, the wind and the moon figure prominently in his poetry. He was no different from the intellectual aristocrat poets of the Heian court in that on his travels he seldom seems to have seen nature through his own eyes. At this period even painters did not actually visit a famous scene in order to paint it and in poetry it was not realism that was important but the use of often-repeated conventional epithets namely *utamakura*. For example, in 1207 the Retired Emperor Go-Toba commissioned four painters to depict scenes of famous places on the *shōji* of the newly built Saishō Shitennō-in temple and when Teika had selected what scenes they were to be, one of the painters said he would like to go and see his particular theme for himself. This artist must have been exceptional since this ran entirely contrary to normal practice and what was true for painters was even more so for poets.

In aristocratic culture spring meant flowers and flowers meant cherry blossoms, regardless of the natural distribution of Japanese *flora*. The aristocracy seem not to have been aware of any other flower and so Saigyō too, thoroughly integrated as he was into that culture and society, did not see them either.

> Would that I could die
> in spring
> beneath a flowering cherry tree,
> lit by full February's moon.

This was regarded by contemporaries as Saigyō's best poem, perhaps because it proved the total submission of the warrior classes (Saigyō was of *samurai* origin) to aristocratic culture.

Minamotono Sanetomo (1192–1219), the third Kamakura *Shōgun*, greatly admired Kyōto culture, married the daughter of an aristocrat and studied poetry under Fujiwarano Teika. After Yoritomo's death in 1199, the power of the Hōjō family greatly increased and Sanetomo's elder brother Yoriie and his son were both killed. Sanetomo himself, after becoming *Shōgun* at the very early age of eleven, was murdered at the age of twenty-eight by his nephew, Yoriie's second son. The third *Shōgun* was no more than a pawn in the power struggle between warrior leaders and it seems likely that he realized this fact.

When it was suggested to him that he quit aspiring for promotion in rank at the royal court, he answered that as he thought he would be the last of the Minamoto clan he hoped for at least some promotion. Two months after this, in spite of his retainers' objections, he planned to go to China and told a Chinese named Chen Ho-Chin to build a Chinese style ship which was completed the next year. However, Sanetomo had to abandon his plans because the ship wouldn't float. It seems likely that he made his plan with the intention of going into exile.

It seems that it was not only the Kyōto aristocrats who were excluded from military power, but also even the *Shōgun* himself:

> In this and that
> What an unstable world it is!
> Some are happy, some are not.
>
> (Kinkaishū)
>
> Reasonable or unreasonable,
> We see everything in this world as
> Nothing but a dream.
>
> (Ibid.)

When Sanetomo wrote of 'this-world', he was undoubtedly thinking about it not in terms of male-female relationship but in political terms. Since in this sphere he was only a puppet in chains not able even to flee from the country, Buddhism and the poetry of the *Shin kokinshū* provided his only avenues of escape and it is perhaps not surprising that the young Sanetomo chose the latter.

The *Kinkaishū*, the anthology of Sanetomo's poetry, was compiled at an unknown date and contains either 660 or 700 poems, according to which manuscript one uses. Many of the poems including the *honkadori*, are based on the *Shin kokinshū*, in terms of style.

> Since the time when you were young and
> First tied your hair with a deep purple ribbon,
> I have never thought that
> Our relationship was shallow.
>
> (Ibid.)

This poem has an introduction which reads 'There was a girl whom I was conversing with in secret. She said that she intended to go some place far away, and so . . .'

Niether in the poetry of Saigyō nor Sanetomo is there any element which enables the reader to visualize the warrior background from which both poets came. Both Saigyō and Sanetomo were converts to the collapsed aristocratic culture and wrote their poems not for the warrior class but for Go-Toba's Imperial Bureau of Waka. However, this does not necessarily mean that all the way through, the poems of the *Kinkaishū* adhere to the elegant and elaborate technique of the *Shin kokinshū*. Here, we can also find the subject matter and rhetoric which Kamono Mabuchi (1697–1769) was later to characterize as a 'masculine style' and Masaoka Shiki (1867–1902) to judge as one of the best since the *Manyoshū*.

> The breakers of the ocean
> Pound and thunder on the rocks,
> Smashing, breaking, clearing,
> They crash upon the shore.

The Kyōto *waka* establishment did not consider such subjects as the frightful waves of the ocean to be normal material for poetry. While Sanetomo thoroughly admired aristocratic culture, there are aspects in which his work transcends its framework, probably because at that period Sanetomo as a poet in Kamakura, was completely isolated as Shōgun. There must have been times when Sanetomo stood alone in silence, gazing at the waves pounding the Yuiga-hama beach.

Many of the aristocrat-intellectuals of the *Shin kokinshū* were positive in their defence of Heian court culture, but on the other hand there were members of the lower aristocracy who adopted an escapist attitude towards the vicissitudes of the times as in the case of Kenreimon-in Ukyōno Daibu and Kamono Chōmei.

Kenreimon-in Ukyōno Daibu's father was a celebrated calligrapher and her mother a famous *koto* player, while she herself was a lady-in-waiting to Kenreimon-in, the second daughter of Tairano Kiyomori and consort of the Emperor Takakura. She was also the lover of Tairano Shigemori's second son, Tairano Sukemori (1158–85). Towards the end of her life she composed more than 300 poems, known as the *Kenreimon-in Ukyōno Daibu-shū*, which were based on her memories of court life, her affair with Sukemori and the fall of the Heike clan and its aftermath. To her the fall of the Heike clan meant the death of her lover and end of the world which had nurtured their love and thereafter she was left with only her memories. She visited Kitayama in autumn, a place that she and Sukemori had 'frequented'. She stood alone looking at the burnt down site of the Heike palace where now only 'foundations were left'. At the Jakkōin temple in Ōhara, she met Kenreimon-in who was alone and ruined at the time.

> I don't know whether
> The present or the past is a dream.
> No matter how much I ponder it
> There is no such thing as reality.

It was not just reality which seemed like a dream to this woman who continued to live out her life in memories of the past 'à la recherche du temps perdu'. She could perceive that which she had not been able to see while living completely integrated into court society. 'I was accustomed to looking at the moon' 'but I felt as if I had seen the starry night for the first time' is a good example. She was accustomed to appreciating the beauty of the moon not out of love for nature but due to cultural convention. However, a realization of the beauty of a starry night is an awakening to a love for nature. When she lost her society, she discovered nature.

Kamono Chōmei (1153–1216) was the son of a Shinto priest, but was prevented from following the same profession himself, as he had desired, by a family quarrel. His entrée to the court of Go-Toba was in his capacity as a poet and perhaps also as a skilful player of the *biwa*, but from the beginning court society was not his metier. When that society began to collapse, Chōmei went off into the mountains near Kyōto where he lived in a small cottage and turned to writing and meditation. There he wrote his most famous work, the *Hōjōki* (1212) and the *Mumyōshō* (date of writing unknown).

The artist who longed for, but could not be integrated into, the aristocratic society sharply observed contemporary Kyōto customs and the *waka* establishment. His perceptiveness found vivid expression in his works. The collapse of the old regime did not mean the collapse of the whole world to him. Rather it meant the discovery of a new world through seclusion and Buddhism. That discovery seems to have created the distance necessary for him to look at things objectively.

The *Hōjōki* was based on Yoshishigeno Yasutane's tenth-century Chinese prose work, the *Chiteiki* (982), but written in Japanese with additional observations supplied by Chōmei himself from his own experience. He begins by describing the desolation and ruin of the capital, proceeds to speak of the cruelty of heaven and earth and the human heart and finishes with an account of the joys of a life of seclusion – all of which exactly follows the pattern of the *Chiteiki*. A large proportion of the text of the *Hōjōki* is essentially a free translation of the Chinese prose of the *Chiteiki*. Take the following passage from the *Chiteiki*:

A man of low rank who has close dealings with an influential family cannot laugh heartily even when he is at his most cheerful; he cannot cry openly even when he is at his saddest. He is anxious in his behaviour, insecure in his mind, exactly like a sparrow or a crow when it comes close to a hawk.

Compare it with this passage from the *Hōjōki*:

Suppose he is a person of little account and lives near the mansion of a great man. He may have occasion to rejoice very heartily over something, but he cannot do so openly, and in the same way, if he be in trouble, it is quite unthinkable that he should lift up his voice and weep. He must be very circumspect in his deportment and bear himself in a suitably humble manner, and his feelings are like those of a sparrow near a hawk's nest.

The author of the *Chiteiki* describes his house in seclusion as follows:

When I got old I built a residence, . . . like a traveller stays at an inn, or like an old silk-worm spins its cocoon.

Compare it with this passage from the *Hōjōki*:

I am now sixty years old, and this hut in which I shall spend the last remaining years of my dew-like existence is like the shelter some hunter might build for a night's lodging in the hills, or like the cocoon some old silkworm might spin.

These two brief comparisons show clearly the similarity between the two works. In his secluded residence Yoshishigeno Yasutane built an Amida hall and collected Chinese books which he enjoyed reading after reciting the *Nembutsu*. In his 'ten foot square hut', Kamono Chōmei had an image of Amida and a collection of books on *waka* poetry and music which he read when he had his fill of Buddhist scripture.

However, the *Hōjōki* as a whole is more than a free translation of the *Chiteiki*. The structure, the simple prose style and the gist of it all reflect the *Chiteiki*, but there are differences. First, the *Hōjōki* depicts the widespread conflagrations, the earthquakes and the epidemics in far more detail than does the *Chiteiki* and far more vividly records the wretched scenes in the streets of Kyōto; this is a clear reflection of the difference between aristocratic culture at its zenith and in its period of decay. Second, there is a difference in the religious tone. In the *Chiteiki*, the performance of the *Nembutsu* is at one with all the other pleasures of seclusion, whereas to Kamono Chōmei it was a practice of real significance: 'I ask myself these questions . . . in my heart there is no answer.

The most I can do is to murmur two or three times a day a perchance unavailing invocation to Amida.'

The *Nembutsu* of Hōnen's age was far more than a simple pleasure of seclusion which was characteristic of the *Nembutsu* of Genshin's time. However, Kamono Chōmei was not completely converted to Hōnen's beliefs. While understanding what they were, he could continue to write *waka* and play his musical instruments despising himself for doing it. The *Mumyōshō* summarizes Chōmei's views and attitudes on both these subjects as purely secular matters unrelated to Buddhism. This work consists of eighty passages of varying lengths all mutually independent and not arranged in any special order, discussing poetry and relating anecdotes about poets ancient and modern (the theory of *waka* is mentioned in passing, but is not Chōmei's essential concern).

The contrast between this work and the neatly structured *Hōjōki* is so vivid that we can see how much the latter owed to the *Chiteiki*. When he wrote the *Mumyōshō* he did not utilize any previous works as a model but wrote about what he himself was familiar with. Obviously he did not pay any attention to the structure as a whole but wrote each item as a portion of the whole for its own intrinsic interest. He was clearly interested in facts in detail and his observation was sharp. For example, on reading of a spring near the Ōsaka barrier in one of Kino Tsurayuki's poems, he hears that this same spring has long since dried up and the location of it is known only to an old monk of the Mii-dera temple. Chōmei visits the monk and receives instructions from him as to how to find the site of the spring which he does only to confirm that it has indeed dried up. Nevertheless, he clearly derives considerable satisfaction from knowing that the spring which appeared in Tsurayuki's poem did once really exist. We can find other examples of such on-the-spot personal verification of facts in *Mumyōshō*. Here again we notice a keen interest in detailed concrete description, a common way of thinking and feeling, which is also a marked characteristic of the indigenous world view, rather than an abstract ordering of the whole. This interest in concrete description may be found in Buddhist tales from the *Nihon Ryōiki* and various picture scrolls from the *Genji Monogatari* scroll.

Chōmei's interest in verifying facts on the spot is a manifestation of the model Japanese concern with the concrete as opposed to the abstract, regarding always the facts are more important than universal principles and everyday experience than transcendental concepts. The *Chiteiki* was modelled on Chinese literary works and the *Hōjōki* was modelled on the *Chiteiki*, which had been written in the manner of classical Chinese literature. In fact the *Hōjōki* represents the late twelfth- and early thirteenth-century Japanization of foreign culture. And that Japanization meant defiance of the transcendental nature of Kamakura Buddhism. What defied it was the this-worldly nature of indigenous thought which, though unconsciously, was totally assimilated in the author's thought, and which permeates every page of the *Mumyōshō*. In this sense, Chōmei represented the deeply rooted traditional mode of thought in this period of transition. However, the *Mumyōshō* tells us more than this. His accounts of the role of poetry in the daily lives of the aristocracy, of feuds between poets and of burning enthusiasm for poetry leaves us in no doubt as to the true meaning of the institutionalization of *waka*.

The new awareness of history on the part of the aristocratic intelligentsia, nurtured by the collapse of the old order, reached its peak of expression in Jien's *Gukanshō* (*c*. 1220). Jien was the son of the *Kampaku* Fujiwarano Tadamichi (1097–1164) and the younger brother of Kujō Kanezane. He was also abbot of the Tendai Sect Enryakuji temple and a formidable poet, the author of a collection of poems known as the *Shūgyokushū*.

The *Gukanshō* is in seven volumes and provides the genealogies of the Emperors of Japan and leading ministers, and an account of the history of Japan from the earliest times to 1219 in fairly cursory form apart from the period beginning with the Hōgen war in 1156 which is treated in much greater detail. The final volume is a combined summary of the whole work and analysis of early thirteenth-century political conditions with suggested remedies. In this respect the work should be seen in the context of the following year's (1221) abortive attempt by Go-Toba to overthrow the Bakufu in the Jōkyū insurrection. In this sense it may be seen as a response to the policies of Kujō Kanezane who previously had known the mind of and acted through the will of Yoritomo. A feature of the *Gukanshō* lies in the conscious use of *katakana-majiri* script. There were two reasons for using such a mode of writing; one was that even among men of learning, there were few who could really understand Chinese; the other was that one could express almost everything in Japanese and be understood by most people. Jien was perhaps the first man to realize the possibilities of expression through the Japanese language and it was an important and original contribution ranking with Dōgen's *Shōbō genzō*, also written in Japanese. Doubtless, as in the case of Dōgen, Jien's decision not to use Chinese must have been not because his knowledge of it was too poor.

The most important aspect of the *Gukanshō* is that it was not a simple chronological record of events from the past, but an attempt to explain these events through a kind of causal relationship. The idea of historical development is also present in *mappō* Buddhist thought and in the *waka* theory of Shunzei and Teika as we have already seen, but the former did not explain the causal relationship between concrete historical events while the latter was confined to the extremely narrow field of the development of form and style in poetry.

The *Gukanshō* was the first work to attempt to explain what had happened and what was happening in the world as the manifestation of underlying causes and reasons, and no work as successful in presenting the past as a series of inter-related events was produced until the *Tokushi yoron* of 1712. Jien attempted to discover some kind of order or system in the past declaring that it was precisely because just such an order and regularity was missing that Japan had been in such chaos since the Hōgen wars. As Jien saw it the world was in order in the age of the Fujiwaras when the Regency flourished, then came the system of Rule by Retired Emperor culminating in the collapse of the rule of the Regents and the menace of warrior power to aristocratic society. It is not surprising that the question of why things turned out this way was posed not simply by the nobility but by the Fujiwara family itself. Since the reason for this was not adequately explained by the Buddhist *mappō* concept, some kind of principle of historical development had to be discovered. This principle was based on the concept of *dōri* (reason) which has different meanings in the *Gukanshō* according to the context in which it is used. It is used both in a metaphysical sense as meaning the absolute nature or essence of things and in a moral sense as meaning justice or 'right'. While admitting that the course of events can be altered by the intervention of supernatural and transcendental power, Jien stresses that the *dōri* should be the basis on which political leaders made decisions. He stresses the idea over and over again that as the Retired Emperors disregarded the Fujiwaras, a chaotic world where the warrior class flourished came about.

The question remains of how Jien related *dōri* in its metaphysical 'absolute' sense to *dōri* in its political sense. The former he termed *Myō* {noumenon (i.e. gods and Buddhas)}, the latter *Ken* {phenomenon (i.e. men)} and recognized seven inter-related categories:

Category 1: *Myō* and *Ken* in harmony and the world permeated with *dōri*.
Category 2: Man alive in the 'phenomenal' world but not cognizant of the change in divine reason.
Category 3: *Dōri* existing in the phenomenal world but considered erroneous from the divine point of view.
Category 4: Reconsideration of considering things to be 'good' when they are later found to be 'bad'.
Category 5: Reaching the proper decision after considering many alternatives.
Category 6: Reaching an improper decision after considering many alternatives.
Category 7: Blind reckless conduct and no one understanding *dōri*.

In only the first three stages is the relationship between *Myō* and *Ken* touched on, the remaining four relating only to purely political matters. The *dōri* or, in other words, the principle which governs historical development is thought of by Jien as a constant factor – if it were not so it would be impossible to understand the changes occurring in different periods as having any rhyme or reason. Also it should be noted that this principle applies only to decisions made by the gods, the Buddhas and political leaders and is in no way related to human and cultural factors beyond this. This firmly relates not only to Jien's views on Buddhism (something which transcends time and culture in its relevance) but also to his political view as a descendant of the Regents and a member of the ruling classes.

The *Gukanshō* was written against the background of sharp tension between Kyōto and Kamakura and its author's attitude towards the warrior classes is well shown by his words; 'now we have the age of the warriors, we are truly in the period of *mappō'*.

However, as a historian, his estimation of the power of the warrior class can be found in the following comment: 'Now is the time when many warriors should find and follow the right path.' No matter how severely we criticize the warriors, we cannot find a better ruling class. Therefore, we should try rather to lead them to the right path. This is his conclusion.

Jien's realism as a historian makes a refreshing contrast to the foolish policies of those Kyōto rulers who entered upon the Jōkyū rebellion.

Fujiwarano Teika defended culture; Kenreimon-in Ukyōno Daibu was in search of 'temps perdu'; Kamono Chōmei retired from the world and made his observations on it; Jien wrote the first Japanese language 'history' of his country. All these were the responses of the last Heian court intellectuals to the new age. What all had in common was a complete lack of sympathy with the warrior classes, the people at large and indeed anyone outside aristocratic society; that they were totally unreceptive of the influence of the new Kamakura Buddhism; and that when writing, they wrote for the people of their own circle and them alone.

THE HEIKE MONOGATARI AND THE SHASEKISHŪ

The culture of the Heian period reached the *samurai* and the people at large by two main paths. The first was through what are known as *katarimono*. The model example of *katarimono* was the *Heikyoku* – ballads on the theme of the Heike wars narrated to the accompaniment of *biwa* music by blind priests known as *Biwa hōshi*. The *Heike monogatari* was in reality compiled on the basis of these heikyoku. The second was through the Buddhist 'sermons' delivered in the temples. It may be thought that the Buddhist *setsuwa* tales of which the *Shasekishū* is a representative thirteenth-century example were collected as materials for these 'sermons'.

We do not know in any certain detail who listened to the recitations of the blind priests or who heard the 'sermons' of the monks, but what is sure is that the audiences were not made up *only* of aristocratic intellectuals and that performances were given not only in Kyōto but further afield in the provinces. It is in the

nature of the audience rather than in the origins of the authors
that the basic difference lies between on the one hand the *Heike
monogatari* and the *setsuwa* tales typified by the *Shasekishū* and on
the other hand Heian court literature typified by *waka* poetry and
monogatari.

In all cases the authors were still either aristocrats or monks,
but the audience began to expand beyond the narrow confines of
aristocratic society. In the thirteenth century for the first time
these authors began to write for social classes different from their
own, resulting in a movement away from the 'writer equals
reader' situation (i.e. where the author was writing purely for his
own circle) towards a situation where the reader (or listener) was
removed from the writer. Naturally the illiterate or almost illiterate audience exerted their own influence on the contents of the
stories they were told and consequently we find new types of
character (not present in the literature for the aristocracy) emerging in the stories. For the first time we begin to see a reflection of
the values and feelings of the ordinary people in literature.

The authorship of the *Heike monogatari* is open to question.
According to Yoshida Kenkō in the *Tsurezure-gusa* (early fourteenth century) Jien employed a learned official from Shinano
Province named Yukinaga, who wrote the work and taught a
blind man named Shōbutsu to recite it. Later, Biwa-hoshi learned
it. Shōbutsu was a native of the Eastern provinces and asked the
warriors of that part of the country all kinds of questions about
military matters and the deeds of heroes which Yukinaga later
wrote down. What Yoshida says is by no means confirmation of
the authorship, but he suggests that while the author was a man
of aristocratic origin he had considerable help from someone else
thoroughly familiar with the customs of the *samurai*.

The theory that the author was an aristocrat is supported by
several features of the *Heike monogatari*, namely that it draws
heavily on chronicles and diaries from these earlier times, that it
is filled with Buddhist terminology and quotations from the
Chinese classics, and that it adopts much the same political
standpoint as the *Gukanshō*. On the other hand, the detailed
descriptions of the lives and customs of the *samurai* of the Eastern
provinces argues for a participation of those thoroughly acquainted with conditions there. In this context, it seems clear that
a *Biwa hōshi* would have been in close contact with the *samurai* (his

audience) and could have learned such details from them. What is important here is not the question of who first recited it but the role played by the audience in relation to the reciter.

The *Heike monogatari* is a chronological record of the rise and fall of the Taira family (the Heike clan) which is traced from its origins through antagonism with the court, the Gempei war, to its final defeat at the hands of Yoritomo. The central characters or 'heroes' are the leaders of the warriors, Tairano Kiyomori in the first part, Kiso Yoshinaka in the middle and Minamotono Yoshitsune in the latter part. However, none of them is the traditional idealized hero of the type appearing in such works as the *monogatari*, fiction of the Heian period, or the *Hōgen monogatari* (Tametomo) and the *Heiji monogatari* (Yoshihira). Kiyomori is criticized both morally and religiously not only (from the author's standpoint) as a desecrator of the dignity of the court and the Regency, but also as a man without any compassion for his wives and lovers, a crude autocrat who even in death desires not the Pure Land, but the head of Yoritomo. Kiso Yoshinaka, the occupier of Kyōto, is depicted as an ignorant and boorish bumpkin and even Minamotono Yoshitsune with his short stature, pale complexion and protruding teeth is hardly a conventional storybook hero.

To the author the world in which these characters move and rule is a world in *mappō* and what governs that world is the principle, as summed up in the opening line of the work, that 'all is vanity and evanescence'.

> Yes, pride must have its fall, for it is as unsubstantial as a dream on a spring night. The brave and violent man – he too must die away in the end, like a whirl of dust in the wind.

There is nothing very original in this opening passage in terms of Buddhist philosophy. It is no more than an expression of an attitude current throughout Heian aristocratic society from the time of the *Ōjōyōshū* onwards and it goes without saying that it bears no relationship to the other-worldly teachings of the new Kamakura Buddhism. In the final chapter the story is told of Kenreimon-in (Kiyomori's daughter) who becomes a nun after the fall of the Taira and in this there is clearly some Jōdo influence at work. In other words, the *Heike monogatari* begins with 'transience' and ends with the joyful seeking of the Pure Land, but the author's attempt to sum up in this way from a Buddhist standpoint is really only a presentation of a typical aristocrat's viewpoint without any relation to Kamakura Buddhism.

The closest to an idealized character in the *Heike monogatari* is Tairano Shigemori who is depicted as the true filial son in the Confucian sense. Moreover he is depicted as having an ability to foretell the future when lying ill in bed; he understands the destiny of his clan and simply refuses all treatment and so dies.

The system of values held by the author of the *Heike monogatari* encompasses awareness of transience and Pure Land teachings, Confucian ethics (as interpreted in Japan), the politics of the aristocrat and the refined tastes of a member of closed aristocratic society – in short all the values held dear by the aristocrat intellectual of the late Heian period. In terms then of its system of values the *Heike monogatari* neither truly reflected the spirit of the Kamakura period nor had within it the capacity to transcend time and appeal strongly to later generations. However, despite the conservative nature of its values, the *Heike monogatari* did succeed both in reflecting the Kamakura period and appealing to later generations in terms of its individualistic and energetic characterization and in its colourful and rhythmic style.

Tairano Kiyomori, for all his faults, acts immediately his feelings are roused, fears no one, not even the Emperor, in a political quarrel and on his deathbed can think only of getting to grips with the Minamoto. His violent energy reduces the idealized Shigemori to a mere shadow by comparison. Kiso Yoshinaka too is no mere bumpkin, but a man skilled in the arts of war. With only 300 men he defies an army 6000 strong and, when only he and four other warriors remain, is prepared to fight on to the death. Yoshitsune is depicted as a man bountifully endowed with agility and resolution who stands in battle at the head of just a few men and still fights on. Such men were never portrayed in the literature of the Heian court. The *Heike monogatari* draws a distinction between the warriors of the Eastern provinces and the warriors of the Western provinces around Kyōto:

> Even a warrior from a small (eastern) estate has at least five hundred soldiers. They are bold horsemen who never fall from the saddle. When they fight, they do not care if their parents or children are killed; they ride on over their bodies and continue the battle.
> The warriors of the Western provinces are quite different. If their parents are killed, they retire from the battle and perform Buddhist

rites to console the souls of the dead. Only after the mourning is over will they fight again. If their children are slain, their grief is so deep that they cease fighting altogether. When their rations have given out, they plant rice in the fields and go out to fight only after reaping it. They dislike the heat of the summer. They grumble at the severe cold of the winter.

In this passage one is perhaps reminded of Tacitus' observations of the wild barbarian tribes in his *Germania*. The author of the *Heike monogatari* did not overlook the fact, as in the case of Tomoe who followed Kiso Yoshinaka, that even the women of the Eastern warriors bore arms and were ready to fight to the death.

Why did the *Heike monogatari* paint such a vivid picture of the lives and deeds of these fighting men? We can only conjecture that it was due to the fact that the audience were no longer composed of the aristocracy and court ladies but of the masses which included illiterate people who demanded such tales. The question remains nonetheless why the author was able to fulfil this demand against the background of his own conservative values. The tenth-century *Shōmonki*, written in Chinese prose, and the *Konjaku monogatari* both touched on the world of the warrior.

After the establishment of the Kamakura Bakufu, the *Hōgen monogatari* and the *Heiji monogatari* both portrayed the clash between the Taira and the Minamoto and yet neither bears any comparison with the *Heike monogatari* in terms of the latter work's depth of psychological portrayal of the warriors. The author/narrator of the *Heike monogatari* not only described warriors, he extolled the world in which they lived. This was not only because it was what his audience demanded, but because the author/narrator himself lived in and shared the world of the ordinary people of the Kamakura period. These ordinary people were worldly, practical and often sentimental – unpersuaded by the doctrines of Kamakura Buddhism – but to them resolution and the ties of the family, the warrior group etc., were part of the necessity of life.

The main text of the *Heike monogatari* is written in *Kana-majiri* and contains many words of Buddhist and Chinese origin. On the other hand there are also many native Japanese onomatopoeic words. It is unthinkable that the audience listening to the tale would have understood the meaning of all the Chinese and Buddhist expressions and the *Heike monogatari* has a great many passages which would demand considerable knowledge of such to be understood.

The great charm of the style of the *Heike monogatari* lies not in the meaning of the Chinese words which are used but the atmosphere they evoke, and in the rhythm of the language, which becomes vividly alive when colloquialisms and onomatopoeic expressions are used. The colloquialisms and onomatopoeic expressions obviously stem from the *Biwa hōshi* narrations, but it is not clear where the Chinese phrases come from.

One theory recognizes the Shōmyō influence on the melody in recitation of the *Heike monogatari*. The *Heike monogatari* might have been influenced in phraseology by the Buddhist texts, the *fūju*, recited in temples. These *fūju* were written in a special style of Japanese close to Chinese prose and from the beginning of the Heian period often used parallel phrases. In particular, the opening line of the *Tōdaji Fūju Bunkō* (a Buddhist text recited in the Tōdaiji temple, and said to be from the early Heian period), stylistically and rhythmically reminds us of the opening of the *Heike monogatari*. The greatest influence of the temple culture on the *Heike monogatari* stemmed from its tradition of recitation and special type of rhetoric and rhythm, rather than from its Buddhist philosophy.

The *Hōbutsushū* (compiled by Tairano Yasuyori), the *Hosshinshū* (compiled by Kamono Chōmei) and the *Senjūshō* (compiler unknown) are all representative examples of late twelfth- or early thirteenth-century collections of Buddhist *setsuwa* tales written in *Kana* with Chinese characters. The *Hōbutsushū*, through the medium of short stories related to Buddhism, explains in question and answer form the Buddhist law and priesthood and how to enter the Western Paradise, while the *Hosshinshū* and the *Senjūshō* contain sermons and parables on Buddhist themes, chiefly emphasizing the importance of the abandonment of worldly desires and family ties. There is no evidence of any account being taken in these works of the teachings of the leaders of Kamakura Buddhism and all might be regarded as popularized expressions of the old Buddhism.

On the other hand, the custom dating from the time of the *Konjaku monogatari* of recording secular tales gave birth in the

Kamakura period to the *Kokon chomonjū* collection of tales (20 vols., 1254). Little for certain is known about the life of the compiler Tachibanano Narisue, but he was undoubtedly an aristocrat well-versed in Chinese poetry and prose, *waka* poetry and *biwa* music and the collection seems mainly to have been designed as a source material providing themes for paintings. The collection is divided into thirty sections containing a total of something over 700 stories of which about two-thirds are set in the Heian period and one-third in the Kamakura period. The central characters of the stories are mostly aristocrats, but occasionally come from other classes. The sketches of human character and psychology fall short of the level attained in the *Konjaku monogatari*, but some of the stories are very skilfully constructed.

Thus *setsuwa* tales of both Buddhist and secular origin existed.

Around the year 1279 the monk Mujū (1226–1312) compiled the *setsuwa* collection known as the *Shasekishū* (10 vols). Mujū was a Zen monk, but the Buddhist views expressed in the tales of the *Shasekishū* embrace the teachings of Tendai, Shingon and Zen Buddhism on an equal footing and even the *honji suijaku* theory is dealt with. According to the *Shasekishū* the inner and outer sanctuaries of the Ise Shrine are no more than different manifestations of Taizō (Womb) and Kongō (Diamond) worlds in Esoteric Buddhism. 'Honji (Buddhist origin) and Suijaku (Shintoistic manifestation) are different in form but have the same sense.' With regard to the various Buddhist sects it states, 'the Buddhist Law is essentially one thing but bad and good sects are derived from people'. It says that if you believe in the Law, you can achieve 'peace and safety in this world' and realize 'permanent life in the next world'.

Naturally, Shinran and Dōgen rejected the *honji suijaku* theory and taught that right and wrong depended not on man but on the Buddha's law. Nor did either of them attempt to promise peace and safety in this world. Here in the *Shasekishū*, the criticism of Pure Land Buddhism concentrates on its exclusive nature. While telling a story of a local official who was a Pure Land believer and was punished by the gods for his lack of respect for Shrines, it says that refusing to admit superfluous practices is the main fault of Pure Land Buddhism. The cult of Amida itself which is the core of Pure Land Sect is not naturally criticized from the standpoint of

'the Buddhist Law is essentially one thing'. With regard to the
Zen Sect, it tells a story of a man who fell into a stream because of
an epileptic fit. He lost consciousness, was carried downstream,
and later came to. He said, 'Precisely because I died, I live;
because I am alive, I will die.' Mujū was a monk of the Zen Sect in
which he held high office and that he could even entertain such
ideas is an indication of how far, even as early as the late thirteenth century, the Zen Sect in Japan had deviated from the
teachings of Dōgen.

In the *Shasekishū* there is not a glimpse of the transcendental
teachings of Kamakura Buddhism as propounded by Shinran,
Dōgen and Nichiren. Instead what we have is a collection of tales
peopled by *samurai*, menials, peasants and peasant's wives
together with an insight into their customs and feelings. The
general tone of the collection is revealed by the following story:

Four monks embarked on a seven-day period of silence. Late at
night, the light went out and one of the monks asked for it to be lit
again. A second monk spoke up and said that since they were all
under a vow of silence the first monk should not have spoken.
Whereupon the third monk reproved the other two for speaking
and the fourth monk, the leader of the group, nodded his
argreement and said 'monks, you should not be talking'.

Another story concerns a rather ignorant but pious monk,
who, weary of the world, decided that he would die and enter the
Pure Land. Accordingly he shut himself up in the seminary to
hang himself. Immediately he became famous on account of this
and famous monks came to say the *Nembutsu* while other monks
and laymen gathered to see the outcome. Meanwhile the pious
monk, so brave at first, had become frightened to die and so
changed his mind, thus earning the scorn of all the people who
had come to see his death and praise him for the manner of it. The
monk was so upset by all this pressure that in the end he took his
own life against his will just to satisfy them.

Yet another monk who decided he wished to hasten into the
Pure Land thought of trying to drown himself, but he was afraid
of going through with it as it was said that if one still had a
worldly desire at the moment of death, one could not enter the
Pure Land. Then he had the idea of jumping from a boat with a
rope tied round his waist so that if he sensed a worldly desire in
himself, he could tug on the rope and an assistant would pull him

to safety. Thus the boat was rowed out into the water and in he jumped reciting the *Nembutsu* as he did so. After a while he tugged on the rope and the assistant pulled him back into the boat, soaked to the skin. This happened two or three times until finally the monk screwed up the courage not to tug on the rope, whereupon 'he heard music in the skies and purple clouds trailed the waves'. And so he entered Paradise.

The *Shasekishū* with its insight into the psychologies of its characters, with its sharp perception of detail and with its general humorous flavour even when telling stories of the supernatural, is a vividly living work. However, the wide-open and perceptive eyes of the author are undoubtedly in reality the eyes of his audience. The masses that existed within Mujū.

All the cultural dramas of the Kamakura period were played out within the framework of a practical and realistic world view which had not changed since the time of the *Nihon ryōiki*.

Chapter 5

The Age of *Nō* and *Kyōgen*

The dual government system of the Kamakura period collapsed in the fourteenth century, owing to a combination of circumstances. The strength of the provincial warrior groups increased greatly bringing dissensions within the Kamakura Bakufu and a consequent weakening of its power to rule. The Kyōto government took advantage of the Bakufu's decreasing power by inviting the aid of provincial warrior leaders from the Kantō region (notably Ashikaga Takauji and Nitta Yoshisada), opposed to the Bakufu, in an attempt to resurrect the old system of rule-by-aristocracy. This led to the Imperial 'Kemmu Restoration' of 1333–6.

However, the same provincial warrior groups who had crushed the Kamakura Bakufu were subject to the Kyōto aristocracy for less than three years. Ashikaga Takauji mobilized his forces, entered Kyōto and re-established a central warrior government. The reigning Emperor Go-Daigo fled to Yoshino where he set up his court (known as the Southern Court), while Ashikaga Takauji set a new Emperor on the throne in Kyōto (thus creating what came to be known as the Northern Court) and throughout much of the remainder of the fourteenth century there was intermittent civil war between supporters of both factions until eventually the Southern Court declined and warrior power was conclusively re-established (Muromachi Bakufu).

The new regime established for itself far wider powers than those enjoyed in the thirteenth century by the Kamakura Bakufu whose existence had depended to an extent on compromise with the court aristocracy. Since the time when the civil wars of the Nambokuchō period (the period of the Northern and Southern Courts) started the court was a mere puppet in the hands of the new Ashikaga (or Muromachi) Bakufu.

At the same time, the new government permitted the regional warrior groups to gain a far wider degree of regional autonomy than had the Kamakura Bakufu which ruled through the *gokenin* retainers. Through this there developed between the late fourteenth and early sixteenth centuries a social system which can only be described as 'feudal'.

During this period there was a substantial change in Japan's economic background. A self-governing peasantry emerged through the break-up of the *shōen*, previously owned by the aristocracy and the great Buddhist temples; there were advances in agricultural production (multi-cropping, improvements in irrigation techniques and fertilization etc.) and the merchandising of agricultural produce; and there was the development of commercial cities built on trade with Ming China. Against this economic background the ruling warrior classes were bound to each other by oaths of allegiance and at the same time to the central government, protection being offered by the Bakufu in return for loyalty.

All this was a far cry from the society of the thirteenth century where the necessity for compromise with the power of the aristocracy had meant the retention of certain aspects of the rule-by-aristocracy system. The Kemmu Restoration which had attempted to resurrect the system of central rule by the court and the aristocracy culminated in the creation of a feudal system dependent on warriors who dissolved their association with the aristocracy, furthered the process of fragmentation of power through civil wars and completely excluded the court from all power. What happened was that the movement designed to turn the clock back to the situation which had existed before the thirteenth century only served to promote new tendencies already emerging in the thirteenth century. Reaction gave birth to progress.

As we have already seen, when the Kamakura Bakufu was established and the power monopoly of the aristocracy came to an end, there was a sharp increase in historical awareness on the part of the aristocracy, as shown by Jien's *Gukanshō*. The final collapse of aristocratic power was typified by an even stronger concern with history on the part of the aristocratic intelligentsia. A good example of this is the historical work *Jinnō shōtōki* (1339), written by Kitabatake Chikafusa (1293–1354) who played a central part in the Kemmu Restoration, was a courtier to Go-Daigo and died fighting for Go-Daigo in the Nambokuchō wars. The *Jinnō shōtōki* the opening line of which is 'Our great nation Japan is the country of the gods', traces the reigns of the Japanese Emperors (both mythical and historical) to the time of Go-Daigo, treating them as descendants of the gods who appear in the *Kojiki*. The purpose of the work was to establish an historical basis for the legitimacy of the Southern Court; it was not at all to explain cause and effect relationships or the historical reasons for changing conditions.

In his account of the reign of Go-Daigo, for example, he ventures certain criticisms of the Emperor's policies (such as his distribution of awards), but he makes no attempt to explain the reasons for those policies and has nothing at all to say about the historical events (in term of cause and effect relationships) leading up to the Kemmu Restoration. The *Jinnō shōtōki* was thus completely different from the *Gukanshō* which while often mentioning supernatural factors in explaining the course of events, always analyses historical cause and effect when discussing the success or failure of actual policies. Therefore, the great inferiority of the *Jinnō shōtōki* to the *Gukanshō* as a work of history lies not only in its distortion of truth (myth and historical reality constantly overlap) but in its lack of intellectual curiosity concerning cause and effect and historical development.

From the viewpoint of a man descended from the line of Regents, but with a certain detachment stemming from his belief in Buddhism, the Tendai abbot Jien wrote the very first 'first-rate' history of the country in Japanese – that is to say, history as opposed to factual chronology and genealogy. On the other hand Kitabatake Chikafusa, who fought in many of the battles of the civil wars, from the viewpoint of the Southern Court wrote what amounts to only 'second-rate' history, but 'first-rate' demagogy. The *Jinnō shōtōki*, embellished with a mixed vocabulary of Confucian, Buddhist and Shintō words, extolled the Emperors as sons of the gods and idealized direct imperial rule.

The aristocracy of the Northern Court centred on Kyōto did not take as militant a posture as Kitabatake Chikafusa. The *Masu kagami*, written in the mid-fourteenth century some time after the *Jinnō shōtōki* deals with the life of the court aristocracy in the period 1180 to 1333 beginning with the cloistered Emperor Go-Toba and his court and concluding with Emperor Go-Daigo in chronological order. We do not know the identity of the author of this work (although some attribute it to Nijō Yoshimoto), but it is certain that he was an aristocrat trained and educated in Kyōto.

The *Masukagami* has two special characteristics. First, unlike the *Jinnō shōtōki* or *Gukanshō* which were written in laconic Japanese with a Chinese vocabulary it is written in a kind of classical style resembling that of the *Eiga monogatari*, thus indicating the author's yearning for the culture of the Heian period aristocracy. Second, and this perhaps relates to the previous point, in content the *Masukagami* concentrates on such matters as court ceremony, love affairs, advancement within the bureaucratic system and the births and deaths of the aristocracy. It begins with the failure of Go-Toba's rebellion (culminating in his exile) and ends with the initial failure of Go-Daigo's rebellion, but this is no more than an historical framework around which to hang tales of the individual Emperors and their courts. Principally, the *Masukagami* shows itself best in its colourful narrations of the love affairs of the aristocracy very much in the style of the Heian period *monogatari* fiction. As for example, incest between the Ise vestal and her brother through a different mother {Part II, Chapter 9 'A Pillow of Grass' (Kusamakura)}; the vows of love exchanged between the empress and one of her servants after the emperor had taken the tonsure. Both of the stories are connected with a woman's pregnancy. These events which have little or no relationship to the great movements of the times are described in infinitely greater detail than, say, the Mongol invasions. The court aristocracy as represented in the *Masukagami* seem to have lived in closed groups perpetuating the value systems of the past while calmly waiting for extinction to overtake them.

However, the combative demagogy of the *Jinnō shōtōki* did not perish and even though the Southern Court itself disappeared the spirit which inspired it did not. In the late thirteenth century before the *Jinnō shōtōki* was composed, the Shintō priest Watarai Yukitada (1236–1305) wrote a work entitled *Shintō gobusho* (at least, he is thought to have been the author) in which an attempt was made to rid Shintoism of the *honji-suijaku* theory and establish Shintō ceremonies (purification, ritual taboos etc.) within a theoretical framework centered on Amaterasu Ōmikami. Kitabatake Chikafusa was under the influence of this work when he wrote in the *Jinnō shōtōki*: 'this great country of Japan is the land of the (Shinto) gods'.

Shintō theory reached its zenith in the late Muromachi period when Yoshida Kanetomo (1434–1511) wrote the *Yuitsu Shintō myōhō yōshū*. This work is arranged in question and answer form and explains that whereas 'Buddhism is the flower and fruit of all things; Confucianism is the branches and leaves of all things' it is Shintoism 'which is the root of all things'. The keynote of the *Yuitsu Shintō myōhō yōshū* is the way it classifies all the elements of Shintoism (purification, ritual taboos, the various Shintō deities mentioned in the *Kojiki* and *Nihon shoki* etc.) into a system somewhat similar to that of esoteric Shingon Buddhism, with subdivisions based on Yin and Yang and the Five Elements. For example, in 'Heaven', 'Earth' and 'Man' there are the five elements of fire, water, wood, metal and earth (or fire, water, earth, wind and air) and each of these is identified with three different gods respectively. Other special features of the *Yuitsu Shintō myōhō yōshū* are the detailed genealogies it gives of the Urabe family (who for generations had been in charge of the Yoshida shrine at Kyōto and to which Kanetomo himself belonged) in an attempt to establish the long tradition of Shintoism as 'Supreme Shintō' (*Yuitsu Shintō*); its stress on the worldly, practical benefits of Shintoism (long life, perfect health and wealth) without any concern with the next world; and its assertion that since Japan is the land of the gods, the Emperor – the leader of Japan – is himself a god. 'This country is the land of the gods; the true religion is Shintoism; the leader of the country is the God-Emperor.'

Earlier, Kitabatake Chikafusa in his works *Gengenshū* and *Shingon naishōgi* had already extended the formalized and mechanistic application of the abstract ideas of Buddhism to the Emperor-God theory in order to justify the Southern Court. The idea was that if the Emperor was a god, no authority transcended the Emperor and if Japan was the land of the gods, no values transcended the Japanese nation. In the sense that it does not recognize any authority, values or principles which transcend the actual community and its leadership, this argument is in marked contrast to Kamakura Buddhism and preserves the fundamental structure of the indigenous Japanese world view. Shintō theoreticians from Kitabatake Chikafusa to Yoshida Kanetomo made use of the structure of abstract Buddhist thought, but did not completely accept its transcendental nature (unlike the leaders of Kamakura Buddhism). Perhaps this is not exceptional as an example of the Japanese intellectual attitude towards a foreign ideology.

The war-like tendencies of the warrior groups continued throughout the feudal period, frequently leading to armed conflicts which occasionally developed into full-scale civil wars typified by the Nambokuchō wars of the fourteenth century, the Ōnin wars (1467–77) of the fifteenth century and the complete disintegration of Japan into civil war in the sixteenth century. The representative literary record of this type of war was the late fourteenth-century *Taiheiki*, to be treated later in this chapter.

Not only were there fights among the warrior ruling classes in the provinces; there was also the constant threat of peasant rebellion, the age of civil war also being the age of armed peasant insurrection. Between 1428 and the Kaga peasants' revolt of 1488 an example of this kind of insurrection is recorded on average once every four years. They were most numerous in areas where agriculture was highly developed, a frequent demand of the peasants being a moratorium on debts. Although limited success was often achieved, the lack of a basic ideology and organized leadership on the part of the peasantry usually enabled the warrior classes to suppress these revolts with relative ease.

However, there were occasions when the rebellions achieved more lasting success. In 1485 there was an insurrection in Yamashiro Province in which the peasantry overcame the forces sent by the Bakufu to deal with them which resulted in Yamashiro Province passing from the control of the Bakufu for eight years. The Kaga revolt of 1488 resulted in the establishment of a provincial assembly composed of peasants, monks and the local gentry which lasted as long as a century. The ideological background to these successful insurrections was provided by the Honganji faction of the Jōdo Shinshū sect of Buddhism. The man who revived the flagging Honganji faction was Rennyo, (1415–99) illegitimate son of the seventh patriarch of the Honganji and himself eighth patriarch. In his missionary travels he took in the Ōmi region centering on Kyōto, the Hokuriku region centering on Kaga and the Kinki provinces and in the essence of his belief he adhered faithfully to the teachings of Shinran, as is clear from his collected letters, with regard to dependence on the unlimited power of Amida and the good opportunity for salvation of men of ill deeds. For him to succeed in his missionary work, however, it must have been necessary to dilute those teachings somewhat with some suggestion of practical benefits in this world. His letters were collected into one volume and in one of these he wrote: 'Praying for personal benefits in this world is like trying to get straws. Praying for eternal life is like trying to get rice plants. If you get a rice plant, you will surely get straws.'

The man with 'a truly believing heart' was in the keeping of the various Buddhas, Bodhisattvas and Shintō gods, said Rennyo, and it was in this world that that protection operated. Another aspect of Rennyo's teaching which appealed to the masses was his egalitarianism in stressing particularly to women, that salvation was completely unrelated to whether one was young, old, male or female. However, like Shinran before him, religious equality was not, in Rennyo's thinking, to be extended to social equality. On the contrary, respecting Shintō shrines, refusing to vilify other Buddhist sects and behaving well towards landlords were all intrinsic parts of Rennyo's teaching ('Deep in your mind you should firmly subscribe to the power of Amida as is maintained by this Honganji temple faction').

However, the tendency on the part of Rennyo's followers to disrespect other gods and Buddhas apart from Amida, to vilify other sects of Buddhism, to refrain from fasting and abstinence and to slight the power of the land-owners is clearly shown by the *Nembutsu Dōjō* – places for *Nembutsu* meetings – especially the one which flourished in the mountains of Yoshizaki in the Hokuriku region. The followers of the Pure Land Buddhism (or Ikkōshū) of Rennyo's time apparently drew conclusions which he himself did not intend to on the basis of his religious egalitarianism. The peasant riots or *Ikkō ikki* of this age were inspired by a widespread feeling of solidarity among the peasantry – a solidarity which brought them into direct armed conflict with the power of the warrior classes.

The culture of this period was marked by two special characteristics. First, the Zen Sect which had risen to prominence in the thirteenth century became secularized through the support it gained from the upper echelons of warrior society. This secularization was principally manifested in artistic terms, being typified by the rise of Gozan poetry and prose and the development of *suiboku* painting in the fourteenth and fifteenth centuries. Also the tea ceremony in *wabi* style which appeared in the fifteenth century belonged to the same general tradition. Gozan poetry and prose was written in Chinese and *suiboku* painting was derived from Sung and Yuan China; in other words, they were imported from mainland Asia and in the main were confined in their practice to the Gozan temples. It is true that *suiboku* painting was soon taken up by the upper echelons of the warrior classes and the tea ceremony spread beyond the narrow confines of the temples, but they did not change their essential character in that they continued to be arts unrelated to the people at large.

In the Muromachi period the 'religious' Zen of the Kamakura period became closely related on one hand to the source of political power and, on the other hand, to art and literature.

There was criticism of and reaction to this kind of tendency in the great Zen temples supported by warrior power, the representative literary expression of this being the late fifteenth-century *Kyōunshū* by the Zen priest Ikkyū. Again, although Yoshida Kenkō was not a Zen monk, his celebrated work *Tsurezure-gusa* (fourteenth century) may be seen as a forerunner of the *Kyōunshū*, criticizing as an enterprise of a solitary individual the customs and practices of the times in which he lived.

Second, the age when the arts were the prerogative of the aristocratic intelligentsia came to an end; specialized artists under the protection and patronage of the Bakufu and the higher grade warrior classes emerged as the standard-bearers of culture. These new artists came from a variety of social backgrounds and the audience for their works seem to have been, on one hand, the aristocracy and the upper echelons of the warrior classes, and on the other hand, the masses including the peasantry, merchants and low-ranking *samurai*. The model examples of literature for the ruling classes were, in poetry, the *Tsukubashū*, in prose, the *Taiheiki*, and in drama, *Nō*, while the literature for the masses was typified by, in poetry, the *Inu tsukubashū*, in prose, *otogi-zōshi* fiction, and, in drama, *Kyōgen*. Thus literature and art were clearly divided into two types for two different classes and although of course they were not mutually exclusive it is the contrasts between them which stand out.

The essence of the contrast lay principally in style and subject matter. The literary style of works for the upper classes, perhaps in pursuit of the Japanese style of the Heian period, used many Chinese words and had a Chinese 'tone' to it. The style of literature for the lower classes was of course closer to the language as spoken at the time and contained many colloquialisms. In subject matter, upper-class literature was frequently set against the aristocratic background of the Heian court while lower class literature took the themes of contemporary rural and popular life. These two special cultural characteristics vividly reflect the structure of feudal society in which the warrior classes had come to rule in place of the court aristocracy and in which the peasantry, through rebellion, had the power to defy their rulers.

THE SECULARIZATION OF ZEN

As it spread into China, Buddhism gave birth to several new and original systems of thought typically represented by the Pure Land and Zen Sects. From the tenth century onwards the Jōdo Sect became popular in Japanese aristocratic society and gradually became popularized after the thirteenth century. The Zen Sect was imported from China at the end of the twelfth century and had been taken up by the upper echelons of warrior society by the last years of the thirteenth century. It seems that these warriors sought their own kind of ideological identity separate from the Buddhism of the Heian aristocracy (Tendai and Shingon) and also separate from the popular Buddhism of the Jōdo Sect. To begin with the Kamakura Bakufu invited Sung Chinese Zen monks to visit Japan. Later, at the end of the thirteenth century when the Southern Sung dynasty collapsed and China was united by the Mongols who proceeded to persecute Zen Buddhism, some Chinese Zen monks, hearing of the Bakufu's protective policy towards the Zen sect, chose to exile themselves in Japan. Altogether eighteen of them in the thirteenth and fourteenth centuries adopted Japanese nationality. At the same time, the most influential of the warrior classes assisted Japanese monks to study in China. Perhaps it was because Japanese trade with Sung China flourished and the passage of ships voyaging between the two countries increased, or because the Japanese Zen monks had a strong desire for mainland culture.

In the thirteenth and fourteenth centuries almost 100 Japanese monks studied in China in this way. Of the 469 monks whose lives are recorded in the *Honchō kōsō-den*, ninety-three are mentioned as having visited China – almost one fifth of the whole. Also the Kamakura Bakufu built Zen temples to which later the Ashikaga Bakufu gave its protection.

In the fourteenth century 'Gozan' (Five temples) – five in Kamakura, five in Kyōto – were established on the Chinese pattern and these were not only financially assisted but actually controlled by the Bakufu. Powerful and influential monks such as Soseki (Musō Kokushi) (1275–1351) not only performed memorial services for their protectors, but frequently were charged with the responsibility of drafting documents and even, on occasion, participated in foreign affairs. In this way the relationship between the Zen and warrior hierarchies grew close, this being the first of the special characteristics in the process of secularization of Zen Buddhism which was disseminated among the *samurai* from the mid-thirteenth to mid-sixteenth centuries. In other words, its institutionalization and close relationship with power was effected.

The Zen sect emphasized the 'difficult practice' over the 'easy practice' of Jōdo Shinshū (Pure Land Buddhism), expounded 'self-help' as opposed to dependence on Amida's power and regarded the attainment of enlightenment as the goal of its adherents. However, although Zen was followed by many members of the *samurai* class, this is not necessarily to say that there were many who achieved enlightenment. Kotsuan Funei, who converted Hōjō Tokiyori to the Zen priesthood, complained that with two or three exceptions, there was no hope that the *daimyō* and *samurai* could attain enlightenment, and so he might as well return to China (*Kotsuan Oshō Goroku*). Mugaku Sogen the teacher of Hōjō Tokinune was so harsh in his criticisms of Japanese Zen monks that the also expressed a desire to return home to China (*Bukkō Kokushi Goroku*).

From a foreigner's viewpoint there is no doubt that the warrior classes' grasp of Zen teaching was tenuous indeed. The situation was like that even in the Kamakura period which produced Dōgen, and so was in the later Nambokuchō and Muromachi periods. The increase in the patronage of Zen temples by the powerful did not imply that there were many warriors prepared to become priests. Even the monks of this period, rather than concerning themselves with furthering Zen as a religious practice (in this sense no figure emerged to match Dōgen) were primarily concerned with their enthusiasm for the culture of mainland Asia, particularly art and literature, which they approached through Zen.

The art produced by the Zen temples in Japan was, first, related to temple architecture itself which can be said to have been modelled on the Zen temples of China (the disposition of buildings and the style of architecture were different from those of the temples of other Japanese sects). Another special feature lay in the construction of gardens, particularly stone gardens such as can be found at the sixteenth-century Daisen-in and Ryōanji.

Secondly, there were the *chōsō* or painted portraits of the Zen patriarchs which may be thought to have exerted a profound influence on the development of Japanese portrait painting in the thirteenth century. Both of these – architecture and portraits – were directly related to religion, but the Sung and Yuan paintings imported from China and the *suiboku* paintings executed by Zen monks in Japan had no connection with Zen, although they did set the main trend of Muromachi period painting.

There was the Zen monk Mokuan (?–*c.*1354) who had already crossed to China by the early fourteenth century and practised *suiboku* painting there; and then in the fifteenth century came painters such as Tenshō Shūbun (?–*c.* 1444–8) and Sōtan (1418–81) who became official artists to the Muromachi Bakufu.

After the sixteenth century this tradition in the *suiboku* style was absorbed into the Kanō school. However, there were also monks who did not become official painters, but left the temples and set up their own studios, such as Sesshū Tōyō (1420–1506) in the fifteenth century and Sesson Shūkei (1504–?) in the sixteenth century. Sesshū in particular achieved the highest standards in Japanese painting, visiting Ming China between 1468 and 1469, travelling extensively in Japan and painting realistic landscapes in *suiboku* style.

The connection between the *suiboku* painting of the Japanese Zen monks and Zen itself is not clear, or at any rate it is difficult to suggest any internal relationship between Zen and the 'mountain and water' (*sansui*) landscapes of the best Zen Japanese artist Sesshū, for example. Certainly, among the paintings imported from Sung and Yuan China there were, in addition to many by Yuan-ti-hua, a great number of Chinese Zen monks, notably

Mu-ch'i, and it seems that a higher value was placed on Mu-ch'i's paintings in Japan than in China itself. However, this alone is not enough to point to any profound relationship between Zen itself and *suiboku* painting. On the whole, it is perhaps best to believe that the Zen Sect of the Kamakura period produced the philosophical genius of Dōgen, while in the Muromachi period it produced the painting genius of Sesshū. In this sense, religious and philosophical Zen turned into cultural and artistic Zen.

The popularity of *suiboku* paintings was also the popularity of the prose and poetry written on them. Chinese language poetry and prose, generically known as *Gozan bungaku*, was written by the Japanese monks of the Gozan temples alongside their practice of *suiboku* painting. In broad terms, the history of this poetry and prose can be divided into three periods. First, the first half of the fourteenth century when many religious eulogies were written; second, the second half of the fourteenth century when secularized, ornate poetry and prose were most popular; and, third, the fifteenth to the first half of the sixteenth centuries when secularization was complete and many poems of homosexual infatuation were written.

The influence of Confucianism is an important connecting thread in Gozan literature throughout all three periods. In the first period both Kokan Shiren (1278–1346), compiler of the *Genkō shakusho* (an historico-biographical work on the Japanese priesthood), and Chūgan Engetsu (1300–75), who lived in Yuan China for eight years, took the view that Confucianism and Buddhism were one. In the second period the same view was adopted by Gidō Shūshin (1325–88) who was both an adviser to the Shōgun Ashikaga Yoshimitsu and one of the leading authors of Gozan poetry and prose. Since the theory of the 'Three-in-One' (Confucianism, Buddhism and Taoism) was popular in Sung China, it seems likely that the learned monks of Japan, who idolized mainland culture and wrote in Chinese, were following Chinese fashion. However, there may have been more to it than that. Chūgan Engetsu wrote in his *Tōkai ichiō-shū*:

> Confucianism and Buddhism are like two faces of a coin.
> Their arguments are like two identical jewels.

In this saying we can sense the compatibility between the teaching that Confucianism and Buddhism were one and indi-

genous Japanese thought. The special characteristic of indigenous Japanese thought is its 'this-worldly' nature and concern
with the matters of everyday life.

Internalization of this-worldliness is the state of mind of the
here and now. Buddhism tends to be reduced to a state of mind,
especially in Zen; Confucianism in Japan was readily reduced to
ethics and lost its political and philosophical aspects – ethics was
interpreted rather in terms of pure mind than exterior rules; thus
Buddhism and Confucianism were considered as two faces of the
same psychic state.

To put this another way, foreign ideology did not serve to
break down the structure of indigenous thought by its transcendental nature nor to rebuild it but to refine it intellectually. The
essence of this intellectual refinement was none other than the
internalization of everyday, 'this-worldly' indigenous thought.
This was not the transcendental religious philosophy of the
Kamakura period – typified by Dōgen – nor was it the transcendental philosophy of history – the way of ancient kings – later
expounded by Ogyū Sorai (?–1728). Only once, in thirteenth
century Buddhism, did transcendental absolutism form the nucleus of Japanese thought. In this way foreign ideologies were
deprived of their exclusiveness, and the easy way in which the
Japanese could accept the theory that Confucianism and Buddhism were one is a model example of this general pattern. Consequently, when the Japanese actually became aware of the 'foreig-
ness' of a foreign ideology and asserted their own indigenous
viewpoint, this almost always took the form of the idealization of
Japan itself, as in the case of Kokan Shiren who wrote in his
Genko shakusho: 'The Chinese are very pure, but they have one
small blemish. The Japanese are totally pure.' 'The small blemish'
means the limited popularity of Mahayana Buddhism in China
due to the presence of Confucianism and Taoism. 'Total purity'
means Mahayana Buddhism itself. But there was more to it than
that. Kokan Shiren also wrote:

All people appreciate natural things. No society has ever estimated
artificial things highly. In Japanese history I see that the foundation of
Japan is based on the natural. Other different countries have never
been so. That is why I praise this country. What I call natural things
here are the three divine symbols of the Japanese Imperial House.
(Genkō Shaku sho)

This resembles the viewpoint of the *Jinnō shōtōki* and also later works such as the *Chūchō jijitsu* written by Yamaga Sokō (1622–85).

Poetry in the Chinese language was written with great skill by Japanese monks who had grown proficient in Chinese through months or years spent studying in China. Sesson Yūbai (1290–1346), for example, spent more than twenty years in China (1307–29) before being arrested during the persecution of Zen and later managing to return to Japan. The *Bingashū* contains 242 poems which he wrote during that period.

> I did not like praises and honours,
> Nor did I fear disdain,
> I just stay away.
> My mind, clear water,
> My body, bound and tied
> For three years in Ch'ang-an.
> I sing what I feel in songs,
> In straight words with no decoration.

This poem tells of Yūbai's experiences in prison in a foreign country and of his feelings towards them. One can only marvel at the self-confidence of this Zen monk with calm intensity.

To take another example, the monk Zekkai Chūshin (1336–1405) lived for eight years (1368–76) in China and the *Shōkenkō*, the anthology of his work, contains 163 poems and 38 prose passages. Among the poetry some Buddhist eulogies are included, but the majority take ancient temples and famous lovers in Chinese classics for their themes, reminding one of the secular poetry of the late T'ang dynasty. We know for a fact that he exchanged poems with the Ming Emperor which the Chinese people praised with the words, 'Those poems bear no Japanese flavour'. The Japanese intelligentsia were also thoroughly familiar both with the Chinese language and the techniques of writing in that language. The characteristic of the middle period of the Gozan literature was that although the Zen monks of Japan did not match up to their Chinese counterparts in terms of Zen philosophy, their literary skills were certainly not inferior.

The third age of Gozan literature was the period in which Chinese language poetry underwent a process of 'Japanizing' by the addition of the element of 'love'. The same situation was to recur later when the Confucian poets of the Tokugawa period began by emulating the work of Chinese poets and eventually began to write love poems in Chinese through this same 'Japanizing' process. It also matches the tradition of Japanese lyric poetry since the time of the *Manyōshū* where an overwhelming number of *waka* masterpieces had been on the theme of love. However, the Zen temples of the Muromachi period did not admit women so the objects of the monks' love were young men, in marked contrast to the poets of the Heian court and the 'Chinese' poets of the Tokugawa period.

Typical of this kind of homosexual poetry are the *Shinden shikō* (1447) of Shinden Shōban (1380–1452), the *Ryūsuishū* (1462) of Tōshō Shūgen, and the *San'eki shikō* (*c*. 1520) of San'eki Eiin. Take, for example, this poem from the *Ryūsuishū*:

We passed the night in the same bed,
And now looking at the pale moon at dawn through the window.
Our two shadows fall on the curtain
A pair of mandarin ducks.
I would celebrate the night's joy of love forever.
Our temple is like the Kimshan Temple on the Yan-tse.

The development of this kind of homosexual poetry and prose was one of the great contributions made by the Zen Sect to the culture of Japan in the Muromachi period, and doubtless the tradition was inherited by the warrior society through the late sixteenth century up to the Tokugawa period.

The Zen temples did not only contribute *suiboku* painting and Gozan literature. They also imported printing techniques and published Buddhist religious texts, as well as Chinese classical literature and the writings of the Japanese Zen monks themselves. These printed editions were generically known as *Gozanban* and were the beginning of large-scale publishing enterprise in Japan. In other words, there developed, probably in the fifteenth century at the latest, an unspecifiably large number of readers of Chinese literature. In the previous period works of literature existed only in manuscript form or in oral tradition and in the ensuing Tokugawa period it was the custom to print most works of literature.

Finally, we come to the tea ceremony which developed in the Zen temples (particularly the Daitokuji) and reached its highest form in the sixteenth century in the hands of Senno Rikyū (1520–91). The custom of drinking tea was imported from China, where there was a tradition that it was introduced, along with the Zen sect, by Eisai who, indeed, is believed to have been the author of a twelfth-century work on the subject, the *Kissa yōjōki*.

From the fifteenth to sixteenth centuries the tea ceremony developed into a kind of comprehensive art form in itself with its own special architecture (the *chashitsu* or tea room), and associated painting and calligraphy (the *kakemono*), and its own style of flower arrangement, ceramics (tea wares, especially the *chawan*), and social conversation.

As early as the fifteenth century there were specialized tea-ceremony experts such as Shukō (1422–1502?), and then in the early sixteenth century came Jōō (1504–55) and in the second half of the sixteenth century Rikyū himself. It is said that all three had associations with the Daitokuji temple, so it may be imagined that there was an intimate connection between the Zen Sect and the tea cult as a comprehensive art form. But there was more to it than that.

The Muromachi period tea ceremony (*sadō* or 'way of tea') gave birth to its own individual aesthetics. The *chashitsu* were purposely small and delicate; in *kakemono* the *suiboku* style and also paintings with very light colours were prized; in flower arrangement just a single blossom was used with studied casualness; crude, irregular shapes were chosen for the tea wares and pleasure was gained from the subdued colours of the tea vessels and the random patterns on the glaze. Shukō called this *hiekaru* (cold and dried) or *karu* (dried); Jōō called it *wabi* (humble) and Rikyū called it *Kōzashiki no cha* (small-room-tea) or *Rojisōan no cha* (Tea in a hut).

Neither in Chinese society nor in any other culture known to the world today has there ever been a system of aesthetic values which prized small and delicate architecture and irregularly shaped ceramics in this way. These paradoxical aesthetic values typified by the tea cult were something unique to fifteenth- and sixteenth-century Japan. How did they come about? Jōō seems to have placed heavy emphasis on what he called 'being able to understand the meaning of the Buddha's law and appreciating the sentiments of *waka* poetry'.

Rikyū, whose words are recorded in the *Nambōroku* (a late

sixteenth-century compilation of his sayings by a pupil) said: 'the performance of the tea ceremony in a small room is the first practice for achieving salvation under the Buddha's law'. Again, in explaining Jōō's concept of the tea ceremony, he quoted Fuji-warano Teika's poem:

> As far as the eye can see,
> No cherry blossoms,
> No leaves in their autumn tints:
> Only a thatched hut by a lagoon
> This autumn evening.

What he was saying was that in terms of beauty there was nothing to choose between the magnificence of the cherry blossoms and the *momiji* and the thatched hut by the lagoon, and in the final analysis the creation of beauty lay in the power of the imagination to discern what was beautiful. Thus Rikyū was able to make a comparison between the 'way of the Buddha' and the 'way of tea' and was able to see a deep internal relationship between Buddhism and the tea ceremony. Of course, the way of the Buddha was not necessarily Zen, but both Jōō and Rikyū followed the path of Zen, and discovered the way of the Buddha through Zen.

Thus, in the post-Kamakura period the Zen Sect was, on the one hand, through its temples, closely knit to political power. On the other hand Zen philosophy developed first into literature, then into painting and, finally, into a kind of life-style with its own special aesthetic values. It is not that Zen influenced Muromachi culture; it became Muromachi culture. In other words, religious and philosophical Zen was secularized through political and aesthetic transformation and this process was accomplished through none other than the 'this-worldly', 'secular' indigenous Japanese thought which, despite Kamakura Buddhism, permeated to the deepest layers of Japanese consciousness.

OUTSIDERS' LITERATURE

We have already seen how aristocratic literature was faithful to the traditions of Heian court culture and the literature of the Zen monks to the forms and styles of Chinese secular poetry and prose. Both writers and readers alike of this type of literature belonged to limited circles and in the sense that they shared the dominant values of those circles, the literature they enjoyed may be regarded as typically 'within-the-group' or Establishment. However, because of the power conflicts within these Establishment groups, there were members who were either expelled or voluntarily chose to divorce themselves from those groups. The majority of people who left the Establishment, for whatever reason, did not write anything and so are unknown to us. Some who did write, like Kamono Chōmei, whose *Manyōshū* was faithful to the *waka* tradition of the Heian court and whose *Hōjōki* followed Chinese prose models of the Heian court, wrote within the framework of the original value systems of the Establishment.

Another group of writers, however, when separated from the court or the Zen temples, discovered a unique world completely different from that of the Establishment and wrote literature from outside the group so to speak. Two representative examples of this kind of writer were Yoshida Kenkō (1283?–1350?) who at the beginning of the fourteenth century composed the *Tsurezuregusa*, and the Zen priest Ikkyū (1394–1481) who in the late fifteenth century wrote the anthology of Chinese language poems known as the *Kyōunshū*.

Kenkō was born into the Yoshida family which had connections at court through its association with the Yoshida Shinto shrine. He entered court as a member of the lower aristocracy and seems to have spent half his life there. It is generally said that the reason Kenkō was able to get so close to the Emperor and Empress, despite his own relatively humble station, was through the influence of a middle-grade aristocrat who was a maternal relative of the Emperor Gonijō.

At about the time of the Kemmu Restoration Yoshida Kenkō, himself without ambition, was in an ideal position to observe the corruption, plots and ambitions of the imperial family and the higher and middle rank aristocracy. When the power situation among those at the top of court society changed, probably Kenkō was left with no choice but to leave the court. Almost nothing is known of the remainder of his life. He became a monk in 1324, but travelled widely and seems not to have taken up residence at a specific temple. Such was the man who wrote the *Tsurezuregusa*. It is not known precisely when this work was written, but it was in or about 1333 according to one theory which, if correct, was at a time when the imperial court's plans for an assault on the Bakufu were ripening towards the eventual civil war, leading to the Kemmu Restoration.

The *Tsurezuregusa* comprises 243 separate fragments with a short preface where Kenkō speaks of 'jotting down all the trivial things which come into my head'. These things are truly diverse and indicate both his strong curiosity and a certain detachment from current values. In this book one finds anecdotes relating to Heian court aristocrats and monks; matters concerned with manners and etiquette; stories of contemporary warriors and merchants; opinions on women, *sake*, where to live, *go*, martial arts, cooking, flowers and birds, the wind and the moon; discussions of the transience of life and the desire for an after-life, and on human psychology especially on its ugly side. When he writes on Buddhist teaching (as in passage 39), his work bears some resemblance to the contemporary *Ichigon hōdan* (a collection of sayings of famous Jōdo monks – compiler and date of compilation unknown). His humorous stories of monks (e.g. 144) almost put one in mind of *Kyōgen* drama; and when he writes of the sorrow and plaintiveness of the changing patterns of the seasons, his tasteful and aesthetic sentiments remind one of the *Makura no sōshi*. He ignored the bad omen of the appearance of an ox (no. 206), was not concerned with the retribution taboos associated with snakes (no. 207), and declared that good and bad fortune does not depend on astrology but on human behaviour (no. 91). Such an iconoclastic attitude reminds us of the *Konjaku monogatari*.

This kind of multi-faceted diversity in one small book had never been achieved before the *Tsurezuregusa* and was seldom to be achieved afterwards. The originality of the *Tsurezuregusa* lies in just this random record 'of all the trivial things which come into my head'.

'The things that come into my head' are isolated from one another and disconnected. There is no logical progression from one item to the next. On the contrary, there are many passages which are even contradictory. For example in passage 1 when speaking of the training a man should receive he says, 'it is desirable for a man to be skilled in the composition of Chinese poetry and prose, for him to have knowledge of *waka* poetry and music and to be able to serve as a model to others when it comes to matters of court ceremonial and precedence'. But on another occasion (122) he writes, 'too many accomplishments are an embarrassment to the gentleman. Proficiency in poetry and music, both noble arts, has always been esteemed by rulers and subjects alike, but it would seem that nowadays they are neglected as a means of governing the country. Gold is the finest of metals but it cannot compare with iron in its many uses.' (Keene)

Again in passage 1, he writes 'the mark of an excellent man is that . . . , though appearing reluctant to accept when wine (sake) is pressed on him, is not a teetotaller!' (Keene), while in passage 175 he vigorously rejects the custom of forcing people to drink at banquets, saying 'If it were reported that such a custom (drinking sake), unknown among ourselves, existed in some foreign country, we should certainly find it peculiar and even incredible'. (Keene)

When discussing love affairs, he writes of the joys of love in the typical idealized way of the Heian court aristocrat (3), and so later (190) says, 'a man should never marry' (Keene) and (6), one would do well 'not to have children'. Since a woman is an object of sexual desire Kenkō has every sympathy with the story of the hermit Kume who (as told in passage 8) lost his magic powers when attracted by a young girl washing clothes in the river. 'This was quite understandable, considering that the glowing plumpness of her arms, legs, and flesh owed nothing to artifice.' (Keene)

On the other hand he says that from a Buddhist point of view, sexual relations between men and women are something to be carefully avoided, to be feared and to be prudent about (9). Kenkō had no consistent system of ideas. The Tsurezuregusa is a record of miscellaneous ideas and images which came, so to speak, into his mind successively without him seriously considering how they were interelated.

However, there is one attitude which is consistent throughout the Tsurezuregusa, an attitude which is revealed in the following random quotations: 'human life is transient' (7); 'the human heart is untrustworthy' (12, 85 etc.); fast 'rise and fall' of people's fate (25); in other words, 'there is nothing which can be trusted' (212).

When Kenkō writes of the treachery of the human heart and 'the stories one hears in this world are usually all falsehoods' (73), it implies that he felt something akin to a 'misanthrope'. What could one do with such a pessimistic view of the world? Yet there is always the possibility of enjoying ourselves alone; 'while they (people) live they do not rejoice in life, but, when faced with death, they fear it – what could be more illogical?' (93 – Keene) On the other hand, there is Buddhism which puts hope in the next life. 'It is admirable when a man keeps his thoughts constantly on the future life and is not remiss in his devotions to the Way of the Buddha.' (4 – Keene) The latter solution is basically Buddhist, but the words used are perhaps not those of a convinced believer in Buddhism.

Doubtless, Kenkō's feeling that nothing could be trusted was the conclusion extracted from his own experience. As to what should be done about such a state of affairs, the author of the *Tsurezuregusa* seems to have been too much bound up with his own 'trivial thoughts' to reach positive conclusions. At least, any conclusions he did reach were essentially not Buddhist. For Kenkō ultimate reality was nothing but a frame of mind in which 'trivial thoughts' appear and disappear successively. As there was no Buddha for him which transcended his disconnected chain of thoughts, so there was no guarantee of the continued existence of his own mind itself. 'Emptiness accommodates everything. I wonder if thoughts of all kinds intrude themselves at will on our minds because what we call our minds are vacant?' (235 – Keene)

This is none other than an internal reflection of the every-day 'this-worldly' nature of indigenous Japanese thought. That is why the world of the *Tsurezuregusa* naturally led to *renga*, which we shall discuss later. The progression from one stage to the next with a linking idea, and then the sudden change of thought; the complete absence of overall structure; all interest centering on the section before one's eyes like the slow and careful unrolling of an *emakimono*. The past is over and done with, the future not something to worry about. This was the concept of time against which the Japanese of the fourteenth and fifteenth centuries lived. *Renga* was one literary manifestation of this, the *Tsurezuregusa* another. In fact, the *Tsurezuregusa* was *renga* in prose.

Ikkyū is said to have been the illegitimate son of the Emperor Gokomatsu and was related to two later Emperors – Shōkō and Gohanazono. He took Kesō Sōdon as his master and according to legend achieved enlightenment at the age of twenty-six on hearing the cry of a crow at midnight. After Kesō's death in 1428, the master's pupil Yōsō became head of Daitokuji and Ikkyū took to wandering around and lived among ordinary people, using the name Kyōun. Later, in 1447, he left the Daitokuji altogether and lived at the Katsuroan residence in Kyōto, and at the outbreak of the Ōnin wars in 1467 he moved to the Shūon-an in the village of Takigi in Yamashiro Province.

When the Shūon-an was burned down during the civil war he toured the provinces of Yamato and Izumi and did not return to the Daitokuji until ordered to do so by the Emperor in 1474. Why did he leave the Daitokuji in the first place? Apart from the poems of the *Kyōunshū* itself we have nothing to go on and so there is no way of knowing the reasons for sure. However, according to this and to the *Jikaishū*, a one volume work which he is believed to have written and only exists in manuscript, it seems almost certain that he had a violent disagreement with Yōsō. Also, and perhaps connected with this, was the strong antipathy he conceived for the secularized world of the Zen temples in this period, a theme which recurs in the poems of the *Kyōunshū*.

The *Kyōunshū* altogether contains more than 1000 of Ikkyū's poems written in the Chinese language. They are all poems consisting of four-lines with seven-words per line. The date of compilation is unknown, and apart from a few poems which themselves bear dates it is impossible to establish a chronological order. The poems can be divided into three categories: first, those explaining the doctrine of Rinzai Zen, the majority of which are, philosophically speaking, extremely speculative in nature and dedicated to the Zen patriarchs, in particular Daitō Kokushi (1282–1337), founder of the Daitokuji. However, there are also poems in this category which reflect Ikkyū's own beliefs. Second, there are poems which denounce and scorn, often in very harsh terms, the customs of the times, particularly those of the Zen temples. Third, there are love poems, including those relating to his love, late in life, for a blind woman attendant.

The poems are not related to theoretical aspects of Zen and it is impossible to deduce from them any theoretical aspects of Ikkyū's brand of Zen. However, since he was not a megalomaniac, there would be no other way to interpret the following poems entitled 'self-praise' than the expression of an extraordinary confidence in Zen.

> Disciples of Kasō cannot understand Zen.
> Who would dare to tell me about Zen to my face?
> For thirty years I've been carrying a heavy burden
> Alone trying to keep it in Shōgen's place.

The same can be said for the next one entitled 'Return into the City from the Mountain.'

> Who can tell how insane my style is?
> In the morning I am in the mountains and in the evening in town.
> If I at the right time hit or shout at Tokusan or Rinzai,
> Even those great masters would be ashamed.

With such self-confidence, he was able to regard most of the other Zen monks as short-sighted frogs at the bottom of a well and could refer to the ruling faction and the masses all as puppets.

> Figures appearing on the puppet stage
> Are the rulers and the ruled.
> We quickly forget they are all made of wood.
> A fool sees them as human!

Over the first two categories of poems there are no disagreements among Ikkyū's biographers, but there are disagreements concerning the third category. In the third category, Ikkyū composed poems on 'fish markets, drinking establishments and brothels' or 'singing songs and making love at night' or 'the pleasure of embracing and kissing' going as far as 'licking a beauty's sexual sweetness'. How is it possible for us to reconcile such poems with the high echelons of Zen priesthood? Hitherto most commentators have supported one of the following three interpretations; first, to put emphasis on his Zen attitudes and completely ignore his dissipation; secondly, to defend his weaknesses as only being human; and thirdly, to suggest that he was having a sly dig at the hypocrisy of the great Zen temples (particularly the Daitokuji Temple headed by Yōsō).

Not one of these theories suffices to explain the *Kyōunshū* and its author. When assessing an historical personality it is intellectually dishonest for any scholar to disregard facts which are inconvenient to the attitude one wishes to take. To say that Ikkyū was morally weak but that this just serves to show he was human is no more than an inappropriate application of present-day middle-class morality, completely ignorant of the Muromachi period and Zen. To the Japanese of the Muromachi period sexual love, whether man for woman or man for man, was not a 'weakness', and in Zen 'humanity' (the state of being human) was not a positive value, but something to be transcended. The 'sly dig' theory is not totally untenable. Some poems, it is true, might lead one to that conclusion, but the majority cannot be explained in such terms. Take, for example, the following poem to which none of these theories applies:

> Disciples of Rinzai cannot understand Zen
> The truth has been transmitted directly to my 'Blind Donkey' hut
> Making love forever through the three lives to come
> The autumn wind at night is a hundred thousand years.

This is not simple dissipation. A person ashamed of his 'weakness' would surely not begin a poem with such a line as 'Disciples of Rinzai cannot understand Zen'. If attempting to satirize the Zen temples and the habits of their monks, Ikkyū would surely not have included such a line as 'The autumn wind at night is a hundred thousand years'. The only possible explanation here must be that 'Zen' equals 'love' equals 'a hundred thousand years in one night'. A hundred thousand years in one night is an assertion of the 'eternal present', transcending time.

Among ancient Zen *kōan*, there is one called 'Old Woman Burns a Monk's Hut'. An old woman builds a hut and takes in a monk who lives there for twenty years performing memorial services. Food is brought to him by a young girl. One day the old woman orders the girl to embrace the monk when she brings the food and report how the monk would react. The girl follows the order and reports that when she embraced the monk, he said 'Naked tree leans on the cold rock. In the middle of winter, there is no warmth'. When the old woman hears what the monk has said, she drives him away and burns and destroys all traces of his presence, screaming, 'how could I have taken care of such a fake degraded nut for twenty years?' Ikkyū, referring to that kōan, composed the following poem:

If the young girl makes a promise with me tonight
In spring the ancient withered willow would burst forth and sprout.

The love in the poetry of the *Kyōunshū* differs greatly from that
of the love poems of San'eki Eiin. The latter, little related to Zen,
convey a more secular world. In the *Kyōunshū* Zen and love are
one and the same thing. Its poems which combine religious
feeling and the rapture of sexual passion are metaphysical and at
the same time sensual, but they never admit the psychological
elements of everyday life.

The world of this poetry came into being in fifteenth-century
Japan through the medium of Zen. This kind of poetry which
appeared in Japanese Zen in the fifteenth century is in a way
similar to that of St. John of the Cross in sixteenth-century Spain
as well as some of the metaphysical poems in seventeenth-
century England, particularly those by John Donne. The like of
Ikkyū had not been seen before in Japan and was not to be
seen after. In the age of the secularization of Zen, only Ikkyū
created a unique and original poetic world by giving flesh
to a foreign ideology and transmitting his experience of sexual rapture through carnal love. His death-bed poem is as
follows:

Ten years ago we made our vows of love
Under the blossoming cherry tree
The greatest love has no end to feeling
I hate to leave her thighs which were my pillow,
Late at night our love is pledged for three lives to come.

Ikkyū died at the age of eighty-seven.

ARTISTIC INDEPENDENCE

In the period of the feudal system literature written in the Chinese language flourished in the Zen temples. Literature written in
the Japanese language, simultaneously with its geographical
spread to a wide area ranging from the Kantō region to Kyūshū,
began to be disseminated among both high and low social classes, including the aristocracy, Buddhist monks, warriors, merchants and peasants. Probably this was related to the develop-

ment of commerce on a nationwide basis and of the changes in status relationships in warrior society. The much wider range of audience for art and literature in the fourteenth and fifteenth centuries stimulated specialization on the part of writers and artists, culminating in the emergence of independent professional men working under the patronage not only of the court and temples but also of the Shogunate and the provincial *daimyō*. We have already mentioned painters typical of this trend such as Sesshū, but there were also the *renga* poets and the authors and actors of the *Nō* and *Kyōgen* drama.

Renga was part of a popularization of the aristocratic culture of the court, while *Nō* and *Kyōgen*, originating as entertainments for the masses, gained the acceptance and support of the ruling classes. In other words, *renga* is an example of a literary form spreading from the top to the bottom of society and *Nō* and *Kyōgen* the reverse. The men who played a decisive role in this social cross-fertilization of literature were the *renga* poets and the *Nō* and *Kyōgen* actors and authors. We know nothing of the lives of most of these people, but in family background they were neither aristocrats nor members of the ruling military classes. The work of some reflected the tastes of the ruling classes (e.g. the *Tsukubashū* anthology of *renga* poetry and the *Nō* drama) and others reflected the habits, customs and lives of the ordinary people at large (e.g. the *Inu tsukubashū* and the *Kyōgen* drama).

In *renga* different poets took turns composing the first and second halves of a single *waka* poem – the amusement deriving from seeing how each succeeding poet in turn would complete his part, the poem gradually developing into a chain. This pastime seems to have been practised by court poets as early as the Heian period, but from the thirteenth and fourteenth centuries onwards it spread beyond the confines of the court and began to become popular not only with aristocrats, but also with monks, warriors and other social classes (the *renga* composed by these lower classes being known as *chika renga* or 'underground' *renga*).

Nijō Yoshimoto (1320–88) was a representative court *renga* poet and the priest Gusai (1284?–1378?, also known as Kyūsei) was representative of the *chika renga* movement. Yoshimoto was a leading court aristocrat of the Northern Court established by the Ashikaga Bakufu. He was a *waka* theorist of note, loved *renga* poetry and collaborated with Gusai in the compilation of the *Tsukubashū*, a *renga* anthology (1356 or 1357). This work in 20 volumes contains more than 2000 phrases. In cases where the whole *renga* was too long, only parts of it (mostly two phrases) were selected for compilation. The contents, subject matter and vocabulary were much the same as in the *waka* poems of the imperial anthologies. Poems on cherry blossoms, birds, the wind, the moon and love all followed the treatment accorded them in Heian court culture and very few poems reflected the age of civil war in which they were written.

In the fifteenth century the *Shinsen tsukubashū* (1495) was compiled also in 20 volumes, principally by the priest Sōgi (1421–1502), and likewise contained more than 2000 phrases which differed little in basic content from those of the *Tsukubashū*. These two anthologies are collections of good *renga* phrases similar to the imperial *waka* anthologies.

The real state of *renga*, however, can perhaps best be judged by the *Minase sangin nanihito hyakuin* (1488), composed by Sōgi and his two pupils Shōhaku and Sōchō, from which I quote the first six phrases, as follows:

> Snow yet remaining
> The mountain slopes are misty –
> An evening in spring.   (Sōgi)

> Far away the water flows
> Past the plum-scented village.   (Shōhaku)

> In the river breeze
> The willow trees are clustered.
> Spring is appearing.   (Sōchō)

> The sound of a boat being poled
> Clear in the clear morning light.   (Sōgi)

> The moon! Does it still
> over fog-enshrouded fields
> Linger in the sky?   (Shōhaku)

> Meadows carpeted in frost –
> Autumn has drawn to a close.   (Sōchō) Keene.

Thus it continues towards a total of 100 phrases (the 100 phrases being the most popular form of *renga* in the fourteenth and fifteenth centuries). Even in these six phrases, we begin with a scene in the mountains in early spring and then progress to a scene by a river bank, then to an autumn evening and, finally, to fields in late autumn. A theme is proffered in the first line which is then in turn developed and a new theme picked up from the preceding line and so forth. Continuity and change, the realization of expectation and the sudden surprising change play between the planned result and the happening by chance. As Sōgi himself said: 'There are set associations between Yoshino Mountain and cherry blossoms and clouds, or between the Tatsuta River and autumn coloured leaves.' The themes and imagery of *renga* followed the conventions of *waka*. Where the difference lay was '*Renga* differs from *waka* only in that it presents unexpected terms.' (*Azuma mondō*)

However, there was more to it than that. Nijō Yoshimoto said: '*Renga* does not join one idea with the next. Success and failure, joy and sorrow, succeed one after another as often happens in this world. Even as one thinks of yesterday, today is gone; when one thinks of spring, autumn has come and the cherry blossoms have become *momiji*.' (*Tsukuba mondō*) In *renga* one forgot the previous thought and gave no consideration to the next, simply producing the next phrase on the basis of the phrase before one's eyes. This corresponds to the modern attitude of 'forget yesterday and give no heed to tomorrow. Live only for the present'.

Time in *renga* is the perpetual present with no beginning and no end, the world of *renga* having no structure being simply a collection of independent parts: just the 'here and now' of everyday life which had been the sole reality in indigenous Japanese thought from earliest times.

It was because *renga*, which developed from *waka*, directly reflected this world view that it permeated to the masses and achieved such unprecedented popularity. During the civil wars of the fourteenth century it was known for troops taking part in a siege to invite *renga* poets to hold *renga* meetings (cf. *Taiheiki* Vol. 7), where each participant was both an author and a member of the audience. The development of 'group literature' in this way is not surprising in a society in which the integration of small groups was a characteristic. Heian court society in creating the *uta-awase* had already refined and institutionalized the literary amusements of the group and *renga*, popular and reaching a wide range of social classes, was its legacy to the Muromachi period.

However, the popularization of *renga* led to the direct reflection in its subject matter of the lives and emotions of the mass of the people which were, it goes without saying, widely divergent from the tastes of the aristocracy with their adherence to the dead Heian culture. While on one hand the *renga* poets sought to gratify the tastes of the aristocracy with their poetry (as in the *Tsukubashū*), on the other hand they created an entirely new form of poetry (the *haikai renga*) which made use of colloquial language, took for its subject matter the themes of everyday life, sought for humorous effect, and included elements of sexual lewdness.

The representative anthology of this kind of poetry was the *Inu tsukubashū* (probably early sixteenth century). This was compiled by Yamazaki Sōkan (dates unknown) and contained more than 1000 phrases, classified under the headings 'the four seasons', 'love poems' and 'miscellaneous poems'. And in addition, there is one part which contains only *hokku*.

Among *haikai renga* there were many parodies of *waka* poems, the poetry of Hitomaro, Onono Komachi and Saigyō frequently being treated in this way. Other poems derived humour from their treatment of the popular themes of the revenge of the Soga brothers and the warrior-monk Benkei. Puns and *kakekotoba* were commonly used devices and one of the special features of *haikai renga* was their frequent specific mention of parts of the body (not seen for example in *waka* poetry or in the *renga* of the *Tsukubashū*) such as 'nostrils', 'mustaches', 'buttocks' and 'testicles'.

Japanese literature from the Heian period onwards seldom mentioned food as such (compared, say, with Chinese novels), but all kinds of everyday food are touched on here, and perhaps only here in *haikai renga*. Sex, both heterosexual and homosexual, was also treated, there being frequent allusion to male and female sexual organs and copulation. This marked contrast between the convention of refined and elegant vocabulary of Heian court *waka* and these vivid depictions of food, sex etc. not only achieved humorous effect, but was also in a sense iconoclastic.

The professional *renga* poets who inherited the culture of the court aristocracy came into contact with the people at large while travelling round the country (as in the case of Sōgi) and doubtless in so doing became aware of the limitations of the aesthetic values of aristocratic culture itself. *Haikai renga* were a manifestation of this new awareness.

It was not only *renga* which was popular among the people at large in the Muromachi period, but also the short ballads known as *kouta*. The *Kanginshū* (early sixteenth century – the preface is dated 1518) contains more than 300 ballads, the majority of which are *kouta*. Among them are songs which were performed on the *Kyōgen* stage and also included are poems and folk ballads written by unknown authors. The majority are very short with no set form and were, it may be thought, beloved by the common people. In *renga* there is little evidence of Buddhist influence and in *kouta* such influence is confined to conventional epithets relating to the transience of life (and even these occur in only about ten per cent of cases). Mostly they were love songs, some dealing with the complex psychology of love, others with sexual passion. Examples of these categories are, respectively, as follows:

> When I had almost given him up
> He came to see me
>
> Though I care about him, I pretended not to.

Examples of the latter category are as follows:

> Bite me, but not too hard,
> or it leaves marks.
>
> I'm a young girl from Tsuruha in Sanuki Province
> And slept with a young man from Awa Province
> He enjoyed my feet, my belly.

As far as the masses are concerned, the central interest of Japanese lyric poetry had not changed from the time of the ancient ballads up until the time of the *Kangin-shū*. The professional *renga* poets were on one hand close to aristocratic society and culture, while on the other hand they were in contact with the people at large. While the main artistic accomplishments are reflected in the *renga* of the *Tsukubashū* and the *Shinsen tsukubashū*, they had to compensate for this with the more popular and vulgar poems of the *Inu tsukubashū*.

In this period there were two traditions of Japanese prose writing. The first is represented by the *Taikeiki* which in describing the civil wars of the fourteenth century used many Chinese words and frequently quoted Chinese poetry. It was written in the late fourteenth century, although the exact date is unknown. The author also is unknown, but no doubt he was a scholar and an intellectual in a position to consult a great many books. There is a tradition that monks were telling stories based on the *Taiheiki* as early as the Muromachi period, and if this is true it is an indication that the work was known to a wide range of social classes from early in its existence. However, the *Taikeiki* was written by an intellectual and most certainly have been meant to be read by a highly educated class – in other words, aristocratic, high-ranking warriors or monks.

The second tradition of prose writing was the long and short novels written in comparatively easy prose. The authors and dates of these works are almost always unknown. The *Gikei-ki*, which tells of the career and the tragedy of Minamotono Yoshi-tsune, and the *Soga monogatari*, which tells the classic revenge story of the Soga brothers, are representative examples of the long novel, both apparently originating as *katarimono*. The short novels are known as *otogizōshi* and these range widely in theme including stories of the love affairs of the aristocracy, homosexual love between monks, warriors' deeds of arms, the success stories of commoners who 'made good', and fanciful tales from China and Japan (including folk stories). The dissemination of these works is unclear, but the probability is that their stories were mostly read aloud to people. Stylistically, there is no great divergence among the *Gikei-ki*, the *Soga monogatari* and the *otogi zōshi*, but all differ radically from the *Taiheiki* and it may well be imagined that they were written for a more popular wider-ranging audience.

The *Taiheiki* (40 volumes) concentrates on the Nambokuchō wars and describes the seemingly endless round of battles fought in the half century 1318 to 1367. Its contents can be divided into three parts. The first section (Volumes 1–12) deals with the battles surrounding the Emperor Go-Daigo's war with the Kamakura Bakufu, leading to the Kemmu Restoration; the second part (Volumes 13–21) with the conflict between the Ashikaga Bakufu (and the Northern Court) and the Southern Court; and the final part concentrates on the struggles between various warrior leaders under the Ashikaga Shogunate. Generally speaking events are described in chronological order and frequently follow facts based on contemporary source material, but not invariably so (for these reasons historians doubt its value as an historical source).

The political standpoint of the author in the first section inclines towards favouring Go-Daigo, while in the second section he criticizes both sides and ends, in the final section, by praising the stability of Ashikaga rule. The underlying viewpoint of the author of the *Taiheiki* is undoubtedly markedly different from that of the *Jinnō shōtōki* which was written in support of the Southern Court.

One of the reasons for this is that the *Taiheiki* details developments subsequent to the Kemmu Restoration and it was difficult to understand these developments purely in terms of a confrontation between the Northern and Southern Courts. The author's understanding of politics was weak in comparison with Jien's and the reasons for the political decisions of the central characters are seldom fully explained. Take, for example, the reasons for Go-Daigo's attack on the Bakufu, the reasons for the revolts of Ashikaga Takauji and Nitta Yoshisada, the essential nature of the disharmony between the supporters of Go-Daigo and Takauji; the reasons for Kusunoki Masashige's faithful support of the Southern Court.

On all these points the author of the *Taiheiki* has little to say and his account of the psychological relationships between the central characters borders on the superficial. By way of contrast, the descriptions of troop movements and so forth are detailed and accounts of strategy, tactics and actual battles occupy a large proportion of the whole work. However, in comparison with the *Heike monogatari*, even the battle descriptions are flat and lacking in colour, while, as suggested above, the insight into the psychology and motives of the central figures is scanty.

Nevertheless, in its depiction of warrior society, the *Taiheiki* provides information not contained in the *Heike monogatari*. One of the most conspicuous facts within the *Taiheiki* narrative with regard to the *samurai* leaders and their followers is the drastic change – the increase and decrease – in the number of the warriors supporting one or the other side. For example, when the forces of Nitta Yoshisada and Ashikaga Takauji met at Hakone,

Yoshisada had 70,000 troops at his disposal as opposed to the 60,000 of Takauji as the forces moved towards each other on the Hakone road. At Takenoshita Prince Takanaga had 70,000 men and the supporters of Ashikaga Takauji 180,000 men. At Hakone Yoshisada had superiority but at Takenoshita Prince Takanaga's army (on the same side as Yoshisada) was routed, partly through treachery. After hearing of the Prince's defeat at Takenoshita the forces of Yoshisada at Hakone were defeated and put to flight and by the time both armies had disintegrated Yoshisada had only 100 men left and Prince Takanaga 300. Since Yoshisada had numeri- cal superiority at Hakone, the fact that his army dwindled from 70,000 to 100 cannot have been due to death and injury. We can only assume that the overwhelming majority of his army, indeed almost all of it, simply joined the side it deemed likely to win. In fact the implicit suggestion of the *Taiheiki* is that most of the warriors who took part in these civil wars were motivated solely by self-interest.

Generals on the route were threatened by far more powerful bandits and outlaws; soldiers on the retreat often became monks without conviction to escape from the enemy. The *samurai* leaders repeatedly betrayed their own leaders and so they them- selves would frequently ask for hostages to prevent betrayal. Those who provided their own wives and children as hostages often went ahead and sacrificed them to realize their own treacherous plans.

The idealization of *bushidō* or the 'way of the warrior' was something which developed under the stable and judicial rule of the Tokugawa family when all the fighting was over. The author of the *Hagakure* appears to have known nothing of the warriors of the Nambokuchō period and the Sengoku period. If he had known, instead of writing about the valour of warriors being prepared to fight to the death, he would have written of their betrayal.

The leaders of the warrior classes relied on the court for author- ization of their power. A typical example of this can be seen in the way both Takauji and Yoshisada when at war with each other sent reports to the Emperor and sought his support. However, the warriors were united in their hostility towards the court aristocracy and it was precisely because of this hostility that Takauji was able to gather a large army to crush the Kemmu

Restoration and prevent a resurrection of aristocratic power. 'If the present aristocratic regime continues as it is, all the *samurai* in the world would be under the control of the insignificant aristocrats in Kyōto and would seem to be just like slaves.' (Vol. 14)

The author of the *Taiheiki* did not overlook the attitudes of Prince Morinaga, the Shogun during the period of the Kemmu Restoration: 'He bathed himself in all the luxury that he desired disregarding what the people said, and indulged himself solely in licentiousness.' (Vol. 12)

Even while praising Kusunoki Masashige as a man 'who combined the virtues of wisdom, benevolence and valour', the author seems to have known where the background to Takauji's power lay. It was derived from the feudal system and the 'world of the warrior'.

However, even in warrior-dominated Japan there were frequent peasant riots which are not even mentioned in the *Taiheiki*. When all is said and done, the *Taiheiki* was written for the ruling classes.

More than anything else it was the *otogi-zōshi* which reflected the aspirations of the mass of the people who were going to develop their power to the point where they would be strong enough to arouse peasant riots; in particular the *shusse monogatari* (stories of worldly success achieved by commoners) such as the *Bunshō sōshi*, the *Fukutomi chōja monogatari* and even the *Monokusa tarō*. These were tales of people who, while accepting the given structure of society and the values which governed it, managed to rise from the bottom to the top.

It has already been mentioned, the peasant riots apart, that there was no particular identifiable ideology underlying the defiance of the ordinary people of Japan in this period. In fact, the idol of the masses was not one of their own class, but the *samurai* who was idolized precisely because he came from a class above their own. This idol in the popular view combined Confucian ethical values such as loyalty and filial piety with traditional aristocratic values including good looks, sexuality and nobility of birth. Therefore it is not surprising that many of the *otogi-zōshi* (and some longer novels too) centre on such characters as Minamotono Yoshitsune and the Soga brothers. This taste for idealized ill-starred heroes is perhaps not fundamentally different from the way the *Taiheiki* idealizes the Kusunokis, Masashige and his son Masatsura.

NŌ AND KYŌGEN

The most original product of the feudal age in literature was probably the dramatic form known as *sarugaku* which reached its peak of development in the fourteenth and fifteenth centuries. There were two types of *sarugaku*: Nō (or *sarugaku no Nō*) a kind of opera which concentrated on singing and dancing, and *Kyōgen* (or *sarugaku no Kyōgen*), which was a form of comic drama with some dancing and singing combined. The repertoire and method of performance of these dramas became fixed between the late sixteenth and early seventeenth centuries and have come down today in those forms. (The oldest surviving Nō plays can be traced to the fifteenth century, but it was in the sixteenth century that most of them were written down. *Kyōgen* relied heavily on improvization and it was not until the seventeenth century that the oldest still extant plays were put into written form. Once many manuscripts of these plays had come into existence, there was a tendency not to expand the repertoire and there were also no substantial changes in the way the plays were performed.)

Sarugaku was already being performed in the Heian period. In the Japanese court of this period the *seigaku* which had been transmitted from China in the Nara period developed into *bugaku* and *gaguku* and it is said that *sangaku* (which involved song and dance, acrobatics and conjuring tricks) absorbed the indigenous songs and dances associated with Shintō festivals and ceremonies and in the eleventh to twelfth centuries became *sarugaku* and *dengaku*.

Dengaku died out in the seventeenth century and so we do not know for certain what it consisted of, but according to one theory, it concentrated on the acrobatic stunts derived from *sangaku* whereas *sarugaku* concentrated on the dance from the same tradition.

It seems that in the late thirteenth century both *sarugaku* and *dengaku* on one hand developed their associations with Shintō festivals while on the other hand playing a role as popular entertainments. In either case both Nō and Kyōgen plays were included. In the fourteenth and fifteenth centuries, this popular entertainment, *sarugaku*, enjoyed its greatest popularity and in one of the *sarugaku* troupes a genius emerged who played the roles of actor, author, and director at the same time with the result that the artistic quality of the drama was heightened.

Drama became, for the first time in Japanese literary history, one of the major forms of expression. (This applies mainly to the *sarugakuno Nō*. We can do no more than guess vaguely about the *Kyōgen* of *sarugaku*.) There is absolutely no source material relating to *dengaku*, but it seems not to have substantially differed from *sarugaku* and it is rather because of this lack of source material and not because of any great difference in social or artistic significance that *sarugaku* is so much discussed today while *dengaku* is almost totally ignored.

In Western literary history, literature developed from classical times on the basis of drama and epic poetry. It was not until the eighteenth century that the novel emerged as an important form. Japanese literature differs widely from that of the West in this respect since in the early period of its development it was firmly based on lyric poetry and the novel. Drama was a fourteenth- to fifteenth-century development. However, there was more to it than that. The important position occupied by drama in Japanese culture from the fourteenth to fifteenth centuries onwards sharply differentiates Japanese cultural history from that of China. In China, the traditional concept of literature included neither drama nor novels and was certainly not written in the vernacular. Perhaps due to this attitude, all ancient Chinese drama disappeared completely. (The so-called Yuan dramas are an exception in that they have survived, but even here there is no tradition of performance. Peking drama is said to have developed from as late as the eighteenth century.) However, in the history of Japanese drama from the fourteenth to fifteenth centuries onwards old forms were preserved and new forms developed.

Why did this important phenomenon take place in the fourteenth and fifteenth centuries – the age of civil war and peasant riots? Probably it was because in this age artists and writers emerged from a completely different social background from the one which had previously produced them. There were perhaps two factors which made this possible. First, the development of agriculture and commerce opened the way for writers and artists to come forth from the common people; and, secondly, quite unlike the court aristocracy who had themselves acquired artistic accomplishments, the new up-start warrior ruling class needed professional artists to provide them with entertainment.

Hardly anything is known of the lives of the Nō actors and authors of this period or of their family backgrounds, with the exception of the celebrated actor/authors of the Kanze-ryū tradition of Nō. There is not even a single name left to us of those who composed Kyōgen. These facts suggest to us that the social position of the author/actor of the sarugaku was quite low and we can surmise that many of them were ordinary people. The aristocracy would certainly have regarded them as the lowest class. For example Oshikōji Kintada (1324–83) wrote in his Gogumaiki, 'this sarugaku is the work of beggars'.

At any rate it was not intellectuals of aristocratic or high-ranking warrior origin who promoted this popular entertainment to the apex of cultural life, but artists of common origin. The same could be said of the renga poets, but they were different in the sense that they were popularizing an aristocratic art form, whereas the authors and actors of Nō and Kyōgen were bringing something popular to the aristocracy.

We can observe here a diffusion of upper class culture descending to the common people, and at the same time a refinement of the lower class culture ascending to the ruling class. We know very little about the audiences of sarugaku performances but certain general points can be made. First, in the fourteenth and fifteenth centuries Nō and Kyōgen plays were performed as part of the same sarugaku programmes, so the audience for both must have been the same. Second, since the patrons of the drama troupes were the upper echelons of warrior society, including the Ashikaga Shoguns and their families, the audiences must frequently have included members of the warrior ruling classes, including the Shoguns themselves, and the court aristocracy. Thirdly, a fifteenth-century document (the Inryōken Nichiroku) says that when the Shōgun went to see a sarugaku performance on the banks of the Kamo River in Kyōto, 'there were innumerable spectators' and 'we could not count the audience at all'.

It is quite certain from contemporary records that members of various lower social classes were also in the audience. Nothing beyond this is known. What is most notable about this, however, is that for the first time in Japanese history members of the ruling classes and ordinary people went to the same place at the same time to watch the same entertainment. Not only had this never happened before, it never happened later either until the creation of the present-day 'mass society'. It was no doubt for this reason that the content of *sarugaku* had on one hand to incorporate elements of Heian court culture (which was admired not only by court aristocrats but new up-start warriors also) and on the other hand had to be related to the interests of the everyday lives of the common people. Roughly speaking, *Nō* catered for the former interest, *Kyōgen* for the latter.

From the seventeenth century onwards the following differences between *Nō* and *Kyōgen* were apparent. *Nō* was a splendid 'opera' in which the actors wore masks, maintained a judicious balance between dance and 'speech' and performed with the accompaniment of an 'orchestra' (flute and drum) and a chorus. In *Kyōgen* the actors did not wear masks (usually) and although some dancing was included, the main emphasis was on mimicry and horseplay. There was no music and no chorus as a rule, but there were exceptions.

The script of a *Nō* play in the fourteenth and fifteenth centuries (and subsequently), was apparently fixed at least to a certain degree, but in *Kyōgen* there was a synopsis only and what followed was left to the actors' improvization. As far as vocabulary is concerned the extant *Nō* plays indicate an extremely stylized literary language, with many quotations from *waka* poems and other classics and many *kakekotoba*, making for a very intricate and distinctive style, whereas *Kyōgen*, relying on the colloquial language of the day, is simple, direct and full of spirit. The central characters of the *Nō* drama are supernatural beings (gods, devils, *tengu*, spirits of the dead etc.) or figures from the history of Japan (famous men or women of the Heian period, celebrated warriors of the *Heike monogatari* etc.). The central characters of *Kyōgen*, on the other hand, are contemporary local ruling dignitaries (*daimyō* etc.) and their followers, or blind men, thieves, monks, peasants, artisans and their womenfolk. There are no supernatural beings or characters from history. The very highest levels of the ruling classes do not figure and most usually the characters come from the lower end of society. In light of all this it seems a reasonable conjecture that *Nō* was designed for the upper classes and *Kyōgen* for the lower classes.

However, some of the central *Nō* characters (Onono Komachi,

Izumi Shikibu, Saigyō, Yoshitsune etc.) also figure prominently as the heroes of contemporary popular fiction for the masses (the *otogi-zōshi Gikei-ki Soga monogatari*). The ordinary folk who watched *sarugaku* not only enjoyed the *Kyōgen* performances, but were doubtless also delighted to see their heroes in *Nō* plays as well. On the other hand, senior members of the warrior classes in this age were not too far removed from popular life to prevent their understanding of *Kyōgen*. The distance between the court aristocracy and the masses of the Fujiwara period was infinitely great. Later the warrior rulers of the Tokugawa period tended to emphasize their distance from the masses in all respects, but in the Muromachi period the gap was much less wide, so that people high and low could enjoy both *Nō* and *Kyōgen*.

The earliest author of *Nō* plays known today was Kan'ami Mototsugu (1334–84). Zeami Motokiyo (1363–1443) was his son and Zeami's son was Jūrō Motomasa (*c.*1394–1431). Apart from these three generations of writers of the Kanze school (as it is known), Kojirō Nobumitsu (1435–1516) (a descendant of Zeami's younger brother), of the Komparu family Zenchiku Ujinobu (1405–*c.* 1470) and his sons all wrote *Nō* plays. Zenchiku was Zeami's son-in-law. There were other writers unrelated to the Kan'ami/Zeami family including Kongō (dates unknown, possibly not one man) and Kyūzō (dates unknown). The reason why the name of Zeami stands so high today as an author of *Nō* plays is that he wrote many of the 240 plays still performed and because he wrote many treatises on the art of performing *Nō* (of the twenty-one works written by Zeami apart from plays themselves, nineteen are on this subject).

The dramatic structure of the plays of Kan'ami is conspicuous by the device of 'confrontation' between two characters. For example, in the play *Jinen koji* there is a violent verbal altercation between a slave dealer aboard a boat and the hero who tries to rescue a girl from the boat; and in the play *Sotoba Komachi* there is a Buddhist philosophical interplay between Onono Komachi (in the form of an old hag) and a Buddhist monk. *Jinen koji* finishes with a dance by the hero and *Sotoba Komachi* with a 'mad dance' by Komachi, but there is no doubt that the peak of dramatic tension is achieved in the 'confrontations'.

In the sense that these plays are concerned with human relationships in this world without the participation of supernatural beings, they are not so very far removed from *Kyōgen*. The same could be said of the plays of Kyūzō of which the *Youchi Soga* is representative. This is based on the famous tale of the revenge of the Soga brothers and as one can see from the brothers' feelings towards their mother, the plot is based on realism and again supernatural beings do not figure.

Zeami, however, developed *Nō* in a different direction. First, in place of the traditional heroes of the masses, he chose for his central characters the warriors of the *Heike monogatari* (Yorimasa, Sanemori, Tadanori and Atsumori) and classical figures from Heian culture (Narihira and the woman of *Izutsu*, old woman in *Higaki*, Tōru and Tsurayuki). Second, he derived dramatic tension not from the 'confrontation' between two characters, but from the anguished inner examination of one character, usually the metamorphosis of a hero. For example, in cases where a warrior is the hero, the whole play consists of the first part in which a wandering monk will meet an old man (the *mae shite* or 'first protagonist') at the site of some ancient battle and the monk hears from the old man the story of the battle, and of the second part in which the monk realizes exactly who the old man is, then the old man assumes his true form as the warrior hero (the *ato shite*) who performs a dance while telling the story of how he met his death and a monk recites the scriptures to appease and pacify the ghost. The *mae shite* can be an old man or an old woman and the *ato shite* is a ghost who performs a 'mad dance'. The first part represents this world, the latter part the next world of the spirits.

The basic structure does not change when, for example in the *Koi-no-omoni*, the plot is concerned with an old man of humble birth who falls in love with a high-born lady and kills himself when she made fun of him. The *ato shite* is the ghost of the old man who dances a 'mad dance' and harshly condemns the woman. In this way the heroes of Zeami's plays almost always change from human beings into spirits, move from this world into the next, from the natural world into the supernatural world.

This is not to say that there were no such plays in Kan'ami's time (e.g. *Kayoi Komachi*) and even before then there were plays (associated with Shintoism) in which a god appeared in the first part as an old man and then in the latter part as his true self. It should be noted, however, that Zeami wrote not of gods in their real or assumed forms, but of actual human beings who crossed over from this world into the next and he seems to have achieved the definitive form of the Nō drama.

Certainly, his style of writing was new to the period and he felt it necessary to justify his standpoint with a series of theoretical treatises just as, 200 years later, Okura Toraaki was to write the *Waranbegusa*, the first theoretical work on *Kyōgen*, when he felt the necessity to defend his own art of *Kyōgen* and distinguish it from early *Kabuki*. After Zeami's time, the majority of Nō authors wrote either the 'realistic' style of play in the Kan'ami tradition or the 'fantastic' style of the Zeami tradition.

The originality of Zeami's Nō plays lay first, in the economy of their presentation; second, in their music; and third, in their dramatic structure as plays.

First, the Nō libretti were short (usually about 3000 characters in length) and the stages were small. We know next to nothing about the performance of Nō in the Muromachi period, but in the productions of today (which are considered to have been fixed in the seventeenth century) the movements of the actors are highly stylized. The very slightest movement of the body indicates a fixed action. For example, a long journey is indicated by a slow circuit of the small stage and the hero's tears and lamentations by a slight lowering of the mask in front of which one hand is held. Large stage sets and scenery are not employed and usually the only small prop used by an actor is a fan. By the imaginative powers of the audience the narrow stage is converted into a grassy plain, the sea shore or a palace. In other words, in Nō there is a minimum of emphasis on the actors' movements, words and stage scenery and maximum emphasis is placed on the imagination of the audience. No other Japanese dramatic form has such economy and probably there are few equivalents anywhere in the world.

Second, leaving aside the question of its origin, the musical accompaniment in present-day Nō performances consists of a single flute and large and small drums. There is little in the way of melody and structural harmony is lacking. It is, on the other hand, extremely rhythmic and the *ma* or pauses are just as important as the music itself – the period of silence when for a moment the short rhythmic beats of the drums and the sharp notes of the flute cease. This extremely ascetic music corresponds to the extreme economy of the actors' body movements.

Third, there are few actors on stage in a Nō play. Usually there is the protagonist or hero (the *shite*) and the deuteragonist (*waki*), who provides the stimulus for the *shite's* internal drama. The *shite* appears first as a human being and then as a ghost, and this structure of concentrating on a single character and allowing him to interchange between this world and the next is unique to Nō. Since death is the 'point of contact' between these two different worlds, the theme of Nō is the passions, especially those of love and battle, which lead to death.

Despite the popularity of Buddhism from the Nara period onwards, Japanese literature, especially lyric poetry, concentrated its interest on 'this world'. Even the transcendentalism of thirteenth-century Buddhism perished with the secularization of Buddhism in the fourteenth and fifteenth centuries, but at the same time a new form of drama emerged (Nō) which concentrated its attention on the 'next world'.

It is impossible to explain these special characteristics of the Nō drama except against the background of the transcendentalism of a foreign ideology. The asceticism of the presentation was a transposition of aesthetic values through the medium of Buddhism and the concern with the hero after death implies the permeation of the 'next worldly' thought brought by Buddhism. Since in Zeami's time Buddhism itself was secularized one might say that it was a case not so much of his art being influenced by religion, but of religion becoming art by him. Alternatively, one might say that in the thirteenth century the transcendental ideology of Buddhism was profoundly and creatively accepted as religion and in the fifteenth century as art.

Such art might not have been created in the framework of the fundamentally secular culture moulded in Heian aristocratic society. The phenomenon in which transcendental Buddhism was accepted as art in the fifteenth century could only have been possible because the origin of Nō, in other words, the origin of *sarugaku*, was totally different from the world of the aristocracy.

It was only the artists (who came from common origins and were capable of getting close to the higher intellectual classes) who were able, in the trend towards the secularization of Buddhism, to 'humanize' next world thought and turn it into art and literature.

Zeami's theoretical works including *Fūshikaden* expounded his aesthetic values and yet also gave technical instructions as to how those values could be given real form by actors on the *Nō* stage. He used the term 'the flower' as one of his central concepts to indicate the effect which the actor must produce in the audience; the other, *'yūgen'*, is the beauty projected by the actor on stage. The 'flower' is to be achieved by 'interesting and unexpected performance, whereas the *yūgen* refers to the actor's inner quality and is reflected in graceful clothing, elegance and gentleness of speech.

The importance of the 'flower' – its positive effect on the audience – reveals his vital concern with his and his own troupes success in rivalry against other *Nō* troupes. The emphasis on *yūgen* suggests that Zeami's aesthetic values were conceived in *conscious* imitation of the traditions of the culture of the Heian court aristocracy. In his theoretical works on *Nō* drama Zeami uses a number of Buddhist terms and concepts, but he does not refer to the fundamental relationship between the Buddhist world view and the structure of his plays. That relationship was essentially *unconscious* and all the more profound for that.

Why did Zeami not only write plays but also write *about Nō* drama? The ostensible reason was to transmit to his heirs a device which could be used by them in clashes with rival schools of thought in *Nō*. The *Fūshikaden* even speaks about some tactics of the *Nō* performance to be used to win competitions. Also it may be thought that after he lost the favour of the Shōgun and was exiled to the island of Sado for unknown reasons in 1434, Zeami was anxious about the future of his troupe and his theoretical works might help to ensure its survival. However, there is no doubt that the main reason was that he had created a new form of *Nō* drama and felt the need to defend it.

Today some 300 *Kyōgen* plays are known (the oldest dating from the seventeenth century) and about 200 of them are still performed. As far as we can judge there was virtually no influence from Buddhist thought on *Kyōgen*; on the contrary there are distinct traces of iconoclasm. For example, in the play *Niō*, one of the two swindlers disguises himself as *Niō* (the Buddha's guard), and the other spreads the rumour that if the villagers bring offerings to the Niō who has descended from heaven, their wishes would be fulfilled. One of the villagers was lame, so he tries to touch the Niō's feet in order to cure himself. This tickled the Niō. He bursts into laughter and reveals himself as a swindler.

There is also the play *Shūron* in which two Buddhist monks, one an adherent of the Lotus Sect, the other of the Pure Land Sect meet while travelling along the road. They begin to boast to one another about the superiority of their respective sects. Each, in an attempt to overcome the other begins to recite the special invocation of his sect (*Namu Amida-butsu* in the case of the Pure Land monk and *Namu Myōhō Renge-kyō* in the case of the Lotus (Nichiren) monk). So wild does the argument become that in the end the Pure Land monk is calling out *Namu Myōhō Renge-kyō* and the Lotus monk *Namu Amida-butsu*!

In other plays, the powerless rituals of the *yamabushi* (monks who wander the mountains) are ridiculed (e.g. *Fukurō Yamabushi*, *Kusabira*). Because of this tendency on the part of *Kyōgen* to poke fun at monks, there were cases even in the fifteenth century of angry monks physically attacking actors and the great Buddhist temples and punishing them from which we may judge that from the very beginning *Kyōgen* was harsh in its criticisms of the clergy.

Many *Kyōgen* plays were based on greater or lesser feudal lords and servants and humour is derived from the ignorance and stupidity on the part of the masters (as in the play *Hagi daimyō*). There was even a case in the Muromachi period where such a play was performed at court and the actors received an official reprimand. In other words, *Nō* and *Kyōgen* were worlds apart, the latter being completely 'this-worldly' and concerned with everyday life. It existed within the framework of the indigenous Japanese world view completely unrelated to Buddhism and frequently ridiculed dignity and pomposity.

But Niō was not of the rank of such Buddhist deities as Bodhisattvas. *Kyōgen* never ridicules Bodhisattvas. *Kyōgen* never attacked Buddhism itself. It was ignorant monks who were the figures of fun and not the beliefs they held. Wise and learned monks were never made sport of. Equally, although jokes were made about stupid *daimyō* in *Kyōgen* plays, the *daimyō* institution itself was not the subject of general attack. The masses of the Muromachi period showed their defiance towards authorities through peasant rebellions, not through the *Kyōgen* drama. The spirit which inspired *Kyōgen* was similar to that which inspired the *Inu tsukubashū; Kyōgen* was not the manifestation of the mass sentiment which underlay the peasant riots.

Where *Kyōgen* displayed its most subtle and clever humour was in the cases where the central theme was psychological haggling between a husband and wife. Take, for example, the play *Nushi* (Lacquer Craftsman) where there is a difference in attitude on the part of a craftsman and his wife towards his master. Whereas the husband makes every effort to welcome this man who has not visited him for a very long time, his wife fearing that this visitor will be a rival to her husband since he lives in the same town tries to hoodwink him. Here there is sharp perception of everyday life and the structure of this small comedy is masterly. This world of Kyōgen shows us in what direction the indigenous world view was able to develop subsequent to the *Konjaku monogatari* through an enrichment of content and stylization of form due to its encounter with the mass audience.

Thus the contrast between *Nō* and *Kyōgen* was not confined to style of language, subject matter and performance, but was truly representative of a contrast in world view. In all ages of Japanese literary history foreign and indigenous world views have coexisted and appeared in various forms of literature. However, the existence of these two contrasting world views as aspects of two dramatic forms performed on the same stage was unique to the fourteenth and fifteenth centuries. Nothing shows more vividly that these world views were not the respective properties of two distinct social classes, but existed as two layers of consciousness within the same individual.

Bibliographical Notes

Most quotations in this book are from the texts in the following two collections:

Nihon Koten Bungaku Taikei (Iwanami) and *Nihon Shisō Taikei* (Iwanami). A few quotations are also from the texts in *Gunsho Ruijū*, *Zoku Gunsho Ruijū*, *Gozan Bungaku Zenshū* (edited by Uemura Kankō, 1935–36), *Gozan Bungaku Shinshū* (edited by Tamamura Takeji, 1967–72), and *Nihon Kagaku Taikei* (edited by Sasaki Nobutsuna).

Besides the collections above, major sources for specific texts and informations are as the following:

CHAPTER 1
Sankyō Gisho, Iwanami Bunko.
Ishimoda Tadashi, *Nihon no Kodai Kokka*, Iwanami, 1971.

CHAPTER 2
Ennin, *Nittō-guhō-junreikō-ki*, Tōyō Bunko (Heibon-sha).
Kōbō-daishi Zenshū
Tsuji Zennosuke, *Nihon Bukkyō Shi*, Vol. I, Iwanami, 1944.
Ishimoda Tadashi and Matsushima Eiichi, *Nihon Shi Gaisetsu I*, Iwanami, 1955.

CHAPTER 3
Hara Katsurō, *Nihon Chūsei Shi*, Fuzanbō, 1906.
Tsuji Zennosuke, op. cit.
Inoue Mitsusada, *Nihon Jōdo-kyō Seiritsu-shi no Kenkyū*, Yamakawa-shuppansha, 1956.

CHAPTER 4
Ishimoda Tadashi and Matsushima Eiichi, op. cit.

CHAPTER 5

Tamamura Takeji, *Gozan Bungaku*, Shibundō, 1960.

Kitamura Sawakichi, *Gozan Bungaku Shikō*, Fuzanbō, 1941.

Sadō Koten Zenshū, Vol. III, Tankōsha, 1960.

Sadō Zenshū, Vol. IX, Sōgensha, 1935.

'Kyōun-shū', edited by Itō Toshiko, in *Yamato Bunka*, No. 41, 1964.

Jikai-shū, a photographed copy of the manuscript in Shūon-an.

Kōhon Inu-tsukuba-shū, edited by Ebara Taizō, private edition, 1938.

Kitagawa Tadahiko, *Zeami*, Chūōkōron-sha, 1972.

Index